The philosophy of
Ang Lee

The Philosophy of Ang Lee

THE PHILOSOPHY OF
ANG LEE

Edited by

ROBERT ARP, ADAM BARKMAN,
AND JAMES McRAE

 UNIVERSITY PRESS OF KENTUCKY

Scholarly publisher for the Commonwealth,
serving Bellarmine University, Berea College, Centre College of Kentucky,
Eastern Kentucky University, The Filson Historical Society, Georgetown College,
Kentucky Historical Society, Kentucky State University, Morehead State
University, Murray State University, Northern Kentucky University, Transylvania
University, University of Kentucky, University of Louisville, and Western
Kentucky University.
All rights reserved.

Editorial and Sales Offices: The University Press of Kentucky
663 South Limestone Street, Lexington, Kentucky 40508-4008
www.kentuckypress.com

17 16 15 14 13   5 4 3 2 1

Library of Congress Cataloging-in-Publication Data

The philosophy of Ang Lee / edited by Robert Arp, Adam Barkman, and James
    McRae.
    pages cm
  Includes bibliographical references and index.
  ISBN 978-0-8131-4166-4 (hardcover : acid-free paper) —
  ISBN 978-0-8131-4169-5 (epub) — ISBN 978-0-8131-4170-1 (pdf)
  1. Lee, Ang, 1954—Criticism and interpretation. 2. Philosophy in motion
pictures. I. Arp, Robert, editor of compilation. II. Barkman, Adam, 1979–editor
of compilation. III. McRae, James, 1976–editor of compilation.
  PN1998.3.L438P48 2013
  791.4302'33092—dc23   2012050799

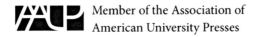

To Zoe and Lexi, who were born in China. *Wo ai ni!*
—Rob Arp

To my mom, who first took me to the movies.
—Adam Barkman

To my wife, Heather, for her steadfast support, and my mentor,
Graham Parkes, who taught me to appreciate
the philosophical side of film.
—James McRae

Contents

Part 2: The Western Philosophy of Ang Lee

INTRODUCTION

Robert Arp, Adam Barkman, and James McRae

Make Movies or Die

"Hi, I'm Ang Lee, and if I don't make movies I'm going to die."[1] Ang Lee used these words to introduce himself to the production company, Good Machine, which would go on to fund his 1992 film, *Pushing Hands.* Lee is one of the most talented and diverse directors in world cinema. He is known for his ability to make provocative and original films on virtually any topic: Victorian romances, kung fu epics, superhero action films, tragedies about forbidden relationships. Lee has produced eleven feature-length films that have garnered critical acclaim and earned him multiple Academy Awards, Golden Globes, and British Academy of Film and Television Arts awards.[2] Though the subject matter of these films has varied widely, they share complex, often controversial themes that make them fertile ground for philosophical inquiry.

The purpose of this book is to explore the philosophy of Ang Lee's films, and the chapters draw from both Eastern and Western philosophies to examine the multicultural themes present in Lee's works, so that readers will gain an insight into Lee's films and the rich philosophical heritage in which they are grounded.

Ang Lee's Career as a Filmmaker

Lee was born on October 23, 1954, in Taiwan, but he did not begin his career as a professional filmmaker until he was thirty-seven years old. Lee's father was a high school principal and a traditional Confucian who emphasized education and filial piety. When Lee failed the national university entrance exams twice, it brought great shame to his father. Lee enrolled in the National Taiwan University of Arts in 1973 as a theater and film major, which embarrassed his father even further because film was not considered a respectable vocation in Taiwan in the 1970s.[3]

In 1978, at the age of twenty-three, Lee moved to the United States and enrolled as a theater major at the University of Illinois at Urbana-Champaign. Because he spoke English as a second language, he turned to directing as a dramatic medium that would circumvent his linguistic limitations. In 1980, he graduated with a B.F.A. in theater and theater direction and enrolled in the master's program in film production at the Tisch School of the Arts at New York University. During this period, he produced a number of acclaimed student shorts and worked as a cameraman for one of Spike Lee's student films. In 1985, Lee finished *A Fine Line,* a forty-three-minute film that he made for his master's thesis. Though his film won New York University's top two awards—for best director and best film—after earning his master's degree, Lee would not work in film for six years.[4]

In 1990, Lee was contacted by the new production company Good Machine, which agreed to help fund his first feature-length film, *Pushing Hands* (1992). Because this film garnered critical acclaim and was a huge success in Asia, Lee was able to gain funding for another low-budget film, *The Wedding Banquet,* which went on to become the most profitable film of 1993 proportionate to its cost and to earn an Oscar nomination for best foreign-language film. This was quickly followed by *Eat Drink Man Woman* (1994), which brought Lee another Oscar nomination in the same category. Lee's early work attracted the attention of Hollywood, and his next three films would be made in English with larger budgets. In 1995, he directed an adaptation of the Jane Austen novel *Sense and Sensibility,* which received seven Academy Award nominations and one win for best adapted screenplay. Lee built on this success with two critically acclaimed, limited-release films: *The Ice Storm* (1997) and *Ride with the Devil* (1999). Coupled with his early trilogy, these three films demonstrated Lee's breadth and depth as a filmmaker, and he quickly developed a reputation as a director who could turn any subject into a tour de force.[5]

In 2000, Lee directed the Qing dynasty martial arts film, *Crouching Tiger, Hidden Dragon.* The film became an international sensation and was nominated for ten Academy Awards, going on to win for best foreign-language film, best cinematography, best art direction—set direction, and best original score. Though Lee was nominated for best director and the film for best picture, he won neither.[6] Lee's success with this film was followed in 2003 by *Hulk,* an adaptation of the popular Marvel Comics series. The director's artistic vision was continually constrained by Universal Studios, which rejected Lee's tragic interpretation of the Hulk in favor of a straightforward action film. Though Lee's skill is evident throughout the film, *Hulk* never achieved its full artistic potential and was poorly received by critics and at the box office.[7]

The failure of *Hulk* sent Lee into a depression, during which he considered quitting his career as a filmmaker. Fortunately, his father persuaded him to make another movie, and Lee turned his attention to *Brokeback Mountain*. In 2005, the controversial film was released to widespread critical acclaim. It was nominated for eight Oscars and won three, including Lee's first best achievement in directing award. However, even though it was heavily favored to win the best picture award, *Brokeback Mountain* lost to *Crash* (Paul Haggis, 2004).[8] Lee then directed the sexually charged spy drama, *Lust, Caution,* in 2007. The film was a huge success in China, albeit with most of the sexual content edited out, but the NC-17 rating it received in the United States limited its release. Although critics mostly praised *Lust, Caution,* Lee's next effort, *Taking Woodstock* (2009), was less successful. Though some critics found the film to be a satisfactory adaptation of Elliot Tiber and Tom Monte's whimsical 2007 novel, most thought it oversimplified the complex issues surrounding the cultural transformation that took place in the late 1960s.

The Philosophy of Ang Lee

Friedrich Nietzsche claimed that all philosophy is autobiography: a good writer should spill his very soul onto the page such that if one understands his work, one understands who he is as a person.[9] In a rare interview, Ang Lee stated, "If you want to understand me, it's all in my films."[10] The director suggests, like Nietzsche, that his works are an autobiography, a window into his values, concerns, and motivations. It is because of this that Lee's films are such a rich source for the philosophy of film.

Philosophy of film is a subdiscipline of aesthetics, the branch of philosophy that focuses on the nature of beauty and art. Though its origins can be traced as far back as Hugo Münsterberg's 1916 monograph, *The Photoplay: A Psychological Study,* it did not gain acceptance as a major area of academic inquiry until the 1980s. Philosophy of film differs from film theory in the sense that it is critically argumentative and questions its own nature as a discipline.[11] Though philosophy of film has largely gained acceptance as a legitimate area of inquiry, there is still some debate about its place in academic philosophy. Part of this dispute stems from the reticence of some academics to accept film as a legitimate art form worthy of serious consideration. However, just as ballet—which was once considered scandalous debauchery—is now acclaimed as high art, film has gradually gained acceptance as a legitimate artistic medium.[12]

One area of debate in philosophy and film hinges on the extent to which a director can be considered the auteur, or author, of the film.[13] Typically a director is given credit for the quality of a film, but is this really appropriate, given the fact that hundreds of people contribute to the work? This question is pertinent for us here because if a director is not the author of his films, how can there be such a thing as the philosophy of Ang Lee? Thinkers such as François Truffaut and Andrew Sarris have argued that the only films worthy of consideration as art are those in which the auteur has complete control of the project, including the screenplay, direction, editing, and producing of the film. This view has been criticized because it seems to overemphasize the role of the director and ignore the particularity of the context in which films are produced.[14] Yet there does seem to be a kernel of truth to auteur theory: although the director is not the only author of a film, he has more control over the project than any of the other contributors. Just as Socrates was a midwife for the truth, good directors encourage and facilitate good performances from their actors and crew. It is in this sense that we can consider the films of Ang Lee to represent a coherent set of views.

Part of Ang Lee's genius as a filmmaker stems from the fact that he is a product of both Chinese and American culture. He draws extensively from the artistic and philosophical traditions of both backgrounds as he writes and directs, and this multicultural approach has made him a diverse and inspired filmmaker. Following Lee's unique fusion of East and West, this book is organized into two major sections: Eastern and Western philosophy. The first section deals predominantly with Asian philosophical themes in Lee's works, such as Daoism, Confucianism, and Buddhism. Although these themes are most prevalent in Lee's Taiwanese and Chinese-language films— such as the Father Knows Best trilogy; *Crouching Tiger, Hidden Dragon*; and *Lust, Caution*—several authors discuss the significance of these concepts in many of Lee's more Western works, like *Brokeback Mountain* and *Sense and Sensibility*. The second section emphasizes Western philosophical traditions in Lee's English-language films. These categories are not meant to be exhaustive or exclusive; Ang Lee is very much a comparative filmmaker in the philosophical sense of drawing what is best from a variety of different traditions to creatively address key issues.

If there is any unifying philosophical theme for Lee's films, it is the struggle for authentic self-identity. As Søren Kierkegaard states, "Anxiety is the dizziness of freedom."[15] A lack of authenticity brings about an existential crisis in which one must resolve the tension between who one genuinely wants to be and who one is told to be by others. Philosopher Charles Taylor states, "The ethic of authenticity is something relatively new and peculiar to modern culture."[16] Taylor sees the quest for authenticity as a response to the "malaises of modernity" in Western society, and he argues that authenticity is found in a person's "horizons of significance," which consist of the context in which one exists, particularly the people within that context. These horizons may be called significant because of their role in the definition of the person. For Taylor, someone is "a self only among other selves. A self can never be described without reference to those who surround it."[17] The self is not formed in a vacuum; rather, it is created dialogically through one's relationships with other persons. The need for dialogical definition is readily apparent when we look at the use of language for self-definition. Human beings cannot have higher-order thought without the aid of language, and no one ever acquires language independent of other people.[18] Thus, the self is essentially interrelational in nature. A person cannot help but exist within a sociocultural environment, and one's experiences within this environment have a marked effect on the person. The role that environment plays in one's definition of oneself is so essential that one defines who one is according to where one is speaking from: one's family, friends, spouse, society, and morality.[19]

The protagonists of Lee's films are typically caught in a struggle to define themselves dialogically in the manner that Taylor describes. In particular, several of his films feature characters who are fighting to maintain a sense of Chinese identity in the face of the globalization of Western culture. Lee's first three films deal specifically with the negative effect that the malaises of modernity have on traditional cultures. Yet even in films that do not explicitly deal with the Chinese diaspora, we find characters working to define their identities in a new sociocultural environment that endorses disparate values. Ultimately, it is only by grappling with these new challenges to their identities that the protagonists can find authenticity.

Lee deals explicitly with sexual identity in virtually all of his films. Three films—*The Wedding Banquet*, *Brokeback Mountain*, and *Taking Woodstock*—

deal with the social conflicts that arise when homosexual men try to con-front and express their sexual identity. *The Wedding Banquet* is a comedy that makes light of the sometimes absurd social masks that gay and lesbian couples are forced to wear to fit in. *Brokeback Mountain* is a tragedy that details the shame, self-loathing, and loss that homosexuals often face in societies that condemn their lifestyle. *Taking Woodstock* echoes the whim-sical tone of *The Wedding Banquet,* yet it deals seriously with Elliot Tiber's struggle for sexual liberation. Other films deal with the sexual and social identity of women. The women of the Father Knows Best trilogy must define themselves against the patriarchal authority that is prevalent in both Western and Eastern culture, particularly in the Confucianism of China. In *Sense and Sensibility,* Elinor and Marianne strive for happiness amid the confines of Victorian chauvinism. A similar conflict is faced by Yu Shu Lien and Jen in *Crouching Tiger, Hidden Dragon,* because traditional Chinese society does not have a place for independent women warriors.

Confucius (551–479 BCE) is arguably the most influential thinker in the history of East Asian philosophy. His philosophy permeates Chinese culture to this day and is a central theme in Lee's films. Living in the chaos and tyranny of the Zhou dynasty, Confucius sought to define a political and ethical philosophy that could return China to the halcyon days of the Shang dynasty. He argued that peace and tranquility only come about when people have cultivated themselves as persons of great moral virtue. The classical Chinese understanding of the person is based on a focus–field notion of the self: like a figure in a landscape painting, an individual is only the focal point of the vast environment of social interactions that define him or her.[20] Thus, Confucius' philosophy is humanistic, focusing on social interaction rather than metaphysics.

Confucius encourages people to cultivate themselves to become *jūnzǐ,* "exemplary persons." This is done by developing core moral virtues, the most important of which is *rén,* which can be translated as "humanity," "benevo-lence," or "authoritative conduct." *Rén* represents the moral sense of a virtu-ous person that tells one what is right to do to promote the various roles and relationships that define one's character.[21] In some ways, this is reminiscent of contemporary feminist care ethics: the right thing to do is that which builds and maintains the complex web of human interrelation.[22] This is bal-anced by an emphasis on *yì,* a sense of moral appropriateness that is based on generalizable ethical principles that define what is right.[23] Confucius also emphasizes *lǐ,* which refers to the rituals and customs that characterize a society and allow it to operate smoothly. *Xiao* refers to filial piety; respect for one's elders radiates concentrically to other groups of people to help all people in one's community flourish as human beings.[24] By cultivating these virtues, Confucius argues that one can become an exemplary person whose authentic self-identity is defined in relation to one's family and culture.

Several of Lee's films deal specifically with Confucian themes. His first three films—*Pushing Hands, The Wedding Banquet,* and *Eat Drink Man Woman*—are meant to be a trilogy that engages in an East–West dialectic by drawing on common themes. In all three films, a traditional Confucian father is struggling to maintain relationships with children who define themselves according to modern Western values. In particular, there is a tension between the *lǐ* (rituals, customs) of China and those of America. The children try to pull away from their fathers, but in doing so, they threaten to defy *xìao* (filial piety).

Daoist philosophy is another core component of both Chinese culture and Ang Lee's films. Daoism supports the ecocentric philosophy that authentic self-cultivation is achieved by following the way of nature. The term *dào* refers to both the way of the natural world and to the undifferentiated nature of ultimate reality. Nature is a dynamic, interdependent process in which particular things are only temporary manifestations of the ever-changing whole. *Dé* is the function or virtue of something, and it refers to the particular forms that the *dào* takes as individual things in the world. Things manifest according to two forces: *yīn,* which is negative, dark, and destructive, and *yáng,* which is positive, bright, and creative. A key principle of Daoism is *wú-wéi,* which means noninterference or nonassertive action.[25] One should not strain against the forces of the natural world but should instead harmonize oneself with its confluence of events. This is done by cultivating the suppleness (*róu*) that is epitomized by living bamboo, which remains strong and flexible even when bent. Daoism has had a great influence on the martial arts of China, Japan, and Korea. The character for *róu* is pronounced *jū* in Japanese and is a foundational part of the martial arts of judo and jujitsu, which teach fighters to yield to an opponent's power in order to throw or submit him.

In *Pushing Hands,* Master Chu is a retired tai chi[26] master who moves to New York to be with his son Alex, daughter-in-law Martha, and grandson Jeremy. There is a tension between Chu's traditional Confucian ethos and the modern Western values of his son's family. Chu's presence prevents Martha from writing her second novel, which interferes with her own quest for authenticity. Alex feels pulled in two directions: on the one hand, he considers himself a contemporary Western individual, while on the other, he is motivated by a sense of filial piety toward his Confucian father. In the tai chi push hands drill, one learns to control one's partner by yielding to his force, which Chu must do to survive and thrive in his new family setting. Thus, the adaptive nature of Daoism must temper traditional Confucian values to help them adapt dynamically to the modern world.

The Wedding Banquet tells the story of Wai-Tung Gao, who is in a happy gay relationship with Simon but feels pressured by his traditional Chinese family to marry a woman. Wai-Tung's Chinese tenant, Wei-Wei, needs a green card, so she agrees to marry him to mollify his parents. The conflict of the film comes from the tension between Wai-Tung's desire to have a relationship with Simon and his filial obligations to Confucian values. The first part of the film is comedic, playing on the absurdity of the situation, but it becomes more dramatic after the banquet, when Wei-Wei seduces her drunken husband, who impregnates her. The duplicitous nature of Wai-Tung's relationships leads to fights with Simon, Wei-Wei, and his mother. Ultimately, Wai-Tung's father reveals to Simon that he knows about their relationship and gives the young man a *hongbao* to signify approval of their union.[27] The film ends with the family reconciled: Wai-Tung and Simon agree to both be fathers to Wei-Wei's child, and Wai-Tung's parents agree to support the unusual relationship. Like *Pushing Hands,* this film represents a struggle for authenticity in the face of the competing interests of traditional Confucian values and a desire for individual freedom.

In Chinese philosophy, there is a tension between Confucianism, a humanistic philosophy that emphasizes social virtues such as ritual propriety, and Daoism, a naturalistic philosophy that endorses moving in harmony with one's environment. James McRae's chapter in this volume, "Conquering the Self: Daoism, Confucianism, and the Price of Freedom in *Crouching Tiger, Hidden Dragon,*" discusses these themes in detail. Lee's films commonly deal with protagonists who are forced to reconcile their natural desires with the demands of their societies in order to authentically cultivate themselves. The Daoist theme of *wú-wéi* is particularly evident in those films that tell the tale of martial artists: *Pushing Hands* and *Crouching Tiger, Hidden Dragon.* McRae's chapter also explores the tension between Confucian and Daoist themes. Though the protagonists can only attain authenticity by breaking from the confines of established social norms, this freedom comes with a price that drives the tragic elements of the story.

Sense and Sensibility explores the tension between following one's natural desires (sense) and adhering to sociocultural norms (sensibility). The drawbacks of these extremes are illustrated early in the story: Fanny Dashwood is an exemplar of stuffy Victorian pretentiousness, whereas the Middletons err on the opposite extreme by being too open and not respecting privacy. The custom of primogeniture compels Mr. Dashwood to leave his daughters no inheritance, though he is concerned for their well-being and begs his son, John, to take care of them. Edward Ferrars wants a relationship with Elinor, but he refuses to break off his engagement with Lucy Steele because he is a man of his word, even though doing so makes him miserable and costs him his inheritance. John Willoughby wants to marry Marianne, but he pursues the wealthy Miss Grey after he is disinherited because he cannot bear to live without money and status. Marianne represents sense and Elinor sensibility, and the film shows that there must ultimately be a balance between the two. This parallels the tension between Daoism and Confucianism in Lee's other films—there must be equilibrium between the natural and the humanistic if one wants harmony in one's life. Renée Köhler-Ryan and Sydney Palmer analyze this theme in detail in their chapter, "What Do You Know of My Heart? The Role of Sense and Sensibility in Ang Lee's *Sense and Sensibility* and *Crouching Tiger, Hidden Dragon*," particularly as it concerns the strong female protagonists in these films. *Crouching Tiger, Hidden Dragon* is Ang Lee's unique take on the traditional Chinese *wǔxiá* martial arts narrative. The conflict of the film revolves around the search for authentic self-identity undergone by the film's two female protagonists, Yu Shu Lien and Jen. Köhler-Ryan and Palmer investigate the parallels between these characters and the strong women protagonists in *Sense and Sensibility*, arguing that feminine discourse can lead to authentic self-cultivation.

In *Brokeback Mountain*, Lee focuses on the conflict between personal identity and social expectations. This work, more so than any of Lee's others, uses silence to tell the story. In the scenes that take place on the mountain, Jack Twist and Ennis Del Mar communicate through silence, yet ironically, when they are in town, even though there is much more dialogue, they are unable to express their feelings in a society that condemns them for who they are. Societal strictures bind both men to lives that they do not want: they marry and have children only because it is expected of them. There is a tension in this film similar to the one seen in *Crouching Tiger, Hidden Dragon*, in which the naturalism of Daoism grates against the humanism of Confucianism. Like the protagonists of Lee's *wŭxiá* narrative, the heroes of this western must pay a terrible price: Jack dies violently in the hands of homophobes, while Ennis is left alone without either Jack or his wife. Michael Thompson's chapter, "The Confucian Cowboy Aesthetic," analyzes the protagonists of *Crouching Tiger, Hidden Dragon* and *Brokeback Mountain* in light of the four cardinal relationships of Confucianism. He argues that the individualism—or cowboy aesthetic—of the characters is ultimately enmeshed in a Confucian framework that grounds individual authenticity in communal relationships. In "East Meets Western: The Eastern Philosophy of Ang Lee's *Brokeback Mountain*," Jeff Bush investigates the tension between the traditional cowboy code that society expects Jack and Ennis to uphold and the unorthodox relationship that defies this ethos even as it defines them. Using the Confucian philosopher Mencius and contemporary ethicists such as John Corvino, he argues that Eastern archetypes of masculinity suggest that one's natural desires and social obligations need not be at odds.

In 1957, the early philosopher of film Rudolph Arnheim argued that silent cinema was superior to talkies because the absence of dialogue forced the viewer to focus upon the images presented by the film.[28] To some extent, Lee's films resemble silent pictures: they feature minimal dialogue, sweeping natural vistas, and strong soundtracks. These features prompted actor Jake Gyllenhaal to describe Lee as "fluent in the language of silence."[29] This is perhaps why American audiences, who typically shun subtitled features, flocked to see *Crouching Tiger, Hidden Dragon:* it is a visual masterpiece with a universal appeal that transcends language. André Bazin criticized Arnheim's acclaim of silent film by stating that the most important dichotomy was actually between films that emphasize image and those that rely on editing. Bazin praises films that stress realism, in which the camera reveals the world "frozen in time."[30] Lee's films emphasize this aesthetic: long shots frame the actors in such a way that the viewer focuses on the whole scene rather than just particular actions or facial expressions. In an interview with the *New York Times,* Lee stated that Yasujiro Ozu's *Tokyo Monogatari* (1953) was one of the films that had influenced him the most as a young man.[31] Ozu is famed for his use of the Japanese aesthetic paradigm of *ma*,[32] which represents the negative space between people or events through which they interact.[33] Lee's use of silence and negative space is addressed in this book in the chapter "Landscape and Gender in Ang Lee's *Sense and Sensibility* and *Brokeback Mountain*," in which Misty Jameson and Patricia Brace discuss how Lee's use of panoramic landscapes enforces the solitude inherent in tumultuous relationships in films such as *Brokeback Mountain, The Ice Storm,* and *Sense and Sensibility.*

Eat Drink Man Woman is the tale of a semiretired Chinese master chef, Chu, who is widowed and living with his adult daughters. All three daughters develop relationships with different men and begin to distance themselves from their father, who has difficulty expressing his feelings to his children through words, so he instead shows his love through the art of cooking. Chu's struggle illustrates the Buddhist theme of impermanence: he has lost his wife and is losing his daughters, and his sense of taste is failing, but it is only by accepting the ephemeral nature of these things that he can find peace. In his chapter "Can't Get No Satisfaction: Desires, Rituals, and the Search for Harmony in *Eat Drink Man Woman,*" Carl J. Dull uses the Confucian philosopher Xunzi to discuss the tensions created by human nature, desire, and interpersonal relationships. Though the harmony of a traditional Confucian family is threatened by Western values and new relationships, it is only by embracing and resolving these new tensions that harmony can truly be maintained. Ronda Lee Roberts deals with the clash between autonomy and Confucian patriarchy in her chapter, "Paternalism, Virtue Ethics, and Ang Lee: Does Father Really Know Best?" She argues that the tension between modernity and traditional values can be resolved through an appeal to Aristotelian virtue ethics, which can create a harmonious mean between seemingly disparate extremes.

Lust, Caution explores Wong Chia Chi's struggle for identity as she works undercover in a plot to assassinate Mr. Yee, a recruiter for the Japanese forces occupying Shanghai. She is forced to transform herself from an innocent college student into a spy, a process that demands the callous sacrifice of her virginity to one of her coconspirators. She must then take on the role of Mrs. Mak and become Mr. Yee's lover so that she can lure him into an assassination trap. Yee is a cold and brutal man, and his first sexual encounter with Chia Chi has all the violence and disrespect of an assault. She then finds herself torn between two selves: the freedom fighter who is working to assassinate a vicious government agent, and the lover who is bound to Yee through their frequent trysts. Ultimately, Chia Chi betrays herself and the resistance to save Yee's life, a sign that her self-identity has become so confused that she has embraced the illusory self she created. In the chapter, "*Lust, Caution:* A Case for Perception, Unimpeded," Basileios Kroustallis uses the phenomenology of Maurice Merleau-Ponty, the aesthetics of Arnol Berlean, and the philosophical anthropology of Thomé Fang to analyze the moral development of the film's main characters. He argues that Chia Chi's behavior is motivated not by a fundamental moral dilemma, but rather by a lack of phenomenological engagement with the cause that she claims to support.

In *Hulk,* Lee attempts to explore the complexities of Bruce Banner's character. Bruce struggles with his self-identity in terms of not only the mixed blessing of his newfound superpower, but also the patriarchal influence of his father, David, whose tainted genes were passed to his son. Adam Barkman's chapter, "The Power to Go beyond God's Boundaries? *Hulk,* Human Nature, and Some Ethical Concerns Thereof," explores Bruce Banner's identity crisis by arguing that Lee's approach is both typically and untypically Eastern in respect to philosophy. On the one hand, Lee's focus on Bruce's relationship with his father is a common Confucian theme throughout Lee's works, but on the other hand, Lee's insistence that there is an unchanging self that unites the Hulk and Bruce is anti-Buddhist and anti-Daoist.

Timothy M. Dale and Joseph J. Foy's "Displacement, Deception, and Disorder: Ang Lee's Discourse of Identity" studies the philosophy of identity expressed in three of Lee's works: *Hulk, Crouching Tiger, Hidden Dragon,* and *Brokeback Mountain.* The authors suggest that the strictures of society force the protagonists of Lee's films to conceal aspects of their identity, a subterfuge that ultimately leads to calamity.

Taking Woodstock is a commentary on both warfare and sexual identity. The film is based on the true story of Elliot Tiber, who helped to bring the Woodstock festival to Bethel, New York. Elliot struggles to define his sexual identity amid the free love movement that defined the late 1960s, particularly the emerging gay rights movement. David Zietsma's chapter, "Subverting Heroic Violence: Ang Lee's *Taking Woodstock* and *Hulk* as Antiwar Narratives," views the film as a critique of the violence that permeates Hollywood productions. He argues that both films depict violence as an obstacle to authentic self-cultivation: the protest movements of the Vietnam era serve as a counterpoint to the imperialism and blind patriotism that have characterized American culture in the twentieth century. In the chapter entitled "*Homo Migrans:* Desexualization in Ang Lee's *Taking Woodstock,*" Nancy Kang explores the existential crisis that homosexuals face in confronting and revealing their identities. She argues that while honesty about homosexual identity can result in death—either physical or social—dishonesty can lead to a miserable, inauthentic existence. She interprets *Taking Woodstock* as a film that endorses a universalist conception of human love, typified by Elliot Tiber's quest for personal liberation.

The Ice Storm continues to explore the theme of authenticity in interpersonal relationships. Both the Hood and Carver families are highly dysfunctional: the parents do not communicate with one another or their children, Ben Hood is having an affair with Janey Carver, and their children suffer from empty attachments to sex, drugs, and violence. All of the main characters are embroiled in an existential crisis in which they struggle to define their self-identities against the ennui of modern life. The catalyst for this change is an ice storm, which acts as a metaphor for the cold, turbulent relationships that these family members share.

Susanne Schmetkamp's "Because of the Molecules: *The Ice Storm* and the Philosophy of Love and Recognition" addresses the dialogical nature of love and sexuality as a way to explain the failed interpersonal relationships of the Hood and Carver families. David Koepsell's chapter, "It's Existential: Negative Space and Nothingness in *The Ice Storm*," uses the philosophy of Jean-Paul Sartre to explore the characters' responses to anxiety and despair that defined the sociopolitical climate of the United States in the early 1970s. George T. Hole's "*The Ice Storm*: What Is Impending?" examines the psychological bases for the characters' suffering from the perspectives of Zen Buddhism and Heideggerian existentialism.

Ride with the Devil deals with the controversial topic of the American Civil War from a perspective that is sympathetic to the plight of both Southerners and slaves caught up in the conflict. Jake Roedel and Jack Bull Chiles are members of a group of Missouri bushwhackers, Confederate irregulars who used guerilla tactics against Union forces. Much of the conflict of the film comes from the tension between individual authenticity and the hostile sociopolitical environment of the Civil War. Daniel Holt is a former slave who is serving as a Confederate scout out of a sense of loyalty to George Clyde, who granted him freedom. His sense of personal debt forces him to support a cause that is fundamentally unjust and contrary to his self-interest. Jake, who was born in Germany, has suffered from the anti-German prejudices of many Southerners, and this makes him sympathetic to the racism that Daniel experiences. In the chapter entitled "All's Fair in Love and War? Machiavelli and Ang Lee's *Ride with the Devil*," James Edwin Mahon uses the philosophy of Machiavelli to resolve some of these ethical and political tensions.

Versatile and Fearless

Ang Lee is renowned as a versatile and fearless filmmaker who continually strives to break new ground by exploring complex philosophical themes through the medium of motion pictures. His films resonate with viewers not only because of his skill as a director, but because they investigate issues that are universally important to human beings. As Socrates states in Plato's *Crito,* "the unexamined life is not worth living." Film is an important medium for philosophy because it vividly challenges us to reevaluate the foundational assumptions on which we base our lives. Ang Lee's films are significant not just as works of art, but also as opportunities for philosophical inquiry.

Notes

1. Sarah Kerr, "Sense and Sensitivity," *New York Magazine,* April 1, 1996.
2. Lee's films have been nominated for twenty-seven Oscars with eight wins, forty BAFTA awards with twelve wins, and twenty Golden Globe awards with eight wins.
3. Whitney Crothers Dilley, *The Cinema of Ang Lee: The Other Side of the Screen* (London: Wallflower Press, 2007), 5–6.
4. Ibid., 6–7.
5. Ibid., 7–11.
6. Internet Movie Data Base, listing of awards for Ang Lee (http://imdb.com/).
7. Dilley, *Cinema of Ang Lee,* 12.
8. Ibid., 4, 14–15.
9. For a full exploration of this idea, see Friedrich Nietzsche's own autobiography, *Ecce Homo,* trans. Duncan Large (Oxford: Oxford University Press, 2009).
10. Dilley, *Cinema of Ang Lee,* 18–19.
11. Thomas Wartenberg, "Philosophy of Film," in *Stanford Encyclopedia of Philosophy* (http://plato.stanford.edu).
12. Ibid.
13. Ibid.
14. Ibid.
15. This is discussed in detail in Kierkegaard's book, *The Concept of Anxiety,* trans. Reidar Thomte (Princeton, N.J.: Princeton University Press, 1981).
16. Charles Taylor, *The Ethics of Authenticity* (Cambridge, Mass.: Harvard University Press, 1991), 25.
17. Charles Taylor, *Sources of the Self: The Making of the Modern Identity* (Cambridge, Mass.: Harvard University Press, 1989), 35.
18. Taylor, *Ethics of Authenticity,* 32–33.
19. Taylor, *Sources of the Self,* 35.

20. For a detailed discussion of the focus–field self in Chinese philosophy, see Roger T. Ames and Henry Rosemont's translation of *The Analects of Confucius* (New York: Ballantine Books, 1999) and David Hall and Roger T. Ames's *Thinking from the Han: Self, Truth, Transcendence in Chinese and Western Culture* (Albany: State University of New York Press, 1998).

21. Ames and Rosemont, *Analects of Confucius,* 48–51.

22. See Carol Gilligan, *In a Different Voice* (Cambridge, Mass.: Harvard University Press, 1982).

23. Ames and Rosemont, *Analects of Confucius,* 53–55.

24. Ibid., 51–52.

25. Hall and Ames discuss all of these concepts in detail in *Thinking from the Han.*

26. Tai chi, or tai chi chuan, is an internal Chinese martial art that focuses on the development of *chi,* or psychophysical energy. It is deeply rooted in Daoist philosophy.

27. A *hongbao* is a traditional Chinese wedding gift consisting of a red envelope adorned with calligraphy. It is supposed to bring good fortune to the married couple.

28. Wartenberg, "Philosophy of Film."

29. Dilley, *Cinema of Ang Lee,* 3.

30. Wartenberg, "Philosophy of Film."

31. Dilley, *Cinema of Ang Lee,* 40.

32. Written the same in both Chinese and Japanese; pronounced *jian* in Mandarin Chinese.

33. Steve Odin, *The Social Self in Zen and American Pragmatism* (Albany: State University of New York Press, 1996), 18–19.

Part 1

The Eastern Philosophy of Ang Lee

CONQUERING THE SELF

Daoism, Confucianism, and the Price of Freedom in
Crouching Tiger, Hidden Dragon

James McRae

Authentic Self-Cultivation

There is a famous Chinese painting entitled *The Three Vinegar Tasters* that depicts the founders of China's three great philosophical systems—Confucianism, Buddhism, and Daoism—sampling a vat of vinegar. Confucius and the Buddha find it distasteful, but the Daoist Laozi considers the vinegar to be sweet. Although this image is primarily meant to show the importance of all three traditions for Chinese culture, it is also interpreted as a Daoist critique of the other two systems, particularly Confucianism. Confucius believes that human nature is sour and must be corrected through education, rules, and social norms, but Laozi thinks that human beings are best in their natural state.

Ang Lee's film, *Crouching Tiger, Hidden Dragon* (2000), explores the tension between Confucian and Daoist philosophies of self-development.[1] Although both traditions agree on many points, they differ on the role that society should play in the cultivation of an exemplary person. The purpose of this chapter is to explore how the tension between these two traditions drives the conflict and character development in the film. The first section discusses the foundational metaphysical assumptions that are shared by Confucianism and Daoism. The second section compares and contrasts Confucian and Daoist notions of self-cultivation as they are illustrated in the film. The final section argues that freedom from social limitations is essential to authentic self-cultivation, but it comes at a price: every character must make sacrifices to attain liberation. Ultimately, *Crouching Tiger, Hidden Dragon* illustrates that authentic self-cultivation is a balance between one's natural freedom and the roles, relationships, and obligations of society.

Chinese Metaphysics: The Correlative Universe and the Focus–Field Self

Laozi (born ca. 604 BCE) and Confucius (551–479 BCE) were contemporaries during the Zhou dynasty (1122–256 BCE).[2] Both were scholars and active in political life: Laozi kept the archival records for the court of Zhou, while Confucius briefly served Duke Ding of Lu.[3] The classical texts, *Shiji* and *Zhuangzi,* both claim that the two scholars met on at least one occasion during which Confucius consulted Laozi about the rites and praised the senior scholar for his wisdom.[4] Because *Crouching Tiger, Hidden Dragon* is set in 1779 CE during the Qing dynasty (1644–1911 CE), the ideas of both Confucianism and Daoism would have become culturally embedded and instantly recognizable to the film's characters. Although Confucianism and Daoism disagree on many aspects of philosophy, they do share a common cosmology that is taken for granted by all Chinese philosophical systems.

The ancient Chinese ontology of Confucianism and Daoism is fundamentally acosmotic: "They have no concept of cosmos at all, insofar as that notion entails a coherent, single-ordered world that is in any sense enclosed or *defined.*"[5] Cosmotic thinking in Western philosophy has been problematic, postulating unhelpful ideas: a belief in an ordering agency, a contrast between reality and appearance, a focus on permanence over the process of becoming, and a preference of reason over sense experience. As acosmotic philosophies, Confucianism and Daoism profess no ordering agency and no contrast between reality and appearance, and they focus on change, the process of becoming, and the validity of sense experience over purely rational thinking.[6] Ames and Rosemont draw a distinction between the Western notion of relation and the Chinese notion of correlation.[7] Western epistemology is typically concerned with relationality, in which an independent self observes its environment as a separate entity. Because the individual is separate from the environment, it is necessary for one to have a set of categories through which experience can be organized and interpreted. In the Chinese notion of correlation, the knower and the known are fundamentally related because the knower is part of his or her environment.

Two key terms are used to define the natural environment: *tiān* and *dào.* Neither term is clearly defined within Confucian or Daoist philosophies because these traditions emphasize ethics over metaphysics.[8] Ames and Rosemont choose to translate *tiān* as "the Inherent Order of the Natural World," though many scholars also render it as "the heavens" or "heaven."[9] *Tiān* is often used as part of the compound *tiānmìng,* which refers to the "propensity of circumstances" or the natural tendencies of things. *Dào* can be translated as "road," "path," or "way," and it holds slightly different meanings for Confucianism and Daoism. Confucius interprets it as the way of self-cultivation, such that "to realize the *dao* is to experience, to interpret, and to influence the world in such a way as to reinforce and extend the way of life inherited from one's cultural predecessors."[10] In Daoism, *dào* refers to the way of nature; it is the absolute first principle of existence— undifferentiated, whole, and full of infinite possibility. The *Daodejing* begins with the passage, "The Dao that can be named is not the Dao." As soon as we start rationally categorizing things, we abstract them from their true, interdependent nature. Taken together, *tiān* and *dào* refer to "the movement and patterns of the natural world."[11] In both Daoist and Confucian thought, when the term *tiān* is used, it refers to the natural world and the interrelation of things within the natural order. In Confucianism, when the term *dào* is used, it usually refers to the path of cultivation one must follow in order to become an exemplary person.[12] In Daoism, *dào* refers not only to this process, but also to the natural order of the world as well; *dào* and *tiān* are used interchangeably.[13] This is important because in Daoism, it is only when one brings one's actions into harmony with the natural world that one can truly be a cultivated person. The Daoist view does not contradict the Confucian view; rather, it has expanded on the Confucian interpretation of *tiān* by combining it with the concept of *dào*. Although *tiān* and *dào* have slightly different overtones, the two terms are used interchangeably in Daoist literature.[14]

Confucianism and Daoism understand the person to be defined by a focus–field relationship with his or her context and the persons within that context. Hall and Ames describe the focus–field self in Chinese culture and philosophy:

> Persons are radically situated as persons-in-context, inhering as they do in a world defined by specific social, cultural, and natural conditions. Persons shape and are shaped by the field of things and events in which they reside. . . . This language of focus and field provides us with a way of talking about the continuity and interdependence of

> the human being and *tian* presupposed in the Confucian worldview. *Tian* is the field, the social, cultural, and natural context, and is in some sense greater than the particular person . . . as well as being implicate within and brought into focus by the particular person.[15]

Tiān is the context in which all things reside and the background against which all things must define themselves. Self-development in ancient China was understood as the art of contextualization—the art of cultivating the person in relation to his or her environment. Because of the acosmotic structure of the Daoist world, there is no single, great context in which all things are taxonomically organized parts. Rather, the world consists of the "myriad things," a plethora of particulars that can be understood from a variety of different perspectives. Thus, since the world is made up of "many particular foci that organize the fields about them," the "art of contextualization involves the production of harmonious correlations of the myriad details . . . that make up the world."[16] These "myriad details" include the natural world and other persons (both familial and sociopolitical relationships). By harmonizing oneself with one's context, one is shaped by that context and in turn seeks to shape that context through one's actions within it.

This understanding of oneness as a function of focus–field relationships is most evident in *Daodejing* 39:

> Of old there were certain things that realized oneness:
> The heavens in realizing oneness became clear;
> The earth in realizing oneness became stable;
> The numinous in realizing oneness became animated;
> The river valleys in realizing oneness became full;
> The lords and kings in realizing oneness brought proper order to the
>   world.[17]

This passage describes the way that all things are defined by their focus–field relationships with their context (*dào*). All things must understand themselves and cultivate themselves in relation to the *dào* (natural world). Each thing—the heavens, earth, the numinous, the valleys, and the lords and princes—are truly developed only when they are understood according to their relationship with the oneness of their context. Any attempt to cultivate oneself without this contextualized understanding results in disaster.

Thus, it is one's relationship to the oneness of the *dào* that brings stability and flourishing to the world.

The characters in the film are fundamentally defined by their relationships with each other and with the natural world. Jade Fox (Cheng Pei-pei) represents the unnatural: she learns Wudan by studying the pictures, but does not understand the underlying principles; she uses Purple Yin poison to kill Li by reversing the natural flow of his blood and vital energy; and she corrupts Jen's (Ziyi Zhang) character by making her into a criminal (a poisoned dragon). By contrast, Li Mu Bai (Chow Yun-Fat) is a representation of what is natural. He is repeatedly associated with the green bamboo forest, which is a symbol of adaptability to nature: his sword has "green" in its name, he uses a tree branch to parry Jen's blade in their first fight, and he later uses the green bamboo forest to his advantage in his epic duel with Jen.

Self-Cultivation in Confucianism and Daoism

During his first confrontation with Jen, Li Mu Bai offers a lesson about the true meaning of the martial arts: self-cultivation. "No growth without assistance. No action without reaction. No desire without restraint. Now give yourself up and find yourself again. There is a lesson for you."[18] Jen clearly has fighting skill, but she lacks the character to control her abilities. Ultimately, martial arts training is dedicated to the cultivation of one's character, and it is on this point that a tension develops between Daoist and Confucian approaches to self-cultivation. Despite being grounded in the same cosmology, Confucianism and Daoism pursue different goals when it comes to self-cultivation. Confucianism can be classified as a type of humanism because it focuses on people and society as the medium through which self-cultivation takes place: the human community is the primary source of value. Daoism is a type of naturalism in which self-cultivation is modeled on the way of the natural world.[19]

SELF-CULTIVATION IN CONFUCIANISM

Confucianism considers the self to be dynamically structured as a function of its relationship to its environment and to other people. There is no permanent, fundamental self that an individual must actualize apart from the influence of society; rather, the self is flexible, constantly changing to meet the demands of its environment to thrive within it.[20] Confucius does not care who a person really is ontologically; rather, he is interested in how a person might cultivate him- or herself through the constant flux of a changing world. In the *Analects,* Confucius argues, "It is the person who broadens the way (*dao* . . .), not the way that broadens the person."[21] One's self is not based on some permanent, ontologically fixed being that one must actualize, but rather on one's act of living appropriately in the world. By cultivating oneself to the highest degree, one brings a richness to the field of which one is a focus. Thus, in cultivating oneself, one broadens the *dao.* An important aspect of every person's context is the other persons within that context: "Authoritative persons establish others in seeking to establish themselves and promote others in seeking to get there themselves. Correlating one's conduct with those near at hand can be said to be the method of becoming an authoritative person."[22] For Confucius, self-cultivation must be accomplished in conjunction with the other people with whom one shares one's context. Realizing (*zhī*) oneself is a process of "realizing others" just as understanding authoritative conduct (*rén*) is a process of "loving others."[23]

The goal of Confucian self-cultivation is to become a *jūnzǐ,* or exemplary person, which is the highest goal that most human beings can hope to achieve. Higher still is the goal of the *shèngrén,* or sage, who is the greatest of exemplary persons and is extremely rare. Average people are *shì,* scholar-apprentices on the path to virtue, while corrupt people are *xiǎorén,* petty people.[24] When Yu Shu Lien (Michelle Yeoh) and Li Mu Bai are discussing the possibility of Wudan accepting Jen as a pupil despite their prohibition against training women, Li comments, "For her, they might make an exception. If not, I'm afraid she'll become a poisoned dragon." The term "poisoned dragon" refers to a martial artist with a corrupt moral character (in Confucian terms, a *xiǎorén*). As Robert Carter argues, the Confucian self is a process "always open to self-improvement, self-transformation, and educational growth en route to sagehood."[25] Thus, while Jen's character has been corrupted by her relationship with Jade Fox, it is still possible that given the right tutelage, she might become an exemplary person. Li and Yu are both exemplary persons (or nearly so), but their repressed love for one another has led them to lives of sorrow and regret rather than fulfillment. Ultimately, all human beings have the potential to become *jūnzǐ,* and if all people would strive to be exemplary, we could have a truly harmonious society.[26]

There are several virtues that one must cultivate to become an exemplary person. The first—and arguably the most important—is *rén.*[27] *Rén* refers to humanity, benevolence, moral character, or human-heartedness (though Ames and Rosemont prefer to use the translation "authoritative conduct").

The Chinese character is composed of radicals for "person" and "two," which imply that one cannot become a cultivated person by oneself. It is thought that this character was originally written using "person" plus "above/ascend," which suggests that *rén* refers to the characteristics of a higher person. It is the ultimate moral principle that makes one fully human. A virtuous person has a natural moral sentiment that makes him or her sensitive to the needs of others and his or her own roles and responsibilities (*rénjiān*). Thus, *rén* reflects the interrelational nature of the focus–field self.[28] In the film, both Li and Yu are exemplars of authoritative conduct, as evidenced by their repeated acts of benevolence toward Jen. Li pursues her as a student even though she fights him and is the pupil of Jade Fox, who slew Li's master. Li ultimately dies as a result, and in doing so redeems Jen's character. Yu agrees to be Jen's sister even though Jen stole the Green Destiny and fought against Yu when the latter tried to prevent the theft.

The second key virtue of Confucianism is *yì*, "appropriateness," which refers to the moral principles that guide virtuous action. The character is composed of the radicals for sheep (*yáng*) and we (*wǒ*) and refers to sacrifices made for the good of the community.[29] These are not categorical imperatives in the Kantian sense, but rather more like the virtue rules that Rosalind Hursthouse describes for virtue ethics: general moral principles that promote the goal of virtue and assist in the resolution of moral dilemmas.[30] Ames and Rosemont argue that *yì* is "one's sense of appropriateness that enables one to act in a proper and fitting manner, given the specific situation" and "that makes relationships truly meaningful in a community of mutual trust."[31] By understanding one's context, one can learn to live productively within that context. In this sense, *yì* is a form of practical wisdom that has pragmatic cash value for one's life. This notion of action-guiding principles is reflected in Yu Shu Lien's words to Jen: "Fighters have rules too: friendship, trust, integrity . . . without rules, we wouldn't survive long."[32] Jen struggles to accept this notion throughout the film. After she steals the Green Destiny, she challenges the martial artists in the tea stall and Star Restaurant. These actions are rude and impetuous—a total violation of the Giang Hu moral code.[33] Her disregard of this code ultimately leads to Li Mu Bai's death.

The third key virtue of Confucianism is *lǐ*, which refers to the rituals, rites, customs, and etiquette that facilitate human interaction.[34] *Lǐ* are the everyday practices that embody and promote the achievement of *rén*, including religious rituals, social customs, and general propriety in action. Ames and Rosemont describe *lǐ* as "those meaning-invested roles, relationships, and institutions which facilitate communication, and which foster a sense of community."[35] These are different from laws in the sense that we "make them our own" by imbedding them as habits. *Lǐ* is part of a continuum that includes both ethics (*yì*) and etiquette (*lǐ*): both are needed to promote social harmony. *Lǐ* is closely related to the fourth Confucian virtue of *xiào*, "filial piety." The family constitutes the immediate social environment for a child and is vital to one's moral cultivation. Respect for those closest to oneself radiates outward concentrically to other groups of people in five cardinal relationships: ruler–subject, parent–child, husband–wife, elder–younger sibling, and friends. *Xiào* is not just caring for other people such as one's parents, but a dedication to helping them flourish as human beings.[36] The demands of both *lǐ* and *xiào* are evident in *Crouching Tiger, Hidden Dragon*. Li Mu Bai and Yu Shu Lien feel that they cannot express their love for one another because they fear that they will dishonor the memory of Meng, Yu's fiancé, who died to save Li. Jen's relationship with Jade Fox is confused by the fact that the latter is both Jen's servant and her martial arts master, which is further complicated when Jen surpasses her master and is offered an apprenticeship with Li Mu Bai. Jen and Yu agree to be sisters, yet Jen finds it difficult to defer to Yu's authority. Jen is expected, as a Confucian woman, to accept a political marriage, yet she has an affair with Lo (Dark Cloud, played by Chang Chen). Ultimately, it is the tension between social expectations and one's natural desires that provides the conflict of the story.

The fifth essential Confucian virtue is *xìn*, which can mean honesty, trustworthiness, fidelity, or integrity. Literally, the character refers to a person speaking, and it implies one being true to one's word.[37] Honesty involves not only a correspondence between outward behavior and inner activity (truthfulness with others),[38] but an internal consistency as well (truthfulness with oneself). This is closely related to the concept of *zhèngmíng*, the rectification of names: one must understand the criteria that define a role and then live to fulfill them to the greatest extent possible.[39] The martial arts involve not only combative mastery, but also the cultivation of moral virtue; a person who masters one but not the other cannot be truly called a martial artist. In the film, Li and Yu are bound by both the Giang Hu moral code, which includes honesty and integrity. This is why they feel they cannot have a relationship: doing so would violate the oaths they swore to Meng, who was Li's true friend and Yu's fiancé.

The Confucian text *Zhongyong* stresses the importance of *zhìchéng*, which can be translated as "creativity" or "utmost sincerity" and refers to a sense of authenticity in self-cultivation. Creativity allows one to act in harmony with one's own natural tendencies, other persons, processes and events, and the transforming and nourishing activities of heaven and earth. Because one's natural tendencies are grounded in *tiān,* when one gets in touch with one's natural tendencies via *zhìchéng,* one will be in harmony with *tiān.* Through this web of interrelations with nature, a person becomes a member of the natural triad of humans, heaven, and earth.[40] Creativity is the attribute that allows one to actively interrelate with one's context. One is not simply defined by one's context; one also defines one's context by creatively interacting with it. Thus, creativity is the key to developing the focus–field self. The developmental process of creativity is described in the *Zhongyong:*

> Creativity (*cheng*) is self-consummating, and its way is self-directing. Creativity is a process (*wu*) taken from its beginning to its end, and without this creativity, there are no events. It is thus that, for exemplary persons (*junzi*), it is creativity that is prized. But creativity is not simply the self-consummating of one's own person; it is what consummates events. Consummating oneself is authoritative conduct (*ren*); consummating other events is wisdom (*zhi*). This is the excellence (*de*) of one's natural tendencies (*xing*) and is the way of integrating what is more internal and what is more external. Thus, whenever one applies excellence, it is fitting.[41]

Creativity allows one to "envelop everything"—all things, persons, and events are consummated as part of one's self. Through this creativity, one consummates one's focus–field relationship with heaven and earth. A relationship with *tiān* makes one cultured (*wén*), which in turn leads to excellence (*dé*).[42] Through creativity, one is not only a reflection of one's environment, but also a unique particular within that environment that stands in sharp contrast to other particulars. Self-cultivation is a creative, active process of contextual interrelation in which one both defines and is defined by one's context, not a passive process in which one sits back and lets one's environment dictate one's person.

Ultimately, Confucius argues that virtue, rather than law, should be the basis of government. All people are part of a moral community, and rulers should lead by example to educate their citizens. If society were composed of virtuous people, we would not need laws to control their behavior.[43] Daoism agrees with this point, though it considers the basis of virtue to be the *dào,* not society.

Because human beings exist in focus–field relationships with their contexts, it is essential for people to model their self-cultivation upon the workings of the natural world (*tiān* and *dào*). Zhuangzi states that all humans are fundamentally defined (given face and form) by *tiān* and *dào,* and it is by coming to understand and emulate their workings that we can develop ourselves into sages.[44] Laozi encourages people to pattern themselves on the natural world,[45] the *Zhongyong* describes how Confucius gained excellence because he modeled himself on the rhythms of nature,[46] and Zhuangzi states, "Virtue resides in the Heavenly."[47]

The undifferentiated whole of the *dào* is manifested as particular things via *dé,* which can be translated as "function" or "virtue." *Dé* consists to two opposing, complementary forces: *yīn* and *yáng. Yīn* represents forces that are negative, recessive, dark, or destructive, while *yáng* designates those that are positive, bright, dominant, or creative. The *tàijítú* (the "diagram of ultimate power," a popular symbol of Daoism) represents the relationship of *yīn* and *yáng* as a constantly changing process: though one force might be more prevalent at a particular time, eventually the other force will prevail, restoring balance to the universe. *Daodejing* 42.93 describes the progressive contextualization of all things in a focus–field relationship with the *dào:* "The way begets one; one begets two; two begets three; three begets the myriad creatures." The *dào* (way) is the field for the *dé* (one), which is the field for *yīn* and *yáng* (two), which are the field for heaven, earth, and human beings (three), which are the field for the many particular things within the world (myriad creatures). *Dào* is the field against which *dé* is defined. *Daodejing* 25 describes the *dào* as "a thing confusedly formed," continually created and recreated in every moment by the interaction of all of the myriad things. In the film, the sword, the Green Destiny, is described as a fusion of polar opposites: peace and violence, enlightenment and death. Sir Te (Sihung Lung) states, "A sword by itself rules nothing. It comes alive only through skillful manipulation."[48] It is only through self-cultivation that one is able to develop the skill necessary to live in harmony with the continually shifting balance of *yīn* and *yáng.*

The *dào* is natural (*zìrán*)—it exists as a function of the interrelation of all of the myriad things that live within it, and it is through this interrelation that these things can be said to be one. In order to be a person in the truest sense, one must naturally and harmoniously interrelate with one's context and the persons within that context.[49] Naturally integrating oneself with one's context does not necessarily mean that one becomes a generic part of a larger, homogeneous whole. In the film, Shu Lien confirms her suspicions about Jen by dropping a teapot and forcing Jen to reveal herself through her natural (yet cultivated) martial reflexes.[50]

The fully cultivated person as a focus–field self is found in the concept of the *zhēnrén,* "genuine person." This term is composed of two Chinese characters: *rén* means "person," and *zhēn* can be translated as "the highest degree of purity and integrity."[51] More specifically, *zhēn* is "the ground of personal, social, and political integration that makes one continuous with one's natural and cultural environments."[52] One who has cultivated oneself as *zhēnrén* has developed that self in relation to one's context and to the persons within that context. Thus, *zhēnrén,* as Laozi and Zhuangzi understand it, represents the cultivated focus–field self. Hall and Ames state, "Daoism and its notion of the 'authentic person' (*zhēnrén* . . .) is a celebration of the pursuit of full contextualization for the always unique person within an ever changing world."[53] Through a careful cultivation of the interpersonal relationships between the self and the environment, sages develop themselves as *zhēnrén.* It is the Daoist sage who is the true exemplar of the cultivated contextual self. When a person successfully interrelates with his or her context and the persons within that context, he or she becomes a sage, a leader by example, and a standard upon which others might base their own development.[54] Zhuangzi describes the development of the sage:

> He who knows what it is that Heaven does, and knows what it is that man does, has reached the peak. Knowing what it is that Heaven does, he lives with Heaven. Knowing what it is that man does, he uses the knowledge of what he knows to help out the knowledge of what he doesn't know, and lives out the years that Heaven gave him without being cut off midway—this is the perfection of knowledge.[55]

The sage has combined the knowledge of humankind and the knowledge of nature to yield a complete understanding of the world in its totality. Furthermore, he or she lives life according to the natural rhythm of *tiān,* existing in true harmony with his or her context.

Zhuangzi states, "True Man breathes with his heels; the mass of men breathe with their throats."[56] In the Chinese martial arts, which are heavily influenced by Daoist philosophy, the concept of rooting to the earth through one's heels is vital. The disciplines of tai chi chuan, *chin na, wing chun,* and *ba gua* (to name a few) all emphasize the way in which a person draws energy from the earth through the *qì* meridians that terminate in the heels. Thus, when Zhuangzi talks about breathing through the heels, he describes the way in which the *zhēnrén* draws his sense of identity from his intimate contact with the earth, and through the earth, with the totality of his context. Whereas uncultivated men consider themselves to be individuals distinguished from the rest of humanity, the *zhēnrén* defines himself through his focus–field relationship with his environment and the persons within that environment. Zhuangzi states, "When man and Heaven [*tian*] do not defeat each other, then we may be said to have the True Man [*zhenren*]."[57] When people interact with nature (*tiān*) in a focus–field relationship and do not treat nature as an other, they cultivate themselves as *zhēnrén*. In the "Hsü Wu-Kuei" chapter of the *Zhuangzi*, the person as *zhēnrén* is described as follows: "Embracing virtue, infused with harmony, he follows along with the world—this is is called the True Man."[58] In the film, Li and Yu are depicted as sages of the martial arts. Both characters have cultivated themselves to the point that they can harmonize with the patterns of the natural world. The only thing that is holding them back from an authentic, flourishing life is their reticence to embrace their love for one another, which is the result of society's artificial expectations.

In *The Propensity of Things,* François Jullien offers a detailed analysis of Daoist ethics. Anything that can be called a force of change in history depends on its context and cannot be abstracted from its context. This also applies to public morality: an act is only considered moral in relation to a particular sociohistorical context.[59] Jullien describes the way in which systems arose out of the necessity of humanity to survive in its continually changing environment. Moral systems are constructed by a society as a tool to keep the peace and bring about the greatest prosperity to everyone in a society. One moral system is not better than another; it is just more effective (using it is more reasonable) at a particular time and place. A particular system is used until it no longer fits the demands of its context (that is, it no longer allows a society to function in harmony with nature); then another system is adopted.[60] The development of civilization is not governed by progress (moving from barbarism to an ideal political state); rather, it is controlled by alternation (moving from a moral/political system that is inappropriate for the particular context to one that is more appropriate). This is not relativism because there is a way to determine whether a moral or political system fits properly into a given sociohistorical context—specifically, do all members of the society prosper when the society adopts the particular moral system? A moral system must promote a society in which all people are free to act, yet act in a way that does not impede the flourishing of other persons. This stands in sharp contrast to the traditionalism of Confucius' *lǐ* and *yì*, which Daoism rejects as stagnant constructs that defy the changing order of the natural world.

Daoist personal morality is an extension of its system of sociopolitical ethics. According to Jullien, Daoism understands human behavior according to two principles: first, every tendency has a natural inclination toward growth; and second, any tendency that is carried to its extreme of growth demands reversal.[61] The goal of personal action is to maintain a harmonious interrelation with nature. Any action that goes against the flow of nature will gradually build up potential for reversion, bringing the actor back into harmony with nature. It is possible for a wise person to logically determine the trend that events are taking and align him- or herself with that trend in order to prosper from it.[62] However, if one's actions do take one away from the flow of nature, there are two things that one must do in order to reestablish harmony. Initially, one should shun excess so as to avoid the imbalance that leads to reversion. Even when imbalance is present, one should avoid further excess to minimize the amount of reversion that will necessarily take place. Then, if reversion does occur, one should go along with it. It would be foolish to oppose necessary change. True skill is the ability to "ride" the change and extract from it the greatest benefit.[63] Reversion is not necessarily a negative thing, so long as one does not try to oppose it. Moral constancy (maintaining harmony with the *dào*) is highly valued for the Daoist because it prevents an individual from becoming imbalanced and inviting reversion. One must be careful to not interpret reversion as a kind of determinism. The Daoist understanding of the world leaves room for human initiative in the ability of an individual to influence a tendency at the early stages of its development (before it reaches the point of no return and must revert). Even when the point is reached where reversion is inevitable, it is up to the individual to manage the change properly in order to reap the greatest reward.[64] In *Crouching Tiger, Hidden Dragon,* Jen rebels against her traditional Confucian roles by swinging to the complete opposite end of the spectrum and embracing the lifestyle of a criminal warrior. The extreme nature of her actions leads to personal disaster and produce a reversion. By the end of the film, Jen begins to achieve a balance between her roles and responsibilities on one hand and her desire for autonomy on the other.

One's harmony with the *dào* is maintained via *wú-wéi*, which can be translated as "noninterference" or "nonassertive action."[65] One should not strain or contrive to accomplish something that goes against nature, but should rather let things happen in their natural ways. Unlike Confucianism, which considers the complex and well-lived political life the ideal, Daoism's ideal is to be simple and harmonious. We should let things naturally manifest their own perfection, stripping away bad habits rather than cultivating new ones. To do this, a Daoist should cultivate *róu,* "suppleness" or "yielding strength." In the film, Sir Te advises Governor Yu (Li Fa Zeng), "Be strong, yet supple. This is the way to rule."[66] Strife is caused in society by bad rulers who directly oppose the ways of nature. The concept of *róu* is so essential in the martial arts that two styles—judo and jujitsu[67]—use the character for *róu* in the names of their arts. When pushed, a fighter does not oppose the force by pushing back, but rather pulls the opponent forward, channeling the energy of the push into a throw that uses the assailant's force against him. Green bamboo is often used to illustrate *róu:* while the limbs of trees snap under the weight of ice and the force of wind, bamboo bends with the pressure and snaps back unharmed. This concept is at play in *Crouching Tiger, Hidden Dragon* in Li Mu Bai and Jen's duel in the bamboo forest. Li uses the flexibility of the bamboo to neutralize the advantage that Jen has with the Green Destiny in her hands. When Yu Shu Lien and Jen fight in the courtyard, Yu repeatedly attempts to pick the right weapon to beat the Green Destiny, but each fails because it directly opposes the superior force of the sword. The only time that Yu scores is when she allows Jen to cut her weapon in half and uses the motion to counterattack. Jen states early in the film that Li Mu Bai's name means "skill," and Li later says, "Real skill comes without effort."[68] Success in the martial arts comes only when one moves in harmony with both the natural world and one's opponent.

The Price of Freedom

Much of the conflict in *Crouching Tiger, Hidden Dragon* comes from the tension between Confucian and Daoist understandings of self-cultivation. The title of the film refers to the two young lovers, Jen and Lo (Dark Cloud). Jen's full name, Jiāo Lóng, means "delicate dragon," while Lo's full name, Xiǎo Hǔ, means "little tiger." Both Jen and Lo are stubborn and self-absorbed, but they show great potential that has not yet been actualized. Hence, the tiger crouches and the dragon is hidden. Ang Lee describes the phrase "crouching tiger, hidden dragon" as a common Chinese idiom "which reminds us never to underestimate the mysteries, the potent characters that lie beneath the surface of society."[69] He further states that "*Crouching Tiger, Hidden Dragon* is a story about passions, emotions, desires—the dragons hidden inside all of us."[70] Jen and Lo impulsively rebel against society's attempts to restrict their desires, while Li Mu Bai and Yu Shu Lien are exemplary persons who are nonetheless miserable because they are unable to express their love for one another. Thus, there is a tension between Daoism's creative freedom to pursue what is natural and the ritual propriety and customary roles of Confucianism.

The plot of *Crouching Tiger, Hidden Dragon* is centered upon Jen's struggle for authentic self-cultivation. Although she is bound by the strictures of Confucian society, she wishes to creatively redefine herself as a warrior. Thus, her character develops as a result of the tension between a desire for autonomy and the social roles, relationships, and obligations that define her. The Japanese philosopher Watsuji Tetsurō describes this as a process of double negation in which the authentic self comes as a result of simultaneously affirming and negating both the individual and the collective.[71] Jen cannot embrace only one of these poles because it is the tension between the two that generates authenticity.

However, there is still a fundamental dispute between the humanistic philosophy of Confucianism and the naturalistic approach favored by Daoism. Confucianism considers Daoism's focus on nature and noninterference to be nebulous and unstructured, while Daoism views the rituals and roles of Confucianism as rigid and confining. Hall and Ames argue that according to Daoism, "The insistent particularity (*de*) of human beings and the possible intensity of their natural feelings is trivialized by recourse to contrived rules and artificial relationships that are dehumanizing, and by strategies for social regulation that privilege an ordered uniformity over spontaneity."[72] In *Crouching Tiger, Hidden Dragon,* the tension between these two traditions is played out through the conflict between the confines of Confucian society and the freedom of the martial lifestyle. The film and the book upon which it is based belong to a genre of Chinese fiction known as *wǔxiá*. The term consists of two characters: *wǔ*, "war" or "martial," and *xiá,* "knight-errant." Thus, a *wǔxiá* is a wandering warrior who lives according to an ethical code that includes Confucian virtues such as *yì* (moral appropriateness) and *xìn* (integrity).[73] *Wŭxiá* are expected to show absolute loyalty to their masters and to the moral code that binds them, even if it means death. Li Mu Bai and Yu Shu Lien are exemplars of this tradition: through disciplined training, they have cultivated themselves into exemplary persons, but the strictness of the *wŭxiá* code has forced them to do things they regret. Ang Lee states:

> Li Mu Bai and Yu Shu Lien are accurate portrayals of two common character stereotypes in Chinese society. They live by a Confucian moral code; they live for the community. In "Giang Hu," you need skills to survive as well as respect from the masses. Jen symbolizes their souls' desire. In fact, Jen is the real hero. Her personality is what defeats Li Mu Bai and Yu. She takes advantage of their humility. Bound by the forces of society, Li and Yu never fully enjoyed the thrills and excitement of youth. They pay dearly for their status; regrets mount as their youth fades.[74]

Yu's fiancé, Meng Si Zhao, was a *wŭxiá* and brother by oath to Li Mu Bai, and he sacrificed himself to save the latter's life. This creates a tension between the cardinal relationships of Confucianism. Li has specific obligations to the friend who saved his life, one of which is to respect Meng's relationship with Yu, yet Li clearly loves Yu and wants her to be his wife. Yu is torn between playing two roles defined by two different relationships: husband–wife and friends. In Confucian China, widows were expected to show fidelity to their late husbands by not remarrying except under circumstances of extreme financial need.[75] Early in the film, Jen comments that Yu could not roam around freely if she were married, and Yu reluctantly acknowledges that this is true. Though she is a warrior, she is still bound by the traditional roles a woman is expected to fulfill.[76] She tells Jen, "I am not an aristocrat, as you are . . . but I must still respect a woman's duties," and "So the freedom you talk about, I too desire it. But I have never tasted it."[77] Both Li and Yu feel as though the Confucian tenets of the *wŭxiá* lifestyle are in conflict with their natural desires. One of the most visually striking shots in the film takes place in the scene in the woods where Li tries to express his love to Yu. Li stands alone in front of a pale wall that separates him from a bamboo forest that shows through the window before him. This image shows how the strict roles and rituals of society separate one from one's natural desires and freedom. That the forest is bamboo—a symbol of Daoist noninterference—

makes the shot even more poignant. The structures of human civilization do not prevent us from seeing the objects of our natural desires, though they can prevent us from attaining them.

This tension between the five cardinal relationships of Confucianism and one's inner desires creates tension for most of the characters in the film. Jade Fox's anger and resentment are born out of her feelings of confinement in the patriarchal Confucian social structure of China. She kills Li Mu Bai's master because even though he was happy to use her for sex, he refused to train her in the martial arts. Wudan's refusal to train women was not uncommon for martial arts in this period of Chinese history: women were expected to be homemakers who showed deference to men, not fighters who could rival a man in armed combat. Jade Fox finds that she cannot reconcile these two disparate roles of lover and student, so she kills Li's master and steals his training manual. The confusion of roles is exacerbated when she becomes Jen's governess. Openly, she is Jen's servant, yet secretly, she is Jen's martial arts master. Jade Fox considers herself to be a great martial artist who has risen to prominence in spite of the confines of patriarchal society, so she resents having to play the meek, humble role of servant to a noble family. As the film progresses, it is revealed that Jen has surpassed Jade Fox's skills because of her ability to read and understand the principles behind the Wudan scrolls. This creates further tension for Jade Fox because the power dynamic of the master–student relationship has shifted. Though Jade Fox's actions are reprehensible, her character becomes somewhat more sympathetic when we understand her to be motivated by a longing to reconcile the tension between her desire for freedom and the strictures of a patriarchal society. Thus, it seems that although ritual propriety can often promote harmonious interaction, when it is taken to an extreme, it can inhibit creative growth and foment unrest.

Jen longs for the freedom of the *wŭxiá* life, but she finds herself bound to the role of a noble woman in a patriarchal society that expects her to be nothing more than a wife. Jen's jade comb is the symbol of a civilized woman. Lo (Dark Cloud) steals it, symbolically stripping her of her status and affirming her inner desire for liberation from traditional Confucian roles. Lo's theft of the comb leads to the emotional and sexual freedom that the lovers share in the cave. Many of Lee's other films explore the theme of societal impositions upon freedom, particularly *Brokeback Mountain* (2005) and *Sense and Sensibility* (1995). Erick Eckholm raises this point in an interview with Ang Lee:

> In discussing *Crouching Tiger,* Mr. Lee frequently made com-
> parisons to *Sense and Sensibility.* . . ."Family dramas and *Sense
> and Sensibility* are all about conflict, about family obligations
> versus free will," he said. The martial arts form "externalizes the
> elements of restraint and exhilaration," he continued, punching
> his fist outward. "In a family drama there is a verbal fight. Here
> you kick butt."[78]

Freedom always comes with a price. Jade Fox is killed by her own darts, which is the price of her freedom from Wudan and her old master, whom Li Mu Bai is trying to avenge. Jade Fox aims at Jen but kills Li instead, destroying Jen's new master. Li's death is the price of Jen's freedom from her old master, Jade Fox, and the price of her rebellion against Li and Yu, who tried to help her as master and older sister. Li is killed by the same poison that killed his master. Metaphorically, this poison might refer to the stiff patriarchal attitudes that led Li to avenge his master rather than focusing on his relationship with Yu. Because of his love for Jen, Lo offers to return to society and make his mark to earn her hand. He fails because he is always recognized as a bandit, which is the price of his earlier freedom. At the end of the film, Jen asks Lo to make a wish before she leaps from the bridge. Lo gets to return to the desert, but without Jen. This is the price of his life as a bandit and Jen's rebellion against her traditional roles: they can love one another, but they cannot be together.

Ultimately, *Crouching Tiger, Hidden Dragon* does not seem to endorse a single philosophical system; there should be a balance between the natural freedom of Daoism and the refined order of Confucianism. Although blind adherence to a patriarchal authority leads to a life of inauthenticity and regret, rebellion against society always comes with a price. Ang Lee states, "The key is to achieve a balance, to seek harmony and reduce conflicts."[79] Just as a true Confucian is not a blind follower of tradition, a true Daoist is not a wild rebel who shuns relationships and obligations. As Jen realizes at the end of the film, a sage is a person who understands that authenticity is a balance between the social and the personal. Confucius and Laozi respected one another because even though their methodologies differed, they pursued the same goal of helping human beings to cultivate themselves into exemplary human beings.

Daodejing 33 states, "To conquer others is power / To conquer oneself is strength." *Crouching Tiger, Hidden Dragon* is the story of Jen's struggle to conquer herself through a process of authentic self-cultivation that balances the traditions, moral principles, and social obligations of Confucian humanism with the spontaneity of Daoist naturalism. When she wholly rejects society by becoming a warrior and criminal under Jade Fox and rejecting Li and Yu's attempts to mentor her, she finds that this extreme type of freedom comes with a hefty price: the loss of the relationships that make this life worthwhile. Similarly, when Li and Yu fail to embrace their love for one another due to a blind adherence to ritual propriety, they also feel this loss. A good person must respect moral principles, beneficence, propriety, filial piety, and integrity, but not at the expense of autonomy and creativity. It is only by balancing these values that we can conquer the self, and it is only by conquering the self that we can flourish.

Notes

1. Confucianism and Daoism are indigenous to China, while the third great tradition, Buddhism, has its origins in India with Siddhartha Gautama. Although Buddhism is an important philosophical tradition and there are some Buddhist themes in Lee's film, here, I focus only on Confucianism and Daoism.

2. Alan Chan, "Laozi," in *Stanford Encyclopedia of Philosophy* (http://plato.stanford .edu).

3. Ibid. Also see Jeffrey Riegel, "Confucius," in *Stanford Encyclopedia of Philosophy*.

4. Chan, "Laozi."

5. David L. Hall and Roger T. Ames, *Thinking from the Han: Self, Truth, Transcendence in Chinese and Western Culture* (Albany: State University of New York Press, 1998), 249.

6. Ibid., 108. Also see Roger T. Ames and Henry Rosemont Jr., *The Analects of Confucius: A Philosophical Translation* (New York: Ballantine, 1998), 23.

7. Ames and Rosemont, *Analects of Confucius,* 24.

8. Hall and Ames, *Thinking from the Han,* 149–150.

9. Ames and Rosemont, *Analects of Confucius,* 45–48.

10. Ibid., 45–46.

11. Hall and Ames, *Thinking from the Han,* 235.

12. For example, the term *réndào* refers to "a way of becoming consummately and authoritatively human." See Ames and Rosemont, *Analects of Confucius,* 46.

13. Ingrid Fischer-Schreiber, *The Shambhala Dictionary of Taoism,* trans. Werner Wünsche (Boston: Shambhala, 1996), 183.

14. Ibid., 183.

15. Hall and Ames, *Thinking from the Han,* 264.

16. Ibid., 40.

17. Laozi, *Daodejing*, trans. Roger T. Ames and David Hall (New York: Ballantine, 2003), section 39.

18. Ang Lee, Linda Sunshine, James Schamus, Richard Corliss, and David Bordwell, Crouching Tiger, Hidden Dragon: *A Portrait of the Ang Lee Film Including the Complete Screenplay* (New York: Newmarket Press, 2001), 80. The dubbed version of the film contains slightly more eloquent dialogue for the fourth sentence: "Give yourself up and find yourself reborn." The screenplay was written by Lee and Schamus in English, translated into Mandarin for the shooting script, and then translated back into English to provide overdubbing that would more accurately match the movements of the actors' lips. As a result, there are subtle differences between the subtitles (the original English screenplay) and the dubbed lines (which are translated from Mandarin). Unless otherwise indicated, this essay makes use of Lee and Schamus's original screenplay for direct quotations.

19. Roger T. Ames and David Hall, "Correlative Cosmology—An Interpretive Context," in Laozi, *Daodejing*, trans. Roger T. Ames and David Hall (New York: Ballantine, 2003), 31–32.

20. Ames and Rosemont, *Analects of Confucius,* 10–11 and 19–25.

21. Ibid., 15.29.

22. Ibid., 6.30.

23. Ibid., 12.22.

24. Ibid., 60–65. Confucius discusses *jūnzǐ* and *shèngrén* in the following passages in the *Analects:* 20.3; 15.17–23; 15.31; 4.16; 4.5; 12.4; 14.24; 16.8; 16.10; 14.29; 17.24; 19.9.

25. Robert Carter, *Encounter with Enlightenment: A Study of Japanese Ethics* (Binghamton, N.Y.: SUNY Press, 2001), 64–65.

26. Ibid., 66.

27. See Ames and Rosemont, *Analects of Confucius,* sections 12.1; 12.22; 7.30; 6:30; 15.24; 14.34; 7.16; 4.25; 15.9; 7.6.

28. Ibid., 48–51.

29. Ibid., 53–55.

30. Rosalind Hursthouse, *On Virtue Ethics* (Oxford: Oxford University Press, 1999), 36–39.

31. Ames and Rosemont, *Analects of Confucius,* 54.

32. Lee et al., Crouching Tiger, Hidden Dragon, 40.

33. Ibid., 108–110 and 110–113. Giang Hu (Jiānghú) is the name for the warrior underworld to which *wǔxiá* like Li Mu Bai and Yu Shu Lien belong. See Chapters 2 and 3 in this volume for more details about the Giang Hu underworld.

34. See Ames and Rosemont, *Analects of Confucius,* sections 3.3–4; 4.13; 8.2; 3.26; 11.1; 3.17.

35. Ibid., 51–52.

36. Ibid., 58–59.

37. Ibid., 53. The character represents an image of a person standing by his or her word.

38. Robert Carter raises this point in a discussion about the virtue of truthfulness in Japanese Confucianism. See his *Encounter with Enlightenment*, 70.

39. Ames and Rosemont, *Analects of Confucius*, 63.

40. Roger T. Ames and David L. Hall, trans., *Focusing the Familiar: A Translation and Philosophical Interpretation of the* Zhongyong (Honolulu: University of Hawai'i Press, 2001), 22. Chinese characters have been silently elided from the quotations.

41. Ibid., 25.

42. Ibid., 26.

43. See Ames and Rosemont, *Analects of Confucius,* sections 3.18; 7.11; 8.18; 12.7; 12.14; 12.17; 12.19; 13.3; 13.6; 14.1; 14.20; 14.23.

44. Chuang Tzu [Zhuangzi], *Chuang Tzu: Basic Writings,* trans. Burton Watson (New York: Columbia University Press, 1996), 72.

45. See Laozi, *Daodejing,* 25 and 47.

46. Ames and Hall, *Focusing the Familiar,* 30.

47. See Chuang Tzu, *Basic Writings,* 104.

48. Lee et al., Crouching Tiger, Hidden Dragon, 43.

49. Hall and Ames, *Thinking from the Han,* 168.

50. Lee et al., Crouching Tiger, Hidden Dragon, 76–77.

51. Hall and Ames, *Thinking from the Han,* 163.

52. Ibid., 165.

53. Ibid., 85.

54. Ibid., 265.

55. Chuang Tzu, *Basic Writings,* 73.

56. Ibid., 74.

57. Ibid., 76.

58. Ibid., 277.

59. François Jullien, *The Propensity of Things: Toward a History of Efficacy in China* (New York: Zone Books, 1999), 178.

60. Ibid., 181–183.

61. Ibid., 194.

62. Ibid., 200–201.

63. Ibid., 199.

64. Ibid., 202–205.

65. Hall and Ames, *Thinking from the Han,* 52.

66. Ibid., 43.

67. *Jūjutsu* is commonly written as jujitsu or jiu-jitsu.

68. This quotation is taken from the dubbed version. The screenplay reads, "Real sharpness comes without effort" (see Lee et al., Crouching Tiger, Hidden Dragon, 80).

69. Lee et al., Crouching Tiger, Hidden Dragon, 76.

70. Ibid., 76.

71. Tetsurō Watsuji, *Watsuji Tetsurō's Rinrigaku: Ethics in Japan,* trans. Yamamoto Sei-

saku and Robert E. Carter (Albany: State University of New York Press, 1996), 114–115. Also see Bernard Bernier, "Transcendence of the State in Watsuji's Ethics," in *Frontiers of Japanese Philosophy 2: Neglected Themes and Hidden Variations,* ed. Victor Sōgen Hori and Melissa Anne-Marie Curley (Nagoya: Nanzan University Press, 2008), 94–100.

72. Ames and Hall, "Correlative Cosmology," 31–32.

73. Ibid., 137.

74. Ibid., 138.

75. Li-Hsiang Lisa Rosenlee discusses this at length in *Confucianism and Women: A Philosophical Interpretation* (Albany: State University of New York Press, 2006). Of course, Yu is not actually a widow because she and Meng were never married, but she is nonetheless expected to show respect for his memory, which interferes with her ability to have a relationship with Li.

76. Lee et al., Crouching Tiger, Hidden Dragon, 54.

77. Ibid., 57–59.

78. Ibid., 83.

79. Ibid., 137.

WHAT DO YOU KNOW OF MY HEART?

The Role of Sense and Sensibility in Ang Lee's *Sense and Sensibility* and *Crouching Tiger, Hidden Dragon*

Renée Köhler-Ryan and Sydney Palmer

> When it comes to emotions, even great heroes can be idiots.
> —Sir Te, *Crouching Tiger, Hidden Dragon*

A Spectrum of Possible Dynamics

When Ang Lee asked Michelle Yeoh to play one of the lead roles in *Crouching Tiger, Hidden Dragon* (2000), he described it to her as "*Sense and Sensibility* with martial arts." However, this too glibly states the relationship between the two films. Comparisons and contrasts between them reveal that each complements the other, rendering a dynamic conceptual framework for Lee's understanding of sense and of sensibility. Lee has a rich appreciation of human subjectivity, in which the person's role within a society defined by codes and norms can, but need not completely, conflict with his or her emotionally defined relationships with others. In effect, for Lee, sense and sensibility form a spectrum that can either destroy or heal those involved, depending on whether they can, individually or with others, integrate the seeming restrictions of sense with the ostensible freedom of sensibility.[1]

Lee explores the spectrum formed by the possible dynamics between sense and sensibility through sisterhood—of blood in *Sense and Sensibility* (1995) and spirit in *Crouching Tiger, Hidden Dragon*—and one finds that, for him, feminine discourse can enable or thwart genuine dialogue and also the very lives of those involved. In *Sense and Sensibility,* Elinor would give up her personal desire to be with the man she loves (the idea of marrying and being happy with him is to her "bewitching" but unattainable without asking him to act dishonorably, by breaking off an engagement with someone he clearly no longer loves), whereas Marianne would, and very nearly does, sacrifice her physical existence for the idea of love (having declared early to her mother, "To die for love? What could be more glorious?!"). Marianne and Elinor together only really start moving toward a balance when all else seems shattered and utterly unfulfilled in their lives. Allowing themselves to be vulnerable and humble enables a reversal of their—and their family's—lives in the worlds of sense and sensibility. In *Crouching Tiger, Hidden Dragon,* we see Lee's view of what happens when sense and sensibility are unable to reach one another in time. Shu Lien and Jen end in a personal and emotional defeat that literally destroys Li Mu Bai, who only too late admits that he has lived sense and sensibility as two separate spheres—as if they could never be united.

We begin by defining the words *sense* and *sensibility* to see how Lee's philosophy as a director renders them as elements of a balanced whole. Along with these definitions, we will outline some of the most pertinent points of Confucian philosophy, of British romanticism, and of Daoism. The main body of this chapter will then illustrate this equilibrium, or lack thereof, between sense and sensibility, in the visual and symbolic language between the sisters in each film. Lee provides a way for the viewer to engage the range of possible interactions between sense and sensibility through imagery. In *Sense and Sensibility,* sense is associated with the door frames in which we so often see Elinor, and sensibility with Marianne's open windows, musical instruments, and outdoor settings. Lee uses these images through both their presence and absence at key moments, creating a space for something more in each of the characters. There is no simple correlate in imagery in *Crouching Tiger, Hidden Dragon.* Instead, associative fields symbolize each character and what she represents. Lee explores Jen's overriding sensibility in terms of ancient Chinese customs of hair, ornaments, and a hair-combing ritual, all of which pertain to marriage rituals. Reading these codes, we find that Jen is effectively married to the Green Destiny, committed to all that she feels it represents. Jen's abduction of the deadly weapon points to her inner drive to break into the world of Giang Hu by stealth and force. Shu Lien, on the other hand, is in a world of sense that is wary of the romantic associations of the Green Destiny, as well as of its well-known destructive power. Shu Lien's unobtrusive way of intersecting with Jen's code of hair ornamentation and ritual is unmatched by Jen's transgression into the more experienced warrior's symbolic order, represented by the Green Destiny.[2]

Lee's Philosophy of Sense and Sensibility

One of the most intriguing aspects of Lee's philosophy is the way in which it blends elements of Eastern and Western thought. As William Leung argues, "The success of *Crouching Tiger* is due in large degree to the bold willingness of Ang Lee and his team to experiment with the juxtaposition of Eastern and Western knowledge, wisdom, and traditions: here bringing to the fore feminist politics in a Wuxia story, there investing a Jane Austen plot with a Taoist twist." Leung argues that Lee finds "meaningful continuity" even across what seems the "widest cultural divide." Lee's enthusiasm for rich characters and complex narratives makes *Sense and Sensibility* and *Crouching Tiger, Hidden Dragon* fitting terrain for his exploration of Western and Eastern notions of sense and sensibility. Seeing these films side by side, one becomes aware of the nuanced notions of the ways that characters embody their defining motifs most when on the verge of transgressing them altogether. We will now explore sense, which is particularly exemplified by Elinor and by Shu Lien; then we will move to sensibility, found in the characters of Marianne and Jen.[3]

Elinor's world of sense in *Sense and Sensibility* can be characterized as one of commonsense principles ennobled by a code of honor that expresses itself in the manners of polite society. This stands in sharp contrast to Marianne's sensibility—the romantic passions that impulsively drive her actions. Lee's playfulness in juxtaposing the tensions underlying the necessary rituals of family meals and of drawing room visits is one of the ways in which he shows that Elinor is all too aware of the simmering of sensibility (as repressed desire, no matter what its object) just beneath the smooth veneer of polite sense. This, of course, makes her rare moments of passionate declaration—to Marianne and finally to Edward—all the more disarming. These bring to the fore the kind of sense that Elinor represents. It is not the crude greediness of her sister-in-law, Fanny, for instance, who refuses to make room for compassion and insists on the letter of the law, by which Elinor, her mother, and her two sisters are immediately impoverished. That Elinor understands the world of business and economics is clear. She sympathizes and feels deeply the implications of losing her father and her home, but unlike the other women in her family she does not wallow in self-pity.[4]

Lee very often shows Elinor, as it were, practicing sense. She gazes and assesses but rarely condemns, and then always finds a way to take action within the limitations that she recognizes and accepts. Her polite enquiries by letter lead to the Dashwoods once again having a roof over their heads. Elinor watches Willoughby rush away from a weeping Marianne and expresses her concern to her mother, but also to herself, without judgment. This capacity to take in what is going on around her makes her someone in whom people constantly confide. Edward does so, but reciprocally. He is the only one able to compel Elinor to speak of herself with no duress whatsoever. Painfully, Lucy Steele also confides to Elinor her secret engagement to Edward. This piece of information devastates Elinor because it affects her future happiness in a way that she cannot do anything about. At an impasse, Elinor is unable to practice her art of making the best of her adopted code of sense. This makes Elinor's concern to alleviate Marianne's suffering even more poignant, when she has again been made confidant, this time by Colonel Brandon, who explains Willoughby's actions to her.

Through Elinor, Lee offers a critique of the utilitarian philosophy of finance, which has trapped all the Dashwood women in cruel economic circumstances, and also of a code of honor that makes no room for sensibility. The director shows her crushed by its constraints when all seems lost, then finally victorious—but only by accidents of circumstance within the world of sense.

In *Crouching Tiger, Hidden Dragon,* in the character of Shu Lien, on the other hand, we find a critique of Confucianism as well as of Daoism. Like Elinor, Shu Lien accepts her role as a woman within a highly ritualized system. However, she is able to surpass the limitations that would normally have been placed on her as a woman bound by Confucian codes, by her high status within the world of the *wŭxiá*.[5] However, before continuing, a few of the points most relevant to this discussion will here be explained, first about Confucianism, and then about the context and ethical codes of the *wŭxiá* warrior.

As Jennifer Oldstone-Moore describes, "Confucian ethics . . . are directed toward the creation of a harmonious society and a virtuous, benevolent state. It is believed that these ideals can be achieved through the practice of *li* (ritual and protocol) and *ren* (humaneness)."[6] Within this ethical way of living, filial piety (*xìao*) is especially important. The one who embodies filial piety knows and respects his or her rank within society. "The most important relationships" that the person of filial piety honors are "those between parent and child, husband and wife, elder brother and younger brother, friend and friend, ruler and subject."[7] Confucianism prioritizes order and harmony within society, both of which are made possible by the practice of filial piety by all its members.

One can see the embodiment of Confucian philosophy in Lee's character of Shu Lien, who consistently shows herself to be a master both of *lǐ* and of *rén*. Importantly, *rén* is the ethical foundation for all actions of *lǐ*. Lee Dian Rainey points out that *rén* has been variously translated as "benevolence, humanity, co-humanity, love, altruism, goodness, the Good, authoritative person, self" before opting for "humanity" as the best translation.[8] Taking into account all these other possibilities, as well as Oldstone-Moore's "humaneness," *rén* is a quality of integrity and stability that a person maintains in all relationships with others, in this way helping to preserve the harmony that makes any community possible. This, as we will argue below, is an important property of sense, portrayed continually by both Shu Lien and Elinor. Behaving in many respects like Elinor caught within family and societal politics, Shu Lien's utter integrity allows her, through *rén,* not simply to follow sets of rules and protocols, but also to soften them, lending them touches of sympathy and humanity without which Confucianism would lose its inner value. Just as Elinor can remember gifts for each of the servants she will leave behind, and go so far as to empathize with Lucy Steele, Shu Lien greets each of her own servants by name and shows as much compassion as she can for Jen.

It cannot at all be forgotten that Shu Lien has a specific place within Confucian society because of her gender. As a woman, it is highly unusual that she is so involved in political affairs. Li-Hsiang Lisa Rosenlee emphasizes that women in the *Five Classics,* the foundational texts for Confucian ethics, were categorized solely within the family setting. Only in family relations did women have significant roles, and woman's filial piety can only be understood in her relationship to her parents, spouse, and children.[9] Lee's Shu Lien is nonetheless able to remain true to Confucianism while playing a meaningful, respected, and accepted role in politics because she works within an additional tradition and set of codes, taken from the world of the Giang Hu.

In his commentary on *Crouching Tiger, Hidden Dragon,* Lee says that the Giang Hu is a warrior subculture, an underworld composed of a loose society of warriors. Stephen Teo identifies Giang Hu as "an illicit space nurtured by conflict and corruption, but functioning as 'an alternate society.'"[10]

Giang Hu has its own codes, which Jen, for instance, deliberately breaks before the tavern fight scene. Giang Hu is a concept deeply entwined with the Chinese genre of *wŭxiá*. Whitney Crothers Dilley states: "The *wuxia* tradition can be translated as 'martial arts chivalry.'"[11] The term *Giang Hu* describes the ubiquitous presence of bandit–knights-errant groups that are part of the underworld while simultaneously keeping it in order. These ways of behavior, which are based on virtues of knight-errantry, take on different meanings depending on the disposition and intentions of the one embodying them. Depictions of Giang Hu have a long tradition within Chinese literature and drama (including cinema), and martial arts movies—referred to as *wŭxiá* films—are a subset of this broader genre. Crucially for Shu Lien's (and Jen's) character(s), women play significant roles within the *wŭxiá* world. In *wŭxiá* depictions of Giang Hu, women are equal to men, even when inevitable differences in sexuality and gender make themselves known.[12] Finally, it should be mentioned that Shu Lien's melding of the worlds of Confucianism and Giang Hu means that she adopts a particular set of *wŭxiá* virtues. Namely, these are "chivalry, altruism, benevolence and justice for the common good."[13] While Giang Hu is more often than not defiant of authority and "in opposition with the government,"[14] Shu Lien can use her prowess as a warrior to support the system of government she understands to be working for the common good. Jen, unable to integrate such virtues in her life, cannot fight on the side of justice. Her warrior code is self-centered and destructive. She adopts the outward appearance of a warrior in the Giang Hu, but she is in fact still well outside that world.

Shu Lien's fighting style, which Lee describes as "hard" and "outward directed," indicates something of the energy and power it takes constantly to deal with and within a world that leaves her little room for her personal emotions. Shu Lien submits to a world where a rigid code of almost inhuman ethical and religious constraints forces her to vie with her inner desires. This way of life is inimical to the way of the Daoist with which Lee identifies the world of sensibility. Watching *Crouching Tiger, Hidden Dragon* after *Sense and Sensibility*, one catches a glimpse of where Lee's Elinor could have gone if chance had not been on her side. We see Shu Lien use the codes that confine her; then we witness her transgression of these in the final fight scene with Jen; and finally we see her devastation when everything turns against her. The physical strength and violence that Shu Lien uses contrast sharply with the struggles of a still Elinor.

If through Shu Lien we can understand more of Elinor's inner life in the world of sense, comparisons between Marianne and Jen illuminate Lee's philosophical grasp of the idea of sensibility. Interestingly, Lee indicates his more ready identification with sensibility than with sense. In the opening credits of *Sense and Sensibility*, Lee's name appears over Marianne playing the piano. At the end of *Crouching Tiger, Hidden Dragon*, he comments that Jen's leap from Wudan mountain reveals that she is "in some ways . . . the real heroic character in the movie." Although he undoubtedly admires Elinor and Shu Lien, his attraction to Marianne and Jen and what they represent is telling. A running joke throughout his shared commentary in *Crouching Tiger, Hidden Dragon* is that all his movies deal with repression, with the human spirit desiring to express what is constantly held back, or what is perhaps inexpressible. This is what Ang Lee as a film director essentially deals with each time he sets out to capture a narrative on screen. Working with so many factors—production team, actors, limited amounts of time and money—he sets out to move his audience, to make them feel as he does about the characters on the screen.[15] But this can only be part of the reason why Lee finds sensibility so compelling. For Lee, sensibility more than sense closes a cultural gap that might otherwise thwart us in our ability to find what cultures can share concerning the human desire for a force that both captures and expresses the true essence of selfhood.[16]

Sensibility, unlike sense, comes immediately and unabashedly from the innermost core of subjectivity, overflowing with a meaning that cannot ever be entirely articulated. Its sometimes violent response to the confines of sense is thus comprehensible. Sense to the person of overriding sensibility seems like complete inauthenticity, a shying away from reality. For both Marianne and Jen, that reality is in touch with nature. For Marianne, nature takes on the meanings given to it by romanticism. In Jen's case, nature has significance within a Daoist way of thinking and living. It is important to highlight and distinguish the main points of each embodiment of sensibility to comprehend better what Lee sees as the relationship between sense and sensibility—or Confucianism and Daoism—and why it is that he seems to prefer sensibility over sense.

To a Western audience, Marianne's love for all things romantic may be easier to recognize and explain. She longs to be moved emotionally, seeking out manifestations of the reverberations of her innermost being in poetry, in storms, in wild nature—the flowers of the field rather than of the hothouse, as she declares to Willoughby. The undercurrents of human emotions are epitomized for Marianne in an idealized sense of romantic love. Such love overwhelms; it is the only thing worth dying for. Its source seems to lie in the romantic sense of the sublime, where feeling is a formless attunement to the forces of nature, which would overwhelm were it not for the power of the subject's imagination. Marianne, we can safely say, is a British romantic, and as such, she follows in the philosophical lineage of Edmund Burke. British romanticism insists that reason and rationality are inadequate to address what is fundamental about human experience. Nature at its most unruly and poetry in its most emotional formulations are the elements of the sublime present in romanticism that are most appealing to Marianne. Her insistence that Edward read aloud "The Castaway" by William Cowper, one of the foremost British romantic poets of her time, is indication of this preference in Lee's adaptation.

Philosophers tend to think of the sublime mainly in terms of Kant's *Critique of Judgment.* However, historically, the British sublime, and the sense of romanticism attendant upon it, is of a slightly different ilk, one derived at least in part from Burke's account of the physiological effects that the sublime has on the human subject.[17] Of course, Kant is deeply indebted to Burke's analysis of the nature of the sublime. However, there are major differences between the two philosophers' accounts. Although Kant emphasizes that the feeling of the sublime can be related immediately to the human capacity to reason in the noumenal realm, Burke was more concerned to elevate the importance of the passions, to the neglect and perhaps even negation of reason. Burke, as Vanessa L. Ryan describes, "maintains that the sublime is a sensory response to the phenomenal world combined with emotion untrammeled by thought."[18] In the feeling of the sublime, the senses are quickened, as is the inner self, but without any influence or interference from rationality.

This theory has ethical implications with which Marianne implicitly agrees. For her, there should be no distance between the strength of the emotions that one feels and the expression of these to the outside world. Her frustration with Elinor for most of Lee's film is based on Elinor's prioritizing of sense on every possible occasion. Marianne is thus more in the tradition of the Burkean sublime inherited by British romanticism rather than by Kant. Kant deliberately uncouples the aesthetic experience—whether of the beautiful or the sublime—from any underlying forms of motivation (this is what he calls the disinterestedness of the aesthetic experience), including the ethical. Where for Kant the sublime can move us and yet leave us essentially untouched in our relationships with others, Andrew Ashfield and Peter De

Bolla note that "in the British tradition there is a consistent refusal to relinquish the interconnection between aesthetic judgments and ethical conduct . . . experiences we have in elevated states, precisely the affective register of the sublime, need not be divorced from those standards we invoke to govern our conduct."[19] Burke's attitude toward the moral implications of the sublime is telling here. The sublime, he says, is necessary so that our passions can be exercised. These enable us to have sympathy for our fellow human beings.[20] (Notoriously, and in contrast, for Kant, only the feeling of respect, which is not emotion in any romantic sense, has any purchase in the moral realm.)

Of course, Marianne's appreciation of sensibility lacks some of the subtleties of Burke's distinctions. Yet with her insistence on the importance of spontaneity of emotion and the need for there to be no gap between what one feels and what one does, she demonstrates some of the attributes of the sublime adopted by British Romanticism. Marianne goes so far as to submit and would not mind being crushed—or so she thinks—by her overwhelming emotions. This is the case, that is, until she integrates something of more subtle sense in her life. So sure is she of the authenticity of her love for Willoughby that she takes for granted that it must be completely reciprocated. That he chooses the crudest form of sense over her—the world of money—is one of the harsh factors that make her question the picture she has nurtured of the truth of emotion. Seeing Elinor's way of facing a similarly cruel fate, she comes to appreciate that there are more possibilities than a choice between wild, pure, romantic love or death.

Only with sense—which is not necessarily, as she describes Elinor's attitude, "acceptance and resignation"—can the throes of sensibility be somewhat sustained. We have no doubt that Marianne marries for love in the end, but there are now no public displays of romantic fervor. Marianne accepts sense, having witnessed its steadiness of strength in her sister. Jen too finds such constancy attractive, but she is unwilling to forgo her inner character by submitting to the codes of Confucianism. Listening to Shu Lien's admonishment to be true to herself, she gives herself over to sensibility, letting nature become her inner force of life.

Jen has seen firsthand the devastation that her unbridled sensibility has wrought, but her choice is not to turn toward sense. Instead, she allies herself with forces beyond herself. This seems to be the true freedom Lee longs to express, where all the life of sensibility is no longer hidden, no longer repressed. The sublime finds expression here in a submission of self that is not purely submissive. Jen is a disciple, in the end, of Daoism, the competing way of life and philosophy in Chinese culture. While within a Confucian framework her attitude to life and final decision of the film cannot be condoned (especially since she essentially turns away from all forms of filial piety), within Daoism, her motivations are comprehensible and even admirable.[21] However, for the purposes of the present discussion, it is important to indicate some of the most pertinent points, especially in comparison with Marianne's British Romanticism. First, there is an ethical aspect to going along the way of the *dào*. In effect, the Daoist believes that Confucian ethical structures stifle true moral action. Eske Møllgaard describes this attitude: "The truly ethical encounter with the other can only happen through an unbinding of the fantastic structures so we again inhabit the 'midst of life.'"[22] In ontological terms, to live the Daoist way is constantly to be in the realm of becoming, rather than to live in accord with the structures of being that Confucianism accepts. The Way (*dào*), furthermore, "transcends beings and forms in time and space."[23] Beyond the world of ordinary and stable lives and breathes the life of the entire cosmos.

This is the second point of comparison with Romanticism and the feeling of the sublime. Daoism gives preeminence to the ways of nature. To feel with and to be with the meaning of the cosmos is to reach true fulfillment. Here N. J. Girardot's description is helpful: "Tao as the Beginning is an enduring and sustaining presence in the world; and, even though it is hidden or lost to man, it is possible to return to an identification with the source of all meaning and life. . . . The continual rhythm of 'beginning and return' is both the macrocosmic life of Tao in nature and the microcosmic true life of man. To rediscover and reestablish in the individual and society the 'primeval beginning' is therefore, the 'bond of Tao.'"[24] In *Crouching Tiger, Hidden Dragon*, the way of the *dào* is identified with the martial school of Wudan. Li Mu Bai has already recognized Jen's possible suitability to be inaugurated into the secrets of Wudan, even though she is a woman. True to her character, Jen does not wait for the rigorous training that would be required of her as a warrior. Instead, she takes matters into her own hands, throwing herself into the life of the *dào*.

Jen asserts herself by letting the cosmos, or nature, live through her, deciding for her what will happen next. If this really is heroic action for Lee, then here one finds admiration for and at the same time an embedded critique of Marianne, who seems to submit too easily to something not really of her inner nature. Of course, this may be a moot point from a Western perspective. To the Western audience not knowing Daoist philosophy, the situation is completely reversed: Jen's leap looks like suicide, and Marianne's acceptance of Elinor's sense appears to be a form of redemption.[25]

Nonetheless, Marianne and Jen both redeem sensibility by each acknowledging a new—and even *the*—dimension of what it means to be human. Through them, we see an active striving to be true to the reality that they feel, but which circumstances constantly stop them from representing. The audience's frustrations and sympathies with each underlines that whether within a Western or an Eastern frame of reference, Lee depictions of sensibility are recognizable as essentially human, as commonly shared. These films about sense and sensibility draw us into something that is more than us, yet a part of each of us. Moved by the characters in his films, forgetting ourselves in that movement, perhaps Lee would like to think that, at least for a moment, we are living his understanding of reality.

The Scenes: Sense and Sensibility in Action

Elinor and Shu Lien live sense both in its constraining code of honor and in profound and nonjudgmental awareness of others that inspires people to confide in them. Marianne and Jen embody the desire to be part of something that extends beyond themselves, the drive and desire to have a connection so valuable that it overcomes them and puts them in relationship to a greater whole, regardless of the value of the object or person in question. In this section, we will look more explicitly at several scenes in each film where Lee explores these tensions directly between the two sisters and particularly in visual forms. In the first key "sister" scene in each film, the championing of sense predominates, be it through the elder sisters' disclosures or lack thereof. The second scenes portray entrenchment: despite the elder sisters' eruptions into expressions of sensibility focusing on matters of the heart, the younger sisters, for all their sensibility, have ridden roughshod over them. But all remain locked in their fundamental orientations. The final scenes show the moments of integration; only in *Sense and Sensibility* does redemption come in time.

SENSE AND SENSIBILITY

The first crucial scene in Elinor and Marianne's relationship as sisters in the heart of their sense and sensibility tension takes place in Elinor's bedroom at Norland, when Marianne comes to discuss her sister's feelings for Edward. It is night, the conversation takes place by fire and candlelight on Elinor's bed, and most of the discussion is filmed in one master shot. Although there are none of the usual visual keys here (no doors or musical instruments), their nonverbal language echoes and reinforces their basic associations. The more Marianne expresses her love of and happiness for her sister, the more Elinor frames and closes herself up. She can barely speak about Edward without getting flustered. As she says less and less, she physically draws up her legs and later crosses her arms as layers of defense. Elinor cannot function without a frame. Marianne, true to her sensibility, treats Elinor's attempts at building a rampart as an opening, a place to discuss matters of the heart more deeply: she perches her chin on Elinor's defensively raised knees and asks if she loves Edward. She treats Elinor's bodily frame and barriers as if they were a door that could open or a fence in a field to be climbed. But when Elinor crosses her arms, Marianne realizes that the discussion is over.

From the beginning of the film, Lee shows Elinor in door frame after door frame: the first shot, where she asks Marianne to play something less mournful; the consolation of their mother; her speech to their staff. In all these scenes, Lee also focuses on Elinor's constant care of others. In this scene, however, the tables are turned, and her sister is trying to care for her. The master shot allows us to see Elinor and Marianne embody the visual associations already built up in the film: Elinor is so at a loss when confronted with genuine love from her sister that she can only close in on herself, while a heedless Marianne is willing to breach barriers to reach the heart of someone she loves.

Elinor's physical retreat embodies her use of sense in this case not just as a form of viewing the world, but also as self-protection against the eruption of feeling and sensibility. Her posture keeps both Marianne out and her own sensibility and emotions in. Marianne's physical gestures here echo her particularly romantic sensibility: she speaks of nothing but feelings and their priority over all else. First, she focuses on her own feelings of happiness for Elinor and sadness at Elinor's ostensible departure. When Elinor stumbles and retreats, Marianne tries to draw her sister into the world beyond reason and rationality, into a spontaneous expression of love. Expressing her love for Edward would be an opening toward Marianne's understanding of the importance of feeling and being, and to a certain degree at their mercy. It would also help to build an implicit feeling of trust between the sisters. Marianne mocks her sister not only because she cannot seem to admit to herself how much she does care for Edward, but also because she so restrains her emotions that she cannot share them with someone she knows and trusts.

Nevertheless, Elinor's self-conscious attempts not to smile as Marianne leaves the room parroting her description of her feelings shows that she has let Marianne breach her defenses of sense, however slightly and briefly.

The second crucial sister scene happens again in Elinor's bedroom, but this time at Mrs. Jennings's in London. This scene captures the two sisters immersed in their own dispositions to a fault. Elinor closes the door and stays in its contours as she reveals that she has already known about Lucy and Edward's engagement. Given the close association between doors and Elinor, her closing one as she takes in the news that Edward will not abandon Lucy is the perfect symbol for what has just happened to her life. Elinor explodes when Marianne asks, "Elinor, where is your heart?" responding vehemently, "What do you know of my heart? What do you know of anything but your own suffering?" Elinor can no longer bear Marianne's romantic convictions and her focus on the heart and emotions above all else. Having set reason aside and opted for the primacy of emotion and spontaneity, Marianne immerses herself in heartbreak to a level where engaging in real empathy is almost impossible. She can understand Elinor's situation only from her own point of view of passion, not from Elinor's perspective of reason and sense. Elinor lashes out so fiercely because she sees in Marianne not only the self-centeredness that such romantic convictions can lead to, but also the element of honesty and truth she feels denied. Here, Elinor's unswerving dedication to the proper codes and behaviors have ground down her reserves, and she does actually respond with tremendous emotion to Marianne—but it is emotion about the primacy of sense and a rejection of the self-centeredness to which Marianne's romanticism has led her. Appropriately, they are both framed in doorways in the latter half of this scene. They are both confined now, each trapped by the extremes of her mode of being as well as the world's limits, and there seems to be no way out. Elinor's vulnerability here is the greatest expression of it to date, but it would seem too late because Edward is keeping his word to Lucy. Because the sisters are trapped, despite Elinor's brief foray into vulnerability and her expression of her deepest desires, Marianne cannot even go to comfort Elinor. As has happened throughout the film, Elinor must take care of Marianne, even though at this moment it is Elinor who suffers most. When Elinor crosses the room to embrace and comfort Marianne, they are both framed in the door that Elinor closed at the beginning of the scene. Lee's filming of this shot reflects the vertiginous combination of isolation and claustrophobia that narrows their lives.

In the third scene, the sisters are brought to the extremes of isolation as sense and sensibility: Marianne is near death, and Elinor (along with the doctor) is stoically caring for her. Again they are in a bedroom, but now it is Marianne's room at the Palmers', where she is lying unconscious. Like the first scene, it is night, so the room is lit by candle and firelight. Throughout, Elinor's actions and words echo Marianne's from the first scene—touching her legs as a sign of love and care; saying things like, "I cannot do without you."[26] However, Lee begins now with an overhead shot, which manifests its difference, despite its many similarities with the previous sister scenes. This unapologetically vertical shot encompasses both sisters. Given the gravity of the situation and the unexpectedness of the shot itself, Lee signals that this is a turning point. At first, they both appear in isolation, with Marianne on the bed and Elinor facing the fire. But from this vertical perspective, we see Elinor turn. Shot from this angle, it is not just a literal turning toward her sister—although it is that. It is also a revolution in her own internal disposition. She turns to Marianne not to take care of her, which would be expected and what Elinor has done throughout, but for help. Her words and actions are pleas to Marianne. This signals Elinor's breakthrough to balancing sense and sensibility in her own being—not only because she is being vulnerable, which started in the scene at Mrs. Jennings's, but because she expresses her love, fears, and sorrow directly to the person involved. In the first two scenes, the sisters talk about Edward, who is not present. In this scene, Elinor speaks of her deepest vulnerability, her fear of being left alone, to the person she fears is going to leave her. In this dire moment, she realizes that her sister is the only person to whom she can be vulnerable. The overhead shot then manifests another critical element: what the Western tradition in Aristotle's *Poetics* would call peripety and what Christian theology calls grace. Fittingly, there are no doors and no frames in this scene. The vertical perspective opens to the unpredictable but essential element of grace and timing, again so critical to the Western paradigm of dramatic action proceeding onward from Aristotle, along with the grace that keeps *Sense and Sensibility* from being a tragedy.[27]

The culmination of this scene takes place on the following morning. Marianne's fever has broken, and Colonel Brandon has brought her mother. Marianne's first words are, "Where's Elinor?" After being reassured of her sister's presence, Marianne is capable of her first ever genuine words to Colonel Brandon: "Thank you." These words are so heartfelt and so unprompted that Brandon is subtly but clearly pierced by them as he quietly leaves the room. Given the sequence of events, Lee seems to be suggesting the following: Elinor has been able to be vulnerable at last to a person she loves deeply, someone who is in fact the person who has been so frustrated by Elinor's inability to express love. Elinor's breakthrough allows Marianne to transcend her confines: the extreme orientation to death that is sensibility undiluted by sense. Not only does Marianne's fever break, but she is also for the first time capable of an authentic response to Brandon. Although she expressed her near desire to be crushed by and for the force of love as the most noble of fates, she has been able to draw back from the brink of romanticism's self-destructiveness. Lee shows how the two sisters were able to cross the thresholds of sense and sensibility to begin integrating what each needs to balance her own disposition—but only on the brink of death.

CROUCHING TIGER, HIDDEN DRAGON

While Shu Lien's shrewd discernment about and concentration in fighting expresses part of her relationship to sense, the visual associations for Shu Lien and Jen's tension around sense and sensibility also centers, rather surprisingly, on hair ornaments and rituals that also ultimately point toward marriage. The scene that sets up the critical importance of these ornaments and their relationship to the sisters occurs early in the film, between Jen and Jade Fox. Once the depth of the symbolism here is uncovered, we can see how Lee dances between the fighting and the hair ornaments to reflect the struggles of Shu Lien and Jen. We will examine the key scene that sets up the significance of combs and hair ornaments and then look at the unfolding of these associations in the three key sister scenes.

The key comb–marriage scene occurs, not accidentally, immediately before Jen steals the Green Destiny for the first time. It is night, she has a red candle burning, and her governess, Jade Fox, comes in to help her prepare for bed. Jade Fox is carrying new pink pajamas that she has made. She begins to comb Jen's hair and speak anxiously about the future as Jen's impending marriage draws ever closer. All of these elements echo the Chinese wedding hair-combing ceremony. This ritual should take place the night before the wedding, and several key components that hint at this are the new pink pajamas, the red candles, and a woman of good fortune picked by the bride who combs the bride's hair and speaks of the future—both of the bride and groom's togetherness and of their fruitfulness in terms of children. There are obviously variations on this scheme in Lee's film, but the fact that these general elements coalesce between Jen and Jade Fox suggests that Jen is then metaphorically married to the sword. She relates to it out of isolation and power, twisting her gift. However, her crippling relationship to the Green Destiny finds its antithesis in her relationship with Lo, which starts by his playfully stealing her beloved comb. Jen and Lo are not married, but the comb comes to symbolize their union. Lo steals it, leading to their feisty, loving relationship, which Jen does not want to leave. Therefore, when they decide that she should return while Lo tries to prove himself in the world, she leaves the comb with him as a symbol of their connection and love; he is to return it to her when they are reunited. The comb reveals that she is not opposed to marriage as such, but that she needs a genuine love capable of meeting her sensibility. When Jade Fox inadvertently performs the hair-combing ceremony, her words about the future are anxious and filled with uncertainty, while Jen's prediction about things being just the same cannot conceal her boredom about the present and coming state of life. Again, this ritual occurs right before Jen steals the sword, leading to Jen's being bound to the sword without any complement and love as protection against the ferocity of her own sensibility.[28]

The day after the sword's theft, Shu Lien visits Jen. Their conversation prompts Jen to say, "Don't distance us. From now on let's be like sisters." Within the bounds of their conversation, this sisterhood is explicitly based on Jen's desire for a connection with a woman she admires, one who she thinks lives her idealized romantic life. However, the subterranean layers of fighting and hair ornaments deepen the tension between sense and sensibility and intimate how difficult their integration here will be. Shu Lien's shrewd assessment of Jen as her opponent from the previous evening based on her calligraphic style alerts us to the first layer beneath the surface of this exchange. In this, Shu Lien reveals her deep grounding in the Giang Hu underworld, but also and most importantly in the Confucian balance of *lǐ* and *rén*, so that she resorts to martial fighting only when needed. It is clear that she knows Jen stole the sword, but she does not pursue her overtly. Shu Lien seems to realize that Jen's theft emerged from her desire for life and connections beyond herself, playful versions of the Daoist orientation that Li Mu Bai himself has. Jen chafes against the Confucian strictures, and Shu Lien's deep practice of *rén* allows her to see the goodness in Jen's longing. However, this does not stop Shu Lien from attempting to teach Jen that even in the Giang Hu world of knight-errantry, *lǐ*, with all its proper protocol, guides one to act on behalf of the common good. Shu Lien's sense and her compassion here are nearly indistinguishable, as she explains how honor exists even in the fighting world, so that she and Li Mu Bai could not get married, much as they want to. She champions sense here, using *rén* to explain *lǐ*, hoping to reach through Jen's sensibility. Jen, however, knows that Shu Lien was her sparring partner, although she seems to assume that Shu Lien is ignorant of this. But clearly part of Jen's enthusiasm for being Shu Lien's sister stems precisely from their fight. Here we get our first glimpse into how Jen constantly underestimates Shu Lien and the many situations in which she finds herself.

The other layer present here, although obscure until the end of the film, is the hair ornament symbolism. At this point in the story, Jen has been bound to the Green Destiny by Jade Fox's inadvertent hair-combing ceremony. Another hair ornament emerges here: Shu Lien's hairpin. She wears it in the opening discussion with Li Mu Bai before she heads to Beijing, and this sister scene is its next appearance. With the exception of her and Jen's final fight, she wears it at moments of significant discussion, often focusing, explicitly or implicitly, on both love or marriage and the Giang Hu underworld: the initial scene with Li Mu Bai, the sister scene, tea with Jen and her mother, Jen's wedding day when they meet Lo, and then from her return home through the end of the film. Its presence at this moment of becoming sisters forms a crucial bond between the women because she wears it again in their final fight and gives it to Jen, first to assure Mrs. Wu that Jen has her blessing to ask for help, and then in their final interaction, when she places it in Jen's hair. It identifies not only Shu Lien, but also her maturity and sense. It identifies her embodiment of Confucianism and its control over personal emotions and desires, as well as her own submission to the proper actions as, in essence, a widow. Her acceptance of *lǐ*, however, is not bitter or rigid. Rather, it is overflowing in *rén*, ironically toward everyone but herself and Li Mu Bai. In this, it is the antithesis of Jen's uncontrolled sensibility.

The next scene, in which Shu Lien and Jen are entrenched in their own dispositions like Elinor and Marianne in their second crucial scene, takes place at Shu Lien's headquarters well outside of Beijing. Twice Jen invokes the sister bond as she struggles with her desire to confide in Shu Lien. As with the first discussion, the main themes are marriage and the fighting underworld, and Jen can now admit that she is in over her head. Her desire to escape Confucian structures and be part of something beyond herself—in essence, to be Daoist—has been warped by Jade Fox and has led her to violate all the rules of *lǐ* in the Giang Hu world. Shu Lien maintains her sense and compassion through the first part of the scene, although it is tempered with her feelings about Jen's behavior. As in their first sister talk, Shu Lien wears her signature hairpin, which she has worn in situations where her shrewd sense and discernment about others' true motives has obviated the need for physical fighting. It therefore is associated with her capacity not to shame or blame, but to deal respectfully with even those who are not behaving honorably. She knows when to soften the rules to allow for the most humane and righteous solution to emerge. She continues her compassionate practice of sense here too as she helps Jen try to get her bearings and become more mature by dealing with her situation, not running from it into a fantasy Giang Hu world. Shu Lien focuses on filial piety as she tells Jen that while Jen can run from marriage, she cannot run from her parents. Surprisingly, Jen does not withdraw at this point; her concern for Lo overrides any suspicion. Jen does become enraged, however, not by Shu Lien's Confucian leanings, but by the news that Li Mu Bai has sent Lo to Wudan. Jen's indisputable gift in having been self-taught from Wudan's manual and her natural Daoist orientation to shake off Confucian strictures and embrace forces beyond herself would seem to be contradicted by her venomous response to Wudan. As mentioned above, this is partly due to Jade Fox's own response to Wudan. But it speaks even more deeply of Jen's romanticism about the Giang Hu underworld—her misunderstanding of it, in fact—which leads to neither Giang Hu altruism nor a true Daoist immersion in the greater flow and source of meaning. With no one worthy of her filial piety, Jen's intuitions and desires derail into self-serving arrogance. Shu Lien finally explodes when this poison in Jen overruns her vulnerability, and she de-sisters Jen. By having Shu Lien fight while wearing her identifying hairpin, Lee makes present all of Shu Lien's prowess, shrewdness, and compassion, and yet says that all this must now be subordinated in this fight to the death. She has used her sense, her balance of *lǐ* and *rén*, unceasingly to avoid such a fight, but she proves, when so pushed, to be greater even than the Green Destiny. As with Elinor and Marianne, though, only the presence of death itself catalyzes a genuine conversion.

The third scene takes place in the night and early morning in an abandoned building near Shu Lien's house. Given that *Crouching Tiger, Hidden Dragon* is Lee's exploration of a failure to integrate in time, it is fitting that the climax takes place inside these ruins (which is similar to Marianne's viewing of Willoughby's abandoned-looking Cum Magna from a distant hilltop). The moment of transformation comes again on the threshold of death: Jade Fox has just died, and Li Mu Bai will die if not administered the antidote. It is this configuration of elements, along with Jade Fox's confession that she was aiming for Jen, that catalyzes Jen into the maturity symbolized by her offer to make the time-consuming antidote. To do this, though, she needs safe passage into Shu Lien's house. Shu Lien thus gives Jen her hairpin, the symbol of her sense, her compassion, her shrewdness, and her strength. She hands it to Jen, who carries it and shows it to Mrs. Wu to prove her good intentions. Jen has stolen the Green Destiny twice and lived her sensibility as a form of continual taking and ravaging. Now, as a mark of her own maturity, she is entrusted with the symbol of everything she has until this point rejected. It is the antidote to Jade Fox's hair-combing ritual, and her new capacity to accept something from Shu Lien, to say nothing of a symbol of Shu Lien's wisdom, opens Jen to life. This moment can also be seen as another instance of Aristotle's peripety, akin to Elinor's transformation in the third sister scene. The sense of a turning point and a change in character grounds both scenes, although here, time has run out. The illumination or discovery occasioned by Jade Fox's admission, although critical for Jen's own growth, does not come in time.

Shu Lien's own relinquishment of this pin, of finally letting go of all the sense, propriety, and honor that has held her back from claiming her love for Li Mu Bai, allows for her fullest moment of integration at his death. Not having it is her antidote, although too late. Li Mu Bai confesses that he wasted his life by not claiming his love for Shu Lien and then promises to stay by her side, even if as a ghost. Shu Lien is undone and says nothing. Instead, she cries, holds, and kisses him, allowing her feelings to flow without hesitation at this final moment. In this ending sequence, Lee explores how sense and sensibility must move in order to begin integrating the other side of the spectrum. Sensibility must receive and accept the firm but gentle hand of sense as it guides toward maturity. And it is sense that must let go and release its control, its Confucian obligations, to allow feeling to emerge. All of this happens when Jen accepts the task of carrying Shu Lien's hairpin. Neither surrenders her native gifts of sense or sensibility, but each has moved to accept and to release her own particular stumbling block. The ultimate recognition of this comes on Jen's return with the antidote. Li Mu Bai has died. Shu Lien makes as if to behead Jen with the Green Destiny but refrains, a piercing balance of her integration of sense and sensibility. She does not return the sword to Jen. Instead, she takes her hairpin from Jen's hand and puts it in Jen's hair. Despite Jen's failure to arrive in time with the antidote, Shu Lien recognizes that Jen has crossed the threshold at last and has rid herself of Jade Fox's poison. Although the comb symbolism with Lo focuses on the goodness of her capacity to love and seek connection with something beyond herself, it is Shu Lien's hairpin that is a truer barometer of their transformations at the end. Shu Lien's ability—once again, and now in the most difficult circumstances—to judge without condemnation challenges Jen to go beyond the selfish romantic desire to live the forces of sensibility. In Jen's facial expression, we witness her realization of the havoc she has wrought. Her only chance to redeem herself is to enable sensibility to live through her more than her selfish will alone.

Seeing a True Heart?

Lee's philosophy of sense and sensibility is evident not only through all these layers of the sisters' metamorphoses, but also in Lee's approach to these stories. As discussed earlier, Lee states that his sympathies lean toward sensibility. However, his method for portraying the struggle clearly manifests his harmonious embodiment of sense and sensibility.

He partakes of Elinor and Shu Lien's graciousness, their *rén*. No matter how entrenched or frozen his protagonists are, he never grows impatient and never condemns. Neither does he deny outright the value to be found in the worlds to which Elinor and Shu Lien seem so overly beholden. He understands the pull, and to a certain degree the necessity, of those worlds. But he wants his characters to be free of its demands when sense asks too much. In a way, we can see him in the voice of Sir Te at the beginning of *Crouching Tiger, Hidden Dragon,* when he says to Shu Lien, "When it comes to emotions, even great heroes can be idiots." Sir Te embodies the Confucian world of order and obedience, the world of *lǐ,* to which Shu Lien has submitted her life. But even this avuncular elder thinks that Shu Lien has taken her obedience to honor too far. In practicing *rén* himself, he tries to free her in order to release both Shu Lien and Li Mu Bai. Sir Te's line encapsulates the whole of both stories. Nothing tests courage and strength better than grappling with emotion and finding that balance between sense and sensibility that will free and honor all involved.

As we also discovered in the analysis of Lee's philosophy, sensibility more easily crosses cultural divides and causes us to identify with deeply human truths wherever we find them. Following this same line of thought, we suggest that it helps cross the gender divide as well, making these two films about more than just the oppression of women[29]; they are about the prisons that all human beings can create for themselves. Lee deals as roundly with men as he does with his female protagonists: Li Mu Bai and Edward are at least as much adversely affected by sense as are Shu Lien and Elinor, and Willoughby and Lo fall victim in different ways to lives devoted to sensibility. These films deal with more or less historical realities about the role of women; Lee never shies away from this. But with his own articulation of nonjudgmental desire for each character to live as fully and truly to the self as possible, he sees that their predicaments cannot be reduced to merely external causes and circumstances. Again, Sir Te's insight is relevant here: he identifies both Shu Lien and Li Mu Bai in their unnecessary *lǐ*, their overbearing obedience to external honor, when they so clearly belong together. Both have ensnared themselves and their own hearts. While we struggle with Jen for the last sequences of the film in her fanatical reliance on the sword, her question to Li Mu Bai, "What do you know about seeing a true heart?" has an uncomfortable truth to it. He can see that she has not been irredeemably corrupted by Jade Fox, but he has failed to see his own and Shu Lien's hearts. When at last Elinor gloriously and uncontrollably breaks down at the knowledge of Edward's unmarried status, his synopsis of their friendship reveals that they both failed to say things at crucial moments that could have clarified their situation.

At every turn, Lee's compassion identifies how all the characters struggle under the weight of both external and internal repression. His own masterful embodiment of balancing sense and sensibility means that he never becomes prisoner of one at the cost of the other, and that he tries to express this wholeness to his audience.

Notes

1. As stated by Michelle Yeoh in "Interview with Michelle Yeoh," on the DVD of *Crouching Tiger, Hidden Dragon* (Sony, 2001).

2. Giang Hu is a concept deeply entwined with the Chinese genre of *wǔxiá* and is discussed further below.

3. William Leung, "Crouching Sensibility, Hidden Sense," *Film Criticism* 26 (2001): 49. Though here we use pinyin romanization for Chinese terms, instances of Wade-Giles romanization have been left intact inside quotations. In this case, "Daoist" appears as "Taoist" in the older Wade-Giles system.

4. One can compare Fanny's most spectacular outburst here with Elinor's. Fanny is outraged when she hears that Lucy is engaged to her brother, Edward. She yanks the

unsuspecting girl's nose, by that same means forcing her out of the room, screeching, "Get out! Get out!"

5. For a detailed analysis of Confucian philosophy, see James McRae's Chapter 1 in this volume.

6. Jennifer Oldstone-Moore, *Confucianism: Origins, Beliefs, Practices, Holy Texts, Sacred Places* (New York: Oxford University Press, 2002), 53. For a detailed exposition of the key tenets of Confucian philosophy, see Chapter 1 in this volume.

7. Oldstone-Moore, *Confucianism,* 53.

8. Lee Dian Rainey, *Confucius and Confucianism: The Essentials* (Oxford: Wiley-Blackwell, 2010), 32.

9. Li-Hsiang Lisa Rosenlee, *Confucianism and Women: A Philosophical Interpretation* (Albany: State University of New York, 2006), 47.

10. Stephen Teo, *Chinese Martial Arts Cinema: The Wuxia Tradition* (Edinburgh: Edinburgh University Press, 2009), 18.

11. Whitney Crothers Dilly, *The Cinema of Ang Lee: The Other Side of the Screen* (London: Wallflower Press, 2007), 136–141.

12. See, for instance, Catherine Gomes, "Crouching Women, Hidden Order: Confucianism's Treatment of Gender in Ang Lee's *Crouching Tiger, Hidden Dragon,*" *Limina: Journal of Historical and Cultural Studies* 11 (2005) (http://www.limina.arts.uwa.edu.au/); Rong Cai, "Gender Imaginations in *Crouching Tiger, Hidden Dragon* and the *Wuxia* World," *Positions* 13, no. 2 (2005): 441–471.

13. Teo, *Chinese Martial Arts Cinema,* 18.

14. Ibid.

15. In *Sense and Sensibility,* Lee went to immense effort to research the rituals, props, and historical and economic affairs of the time. In *Crouching Tiger, Hidden Dragon,* he concentrated more on "regulating" his actors, as he says of the actress who plays Jen. Not only did they need to learn the nuances of a mostly unfamiliar language, but Jen also needed to learn calligraphy and horseback riding so that the space between learning and doing closed and looked seamless on screen.

16. For the Daoist underpinnings of Lee's interpretation and representation of sensibility through Jen, the following is an invaluable resource: *The Book of Chuang Tzu,* trans. Martin Palmer with Elizabeth Breuilly (London: Arkana, 1996).

17. Vanessa L. Ryan, "The Physiological Sublime: Burke's Critique of Reason," *Journal of the History of Ideas* 62, no. 2 (2001): 265–279.

18. Ibid., 273.

19. Andrew Ashfield and Peter De Bolla, introduction to *The Sublime: A Reader in Eighteenth Century British Aesthetic Theory* (Cambridge: Cambridge University Press, 1996), 2.

20. Edmund Burke, *A Philosophical Enquiry into the Sublime and the Beautiful,* ed. James T. Boulton (New York: Routledge, 2008), 44.

21. For a detailed discussion of the main points of Daoism, see James McRae, Chapter 1 in this volume.

22. Eske Møllgaard, *An Introduction to Daoist Thought: Action, Language, and Ethics in Zhuangzi* (New York: Routledge, 2007), 24.

23. Ibid., 17.

24. N. J. Girardot, *Myth and Meaning in Early Taoism: The Theme of Chaos (Huntun)* (Berkeley: University of California Press, 1983), 49.

25. However, see Stephen Teo's comment: "Mount Wudang is the sacred mountain of Daoism, and by casting herself off it, Jen is not attempting self-oblivion but rather she is, metaphorically speaking, launching herself as a seeker on the path of the Dao, and to reach immortality. In contrast, Li Mubai has perished without reaching the bliss of enlightenment." Teo, *Chinese Martial Arts Cinema,* 176.

26. In the first scene, Marianne asks Elinor, "How shall I do without you?" and rests her chin on Elinor's defensively raised knee. She continues by asking Elinor not to live too far away. In this scene, Elinor does not ask but rather states, "I cannot do without you," while she touches Marianne's legs. Her refrain during this scene is "Please try," and it ends with her plea, "Do not leave me alone." What Marianne warmly and playfully asks for in the first scene, Elinor here reverses and begs for in full vulnerability.

27. "A Peripety is the change of the kind described from one state of things within the play to its opposite, and that too in the way we are saying, in the probable or necessary sequence of events." Aristotle, *Poetics,* in *The Basic Works of Aristotle,* trans. Ingram Bywater, ed. Richard McKeon (New York: Random House, 1941), 1465.

28. In the commentary on the DVD of *Crouching Tiger, Hidden Dragon,* Lee says Jen and Lo's love scenes are up to this point in his career his most romantic.

29. For one of many articles that presents a feminist reading and critique of *Crouching Tiger, Hidden Dragon,* see Rong Cai, "Gender Imaginations in *Crouching Tiger, Hidden Dragon* and the *Wuxia* World," *Positions* 13, no. 2 (2005): 441–471. In emphasizing that cinema is an erotic art form, Cai's critique misses the point somewhat: Lee is not objectifying his female characters as erotic. The complexity of the characters we have discussed transcends the limitations of gender alone.

THE CONFUCIAN COWBOY AESTHETIC

Michael Thompson

Depictions of Isolation

Early in the nineteenth century, French emissary and political thinker Alexis de Toqueville (1805–1859) observed a tendency among Americans, especially those of the new Western states, toward an isolation and individualism wherein its members had little or no knowledge of the history of their neighbors and little or no social interactions with those nearest them.[1] With the Louisiana Purchase and manifest destiny, the character of the settlers in these new territories was one of rugged individualism and was marked by an independence and lack of sociability with the other few inhabitants of the lands.[2] Cowboys are presented as the heroes par excellence of this expansion. The West was settled by cowboys and isolated pockets of humanity with little or no interaction with others around them—or that is what we have been taught.

Cowboys have long been an object of cinema. Many of our most revered Hollywood heroes, such as John Wayne and Clint Eastwood, have depicted this very American attitude of individualism. In several films by Ang Lee, we find a similar expression of the isolation and independent spirit that has come to symbolize the West and its inhabitants. In particular, we find literally self-sufficient and isolated cowboys in the characters of Ennis del Mar (Heath Ledger) and Jack Twist (Jake Gyllenhaal) in Ang Lee's *Brokeback Mountain* (2005). Disconnected from mainstream society because of their sexuality and occupations, both Jack and Ennis find themselves silently suffering in the midst of their cultural epoch, cut off from each other and society at large. As a result of social constraints and their lack of conformity to the social mores deemed proper at the time, these characters remain isolated throughout the movie. In addition to this remarkably American depiction of cowboy lifestyle, Ang Lee explores similar themes of individualism in the comparable period of the Chinese Qing dynasty (1644–1911; the movie takes place in the late eighteenth century), with its sparsely populated western states and more urban areas in the east. Characters in *Crouching Tiger, Hidden Dragon* (2000)—Li Mu Bai (Chow Yun Fat), Shu Lien (Michelle Yeoh), Jiao Long/Jen (Zhang Ziyi), Lo/Dark Cloud (Chang Chen), and even Jade Fox (Chen Pei-pei)—seem to parallel the individualism found in *Brokeback Mountain.* Especially striking is Jen's desire for the adventurer's life, a life without family or constraint of the norms and mores of society as she interprets the Giang Hu (Jiānghú, "warrior underworld") lifestyle of Li Mu Bai and Shu Lien. In these graphic depictions, this rugged individualism often comes into conflict with societal expectations—that is, within the social settings found in both Eastern and Western cultural dynamics. The common understanding is that one must decide whether to act according to social expectations at the cost of personal desire, or whether personal desire outweighs social acceptance.

Western audiences often perceive the action in such movies as a development of personal desires regardless of social impact. Our film protagonists are often presented as just such isolated individuals, who carry themselves through their lives and the plots of these movies as disconnected from the rest of the world. These "cowboys" are indicative of a general mind-set of American audiences, one that was practiced in the actual westward expansion of the United States. However, I suggest that Ang Lee promotes neither this lifestyle nor this attitude. Rather, he uses this attitude in his characters while juxtaposing them against society in order to explore the social determinations of our identities and to elaborate an Eastern notion of Confucian social interconnectivity, but one that resonates as remarkable for all notions of society and individuality.

Confucian Social Dynamics

One possible backdrop for comprehending Lee's understanding of society is through the lens of traditional Chinese Confucian social dynamics. Of the basic teachings of Confucius (551–479 BCE), the five basic relationships, filial piety, and propriety are of central concern in many of the depictions of Ang Lee's films. (We can see a similarity in the American Western culture of etiquette, or doing what is proper.) A Confucian society is one wherein individuals find themselves in constant social interaction, embedded in a web of social relationships.[3] In contrast to the cowboy aesthetic, as I call it, a Confucian outlook on social dynamics denies radical individualism—a Western notion of a self-contained, individual identity or persona that is the core of any social interaction, and one that is achieved by oneself and maintained throughout the diverse unfolding of one's life—in favor of the idea that all the characters are defined first by these relationships, after which they perform individual actions.

On a superficial level, Lee appears to promote the cowboy aesthetic. Yet there are several key scenes (and an underlying context throughout both movies) that imply that even a life of adventure gains its definition and meaning by its social connections and interactions. For an Eastern audience, the relationships between comrades–colleagues, master–student, older sibling–younger sibling, and/or lovers are apparent in the oblique references made throughout. Notably, Eastern audiences attuned to Confucian teachings can find examples of li^4 in various dialogues in *Crouching Tiger, Hidden Dragon.* In *Brokeback Mountain,* the characters better fit the American notion of rugged individualism, but here too, Lee shows his delicate handling of the same theme. At the opening of the movie, Ennis and Jack's characters seem motivated by individual concerns, the pursuit of individually self-satisfying activities, or both. Quickly, however, one realizes that Ennis is not simply a lone cowboy but is connected to Alma in a profound way, one that determines much of his behavior. Jack himself never desires an isolated independence, but he dreams of owning or operating a ranch with someone for whom he cares. That Ennis cannot publicly reciprocate Jack's desires stems from socially generated sexual norms in a dominantly heterosexual culture. Both men act as society expects by working and marrying.

Lee's repeated illustrations of the difficulties involved in social interaction and propriety in conflict with personal desire and ambition echo a further development of Confucius' thought in the writings of Xunzi (310–220 BCE). Xunzi's contribution to Confucian thought elaborates just such social and personal tensions, providing a recommendation that sublimates personal desire in favor of social order—that, in fact, personal desire is dependent on our social definitions.[5] In this essay, I explore the five basic relationships in Confucian philosophy and how the characters in both films, despite their individualism, fulfill their roles within the community. Moreover, Lee's individualism—his cowboy aesthetic—while sympathetic to American audiences, is really character development within the Confucian setting as understood by Xunzi, and it is within such a context that one finds Lee's philosophy of individual and community.

Confucius and Xunzi

It was through the life and teachings of Confucius and his followers that a well-established system of social interconnections was developed. An important aspect of Confucius' teachings was the recognition and establishment of social divisions. In the *Analects,* Confucius identifies five basic relationships and emphasizes the importance of education and cultivation of these relationships in order to ensure both personal success as well as societal harmony.[6] Among these relationships, Confucius recognizes an inherent imbalance of equality and power between the two participants.[7] Clearly a power disparity exists between ruler–subject and parent–child, but Confucius' point appears to be that even among the most seemingly equal relationships—husband and wife when they agree to equally share responsibilities, or friends of the same age and history—inequality is bound to appear. Simply, between husband and wife there may be equality of financial responsibility, but there are inexorable differences rooted in biological inequalities. Between friends, even those of the same age and history, discrepancies about finances, talents, or opportunities illustrate the inequality Confucius finds inherent in any relationship.

This disparity between people, resources, abilities, and opportunities results in society separating into factions and competing against one another. Recognizing the potential for calamity, Confucius seeks to establish the proper relationships between the participants of relationships in order to ensure societal peace and commerce. Confucius recommends that the power dynamics of the state be modeled on those of the family, and he seeks to establish social harmony and order through the notion of filial piety, or propriety. Depending on the role played within a relationship, superior or inferior, specific measures and rituals are enacted to recognize the relationship and to respect both the other and also the relationship itself. These measures are codified in dress, speech, religious ceremony, and occupation, and to dress, speak, and perform or pursue appropriate careers in life is to maintain a system of recognition and harmony in society.

In addition to the five basic relationships so obvious in human practical experience, Confucius also considers human nature. Like many philosophers, Confucius wonders whether humans are inherently good or bad.

Upon consideration, Confucius concludes that humans are not intrinsically good or bad; we are a mixture of both good qualities, which can be enhanced by education, and bad qualities, which should be combated through education and ritual. Confucius emphasizes culture and education in order to cultivate human nature so as to enhance what good qualities we possess and to suppress those less than noble tendencies found in us. Because education and knowledge are so heavily emphasized, Confucius also notes that it is our personal responsibility to develop these relationships and build our knowledge of ourselves as well as the world around us. Social interaction is at the very heart of personal development through education.

The inheritors of his legacy variously interpret Confucius' doctrine on human nature. Mencius (372–289 BCE) interprets Confucius' doctrine and teachings to imply that humans are naturally good, and it is through teaching that we cultivate these inherently good qualities. Mencius contends that humans are born with certain dispositions such as compassion, modesty, shame, and courtesy, and that the course of education and maturity is to simply cultivate these already inherent qualities.[8] Xunzi takes a darker approach. Xunzi understands Confucius to be using education, instruction, and propriety to remedy the darker parts of our human nature—those parts that deny the social conditions of humanity and seek to pursue their unabated self-interest. He devotes an entire book, *Man's Nature Is Evil,* to disprove Mencius' claims of human decency.[9] Xunzi concludes that because we must repress certain portions of our nature, Mencius' optimistic approach is not practical for the preservation of harmonious society. If we only focus on the positive qualities we are born with, the darker forces are left unchecked and can grow uncontrollably. Rather, we should focus on the darker portions of our nature, educate ourselves, and force ourselves to recognize the boundaries and roles we play in our social relationships.

Moreover, because of this inherently selfish nature, Xunzi elevates the social hierarchy found in Confucius' teachings to an even greater level of importance. It is only through the divisions of society according to the five basic relationships that one can find the proper instruction to combat our evil urges. Left to our own devices—that is, without proper instruction from a person in superior position—our desires, left unchecked, would grow, inevitably leading to conflict for resources between individuals, and eventually the decay and destruction of peaceful society. According to Xunzi, if we are not a highly organized social group recognizing each other's roles and strengths (as well as shortcomings) within our society, but rather entirely self-occupied individuals, we will eventually conflict with one another, and little good can come from this.[10] This intentional focus on our often self-ish desires and the suppression of these darker tendencies—this Xunzian approach to our personal and interpersonal lives—finds graphic depiction in the representations of cowboy in the films of Ang Lee.

American Cowboys

Brokeback Mountain presents us with two parallel cowboy stories. At the opening of the movie, we find Jack Twist, estranged from his parents, and Ennis del Mar, orphaned at an early age, applying for a job in the hard-scrabble life of Montana sheep ranching. The initial encounter of the two, strangers applying for the same job, illustrates the isolation and emotional barriers such a life engenders. At the office of Joe Aguire (Randy Quaid), neither men attempts to make conversation or small talk. Rather, they simply stare mistrustingly at each other. After they both get jobs, Jack tending to the sheep and Ennis performing domestic responsibilities at camp, their conversation remains terse and emotionally distant. Jack is just a hired hand trying to earn enough money to continue his rodeo pursuits. Ennis has some loyalties to Alma, his fiancée, but he must endure isolation and loneliness to afford a start to life with his future bride. Both men are simply trying to make ends meet in order to afford their desires once the summer comes to an end. To claim they are emotionally distant and reluctant to share their lives with each other—or anyone, for that matter—would be an understatement. Ennis himself suggests that the short telling of his parents' death was more than he had spoken in a year. Their love affair begins after a late night of drinking and commiserating about their loneliness. Yet it is just such a setting that bespeaks the cowboy aesthetic as we have come to find it in today's culture. Cowboys are depicted as emotionally distant, isolated individuals who need no one and who can sacrifice personal intimacy for the sake of the jobs that provide for them.

Their departure from the mountain demonstrates the need for a com-partmentalization and separation of intimacy from the lives they will resume when returning to civilization. After the brief summer affair, Ennis informs Jack that it was merely a "one time thing" and punctuates his refusal to con-tinue an intimate relationship by punching Jack. Ennis plans on returning to his emotionally solitary former life, despite his impending marriage. Jack plans to return to live in his truck and continue to ride bulls in the rodeo.

Ennis's need to distance himself from someone with whom he has had an intimate connection is the product of two reasons: the social stigmas of homosexuality and his previous obligations to marry. This graphic depiction is at the heart of the cowboy aesthetic: sacrificing personal desire (for intimacy and connectivity with Jack) for duty and obligation (upholding societal expectations of marriage). Ennis must do what is right by returning to his previous romantic encounter with his fiancée, his family, and his familial obligations while maintaining the image of socially acceptable heterosexuality despite his fondness for Jack. Severing this most intense connection with another living person is difficult, as illustrated by Ennis vomiting at their abrupt and awkward departure.

It is only after several years have passed that we realize Ennis's deep fondness for Jack, when Ennis receives a postcard from Jack declaring his imminent arrival. At this meeting, the turmoil of desire and propriety is manifest in the violence of their embrace. Even after removing themselves from society and enjoying each other's company, even daydreaming of a future life together, Ennis removes himself once again by suggesting the implausibility of living and running a ranch together. Both men must return to their lives, families, and responsibilities; they must table their personal needs in favor of social acceptability and duties. The freedom both men desire can only be had in isolation, removed from the prying eyes of society. Even after Alma discovers Jack and Ennis's secret when she covertly observes them during an embrace, the longed-for liberty cannot be obtained. Despite Jack's sudden appearance and suggestion of a life together, social responsibilities prevent Ennis from engaging with him for longer than a few days at a time. Their intimacy and involvement must remain removed from society and can only be indulged in brief engagements a few times a year. As the movie progresses, we find Jack established as husband and father, yet unsatisfied with the socially acceptable married life, choosing to secretly pursue extramarital affairs. We find Ennis divorced, living alone, although sometimes with girlfriends, distant from his children and simply tolerated by family at holidays. Work appears to come first, then family. Only in brief instances do we witness the deep connection he shares with another human being; even Ennis's romantic affairs appear impersonal.

Essential to the cowboy aesthetic as presented in typical western movies (even though this is not a typical example) is the notion of loving from a distance (often unrequited), a love that is only rarely indulged in, after which a great distance of time or geography is necessary. The relationship between Jack and Ennis embodies this ideal, yet we also see it in their grasping at other interpersonal connections throughout the film. It seems as if cowboys are only allowed the luxury of true intimacy a few times in their solitary existence.

Chinese Giang Hu

Unlike the American cowboys, like those seen in *Brokeback Mountain,* Chinese cowboys are depicted through the lifestyle of the Giang Hu, persons living in a shadowy subculture composed of warriors, thieves, prostitutes, and performers. Here we find both noble and ignoble characters who must often sacrifice personal desire for the obligations of this quasi-secret society. Indicative of their cowboy nature is the requirement for intense training and dedication to their martial arts (or performing arts), including the isolation needed to master themselves and their skills. This dedication to occupation leaves little room for intense social connections and necessarily results in a solitary life.

At the opening of *Crouching Tiger, Hidden Dragon,* we find a prime example of the Giang Hu lifestyle: martial arts master and legendary swordsman Li Mu Bai has abandoned his quest for enlightenment through deep meditation. He indicates that he desires to abandon his old way of life and begin life anew with someone or something that called to him—and that called him back from the highest attainment of his martial training. In short, Li Mu Bai wishes to shed his old life and quit the warrior's lifestyle, retire, and enjoy a life more connected with others. In particular, he wishes to retire into domestic life with Shu Lien now that he is entering his latter years. To do so, he must give away his most powerful possession, the sword known as the Green Destiny, a symbol of the Giang Hu life, and start over with the woman he loves. He desires to abandon his duties to his training and to engage in interpersonal interactions. As a *biao shi,* a Giang Hu guardian or escort, Shu Lien's shock at such an announcement indicates just how extraordinary such a step is to the members of this culture. A lifetime of training has prepared him for the final step of enlightenment, but Li Mu Bai does not wish to complete his training to become the ultimate, isolated, independent, enlightened Chinese cowboy. Unfortunately for the romantic tale of Li Mu Bai and Shu Lien, only brief moments are permitted during which they try to close the great distance that has separated their longing; yet even these are awkward and interrupted moments. Li Mu Bai must fulfill his obligations and exact revenge on the rogue who killed his master. He cannot abandon obligations in favor of his personal interest. Rather, his obligation to fulfill his social role prevents his romantic desires.

Lee juxtaposes the character of Jen against the character of Li Mu Bai. Unlike Li Mu Bai, she is in late adolescence or early adulthood. At the opening of the movie, we find Jen, the daughter of an important governor, preparing for her wedding to another prominent citizen. Ensconced within her web of family, reputation, and political connections, Jen appears to be immersed in social dynamics and responsibilities. Quickly we discover that she is no ordinary teenage girl but has, through the tutelage of a Giang Hu outlaw, Jade Fox (murderer of Li Mu Bai's master), been secretly learning the martial secrets of the Giang Hu.

Jen's story is a complicated one. Not only has she been trained in martial arts, actually surpassing her teacher while keeping this knowledge secret to herself, but she also had occasion to live life free of familial obligations and restraint during her brief affair with Lo. Because of her independence and determination, in addition to her martial arts, Jen pursues Lo outside the bounds of civilization and society in order to retrieve what was rightfully her own: her comb. A short but passionate affair ensues, yet society and family cannot be ignored. Inevitably, Jen returns to civilization, all the while longing to be free from societal constraints to live and love when and where she sees fit—in short, to live the Giang Hu lifestyle. The theft of the Green Destiny offers her just the occasion to pursue such an independent life. Jen desires the Green Destiny so that she might become independent, while Li Mu Bai wishes to be free of it so he might engage with others.

The Cowboy Aesthetic

By examining the main characters of these two films, one can now see a central issue Ang Lee is trying to depict in these projects. The protagonists in his films are complicated and conflicted individuals; they are modern depictions of cowboys. These cowboys share similar and essential characteristics.

The first characteristic of cowboys is an intense passion, often a twofold passion. Ennis is characterized by his love for Jack and his love for his family. Li Mu Bai is a master swordsman but also possesses an unspoken love for Shu Lien. Jack also loves Ennis, but he dreams of building a ranch and living with the man he loves. Jen is passionate about Lo but also desires independence from familial and social obligations. That these personal desires and passions are thwarted by external influences is precisely the conflict the cowboy encounters: should one indulge in personal desire, or should one perform expected functions?

Such intrapersonal conflict is often visually depicted in the violence that the cowboy lifestyles elicits. The violence of the physical affection of Ennis and Jack, the beautiful but physical violence of Giang Hu, and the emotional violence implied by the vacillation between indulging in personal desire and commitment to obligations are central to the plot and development of these movies. This conflict indicates an internal recognition of the difficulties of reconciling personal inclination and societal duties. The care of the self often comes into conflict with societal constraints.

Chief among these societal constraints is family. No person is without family. As summarized in the Lo chapter of *Crouching Tiger, Hidden Dragon*, survival is important, and family and friends provide shelter and strength while this treacherous world is navigated. We owe a great deal to our friends and family, and we often desire to establish families to aid us throughout our lifetime. Despite the appearance of the contrary, not even a cowboy can make it by himself. Yet family also places a great burden on the cowboy, so recourse to wilderness and isolation is necessary.

When obligations to society or when personal desire overpower these obligations, recourse is made to wilderness, where there are no rules. In the wilderness, Jack and Ennis may pursue their romantic involvement outside the prying eyes of society. In the wilderness of the forest, Li Mu Bai can express his love for Shu Lien. In the wilderness of travel and the desert, Jen can indulge her independence from and love for Lo. Ang Lee depicts these moments as fleeting and few, but as essential to the cowboy. In typical Hollywood depictions, it is quite the reverse; it is only after long periods in rugged isolation, during which the cowboy satisfies his need for solitude, that he enters town and reengages with society. But herein lies the true correction Lee presents in his films. The truth of human existence is not the cliché of the isolated cowboy; rather, it is in our interconnections that we find who we truly are.

The Confucian Cowboy

Lee's cowboys are always already in context: they are constantly connected, although usually in a way that is not apparent at first viewing. None of Lee's protagonists act in isolation. Rather, they are always connected to and acting within societal bonds. Fortunately, these bonds are given excellent representation in the philosophy of Confucius and its development through the Chinese philosopher Xunzi. When seen through this perspective, we realize that there are no cowboys as Americans have come to depict them in movies, and that despite historical and Hollywood presentation, no one is an isolated individual beyond the constraints of society. In fact, it is through society that one finds meaning in the rare moments of isolation. Furthermore, it is society that is the foundation of the cowboy aesthetic.

Confucian doctrine, as communicated through the works of Xunzi, delineates five basic relationships through which we can comprehend our social roles and our appropriate places in social contexts and to whom we owe deference and respect.[11] In declining strength of deference, the relationship between ruler and subject is the one wherein we find the strongest deference and greatest need of respect; subjects are to defer to and respect authority figures to the greatest degrees. This structure is also evident in the teacher–pupil relationship. At the opposite end of the spectrum, little deference is given between friends of equal bearing, while respect is always to be maintained. Never should one exhibit disrespect to either element in the relationships, nor to the relationships themselves. Xunzi suggests that it is through proper understanding of our roles and status in our interpersonal relationships that we can respect ourselves, others, and the institution of relationship. By constraining our own ego-centered self in deference to these relationships and society at large—that is, by cultivating a sense of $l\breve{\imath}$ (propriety) and $y\breve{\imath}$[12] (sense of duty) to those in positions of authority or deference—we establish a harmonious, secure society. Society becomes disjointed when people place themselves above or outside these relationships and unilaterally pursue their own selfish interests. Unlike the typical American attitude, which suggests that individuals are the basis for society, Confucius and Xunzi claim that it is society that allows for individuals to grow, mature, and cultivate themselves.[13] Thus, for the Confucian cowboy, the recognition and maintenance of the great relationships form the basis for individual thriving. This is precisely one theme that we see in both of Ang Lee's films about cowboys.

In *Brokeback Mountain*, it appears that Jack and Ennis are isolated individuals pursing their own desires. At the opening of the movie, they are both immature, damaged individuals with no deep relationships; they are isolated and alone. Of course, they have their individual narratives and histories, which have formed them, but because of circumstances, they have either lost contact or have severed ties with those with whom they should have basic relationships, thus implying that they are incomplete. Only through the cultivation of relationships—between parents and children, and between lovers (husbands and wives in the traditional formulation, or here, between two men)—can Jack and Ennis, but Ennis especially, heal the wounds of isolation and grow. They are defined by their familial relationships, and they are defined by their relationship to each other. Neither is as isolated as he initially appears. Nor is their isolation ever complete. Basic bonds ground their seeming isolation and help them constitute meaning in moments of solitude or reverie.

In *Crouching Tiger, Hidden Dragon,* the social bonds are more apparent, if not more subtly Confucian. The bond between Li Mu Bai and Shu Lien is one of friendship and camaraderie, and they never transgress this bond, despite longing to change their relationship to one of romance. Lee suggests that the proper cultivation of this friendship lends itself to the growth and cultivation of desire for something more. Other characters represent the breakdown and purposeful neglect of relationships. Jade Fox and Jen do not respect relationships in their quest to become Giang Hu warriors. Jade Fox's long history of self-importance, rather than societal importance, creates a fractured society that the protagonists seek to mend. Jen is at a crossroads: she must decide whether to wholeheartedly pursue the lifestyle taught her by Jade Fox, or to seek to reestablish relationships with her lover, Lo; her surrogate sister, Shu Lien; her potential master, Li Mu Bai; and even her family. Despite failing at some of these, Jen's redemption arrives when she casts aside her own personal desires and reestablishes the basic Confucian relationships, even at her own peril.

It is precisely the reconnection and cultivation of relationships, despite the fact that some of the relationships have expired—that is, a cultivation of respect for the relationships—that ends both cowboy movies by Ang Lee. In contrast to the typical American cowboy aesthetic, with its empty and hollow understanding of individualism, and which attempts to establish an impossible orientation between the protagonist and others, Lee presents us with an alternative, distinctly Confucian understanding of personal and interpersonal connectivity. The American cowboy aesthetic is an empty and false ideal that does not follow from the actual circumstances of life. Lee understands the hollowness and impossibility of isolated individuality and deftly reminds us of this in his films. Citing Aristotle, the German philosopher Friedrich Nietzsche (1844–1900) reminds us that only gods and beasts live in isolation.[14] None of the characters in Lee's films are either, and so they must be connected to the world. So, too, are all of us; we live among one another, never in utter isolation. Remembering and respecting the relationships in our lives is what gives us our bearing and provides the backdrop against which we cultivate ourselves.

Notes

1. Alexis de Tocqueville, *Democracy in America,* trans. Harvey C. Mansfield and Delba Winthrop (Chicago: University of Chicago Press, 2000), book 1, chap. 3.

2. By individualism here, I mean a Western notion of a self-contained, individual identity or persona that is the core of any social interaction, one that is achieved by oneself and that is maintained throughout the diverse unfolding of one's life.

3. See Confucius, *Analects,* in *The Analects of Confucius: A Philosophical Translation,* ed. Roger T. Ames and Henry Rosemont Jr. (New York: Ballantine, 1998).

4. *Lǐ* refers to the rituals, customs, rites, and etiquette of Confucian society. For a detailed exposition of this and other key Confucian concepts, see James McRae, Chapter 1, this volume.

5. Xunzi, *Xunzi: A Translation and Study of the Complete Works, Books 1–32,* 3 vols., trans. John Knoblock (Stanford, Calif.: Stanford University Press, 1988, 1990, 1994).

6. The five great relationships are ruler–subject, parent–child, husband–wife, elder sibling–younger sibling, and friend–friend. See James McRae, Chapter 1, this volume, for more information about these relationships.

7. Confucius, *Analects,* book 12, section 11; see Xunzi, book 7, "On Confucius," in *Xunzi,* 2:53–62.

8. Mencius, "Tăng Wăn Kung, Part I," in *The Works of Mencius,* ed. James Legge (New York: Dover), 234–260.

9. Xunzi, book 23, "Man's Nature Is Evil," in *Xunzi,* 3:139–162.

10. Ibid. Also see Xunzi, book 10, "On Enriching the State" in *Xunzi,* 2:113–138.

11. Confucius, *Analects,* book 1, section 1; Xunzi, books 9–13 in *Xunzi,* 2:85–204. See also Henry Rosemont Jr., "State and Society in the *Xunzi:* A Philosophical Commentary," in *Virtue, Nature, and Moral Agency in the Xunzi,* ed. T. C. Kline and P. J. Ivanhoe (Indianapolis, Ind.: Hackett, 2000), 1–38; and the chapter on Xunzi in Philip Ivanhoe's *Confucian Moral Self Cultivation* (Indianapolis, Ind.: Hackett, 2000), 29–42.

12. *Yì* refers to moral appropriateness, or the generalizable moral principles that allow one to adjudicate moral disputes. See James McRae, Chapter 1, this volume, for a detailed analysis of *yì.*

13. Xunzi, books 2–4, in *Xunzi,* 1:143–195. Jonathan Schofer, "Virtues in Xunzi's Thought," in Kline and Ivanhoe, *Virtue, Nature, and Moral Agency,* 69–88.

14. Friedrich Nietzsche, *Twilight of the Idols,* in *The Portable Nietzsche,* trans. Walter Kaufmann (New York: Penguin Books, 1977), Maxims and Arrows: "To live alone one must be a beast or a god, says Aristotle."

East Meets Western

The Eastern Philosophy of Ang Lee's *Brokeback Mountain*

Jeff Bush

Introducing the Cowboy

Ang Lee's 2005 film, *Brokeback Mountain,* is an adaptation of Annie Proulx's 1997 novella about the intense connection between two cowboys who first meet while sheepherding on a mountain in Wyoming in 1963. Both the film and the novella emphasize the anfractuous nature of the cowboys' emotional and sexual relationship over the next twenty years as they struggle against society's disapproval and strive to maintain the intensity of their initial meeting. Here, I argue that Lee's film connects the genre of the western with Eastern philosophy, which helps us to view homosexuality in a new way. First, I discuss the representation of the hero in the western as a heterosexual archetype. This leads to a discussion of the implicit homosexuality in the western as illuminated by queer theory, that area of critical theory that investigates issues surrounding gender, sexuality, and sexual acts.[1] Second, I argue that, rather than replicating western archetypes or queer theory, Lee's *Brokeback Mountain* parallels both the Eastern philosophy of Mencius (372–289 BCE) and the contemporary philosophy of John Corvino.[2] Third, I explain how Lee takes the western in a new and different direction and that his representations of the main characters in *Brokeback Mountain,* Ennis del Mar (Heath Ledger) and Jack Twist (Jake Gyllenhaal), help us to see connections between Mencius and Corvino. Finally, I suggest that *Brokeback Mountain* captures, in cinematic form, the symbiosis of the cardinal relationship of friendship and the moral concept of *rén,* which furthermore helps us to view homosexuality in moral, rather than sexual, terms.

Since the birth of cinema—and indeed modern visual media itself—the cowboy has exemplified an American heterosexual archetype that still resonates today in its attempted synthesis of masculine iconography and a post-Enlightenment ideology that promotes the cause of the individual. The cinematic template for this archetype was first sketched out in the silent era by Tom Mix, who represented the very essence of a cowboy—be-Stetsoned, athletic, and straight acting. This template was given color (if not shade) by John Wayne, who not only had similar physical attributes to Mix (with the addition of a suitably manly Midwestern drawl), but also managed to elevate the western hero to icon status, symbolizing American values and ideals. Wayne came to embody the personal qualities of independence and stoicism, as well as the value systems of duty and courage, that we now associate with the western hero. Subsequently, the western hero, as an all-American heterosexual archetype, became a simple and powerful image easily utilized by advertisers and presidents alike.

Queer Theory

With its provocative and easily marketable forms (Stetsons, plains, sunsets, horses, rifles) and its powerful belief system of independence (duty and courage), the western has always been ripe for cashing in on not only by advertisers and politicians, but also by groups who have traditionally felt marginalized by the values held up to be ideal in the western. There was something inevitable about the deconstruction of the western by queer theory in the 1980s and 1990s, given that queer theory's objects of interest include heterosexual iconography, fantasy, and masculinity. Queer theory makes it seem that there was always already something queer about the western, and it gives us a way of talking about the western divorced from political ideology or advertising messages. It has provided us with a way of looking at the western as always already containing disruptive spaces that threaten to destabilize the genre itself.

However, there is something disappointing about the emphasis on campy dialogue and phallic imagery that too often preoccupies queer theory. Indeed, we only have to watch *Destry Rides Again* (George Marshall, 1939) or *My Little Chickadee* (Edward F. Cline, 1940) to see a representation of the western with its tongue already firmly in cheek. In the middle of the twentieth century, the western genre was exploited in advertising and in politics for its style rather than its substance. Similarly, queer theory places as much emphasis on form rather than meaning in its deconstruction of the western. We never truly get to the meaning of the western via readings informed by either classic western theory or queer theory; often, we are merely served an advertisement for consumerism.

Queer theory did introduce us to a typical western trope: the juxtaposition of a masculine individuality and a feminizing society. We see this in the conflict between Montgomery Clift's Matt and John Wayne's Dunson in *Red River* (Howard Hawks and Arthur Rosson, 1948) and Robert Wagner's Joe and Spencer Tracy's Devereaux in *Broken Lance* (Edward Dmytryk, 1954). These are oppositions all too familiar in the field of psychoanalysis and deconstruction. Jacques Derrida (1930–2004) would have perhaps referred to the representation of the square-jawed, resilient cowboy as exemplified by actors John Wayne, Gary Cooper, and Clint Eastwood as phallogocentric, a concept that was originally targeted at Lacanian thought.[3] These are representations that see meaning in the phallus, and that provide an overemphasis on the role of a particular (and masculine) form over a more general (asexual) meaning. Indeed, initially, Ennis and Jack appear—like Wayne, Cooper, Eastwood, and others—to perpetuate the phallogocentrism that can be seen to underlie the western archetype. On first sight, they appear similar: they are square-jawed, simple, straight-talking cowboys conventionally attired in denim, with the obligatory Stetson hats and cowboy boots. They size each other up à la Clift and Ireland in *Red River,* who, in a scene with clear homoerotic overtones, admire each other's weapons. However, Lee denies an all too aware audience this kind of visual titillation, as Ennis appears unsure, nervous, lacking in confidence, and unwilling to participate in the dance of seduction that Jack initiates.

Furthermore, as *Brokeback Mountain* slowly accumulates detail, the iconography of the western seems to dissipate as Lee charts a real relationship, in a real landscape, between two shepherds on a mountain, then in their separate, disparate, and frustrated lives. The details, as they slowly build up, are rooted in naturalism, a feature of Chinese filmmaking that emphasizes human interconnectedness over (capitalist) iconography. In the film, Lee often presents scenes in an unwestern way that illustrates gentle and quotidian humor:

ENNIS: You're supposed to mind the sheep, not eat them.
JACK: Why is it always so friggin' cold? We oughta go south where it's warm, you know, we oughta go to Mexico!
ENNIS: Mexico? Hell Jack, you know me, about all the travelin' I ever done is round a coffee pot lookin' for the handle.

This scene is reminiscent of the gentle humor that we see in Eastern films where, interestingly, sheepherding is exploited for comic effect. It is also particularly admirable how Lee never shies away from presenting poverty naturalistically, without imposing a point of view. He never feels as though it has to be camped up (*Calamity Jane,* David Butler, 1953), anesthetized (*True Grit,* Henry Hathaway, 1969), or made more gritty and masculine (*Unforgiven,* Clint Eastwood, 1992). Lee tells us that to be poor in the West is to live a life that is grim, gray, and soul-destroying. There is nothing iconic about Ennis and Jack in the first part of the film. In his depiction of the developing relationship between them, Lee's approach is resolutely unromantic, and he is clearly not interested in passively representing archetypes. He doesn't show us the pioneer spirit of the West but rather a culture in thrall to immediate gratification and consumerism, the signposts of which sit on the shelves in the backgrounds of our lives like the tins of manufactured food in the supermarket where Ennis's wife works, and which Ennis knocks down in his rush to have an illicit encounter with Jack.

Gay Cowboy Movie

The script of *Brokeback Mountain* floated around for seven years, unable to find realization, and was referred to derisively as "the gay cowboy movie." Interestingly, when it was eventually released, it was rejected as not gay enough by some queer critics. The film was then and remains now an anomaly, which is why it was perhaps unsurprising that the Academy snubbed it for the more conventional, and mediocre, *Crash* (Paul Haggis, 2006) at the 2006 Academy Awards. Some critics also complained about the tameness of the sex scenes, perhaps expecting a film about homosexuals to, at the very least, contain some appropriately shocking and graphic gay sex. *Time* magazine appeared to categorize it as a revisionist western: "An anti-romantic West, a place of trailer parks and honky-tonks, of small, thwarted hopes, wrangling wranglers and sweet dreams." Then it dismissed it as "melodrama" that failed to "emote." Daniel Bulger, however, claimed that it was an instance of queer cinema.[4] Indeed, the symbiosis of cowboys and homosexuality, as queer theory has shown, is nothing new, and if we are forced to categorize *Brokeback Mountain,* it does make sense to see it as part of the trend in the 1990s to reclaim cinematic genres and put a queer stamp on old favorites. Todd Haynes's *Far from Heaven* (2002), for example, attempted to make explicit what was implicit in Douglas Sirk's 1950s melodramas, and Lee's *Brokeback Mountain,* it could be argued, attempts to do the same for the western.

The film's subject matter, at the very least, owes much to a tradition of queer cinema that sought to reclaim cinematic archetypes for a queer audience. In Vito Russo's seminal book, *The Celluloid Closet* (1995), he explains that, in silent-era Hollywood, it was not unusual to see overtly homosexual characterization. Indeed, seeing depictions from this time, it is genuinely surprising how stereotypes, such as the limp-wristed and lisping fashion designer, were already well established in the early twentieth century. However, the Hayes Code, a series of censorship rules adopted by Hollywood in the early 1930s, attempted to ensure that depictions of overt sexuality were censured. This had positive and creative effects: stereotypes were made less explicit, and references to sexuality became implicit. Perceptive—and gay—audiences might notice a cruising scene in *My Darling Clementine* (John Ford, 1946) and be highly sensitive to the androgyny of *Johnny Guitar* (Nicholas Ray, 1954) and *Calamity Jane.* For a brief time, then, during the golden age of the western, there was a subtle language of homoeroticism in Hollywood movies. The end of the code, however, saw the paradoxical return of stereotypes that were adapted to the new era of gay liberation and gay visibility.[5] This enhanced visibility unfortunately meant that in the 1960s and 1970s, homosexual characters in mainstream cinema were either lonely, unhappy characters, as in *The Boys in the Band* (William Friedkin, 1970), or characters with sociopathic, even psychopathic, tendencies, as in *The Detective* (Gordon Douglas, 1968). Russo does not comment on the profound irony that Hollywood—the great temple of Western consumerism—anticipated the lucrative potential of the pink dollar even before it was an established phenomenon. To notice this, however, would necessitate an acknowledgment of the complicity between gay culture and Western consumerism that unfortunately has still yet to be fully acknowledged and addressed in both straight and queer criticism.

Mencius, Eastern Philosophy, and Male Sexuality

Although it does owe some gratitude to queer cinema, Lee's representation of Proulx's novella transcends this cinematic genre in unusual ways, and the film itself rises above and beyond a representation or a critique of phallogocentrism. Western melodrama is explicitly, and queer cinema implicitly, consumer oriented. *Brokeback Mountain* is not typical of either of these genres in this respect. Instead, it is an attempt to present male sexuality from the point of view of Eastern philosophy.

The idea that Eastern thought can be used to support a theory of sexuality might seem odd. Indeed, in many ways, Eastern thought appears just as rigid with regard to gender roles as Western thought. Confucians, for example, view society as hierarchical and determined by the five cardinal relationships.[6] Whereas shamanistic traditions tend to see sexuality and gender as being in flux and are less concerned with gender roles, Confucians place enormous emphasis on the genders and their respective roles, and homosexual tendencies—as much for Confucians as for Plato in *The Laws*[7]—are seen as a natural defect or a disease that needs to be cured. There is a strain of Confucian thought, however, that allows us to view sexuality in terms of morality. We find this in the Confucian philosophy of Mencius. Mencius' thought has no mind–body dualism, as we think of it in the West. Instead, human beings are thought of in terms of mind and heart, or *xīn*. His fellow Confucian, Gaozi, proposed a view of *xìng* (nature) as a purely physical or biological concept in which human beings are viewed in terms of consumption and procreation. In his doctrine of natural goodness, or *xìngshàn*, however, Mencius rejects this biological view of *xìng*. This is memorably and vividly depicted in his famous example of a beggar who rejects food that is offered to him in an unpleasant and disrespectful manner: "Suppose there are a basketful of rice and a bowlful of soup. If I get them, I may remain alive; if I do not get them, I may well die. If they are offered contemptuously, a wayfarer will decline to accept them; if they are offered after having been trampled upon, a beggar will not demean himself by taking them."[8]

Mencius' example illustrates how human beings are not primarily interested in eating and having sex but have ethical predispositions. In Western thought, human beings are marked by the intentional stance where we are constantly alert for the representational possibilities that the world presents to us. The equivalent in Mencius' thought is a kind of ethical stance where human beings move through the world in an ethical direction and relations between human beings can be seen as a form of ethical dynamics:

> If men suddenly see a child about to fall into a well, they will without exception experience a feeling of alarm and distress. . . . From this case we may see that the feeling of commiseration is essential to man, that the feeling of shame and dislike is essential to men, that the feeling of modesty and complaisance is essential to man, and that

the feeling of approval and disapproval is essential to man. These feelings are the principles respectively of benevolence, righteousness, propriety, and the knowledge of good and evil. Men have these four principles just as they have their four limbs.[9]

Mencius views these ethical predispositions in terms of the four sprouts, which are universal but become particular as we grow and develop, as we move from ethical beings to moral subjects. He names these moral concepts *rén, lǐ, yì,* and *zhī.*[10] *Rén* is benevolence or compassion and is demonstrated in our (cardinal) relationships with rulers, parents, brothers, spouses, and friends. It is perhaps the most foundational concept in Mencius' philosophy, the concept that binds all others together, and he suggests that it takes on greater prominence in relationships that are immediate rather than deferred. Thus, we can say that it is most prevalent in friend–friend relationships, which are near the bottom of the hierarchy of cardinal relationships. We shall see that this has resonance with the philosophy of Corvino. *Lǐ* is concerned with rules and rituals, with conducting oneself appropriately and showing respect to others. *Yì* is concerned with propriety, values, and attitudes; it arises from our innate sense of shame and the desire to avoid dishonor. Finally, *zhī* is concerned with wisdom and also judgment. It helps us to adapt *lǐ* and *yì* and integrate them appropriately in our lives, as sometimes social rituals and social values need to be assessed according to context. Mencius explains how ethical beings become moral subjects in these four concepts.

Mencius' ethical predispositions, and the moral concepts that define them, reveal that there is a delicate balance between the individual and the social, as well as a fluid relationship between the four moral concepts. Unlike in Western thought, such as Cartesian dualism, where moral subjects are divided from ethical beings, in Mencius' thought, we are always already ethical beings. Acceptance and accommodation are key to Mencius' philosophy. He argues that society needs to accept an individual's innate goodness, and that an individual needs to accept a helpful hand from society to guide him. His view of the relationship between subject and world is akin to the difference between ethics and morals in the philosophy of Kant. However, in Kant, transcendental idealism connects the person with principles; in Mencius, something natural within human beings connects the ethical with the moral: the four sprouts that ground human beings and that need to be nurtured and developed over time. This growth is not from bad to good, nor from pre-Oedipal to Oedipal, because of our intrinsic and natural sense of morality. Mencius' view of humanity is contextual rather than conceptual, and as a consequence, patience, deferral, and moral judgment are all integral to his philosophy.

Corvino's Position: Homosexuality and Ethics

A clear difference between the philosophy of Mencius and the philosophy of Corvino lies in the differences they perceive between individual and society. Unlike Mencius, who is concerned with the maintenance of social rituals and behaviors, Corvino is concerned with the formation of identity, and in particular the formation of sexual identity. This is most apparent in Corvino's views on marriage. He highlights how our attitudes to sexuality are entwined with our attitudes toward marriage, acknowledging that there is an implicit assumption that being married means being in control, and not being married means being out of control. This is, he argues, a false dichotomy:

> Either heterosexual marriage on the one hand, or rampant selfishness on the other. This dichotomy, as I have said, arises from a false view of human nature. Human beings are simply not exclusively selfish, and so they do not need to be pressured into marriage in order to be saved from their egoism and individualism. Love of parents and friends is every bit as spontaneous as love of self. A person who finds no happiness in the happiness of others is not a typical specimen of humanity but a sociopathic freak.[11]

Marriage, he suggests, is a valuable institution, but one that should be viewed as a set of meaningful guiding principles rather than a form of social control. He thus places more emphasis on individual autonomy than on social hierarchy—the right to choose whether to marry or not, despite what society says is right or wrong. On the face of it, it seems Corvino's Western position is diametrically opposed to the relationship between *rén*, *yì*, *lǐ*, and *zhī* so central to Mencius' philosophy. Indeed, the difference between the two seems to illustrate the classic East–West conflict between traditional Confucian ethics and a contemporary Western view grounded in autonomy and voluntary informed consent.

If Corvino's emphasis on personal autonomy can be seen to oppose Mencius' emphasis on social hierarchy, he nevertheless shares with Mencius an antiempiricist view of ethics as a priori. He suggests that it is an odd thing to say that sexual behavior is gay identity because "gay relationships like straight relationships, include countless behaviours beyond sex: movie dates, long walks on the beach, quiet evenings at home, and plenty of mundane 'or better and for worse' stuff." Corvino sees diversity and context as just as important in the construction of gay identity as the way in which one engages in sexual activity. He also considers it odd to equate identity with behavior because "gay identity is usually connected to gay community, where the vast majority of relationships are non-sexual." Corvino's main point is that sexuality is as much dependent on ethics as it is on the act of sex itself: "To the extent that my sexual behaviour is tied closely to my experience of intimacy and isolation, pride and shame, power and vulnerability, joy and loss—all profound human emotions."[12] His view here is not that dissimilar from Mencius: meaning and context are seen to play an important role in the construction of gender identity. He suggests that although there are clear roles regarding gender roles, we cannot think of them as set in stone. Instead, they are all deeply implicated by morality. Like Mencius, Corvino believes that we should view human beings as essentially good but requiring some guidance, and that although rituals are important, they need to be contextualized.

Corvino's primary concern is the moral nature of homosexuality. He does not see homosexuality as a symptom of phallogocentrism—as, say, Jacques Lacan (1901–1981) might—and wishes us to view human beings, homosexual and heterosexual, as defined by our intrinsic ability to make moral judgments rather than by the extrinsic sexual form toward which our desire is directed. In "Why Shouldn't Tommy and Jim Have Sex? A Defense of Homosexuality," he deconstructs the view that homosexuality is unethical. He lists six supposedly moral arguments that people who oppose homosexuality often refer to in order to undermine its validity. In the first statement, "homosexual sex is unnatural," Corvino makes the point that there are many things that people value that are unnatural, such as clothing, houses, medicine, and government. He also states that many things that people detest are natural, such as disease, suffering, and death. In the second statement, "what is unusual or abnormal is unnatural," he refers to the fact that relatively few people read Sanskrit, play the mandolin, breed goats, or are ambidextrous, and that these are not immoral merely because of their lack of frequency. Quoting the Ramsay Colloquium, which opposed homosexuality, he states: "The statistical frequency of an act does not determine its moral status."[13]

In the third statement, "what is not practiced by other animals is unnatural," he refers to Anne Perkins's study of gay sheep, and George and Molly Hunt's study of lesbian seagulls to suggest that some animals do form homosexual couplings. He comments that animals also don't cook their food, brush their teeth, participate in religious worship, or attend college. In the fourth statement, "what does not proceed from innate desire is unnatural," he contrasts the view that homosexuality is natural and biological with the view that homosexuality is a lifestyle choice; he agrees with both but supports neither. On the one hand, saying homosexuality is a lifestyle choice is true to a certain extent, as there is inevitably an element of choice in our desires. On the other hand, saying that homosexuality is natural and biological does not mean it is naturally good and that all homosexuals are good. Neither case determines whether homosexuality is moral or not. In the fifth statement, "what violates an organ's principal purpose is unnatural," he comments that many of our organs have multiple purposes. Our mouths, for example, can be used for talking, eating, breathing, licking stamps, chewing gum, and kissing men and women. In the final statement, "what is disgusting or offensive is unnatural," he comments that plenty of morally neutral activities, such as handling snakes, eating snails, performing autopsies, and cleaning toilets, disgust people. Corvino's conclusion on the view that homosexuality is unnatural, and consequently unethical, is "at best expressed as an aesthetic judgement, not a moral judgement."[14] His balanced views on sex difference and sexuality reveals much about his philosophy in that he encourages us to interpret sexuality according to meaning (ethics, morality) rather than forms (images, language). Corvino ultimately suggests that we can view homosexuality in terms of an ethical relationship between two people.

Eastern with a Twist

The distinction between a Western value system premised on personal autonomy and an Eastern one that is underpinned by social hierarchy is dramatized in *Brokeback Mountain* by the relationship between Ennis and Jack. Their relationship reminds us of the profound sense of *rén* that exists among friends in Mencius' thought. Bulger suggests that Ennis and Jack identify with each other because they are separated by similar social constraints—namely, the illegality and social stigma of homosexual relationships—and that, in their infrequent meetings, they "find a way to be queer to survive."[15] However, there are tensions and oppositions in their relationship, and their attitudes to being queer are strikingly different. For Ennis, the social and the moral are interdependent. He interprets his life holistically and sees himself as a subject in a group as well as a sexual person with physical desires. Jack, however, sees a distinction between the individual and the society, the subject and the person, the social and the sexual. Independence, wealth, status, and appearance (or forms) are priorities in Jack's life, whereas family, cultivation, work, and connectedness are priorities in Ennis's life. One could say that Ennis is concerned with observing hierarchy, following *yì* and *lǐ*, and adhering to the cardinal rules regarding social relationships. Conversely, one could also say that Jack feels oppressed by strict gender and social roles, and seeks to flout hierarchical rules. We cheer for Jack, who attempts to throw off the shackles of these roles, which, for him, oppress rather than contextualize his personal autonomy and freedom. However, there can often be detected an implicit sense of consumerist entitlement underlying Jack's self-conscious, and Western, individualism, which Lee does indeed highlight. Ennis, on the other hand, seems to understand that he must be other than Western to survive—patience, deferral, and acceptance are un-Western (and queer) qualities that lie at the center of his life. He lives a simple, pared-down life in which things, images, and forms are not as prevalent as they are in Jack's. Jack seeks out male company in the form of a male prostitute, then, fatally, picks the wrong person. Jack, it seems, needs sexual gratification more than Ennis; but for Ennis, their relationship is deeper and more profound.

It is in the character of Ennis that the philosophies of Mencius and Corvino converge: he represents a startling view of sexuality intimately connected to society and deeply moral. Through Ennis, Lee gives us a sense of how sexuality can be seen in terms of *rén*—in terms of context, cultivation, and morality. Unlike Ennis, Jack appears unwilling to accept a life of deferred gratification in which his sexuality is cultivated. It is not at the center of his life but rather always in the background, acquiring depth and quality as the years progress. It is genuinely touching when Ennis weeps after Jack reveals to him that he has sought homosexual affection elsewhere, and one gets the feeling that Jack's actions represent a rejection of Ennis's philosophy. Through Ennis, Lee seems to ask why gratification needs to be regular and immediate, and why sexuality cannot be cultivated and consistently pruned and developed.

Masks, Ethics, and Friendship

The audience finds it difficult to formalize the relationship between Ennis and Jack in *Brokeback Mountain*. The two men seem at odds throughout—asymmetrical and unable to relate to each other—which Lee emphasizes throughout the film. As *Time Out* comments: "Jack is exuberant, more romantic, and a dreamer who rides rodeo and hatches impossible plans; Ennis is unadventurous and afraid of himself, takes solace in violence, holds back emotionally, and creates excuses for stagnation."[16] One of the principal differences between them, which affords much dramatic conflict, is that Jack appears more at ease with his sexuality than Ennis, who, it appears, has profound internal conflicts. Ennis's apparent internalized homophobia is indirectly explained by him as the haunting childhood memory of a gay bashing:

> ENNIS: I tell ya there . . . there were these two old guys ranched up together, down home. Earl and Rich. And they was the joke of town, even though they were pretty tough ol' birds. Anyway they . . . they found Earl dead in an irrigation ditch. Took a tire iron to 'em. Spurred him up, drug him 'round by his dick 'till it pulled off.
> JACK: You seen this?
> ENNIS: I wasn't . . . nine years old. My daddy, he made sure me and brother seen it. Hell for all I know, he done the job.

It is easy to view Ennis as out of touch with his feelings and racked with internalized homophobia. Indeed, Jack appears more queer than Ennis from the outset; he is more sexualized, mimicking the movements of a stallion, manipulating his body, and adopting poses to attract Ennis's attention. As the film progresses, he appears more conscious of appearance and clothes, more Western, more defined. We learn that he wants more, and he is not ashamed to go get what he wants, even if society disapproves. He goes cruising, for example, and sleeps with a male prostitute. In contrast to a more liberated Jack, then, it is easy to dismiss Ennis as a closet case and proclaim Jack as the true hero of *Brokeback Mountain*. Toward the end of the film, Jack confronts Ennis by the lake at the foot of Brokeback Mountain. After years of infrequent and ultimately unsatisfying meetings, he spits at Ennis: "You have no idea how bad it gets. Brokeback Mountain is all we got! I wish I knew how to quit you!" In these words, Jack appears to hold out a banner for all those gay men and women who have felt marginalized, rejected, and denied relationships, not only because they live in an oppressive and homophobic social hierarchy but because this very hierarchy functions, at the micro level, as the thought police, which often prevents homosexuals from having truly intimate relationships. In his simple words, Jack appears to be the voice of an oppressed minority and a hero for queer cinema.

However, Lee's focus is always on Ennis, and in particular his naturalism. His reaction to Jack's impassioned speech is totally unexpected. He crumples in Jack's arms, tearfully murmuring, "Why don't you let me be?" Lee then immediately flashes back to Ennis cradling Jack twenty years previously, emphasizing his tenderness:

> ENNIS: [*with his arms around Jack*] C'mon now, you're sleepin' on your feet like a horse. My mama used to say that to me when I was little. And sing to me . . . [*humming*].

Lee evokes a scene of authentic intimacy here that undercuts Jack's almost agitprop speech. In the juxtaposition of these scenes, we see a contrast between appearances and emotions, melodrama and naturalism, masks and authenticity. In Ennis's reaction, Lee is making a philosophical point. He gives us an Ennis who refuses to participate in either the masquerade of being an archetypal cowboy or the masquerade of proclaiming a queer identity. We never see Ennis posing or in a static tableau, as we often do with Jack. Instead, we always see him in context: a nervous teen shepherd; a young father and husband making mistakes; an older, loving father; and an old man in grief. It is intriguing, also, that the facial features of Ennis are not as defined or cinematic as Jack's. Jack's soulful eyes and flashing smile are striking. Ennis's, however, seem curiously vague, with tight lips and a nervous, evasive demeanor. His face is almost a mere suggestion of a face, or a mask, and this has the effect of foregrounding the masquerade. The notion of the mask underpins much thought on sexuality in the West, which involves the adoption of imaginary masks in order to be and to have the object of desire. This all feeds into the opposition between definition (Jack) and lack of definition (Ennis) that Lee consistently exploits. Indeed, Ennis himself defines his relationship with Jack as a thing rather than a relationship: "Bottom line is . . . we're around each other an' . . . this thing, it grabs hold of us again, at the wrong place, at the wrong time, and we're dead." Lee resists the urge to define their relationship in conventional and Western ways. Indeed, we hear this resistance toward definition in the following dialogue:

ENNIS: This is a one-shot thing we got goin' on here.
JACK: It's nobody's business but ours.
ENNIS: You know I ain't queer.
JACK: Me neither.

It is perhaps easy to see their unwillingness to identify themselves as homo-sexual as symptoms of denial and consequences of homophobia and preju-dice. Of course, Jack eventually wants a relationship, and his final speech is a paean to the idea of a homosexual relationship as well as a critique of the internalized homophobia that prevents this. However, Lee gives us a real sense that there are other ways to be homosexual and other ways to feel about being homosexual in his depiction of Ennis and Jack. Ennis and Jack resist wider societal norms in their homosexual relationship, but they also resist the norms beginning to be established by the gay community by refusing to see themselves as having a relationship. Their relationship opposes the traditional notion of male–male relationships in westerns, but their unwillingness to have a relationship also opposes the aspirations of gay men and women to have their relationships legitimized by society. Lee almost presents Ennis and Jack as resistance fighters, engaged in a battle on two fronts, in order to critique a West that is burdened with forms that pressure individuals toward normativity.

We misread Ennis's unwillingness to participate in the masquerade of sexuality as internalized homophobia when it is actually a keen desire to maintain relationships based on *rén*. Mencius says that relationships between friends are where *rén* is most intense. Lee dramatizes this, and in so doing, he seems to suggest that the basis of a homosexual relationship does not have to be characterized by physical intimacy but rather ethical intimacy. This view of relationships between homosexual men as ethical, rather than physi-cal, is a view that can bring together the thought of Mencius and Corvino.

Zhī Moments

In Mencius' philosophy, *zhī* is the moral concept that enables us to contex-tualize rituals, rules, and codes. It is the very negation of dualism. We see this dramatized in *Brokeback Mountain* in the representation of peripheral characters. The western is renowned for its dialectical structure—cowboys versus Indians, landscape versus human, masculine individuality versus feminine (and femininizing) society, and, of course, good versus evil—but

Brokeback Mountain avoids such oppositional tropes. Indeed, there are no clear villains in the film, there is never a clear moral opposition between heterosexual and homosexual. It is significant that, apart from Ennis's half-remembered recollection of a gay bashing, there is little demonstrable homophobia apparent in the film. There are only two other characters in *Brokeback Mountain* who are aware of the "thing" between Jack and Ennis: Jack Aguirre (Randy Quaid), the ranch foreman, who sees them wrestling half-naked on the mountainside; and Alma Bears (Michelle Williams), who catches the briefest glimpse of her husband locked in a passionate embrace with Jack in a scene handled with particularly adept camera work by Lee in its capture of a moment of Bears's emotional devastation.

Aguirre makes Jack aware that he suspects that their relationship was more than professional: "You boys sure found a way to make the time pass up there. Twist, you guys wasn't gettin' paid to leave the dogs babysittin' the sheep while you stem the rose." Bears also makes Ennis aware that she has suspicions about Ennis and Jack's friendship: "Don't try and fool me no more, Ennis; I know what it means! Jack Twist. Jack Nasty! You didn't go up there to fish!" In the film, two casual glances from Aguirre and Bears threaten to expose Ennis and Jack, but neither contacts the police. Instead, they choose to keep Jack and Ennis's relationship a secret.

One could suggest that they do this because, as Corvino suggests, heterosexuals and homosexuals are both moral beings who are continually making moral judgments and decisions, even in the most spontaneous and legally dubious circumstances. The shocking private events that are witnessed by third persons in *Brokeback Mountain* are never made public, which fits into the view, argued by Mencius and Corvino, that we don't actually believe that people are inherently selfish (Confucians) or saintly (Daoists); instead, we are always accommodating others and making allowances for them. Lee portrays the wider society sympathetically, but the boundaries between what is natural (Daoists) and what is social (Confucians) are never clear. Ennis represents the middle route, which is also the route of the viewers, who are encouraged to navigate their way through the complex social relationships and to see that there is a complex and sometimes tragic relationship between the natural and the social. With this in mind, it is interesting that some heterosexual married men were standing and applauding at the end of the film in American heartlands when it was released.

Bulger suggests that *Brokeback Mountain* affords straight and non-straight audiences alike pleasurable queer moments. I would suggest that these moments are more like Eastern, rather than queer, moments—or, rather, they are more like *zhī* moments. Film critic Roger Ebert suggests that Ennis and Jack's relationship could be a metaphor for two lovers from different religions, but I suggest that it is about two philosophies, one based on meaning and the other on form.[17] Lee shows us, via Ennis, that sexuality is contextual as much as it is conceptual. Indeed, Ennis's progress adheres to Mencius' concept of subjectivity as cultivation: he comes to love and care for his children; he comes to accept his sexuality in his own way and in a way that accommodates the wider society; he commemorates Jack in a dignified way, visiting his elderly parents, collecting his ashes, keeping his postcard and shirt as mementos. Although he makes mistakes and does not find love again, over time, Ennis gradually does the right thing in his life while retaining a sense of his own distinct identity. The scene at the film's end, where Ennis clasps the frayed postcard and presses Jack's faded shirt to his chest, is a moving sign of his distance from, and simultaneous defiance toward, a society in which both heterosexual and homosexual roles are marketing strategies that serve to perpetuate a consumerist culture. To Ennis, the small postcard and Jack's tattered denim shirt are cherished objects of meaning rather than ephemeral objects of desire.

In this final scene, Lee suggests that human sexuality is not about having a defined identity (in order to become a consumer), or being in a relationship, such as a marriage. Rather, the essence of sexuality is learning from mistakes and making moral judgments—the message of Corvino. The scene is an epiphany that depicts *xīn;* our thoughts and actions are characterized by affairs of the heart. The final message of the film recalls Corvino's question: why shouldn't men have intimate, even sexual, relationships? The answer lies in a synthesis of Corvino's and Mencius' views: because homosexuals and heterosexuals are moral beings, friends connected ethically via *rén,* homosexuality can be defined as an ethical friendship. An emphasis on masculine iconography and picturesque tableaux binds together the western, queer theory, and capitalism, and Lee offers an anticonsumerist vision of both the western and homosexuality. In this sense, *Brokeback Mountain* presents a different history of male sexuality than one defined by either the traditional western or queer theory; it presents a history of male sexuality that implicitly references Mencius and Corvino. *Brokeback Mountain* is a work of great understanding: it is neither conventional western nor queer cinema, but rather an Eastern western about homosexuality.

Notes

1. There are many philosophers doing work in queer theory, including Judith Butler at the University of California–Berkeley. For more on the discipline, see Annamarie Jagose, *Queer Theory: An Introduction* (New York: New York University Press, 1997); and Alexander Doty, *Making Things Perfectly Queer: Interpreting Mass Culture* (Minneapolis: University of Minnesota Press, 1993).

2. Mencius was a follower of Confucius. For more on his thought, see Kwong-loi Shun, *Mencius and Early Chinese Thought* (Stanford, Calif.: Stanford University Press, 1997). See also the entry "Mencius" in *Stanford Encyclopedia of Philosophy* (http://plato .stanford.edu). John Corvino, one of the world's foremost experts on gay rights, is the editor of *Same Sex: Debating the Ethics, Science and Culture of Homosexuality* (New York: Rowman & Littlefield, 1997).

3. Jacques Lacan (1901–1981) was a prominent psychoanalyst, psychiatrist, and follower of Sigmund Freud (1856–1939). Jacques Derrida, *The Postcard: From Socrates to Freud and Beyond,* trans. Alan Bass (Chicago: University of Chicago Press, 1987), 465.

4. Richard Schickel, "Movies: A Tender Cowpoke Love Story," *Time,* November 20, 2005 (http://www.time.com/); Daniel Bulger, "Queer Cowboys: Alternative Space in *Brokeback Mountain,*" *Film International* (http://filmint.nu/).

5. Vito Russo, *The Celluloid Closet: Homosexuality in the Movies* (New York: Harper and Row, 1995), 107.

6. The five cardinal relationships (ruler–ruled, parent–child, husband–wife, elder–younger sibling, and friend–friend) are discussed in detail in Chapters 1 and 3 of this volume.

7. Plato, *The Laws,* in *Plato: Complete Works,* ed. John Cooper (Indianapolis, Ind.: Hackett, 1997), 1318–1616.

8. Mencius, *Mencius,* trans. Irene Bloom (New York: Columbia University Press, 2009).

9. Mencius, *The Works of Mencius,* trans. J. Legge (Toronto: Dover, 1990).

10. For a detailed exposition of the key virtues of Confucian philosophy, see James McRae, Chapter 1, this volume. Note that although Mencius builds on the foundation of Confucian philosophy, his interpretation of these virtues differs slightly from that of Confucius, particularly concerning the affective nature of *rén.*

11. Corvino, *Same Sex,* 76.

12. John Corvino, "Are We Defined by Our Sexuality?" (http://www.fpride.org).

13. John Corvino, "Why Shouldn't Tommy and Jim Have Sex? A Defense of Homosexuality," in *Contemporary Moral Problems,* ed. James E. Wight (Belmont, Calif.: Wadsworth, 2006), 310.

14. Ibid., 312.

15. Bulger, "Queer Cowboys."

16. *Brokeback Mountain* review, *Time Out,* December 21, 2005 (http://timeout.com).

17. Roger Ebert, *Brokeback Mountain* review, *Chicago Sun Times,* December 16, 2005 (http://rogerebert.suntimes.com).

Landscape and Gender in Ang Lee's *Sense and Sensibility* and *Brokeback Mountain*

Misty Jameson and Patricia Brace

The *Yīn* and *Yáng* of the Picturesque

In his 1757 work, *A Philosophical Enquiry into the Origin of Our Ideas of the Sublime and Beautiful,* English philosopher Edmund Burke discusses these two concepts as they relate to human perceptions of landscape aesthetics in their most basic form: first, the sublime, which causes terror in the observer, and second, the beautiful, which causes pleasure. Later, William Gilpin would temper these two notions with his idea of the picturesque, which mitigates these extremes, mixing the sublime with the beautiful. The picturesque focuses on freedom and lack of control in the outdoors—wild, broken trees; storms; Gothic ruins in disrepair—corresponding to more tumultuous human relationships such as unfettered sexual desire, passionate devotion without hope of reciprocation, and secrecy. On the other hand, the beautiful can be seen in controlled, manicured gardens found in small, subtle, well-mannered landscapes and interiors, corresponding to socially sanctioned relationships, often more pleasing in public than in private. These notions of landscape aesthetics, of course, are not exclusive to Western philosophy; in Chinese tradition, questions of the spiritual in landscape, of man finding that "he is in symbiosis with the landscape," have to do with "man and the landscape as both being produced by *qi*, breath-energy":

> Everything in the universe originates in the same breath energy, which thanks to the regulation internal to its two constitutive factors, *yin* and *yang* (such as the *li*) leads to every manifestation of

existence, properly arranged. It leads to the infinite diversity of beings, man included, and to their relations with one another and their cohesion within a landscape.[1]

Thus, these principles, the sublime/*yīn* and the beautiful/*yáng,* reflect the dualities of nature as well as its essential oneness: man can be part of a landscape yet simultaneously be an observer of it, or a landscape can be picturesque, both delightfully beautiful and awe-inspiringly sublime. Taiwanese director Ang Lee combines these Western and Chinese traditions in his creation of visual, cultural, and emotional landscapes in his films, particularly *Sense and Sensibility* (1995) and *Brokeback Mountain* (2005).[2]

Sense and Sensibility

In Europe, a carefully controlled and geometrically regimented hybrid of Italian- and French-style landscaping was all the rage for the estates of the royals and aristocracy just before Jane Austen's time. André le Nôtre, royal gardener to King Louis XIV of France, set the fashion with his designs for the Tuileries Palace in Paris (1660–1664) and Versailles (1661), which was followed for the next 100 years. A central avenue along the long axis of the grounds provided a sweeping vista to those looking out from the large manor house or castle, as well as those walking or riding through it. Branching out from this avenue were pathways leading to carefully arranged individual plots, planted with flowers, shrubs, and topiary. At their center were often a large sculpture and a water feature, either a calm reflecting pool or an elaborate fountain. Aesthetic qualities of perspective, light and shadow, color, progression, and balance were all carefully planned to give the viewer the perfect experience of a man-made, controlled landscape. Large trees were planted on the boundaries of the gardens as a transition to the surrounding countryside, and cut though these groves were shadowed walkways, ostensibly to keep delicate complexions out of the sun but often a favorite trysting spot for couples.

Although Le Nôtre did work in England (most notably for King Charles II at Greenwich in 1662), another style emerged there by the 1750s, pioneered by William Kent (1685–1748) and popularized by Capability Brown (1716–1783), which subverted the controlled look of the French style with an equally planned landscape that created the look of nature.[3] A famous English estate, Blenheim Palace, home of the Churchill family, gave over 5,000 acres of its parkland to Brown's designs. The Italian- and French-style gardens were minimized, and large expanses of lawn (economically kept clipped short and walkable by flocks of sheep) gave way to pastures and groves. Set among them like jewels in a crown were elaborate water features, including lakes, which mirrored the manor house in their still surfaces, and huge powered fountains. Kent, Brown, and their followers wanted to create a fantasy pastoral, recalling the Elysian Fields of the classical gods, to show off the knowledge and education of their patrons. To that end, they also planned so-called imitation Greek temple follies and ha-has (barrier ditches), rather than fences, to mask human intervention in the landscape. Truly wild nature was embraced by those who favored the more rugged mountains of Wales, the Lake District in the north of England, and the Scottish Highlands, with ruined Gothic abbeys and castles for their sojourns into what was becoming known as the romantic picturesque.[4] This conception was strongly influenced by the aesthetics of philosopher Edmund Burke on the beautiful and the sublime, which provided a useful way to discuss the contrast between the controlled Brownian landscape and the picturesque wild.[5] Both of these late eighteenth- and early nineteenth-century English landscape trends may be found in the works of Jane Austen and are expressed in the Ang Lee–directed version of Austen's novel *Sense and Sensibility* (1811).

Austen's *Sense and Sensibility* was the first of her novels to be published. It was written over several years starting in the late 1790s and ending in 1809–1810, during which time many of the same life-changing events experienced by the Dashwood family in the novel also happened to the Austen women. With her father's sudden death in 1805, Jane, her mother, and her only sister (she had six brothers) were forced to rely on the kindness of relatives, first sharing the home of her second youngest brother, Francis, and his wife. Her third brother, Edward, had been adopted at age sixteen as heir to a large estate, Godmersham, in Kent.[6] The women often visited there, eventually settling into Chawton, a cottage on the estate, where the writing of *Sense and Sensibility* was completed.[7] The physical landscape of the everyday world that Austen's characters inhabit was one with which she was intimately acquainted; she lived in it. They are the same kind of cottages and manor houses on grand estates with gardens and parks where she walked and rode her horse. Where one did and did not belong was a matter of status, but how one gained, kept, or lost that status was always a tricky proposition. As Edward Copeland reminds us in his introduction to an edition of the novel, "For Austen, the gradations of society in 1790 seemed infinitely more vexed by signs of status that were paradoxically both non-negotiable and, of course, already under covert negotiation."[8] Just as a Capability Brown landscape had an underlying plan and order hidden under its grassy fields, wildflower plantings, and groves, there are characters in each Austen work maneuvering sub rosa to renegotiate their lives despite things like an unwanted secret engagement, an illegitimate child, or the loss of wealth. These interior landscapes are often reflected in the setting choices used in the novel and the film of *Sense and Sensibility* as exterior landscapes.

That Austen considered landscape an important consideration in the settings of her novels has been given thorough study.[9] In Alistair M. Duckworth's *The Improvement of the Estate* (rev. 1994), he discusses the philosophical, political, and sociological milieu in which she was writing and its implications in her treatment of land use within her work.[10] He identifies two sorts of park admirers in the late 1700s: those who preferred the "spacious park landscapes of Lancelot Capability Brown (1715–1783)" and "enthusiasts for the picturesque [who] sought out wild scenery."[11] Duckworth cites the influence of several contemporary writers on landscape, including Horace Walpole (1717–1797), a Whig who thought that the English garden was an expression of liberty while the regimented French style smacked of despotism. On the side of the picturesque was William Gilpin (1724–1804), who traveled throughout Britain and wrote his *Observations,* in which he gave direction to his readers wanting to follow in his footsteps. He pointed them toward landscapes with "rugged scenery" and "irregular water stained ruins" and gave them a proscriptive formula for appreciating the picturesque in both art and nature.[12] In 1818, Austen's brother, Henry, wrote of her that she was "at a very early age enamored of Gilpin on the Picturesque," and she was undoubtedly also aware of Walpole, whose writings would have been "found in the libraries of the polite."[13] The author also lived and worked within these landscapes: "At Chawton, the formal gardens of the Jacobean house had been replaced with a more modern landscape between 1763 and 1785. At Godmersham, a Palladian house sat in a park between wooded downs, on one of which a Doric temple gave an Arcadian air to the scene."[14] Austen makes her characters come alive for the reader not just with her gift for writing conversation, but also with her elegant descriptions of their manners and the surroundings they inhabit. Translating this to film required a writer and director willing to delve into the language and visual style of late eighteenth- and early nineteenth-century England. The selection of Ang Lee, a Taiwanese director who had not yet directed a film in English, for a British literary classic may at first blush seem odd, but his willingness to immerse himself in the period and his understanding of traditional Chinese visual aesthetics made him an excellent choice.[15]

Ang Lee's *Sense and Sensibility*

The Academy Award–winning screenplay of Ang Lee's *Sense and Sensibility* was written over five years by actress Emma Thompson, who also portrayed Elinor Dashwood in the film. The producer of the film, Lindsay Doran, describes the first meeting of Lee and Thompson: "And he [Lee] spoke of the deep meaning that the title held for him—Sense and Sensibility, two elements that represent the core of life itself, like Yin and Yang, or Eat, Drink, Man Woman. . . . He immediately recognized the universality of this story and these characters."[16] His careful attention to both the emotional and physical landscapes of his characters would serve him well in bringing Austen's story to the screen. Filmed in England at several National Trust historical managed sites, the quality of both the interior and exterior landscapes strives to be as close as possible to those of Jane Austen's experience of the late eighteenth and early nineteenth centuries. These include Montacute, which was used as Cleveland, the Palmer family estate; Compton Castle, Devon, which was used as Willoughby's home, Combe Magna; and the Effort House on the Flete estate in Devon, which was used for Barton cottage exteriors.[17] At Saltram House, Devon, which was used as Norland Park, a National Trust volunteer reminded the film cast and crew: "This house is much older than you and deserves your respect."[18]

The aesthetic structure and conventions of interior and exterior landscapes parallel the lives of the women and men in Jane Austen's novels. Control and careful planning create the efficiently run household, from the layers of servants and gardeners to the proper behavior of the household dependents. The four Dashwood women, Elinor (Emma Thompson), Marianne (Kate Winslet), Margaret (Emilie François), and their mother, Mrs. Dashwood (Gemma Jones), begin the film as residents of Norland Park, a large country estate in England at the turn of the nineteenth century. Mr. Dashwood lies on his deathbed, and they await the arrival of the only son, John (James Fleet), born from an earlier marriage. When they learn that the entire estate may only pass to the son, and that no provision has been made for dowries for the daughters, the women are forced to leave the only home they have ever known for a small cottage on the estate of Mrs. Dashwood's cousin. Elinor explains the situation to Margaret: "Because houses go from father to son, dearest—not from father to daughter. It is the law." With this downturn in fortune, the three daughters' marriage prospects also diminish because an alliance of families or a young heir with an estate in need of an influx of capital was often an impetus for unions. To make a good marriage was the main goal for which young women were trained in the rules of polite society. These rules were even put out in late eighteenth- and early nineteenth-century conduct books, as described in Deborah Kaplan's *Jane Austen among Women:*

> The heyday of print versions of this ideology—1760 to 1820—covered Jane Austen's lifetime. According to this ideology, men and women married for love and esteem. They experience passion within their conjugal relations and, when that faded, they sustained an affectionate friendship. They spent much of their time in one another's company and in the company of their children to whom they were lovingly attentive. And the setting for these relationships was the home, over which the women reigned.[19]

The death of Mr. Dashwood and the subsequent arrival of John Dashwood and his wife displace the elder Mrs. Dashwood as head of the household, and this leads to conflicts over the management of the home, from the deportment of the daughters to the guest accommodations.

In *Sense and Sensibility,* Austen uses socially and politically charged home and landscape management as a way to show approval and disapproval of specific characters. The heir's wife, Fanny Dashwood (Harriet Walter), is introduced as a villain; we see her and John work their way across the English countryside by carriage toward Norland Park, discussing how much of a promised legacy he will bestow on the Dashwoods. The women are entitled to an income of £500 a year, but on his deathbed, Mr. Dashwood extracted a promise from John to help them beyond this amount. By the time they arrive, Fanny has talked him down from a gift of £3,000 to "the occasional gift of game and fish in season"—something she obviously feels has little value. Fanny disparages the products and beauty of the outdoors on other occasions, such as when her brother, Edward (Hugh Grant), on a visit to Norland while the four Dashwood women are still in residence, asks her about her plans for the walnut grove (a valuable tree prized by both woodworkers and dyers). She responds, "Oh yes, I shall have it pulled down to make room for a Grecian temple." Edward's reply, "How picturesque," may show a deliberate misreading of the two landscape trends popular in the day. A man of Edward's class would surely have been aware of the Capability Brown–styled follies, which consisted of newly created "ancient" classical ruins dotting the created landscape to lend an Arcadian look. This is in direct opposition to the picturesque, which is a wild romantic and Gothic, not classical, ideal.[20] Greedy Fanny is all about appearances; she values little except that which will help her increase and maintain her family power and position. The potential and real economic usefulness of the gardens and lands isn't so much about the profit from the things grown and sold, but on how others of her class will see them. It is fashion, not finance, that concerns shortsighted Fanny.

The women of *Sense and Sensibility* are expected to rein in anything in their natures that is not considered socially proper when appearing in society in much the same way as an eighteenth-century English garden was a carefully created manufactured landscape that followed proscribed rules. Yet this land's beauty is found in both careful plantings (sense) and the looser (though still manufactured) sensibility of the extended landscape of lawns and groves, even unto a wilder picturesque landscape. Like that land, the Dashwoods must have both sense and sensibility. As Anderson and Kidd argue, "Although Elinor demonstrates more self-control than Marianne, both sisters manifest intense sensibility."[21] If one sister may be seen to embody the picturesque, it is the youngest girl, Margaret, who is the wild child, climbing up into tree houses, avoiding Fanny by hiding under tables, and longing for the greater world she sees in her atlas. It is interesting that the first connections she makes with both Edward and Colonel Brandon (Alan Rickman) are in reference to that atlas and the greater world beyond England. Edward engages Margaret over a question of the position of the Nile, and Brandon delights her when he says, on the occasion of their first meeting, that the East India "air is full of spices." Both men also engage her in outdoor pursuits: Edward teaches her mock swordplay, and Brandon entertains her with lawn bowling at his estate, Delaford.

The middle sister, Marianne, is usually seen as emotion personified—she is sensibility, fighting the constraints placed on her by the dictates of society. She is a romantic looking for a grand passion, something beyond the rigid control others expect of her. She feels that Edward's sedateness makes him a poor choice for Elinor, asking her mother, "*Can* he love her? Can the ardor of the soul really be satisfied with such polite, concealed affections? To love is to burn—to be on fire, all made of passion, of adoration, of sacrifice, like Juliet, or Guinevere or Heloise."

When reminded that her three examples all "made rather pathetic ends," she cries that to die for love would be glorious, opines that she shall never find a man to love, and enumerates her requirements in a suitor: "I require only what any young woman of taste should—a man who sings well, dances admirably, rides bravely, reads with passion and whose tastes agree in every point with my own."

Where Shall She Find Such a Paragon?

The Dashwoods are offered a cottage on Barton Park, the country estate of a distant relative, Sir John Middleton (Robert Hardy), and his mother-in-law, Mrs. Jennings (Elizabeth Spriggs). Described in the screenplay as "a very comfortable looking country seat with fine grounds," it nonetheless has "wild countryside" and "impossible trees" ready to snag wild child Margaret's petticoats as she climbs them.[22] The isolated figure of Marianne caught out in more picturesque wild nature and in need of rescue occurs twice in the film, and both occasions form important turning points for her character. First, after she sprains her ankle while on a walk through the fields around their cottage with Margaret, she is found and carried home by a mysterious handsome stranger who appears out of the concealing mists. In her script for the film, Thompson describes the scene:

> We hear the thunder of hooves. CU Margaret's terrified expression. They seem to be coming from all around. She wheels and turns and then—Crash! Through the mist breaks a huge white horse. Astride sits an Adonis in hunting gear. MARGARET squeals. The horse rears. Its rider controls it and slides off. He rushes to MARIANNE's side.[23]

Here is the clichéd knight in shining armor arriving on a white horse to save the day. He sweeps her up in his arms and returns her to Barton cottage.[24] Marianne is entranced by the dashing aristocratic gentleman, who belatedly introduces himself as John Willoughby (Greg Wise) of Allenham and Combe Magna. For Edmund Burke, aesthetic pleasure could just as easily be found in Marianne's terror of being lost on a dark, foggy hillside in the middle of a downpour as in Elinor's gentle horseback ride with Edward through a carefully cultivated garden on a sunny day. As

Burke describes it, "The passion caused by the great and sublime in nature . . . is Astonishment; and astonishment is that state of the soul, in which all its motions are suspended, with some degree of horror. In this case the mind is so entirely filled with its object, that it cannot entertain any other."[25] Marianne's fixation on Willoughby is due in part to his arrival at this uniquely sublime moment in a picturesque landscape; it "fills her mind" with him as "its object."[26]

Several of the couple's subsequent scenes together are set in the outdoors or have some reference to a more untamed nature. When recovering from her injury, Marianne receives a hothouse bouquet from her other suitor, the seemingly dour Colonel Brandon, but she greatly prefers the wildflowers Willoughby brings, as he tells her, "Since you cannot venture out to nature, nature must be brought to you." They discover a mutual love of Shakespeare's sonnets and focus on one concerned with wild nature, number 116, which they never actually finish reciting in the film:

> Let me not to the marriage of true minds
> Admit impediments. Love is not love
> Which alters when it alteration finds,
> Or bends with the remover to remove.
> O, no! it is an ever-fixed mark.
> That looks on tempests and is never shaken.

This seems to refer to the storms in which Marianne is caught and from which she must be rescued, a victim of her overwrought sensibilities. Her subsequent interactions with Willoughby are all done in short, romantically staged scenes, always with a somewhat disapproving audience—for example, their almost uncontrolled wild ride in Willoughby's curricle (the eighteenth-century version of an expensive sports car) as he springs his horses to racing speed, scandalizing the other parishioners outside the church. In a scene of public intimacy, in Caravaggiesque light, Colonel Brandon tries not to look as Marianne happily traces Willoughby's profile in silhouette as the younger man sits behind a candlelit screen at a house party. In another, Elinor watches, unobserved, as Willoughby cuts off a lock of Marianne's hair and presses it to his lips. The scene we expect to come, however, takes place off screen. Willoughby has asked for a meeting with Marianne, alone, but instead of showing us their meeting, we only see Marianne's tearful reaction. This is followed by a scene where Willoughby acts evasive, telling her

family that he must leave immediately for London, with "no idea of returning immediately to Devonshire," and then flees the cottage for the outdoors.
Soon thereafter, Mrs. Jennings, believing she is doing them a favor, invites
Elinor and Marianne to accompany her to London, hoping for a reconcili-
ation between the couple. Instead, leaving the peaceful Devon countryside
for the urban metropolis brings heartbreak to them both.

The second occasion with Marianne in isolation and caught out in nature
is very much of her own doing, when she learns the details of Willoughby's
marriage to the wealthy Miss Grey. In a misguided attempt to have a sad
romantic end for love, like those she earlier idealized, a bereft and self-
destructive Marianne sets off from the Palmer house gardens toward Willoughby's estate, on foot, and is caught in a terrible downpour. As Emma
Thompson describes it, when scouting for a setting for Marianne's escape,
Ang Lee discovered the famous Montacute "brain hedge":

> Ang is thrilled with all the topiary in the gardens. He had Marianne
> walking by this extraordinarily wiggly hedge. Apparently it snowed
> one year and the snow froze the hedge. When the thaw came, they
> cut away the dead bits and continued to grow the hedge—in the
> shape of a wild snowdrift. It looks like a brain. "Sensibility," said Ang,
> pointing to it triumphantly. "And sense," he continued, pointing in
> the other direction towards a very neat line of carefully trimmed
> flowerpot-shaped bushes. The stone and lines of Montacute—grand
> almost too grand though they are—give this part of the story a
> Gothic and mysterious flavor.[27]

As she stares at the castellated Gothic Combe Magna from a hill above it,
she recites Shakespeare's sonnet 116, once again stopping at the line about
tempests, then whispering Willoughby's name. This is the height of the
picturesque, almost exactly reenacting the circumstances of her earlier
sublime encounter with Willoughby. This time, however, she is found by
Colonel Brandon, who had been looking for her, worried her overwrought
state might lead her into danger. As indicated by the screenplay: "EXT.
CLEVELAND. GARDEN. DAY. ELINOR'S POV of BRANDON walking up to the
house with MARIANNE cradled in his arms. It is like seeing Willoughby's
ghost."[28] Marianne falls very ill with a high fever, and the attending physi-
cian tells Elinor to prepare herself for her sister's death. At this point, the
sisters switch places on the sense versus sensibility scale. Elinor is devas-

tated and gives in to her emotional despair in a short speech wonderfully acted by Emma Thompson:

> Marianne, please try—I cannot—I cannot do it without you. Oh please, I have tried to bear everything else—I will try—but please dearest, beloved Marianne, do not leave me alone. [*She falls to her knees by the bed, gulping for breath, taking* MARIANNE's *hand and kissing it again and again.*][29]

Marianne's near-death experience finally seems to (apologies, but the cliché is apt here) knock some sense into her. She sets new goals for herself—she will read not just romantic poets—but further her education supplemented by books from Colonel Brandon's library. She also peruses the family ledgers, perhaps taking over the duty from Elinor. Just as her new affection for Brandon is symbolized by their sedately reading poetry together and the arrival of his gift of a cottage-sized piano for her, her new maturity and confidence allow her to see the sense in his suitability. He was immediately taken with Marianne from the first moment he set eyes on her because she reminded him of his tragic first love. Brandon's personal connection to Willoughby—who was in fact the man who impregnated, then abandoned, the colonel's ward, Beth, daughter of the woman he had been forced by his family to abandon, Eliza—made it all the more painful for him to see Marianne get involved with him. He is a steady country gentleman, retired from the military and now looking to settle down in the country on his large, well-managed estate. Follies and ha-has are not for Brandon, as Duckworth states: "Colonel Brandon's Delaford, with its great garden walls, dovecote, stew ponds and canal, all in close proximity to the parsonage and village, testifies to Austen's fondness for estates that have missed or rejected the hand of the improver."[30]

    In a small, telling scene, soon after they first meet, Marianne is trying to cut bulrushes for basketwork on the banks of a pond in Barton Park. It is hot, and she is overdressed in a hat with netting, heavy gloves, and long-sleeved dress. Her small knife is blunt and practically useless. Out of nowhere, the colonel silently appears and hands her his hunting knife, which slices through the tough stems with ease. He knows how to live with nature, and he wants to make life easier for her, but Marianne's disgruntled reaction says she would rather keep sawing away, cursing the dullness of her knife, than accept help. It's a reflection of her initial dismissal of Brandon; there is no

struggle for his regard, no romantic denial and possibility of extreme emotion the way there is with Willoughby. It will take the humiliation of Willoughby's ballroom denial of her in London, the return of her love tokens
from him, and her subsequent illness for Marianne to see the important
differences between the two men. Both may present the appearance of heroism in their parallel rescues, but the truly honorable man, as reflected in his
care for both Marianne and his estate, is Brandon.

The sister who is usually read to represent sense is Elinor, the eldest,
who keeps the family accounts and others' secrets. Her love is Edward Ferrars (Hugh Grant), a quiet, diffident man with an underlying sharp sense of
humor.[31] In their scenes together, we see that they are controlled when they
are in the interior spaces of the manor houses and even the cottage—for
example, in the painful scene where Elinor must stoically endure Edward's
confrontation with his erstwhile fiancée, Lucy Steele (Imogen Stubbs),
which takes place in the London house of Mrs. Jennings. When inside, he
is regimented, trapped by his long-ago promise to marry another, but when
they are outside, Elinor and Edward are freer to speak and to enjoy being
together. On their first walk together in the gardens at Norland Park early
in the film, Edward confesses to Elinor, "I hate London, no peace. A country living is my ideal—a small parish where I might do some good, keep
chickens and give very short sermons." When they go horseback riding in
the estate fields, she is confident enough with him to bemoan her state as
a woman, having "no hope whatsoever of any kind of occupation" or any
way to earn a living.

They are also together outdoors in the stable yard when Edward tries
to explain to her that he cannot be the suitor she expects him to be. It is
the day before they are to leave for Devonshire and the cottage, and she
has come to say good-bye to her riding horse, an animal that they cannot take with them and that represents all she has lost of her genteel life.
We are reminded of the closeness indicated in the previous scene of them
riding together, and, like Elinor, we expect him to make some sort of love
declaration. His convoluted explanation of why he cannot is interrupted
by a determined Fanny, eager to keep her brother out of the clutches of
a woman she deems totally unsuitable. Fanny appearing in this setting is
especially jarring because it cuts off his confession of the important truth
of his secret engagement, and because it extends her unwanted household
authority over Edward and also over the stables, which had been a safe
place for Elinor. Fanny sends Edward off to London with a summons from

their mother, and the Dashwood women depart Norwood for Barton cottage soon thereafter.

Elinor keeps a tight rein on her emotions; she is always the responsible eldest daughter. Her emotional control and isolation are self-imposed. We see it slip only a few times. First is her terror at the isolation Marianne's death would bring her, as discussed earlier; second is when Marianne learns of Edward's engagement and chides Elinor for her lack of feeling; and third when she learns that Edward is free of his promise to Miss Steele.[32] Even in the previous scene, which sets up the latter by having her learn of his supposed marriage, her reaction is markedly different from Marianne's ill-advised tramp through the storm to Willoughby's house upon hearing the same sort of bad news. In a scene shot but deleted from the finished film, Elinor and her mother are standing outside in the cottage garden in the evening after the servant, Thomas, has told them he met the new Mrs. Ferrars in the village. As her mother tries to apologize for neglecting her, Elinor says simply, "I am very good at hiding," and "There is a painful difference between the expectation of an unpleasant event and its final certainty."[33] She has had some time to immure herself to this eventuality ever since Lucy confided the secret engagement; she has known that if Edward were an honorable man, this would be the outcome. She even presented Colonel Brandon's well-meaning offer of a parish church to Edward, who had been disinherited by his snooty family, an encounter that she must have found extremely painful and awkward. What brings out Elinor's strong emotional response is surprise. Soon after the delivery of the gift piano, Marianne plays and sings through an open window while the rest of the family is occupied outdoors. Margaret plays outside, Mrs. Dashwood sits mending one of Margaret's dresses, and Elinor is pulling weeds. A rider approaches, and, expecting the colonel, they are surprised when Edward arrives. They beat a hasty retreat into the cottage and quickly try to make themselves ready for company. In the stilted conversation that follows, Edward finally tumbles to the fact that they do not know the truth of the situation: Lucy threw him over for his brother, Robert, and it was the two of them who had been married.

ELINOR *rises suddenly,* EDWARD *turns and they stand looking at one another.*
ELINOR: Then you—are not married.
EDWARD: No.
ELINOR *bursts into tears. The shock of this emotional explosion stuns*

> *everyone for a second . . .* [all exit to garden except Edward and
> Elinor]
> ELINOR *cannot stop crying.*
> EDWARD *comes forward very slowly.*

As he apologizes for not revealing his engagement sooner and declares his love for her, Elinor doesn't say a word in the script; she just continues to cry with what Thompson describes as "tears of released emotion, of pain and of happiness."[34] This is a woman who always had a well-reasoned, often witty retort or answer to anything, and she has no words. She is consumed by her sensibility. The scene then totally removes us from the lovers, shifting to the outside garden, where her mother and sisters wait. As a parallel or foil to the off-camera conversation between Marianne and Willoughby when she was expecting his proposal earlier in the film, it is an interesting choice: rather than let the viewer in on Elinor and Edward's private indoor conversation, we get Margaret's garden tree house–view narration, "He's sitting next to her!" then, "He's kneeling down," which she had always expected a proper suitor to do.

The film ends with another outdoor scene, this time in the Barton parish churchyard as Marianne, in an elaborately embroidered gown, and Brandon, in military regalia, leave their wedding. The entire village has turned out, parading to the church, including "children, farmers, laborers, shopkeepers and all our principals."[35] Wildflowers, Marianne's favorite, are strewn about. As they step into the carriage, Brandon throws fistfuls of golden coins in the air, a customary gesture for the bountiful lord and lady of the manor. The scene then shifts to a hillside far above the church, where the wedding bells are heard faintly pealing. Willoughby sits on his white horse, isolated and alone in the landscape. He has given up his true chance at happiness so he could preserve his estate—the £50,000 a year that Miss Grey brought to their marriage allowed him to redeem Combe Magna from his debts after his behavior with Brandon's ward caused his aunt to disinherit him. He is as trapped by the dictates of eighteenth-century societal expectations for men as are the Dashwood women by female ones; however, their stories have come to a more romantic and satisfying end than his. In this female-centered film, both Elinor and Marianne have married well, and to men they apparently love. Edward and Elinor have his country parish dream career, and Marianne has won the marriage market's great prize: a good and kind man of landed wealth and status.

Brokeback Mountain

At times in its history, primarily after World War II, Hollywood filmmaking has relied heavily on male-centered genres or styles, such as the war drama, the western, or film noir, that specifically place greater emphasis on homosocial male relationships than on romantic notions of heterosexuality.[36] These films, particularly westerns or film noirs, also reveal a tendency toward an implicit, systematic distrust of women in both their narratives and formal techniques. This distrust of women, or more specifically of the feminine, provides male characters and audience members alike with suitable forms of homosocial bonding, along with both acceptable and unacceptable codes of masculine behavior. Because of its long history in American cinema, the western, perhaps more than any other genre, has been studied for how it has shaped cultural ideas about gender, with its traditional ideas of an active masculinity (*yáng*) and passive femininity (*yīn*). Although Jim Kitses's "Notes on the Western" (1969) does not directly address gender issues, it is still the touchstone for criticism on this genre, especially his "shifting antinomies" of (masculine) wilderness versus (feminine) civilization.[37] Westerns have an aesthetics of isolation encoded within their iconography, as the traditional cowboy or gunfighter is torn between his role as an individual and the concerns of the community, a community he defends but does not represent. Key to this dichotomy, of course, is the physical environment: the landscape of the western is a palimpsest of previous ideas about the West, from paintings to literature to prior representations of the West on film, particularly the films of John Ford. Western landscapes are loaded images, symbolizing "the ideological promise of America—freedom, openness, redemption, reinvention," and with this in mind, "it is possible to see the validity of the claim that *Brokeback Mountain* queers the Western, that setting a saga of same-sex love in the American wilderness both naturalizes and nationalizes it."[38] Thus, Ang Lee's *Brokeback Mountain* is in some ways the ultimate western, presenting us with the logical progression, in post–World War II Hollywood narratives, from the failure of heterosexual romance in noir films to increased homosocial bonding and finally to homosexual romance. It is only on and around the wilderness of Brokeback Mountain that Ennis Del Mar and Jack Twist are free to be themselves, to have the relationship that provides the only saving grace allowing them to continue their lives within civilization, which is limned by Kitses as the community of "restriction," "institutions," "illusion," "compromise," and "social responsibility."[39] Like most traditional westerns before it, *Brokeback Mountain* presents a wilderness that is sublime yet masculine (*yáng*), and a civilization that is beautiful yet feminine (*yīn*), emphasizing the reliance of these principles on one another; they are inseparable, defined by what the other is not. However, whereas most other westerns either do not reveal what happens to the hero when he enters civilization or do not allow him to enter it at all, Ang Lee's *Brokeback Mountain* highlights this bit of suppressed narrative and also presents the culturally accepted idea of freedom in America—freedom from the repressions of class, race, gender, or sexuality—as an illusion, and a costly one at that. This critique is indirect, at times almost oblique, presented through the minutiae of these men's lives and through the composition of intricate, picturesque landscapes, both natural and human, sublime and beautiful, that symbolize the characters' inner thoughts and feelings as well as the *yīn* and *yáng* of traditional Chinese philosophy. Ang Lee's landscapes primarily make meaning within *Brokeback Mountain* through his specific aesthetics of isolation, in which neither sweeping vistas nor crowds of people are presented merely for contemplation; their scale, beauty, and complexity emphasize the isolation, and sometimes the simple loneliness, of the individual within them.

With the unusual focus on both wilderness and civilization, or the dualistic *yīn* and *yáng* of the landscapes, in *Brokeback Mountain,* some viewers feel as though the western part of the film ends at the forty-minute mark when Ennis and Jack leave Brokeback Mountain, abandoning the traditional western landscape for life in the community (among women) and making only infrequent return trips to what becomes the only real home—the only real domestic partnership—they know. Reviewers and critics of the film have noted the sharp contrast between shots of the exteriors and wilderness and of the interiors and community within this film and the symbolic nature of both: "The expansive images from the film's early scenes . . . shrink to the dimensions of crowded kitchens, closets, trailers, and window-framed views. The awesome scale and reach of the mountain is reduced to a postcard."[40] All the promise and potential of Jack and Ennis's natural isolation early in the film is denied by the confines of their culture; society only brings an unnatural isolation through repression and captivity, much as civilization is often presented in the films of John Ford. Interior shots of Jack and Ennis show them framed within doorways and pushed between corners, with low ceilings looming overhead; these shots are tightly framed during significant moments to reinforce the men's inability to escape society's dictates. Their wives, Lureen and Alma, are often shot in a similar way to reinforce their own gender confines; as Harry M. Benshoff and Sean Griffin claim, "everyone is trapped" by traditional notions of gender in this film.[41] On the other hand, as in the westerns of John Ford, the exterior landscapes in *Brokeback Mountain* are shot in a painterly, romantic, and nostalgic manner, grand in their suggestion of an almost palpable longing for freedom. These landscapes also serve as a kind of ode to the natural environment and the rapidly disappearing space, both literal and imaginary, of the West.

Wilderness Space

Like almost all other western films, *Brokeback Mountain* defines its wilderness space as male through the absence of the feminine, by the work men do on the land, and by their unspoken bond to take care of each other. Their job of tending the herd is both biblical and maternal, but it is a sanctioned version of the feminine, as is the domesticity of the camp, which is reminiscent of a variety of westerns from *My Darling Clementine* (John Ford, 1946) to *Ride the High Country* (Sam Peckinpah, 1962), which is directly referenced in the screenplay.[42] The men's relationship to the land presents us with a kind of pastoral ideal, something that, once they return to civilization, seems increasingly dreamlike, lovingly punctuated by music and the sounds of the natural world. Whenever Ennis and Jack meet after their initial encounter on Brokeback Mountain, the music changes or simply appears, marking a shift in tone for the viewer by breaking the tensions that have been building for the men in their "real" lives in civilization. Indeed, sounds are crucial in the movie for the dichotomy between wilderness and civilization: "The noise of the Laundromat above which Ennis lives with his wife and squalling daughters is in direct contrast to the natural sounds of the wilderness in his scenes with Jack; the chug of the company adding machine and combine harvesters of Jack's life only adds to his sense of suffocation."[43] However, the sound of the wind blowing is almost constant whether the men are in the wilderness or civilization (especially Wyoming), beginning the day after Ennis and Jack's first sexual encounter.[44] As the two men separate that day for work, they for the first time seem alone and unsure, and the environment reflects this: it is windy, cloudy, dark, and getting cold. Neither looks to the other's location; each spends his time doing his job and silently thinking about the night before. Ennis guiltily finds the remains of a sheep slaughtered by a coyote, the result of his failure to return. As the two men meet at the end of the day, each has decided that nothing is wrong with what they have done, and both tacitly agree to let nature take its course:

ENIS: It's a one-shot thing we got goin' here.
JACK: Nobody's business but ours.
ENNIS: You know I ain't queer.
JACK: Me neither.

The protest of "I ain't queer" is, of course, the conditioned response of someone raised in a homophobic culture who is, at nineteen, searching out his own way of being a man; it is the most insidious way that civilization intrudes on the wilderness in *Brokeback Mountain*. The last shot of this conversation cuts immediately to the camp at night; after the blue-gray clouds of the day, the camp is bright white with moonlight, the fire, and their reflection in Ennis's shirt and the tent. Jack is preparing himself for bed in the tent, and Ennis sits beside the fire trying to decide whether to stay or go. Clearly, this mise-en-scène suggests a honeymoon: a young groom anxiously, nervously waits while his bride prepares herself for his arrival. Their isolation and the wilderness itself both naturalize (to borrow Kitses's term) Ennis's decision to stay with Jack instead of going out into the windy darkness to tend the sheep. This natural marriage will outlast, in commitment and feeling, the men's real marriages once they return to civilization. Therefore, the sound of the wind echoing in both the wilderness and in civilization—through Alma's hair as she takes clothes off a line, for instance—is symbolic of the duality of the men's lives: in all of their attempts to be "normal," they still are two men in love with each other in a culture that will not accept such a relationship. Despite their love for each other, they still are unable or unwilling to be together. In fact, even this ideal wilderness sequence is marked, when Joe Aguirre spies on their camp, by the presence of society and the repression (or worse) both potentially face once they leave Brokeback Mountain. Aguirre's intrusion also reminds us that these cowboys, who are really sheepherders, must tend to their herds on government land and follow (or choose to break) government rules; their ideal wilderness has been created by civilization and cannot exist without it.

This beginning (or "western") section of the film invites us to interpret the characters' environments psychologically and emotionally, particularly Ennis, whose emotions and thoughts often come through his actions or his facial gestures. Both men's faces, whether taciturn, sad, joyous, or confused, are as much a part of the western landscape as is Brokeback Mountain itself, and their feelings are finally given free rein once they are allowed to return to the harsh yet comforting isolation of the wilderness where the weather changes as often, and as sometimes as severely, as Ennis's and Jack's moods and emotions. After Joe Aguirre visits the camp and leaves, for example, a violent thunderstorm erupts with severe wind, lightning, and hail; the environment itself seems to be warning Jack and Ennis of civilization's impinging upon their isolation. When Aguirre gives the order for the men to bring the sheep down, Ennis, who is clearly brokenhearted but has no idea how to express his emotions, sits alone, diminutive and diminished, in a clearing with fir trees rising up behind him, streaks of snow climbing down the mountain toward him as large shadows move above him. This aesthetics of isolation allows us to understand the landscape as empathetic, reflecting the men's passions, impassivity, or even stubbornness; it also helps us to understand how confining, even cruel, the trappings of civilization—a wife, children, debt—are for these men.

Ara Osterweil calls *Brokeback Mountain* a "strange fusion between a Douglas Sirk melodrama and a John Ford Western," but bringing together the western and melodrama is not as strange or unusual as one might think.[45] In fact, David Lusted devotes a section of *The Western* to melodrama. Lusted defines such films as those in which "the psychological pressure on the male hero to act in accord with social rather than individual need, or to live within unchosen moral contradictions, leads to trauma," and he cites such titles as *Colorado Territory* (Raoul Walsh, 1949), *Pursued* (Raoul Walsh, 1947), *The Man from Colorado* (Henry Levin, 1948), *Jubal* (Delmer Daves, 1956), *The Hanging Tree* (Delmer Daves, 1959), *Warlock* (Edward Dmytryk, 1959), *I Shot Jesse James* (Samuel Fuller, 1949), and *The Singer Not the Song* (Roy Ward Baker, 1961)—the last three being examples of films that explore "homosexual relationship[s] obliquely and as a symptom of hysteria."[46] Although *Brokeback Mountain* certainly fits this definition of the western as male melodrama, it is careful to avoid the hysteria that has plagued other, earlier films (*Warlock* is an interesting and pertinent example) in which homosocial bonding becomes more complex than friendship. In place of hysteria, *Brokeback Mountain* presents the very real, very honest fear and paranoia both Jack and Ennis express in moments such as those when Jack looks around nervously after a tense conversation in a bar with a rodeo clown who saved his life, or when Ennis reveals his painful childhood memory of a man brutally killed because he was suspected by the community of being gay. Ang

Lee's western is thus a grown-up story about harsh realities, about men with real lives—not stereotypes or icons, but human beings. What some may see as an irreconcilable melodrama is simply realism for the western as opposed to mythos: *Brokeback Mountain* is "edgily realistic," with characters who are "remarkably detailed both in terms of individual psychology and social and economic setting."[47] These details only add to the pathos of the film, making the characters' isolation within civilization, surrounded by their families, seem more tragic yet all too genuine: we see them succeed, but much more often fail, as employees, husbands, and fathers.

For Annie Proulx, "an accumulation of very small details gives the film authenticity and authority," including the "speckled enamel coffeepot." Indeed, all these details "accumulate and convince us of the truth of the story. People may doubt that young men fall in love up on the snowy heights, but no one disbelieves the speckled coffeepot, and if the coffeepot is true, so is the other."[48] The coffeepot—just one unadorned, accurate detail—is symbolic of the men's economic condition, their work as cowboys, and their ideas of masculinity. To be men, Jack and Ennis must own certain things, must wear certain clothes and certain shoes, must get married and have children. These choices are really not choices at all but rather conditioned reflexes. These details, then, do more than simply provide characterization or setting; they help provide the code of masculine behavior keeping these men apart.

For twenty years, Ennis and Jack attempt to closet themselves, to conceal their true identities and their dreamlike relationship on and with Brokeback Mountain. Not to do so might mean ostracism or even death, so for them to understand their relationship, the men must put it in a natural context and make it part of their culturally defined masculine jobs as cowboys; as Jack says to Ennis, "Brokeback got us good." Ennis is not so ready to see his relationship with Jack as natural and instead blames Jack—in their last, most hurtful argument—for his homosexuality: "It's because of you, Jack, that I'm like this." In an attempt to reinforce his own masculinity, he also derisively marks Jack as other: "I heard about what they got in Mexico *for boys like you*" (emphasis added). While Jack and Ennis have jokingly discussed the women they may (or may not) be sleeping with, Ennis threatens Jack when he realizes that Jack may have had sex with another man—not necessarily because of his own internalized homophobia, but because of his emotional turmoil: this means Jack has cheated on him.

After Jack's death, when Ennis visits the Twist household, Jack's father tells him that the last time he saw Jack, Jack "got another fella's goin' a come up here with him and build a place and help run the ranch, some ranch neighbor a his from down in Texas," and the anguish on Ennis's face powerfully confirms his love for Jack, his fears, and his feelings of betrayal. When Ennis discovers his own shirt hanging inside Jack's in the closet upstairs, it is a heartbreaking moment for him, but these shirts are the most perfect emblem of the dual nature of their lives and the hidden nature of their love. Ennis leaves the Twist home carrying not only these two shirts, but also the austerity and tragedy of his relationship with Jack in what seems to be a renewed commitment to him, uttered as the last lines of the film: "Jack, I swear." Always unprepared for his feelings for Jack, Ennis has retreated further into his own personal isolation over the years, divorced from Alma, spending little time with the daughters he loves, fearful that other people know the truth or that he is an aberration. All this weighs heavily on Ennis, who, during his and Jack's last meeting, tearfully acknowledges, "I'm nothin'. I'm nowhere," and the screenplay describes this agonizing moment: "Like vast clouds of steam from thermal springs in winter, the years of things unsaid and now unsayable—admissions, declarations, shames, guilts, fears—rise around them."[49] The great burden of living the lie of their real lives has become too much for these men who can certainly be viewed as traditional western heroes: loners who neither belong completely to the wilderness or to civilization, isolated from others and each other, their silences and strengths an attempt to cover their loneliness and sorrow.[50]

Although both men have been reared and conditioned to suppress anything that might even appear feminine (that is, weak) within themselves, everything about Ennis, more so than Jack, reveals his heterosexual conditioning. Ennis's clothes, speech, and mannerisms, but particularly his emotional repression, which leads to explosions of violence and temper, all are traits of someone who has been taught to see true masculinity as laconic stoicism and little else. In one of the most famous images from *Brokeback Mountain,* the camera, at a low angle, looks up at Ennis standing in faded jeans, a denim jacket, and his cowboy hat as fireworks blaze through the night sky above and behind him. Ennis is isolated in the foreground, turned in the direction of the camera, with Alma and his daughters in the background to his left, as he looks down at the men he has beaten up and threatened while protecting his family. It is an iconic image, and in some ways, Ennis's behavior is simply an act: he conducts himself in the manner that he feels is expected of a man who is both husband and father. But in other ways, this outburst is just another example of the repressed anger and resentment rising to the surface in a man whose life is spent hiding his genuine feelings and needs. It is a complex moment that questions traditional notions of masculinity and male behavior within the western genre while ostensibly reinforcing those ideas. With part of its focus on appropriate codes of masculine behavior, this scene is also one of many in the film in which melodrama and the western overlap. With Lusted's definition of the western melodrama in mind, it can be viewed as a moment in which the psychological pressure on Ennis bursts, resulting in trauma for his family and further isolating him.[51]

It is the unique mixture of western and melodrama, realism and dream, in *Brokeback Mountain* that has resonated with so many audiences. This film, however, is not truly a universal love story, as Roger Ebert has said in his famous review. Despite the lack of sustained overt references to specific events in the decades that pass as the story moves forward, this film is specifically of its time period and even more specifically American.[52] The often dreamlike scenes on Brokeback Mountain itself are a reminder of all the cultural and personal baggage, the prejudice and misunderstanding, that Ennis and Jack try to leave behind, and a further reminder that they are never allowed to be free of their time and place. The attention to detail and grounding within a specific setting are qualities common to most of Ang Lee's films, and when considering Lee's aesthetics of isolation, we might do well to think of another prominent Asian director, Wong Kar-Wai, who is also famous for his attention to detail and his romantic stories of characters isolated by their inability to act or to find the right moment to be together.[53] In this meditation on isolation, Wong Kar-Wai can be viewed as a director of time, creating color-saturated timescapes of longing, while Ang Lee can be defined as a director of space, carefully composing landscapes (or cityscapes) as reflections of characters' inner states, their sorrows, joys, and ambivalence, but above all their isolation from other characters and even from the very world that paradoxically symbolizes their yearning for connection.

Duality and Oneness: The *Qì* of Gender and Landscapes

Sense and Sensibility and *Brokeback Mountain,* perhaps more so than any other of Ang Lee's films, allow the director an extended exploration of the *yīn* and *yáng* of gender issues, particularly the oppression inherent in traditional notions of femininity and masculinity. Lee presents this exploration through symbolic landscapes that are both wild and tamed, free and repressed; each film encapsulates a distinct moment in time and a distinct place as well, adding to the specifics of his critique. Characters belong yet simultaneously do not belong within these environments because of their gender, economic constraints, or sexuality, placing them on the boundaries of their societies. These may be literal, as when the Dashwoods leave their manor home to take up residence in a relative's cottage, or more figuratively as Marianne's emotionally uncontrolled behavior in the company of Willoughby scandalizes polite society. In *Brokeback Mountain,* just as they travel from their closeted homes to the freedom of their once-a-year trips back to the mountain, Ennis and Jack negotiate the emotional costs of their real and secret lives. The contradictory, even simply confusing, existence in which these characters find themselves wandering is reflected in Lee's aesthetics of landscape, his use of a meaningfully charged, symbolic environment where characters' emotional and social isolation, passions, fears, and frustrations are mirrored in the natural and man-made worlds around them. The seemingly contradictory forces of *yīn* and *yáng* are shown to be interconnected; opposites exist only in relation to one another, often simultaneously. This aesthetics is subtle and rewarding for the attentive viewer; these empathetic landscapes enrich our understanding of historically defined gender roles and codes as well as the basic human need to stop wandering and to find a place in our communities and in our world.

Notes

Pat would like to first thank Misty Jameson for her willingness and grace over the last year working long distance on this chapter. Second, to her Uncle Kerry, who always gave her great books and continues to encourage her interests in literature and film. Third to her Aunt Kathy and Aunt Debby for always being there for her, no matter what.

Misty would like to thank Pat Brace for her seemingly infinite patience and would also like to thank Andy and Sophie (and all the cats!) for making her nonacademic life worthwhile.

1. François Jullien, *The Great Image Has No Form, or On the Nonobject through Painting,* trans. Jane Marie Todd (Chicago: University Press, 2009), 135. For a detailed explanation of *yīn, yáng,* and *qì,* see James McRae, Chapter 1, this volume.

2. For additional discussions of Ang Lee's use of traditional Chinese aesthetic motifs, see Whitney Crothers Dilley, *The Cinema of Ang Lee: The Other Side of the Screen* (New York: Wallflower Press, 2007), and Ellen Cheshire, *The Pocket Essential Ang Lee* (North Pomfret, Vt.: Trafalgar Square, 2001).

3. See Derek Clifford, *A History of Garden Design* (New York: Praeger, 1963); Mark Laird, *The Flowering of the English Landscape Garden: English Pleasure Grounds, 1720–1800* (Philadelphia: University of Pennsylvania Press, 1999), and *Encyclopedia of World Art,* vol. 8, *Landscape Architecture* (New York: McGraw-Hill, 1959–1987), 1096–1099.

4. Alistair M. Duckworth, "Landscape," in *Jane Austen in Context,* ed. Janet Todd (Cambridge: Cambridge University Press, 2005), 278.

5. Edmund Burke, *On the Sublime and Beautiful,* vol. 24, part 2, ed. Charles W. Eliot (New York: P. F. Collier & Son, 1909–1914).

6. The couple who adopted Edward would have used this practice because they had no legitimate sons to inherit or daughters to marry off in their family.

7. Jane Austen, *Sense and Sensibility,* ed. Edward Copeland (1811; reprint, Cambridge: Cambridge University Press, 2006), xxiv.

8. Ibid., xlvii.

9. See also Mavis Batey, *Jane Austen and the English Landscape* (London: Bran Elms, 1996); Peter Knox-Shaw, *Jane Austen and the Enlightenment* (Cambridge: Cambridge University Press, 2004), chap. 2, 75; Marilyn Butler, *Jane Austen and the War of Ideas* (Oxford: Clarendon Press, 1975); Alison G. Sulloway, *Jane Austen and the Province of Womanhood* (Philadelphia: University of Pennsylvania Press, 1989), chap. 7, 202–206.

10. Alistair M. Duckworth, *The Improvement of the Estate: A Study of Jane Austen's Novels,* rev. ed. (Baltimore, Md.: Johns Hopkins, 1994), and Duckworth, "Landscape," 278–288.

11. Duckworth, "Landscape," 278.

12. Ibid., 279.

13. Ibid.

14. Ibid., 280.

15. When asked a question about scouting locations for the film, Lee gave credit to Emma Thompson: "She was very generous about taking me to museums to go through paintings from that particular time so I could see the spirit of romanticism coming up, the rise of metropolitanism, and the industrial revolution. She introduced the whole deal to me: landscape design, drawing, painting. It took a long time." Whitney Crothers Dilly, *The Cinema of Ang Lee: The Other Side of the Screen* (London: Wallflower Press, 2007), 97.

16. Emma Thompson, *The* Sense and Sensibility *Screenplay and Diaries: Bringing Jane Austen's Novel to Film* (New York: Newmarket, 1996), 15.

17. See WhereDidTheyFilmThat.co.uk (http://www.wheredidtheyfilmthat.co.uk) and Movie Locations (http://www.movie-locations.com/).

18. Thompson, Sense and Sensibility *Screenplay and Diaries,* 217.

19. Deborah Kaplan, *Jane Austen among Women* (Baltimore, Md.: Johns Hopkins University Press, 1992).

20. In the novel but not the film, there is an aesthetic debate between Marianne and Edward over the nature of the picturesque, in which he denies all knowledge of it and she concedes that the "admiration of landscape scenery is become a mere jargon. Everybody pretends to feel and tries to describe with the taste and elegance of him who first defined what picturesque beauty was" (1:18). But there, too, it is, as Duckworth says, a "false modesty" ("Landscape," 285), as he obviously knows the correct vocabulary to describe the scene in picturesque terms. See also Knox-Shaw, *Jane Austen and the Enlightenment,* 75, and Austen, *Sense and Sensibility,* 460.

21. Kathleen Anderson and Jordan Kidd, "Mrs. Jennings and Mrs. Palmer: The Path to Female Self-Determination in Austen's *Sense and Sensibility*," *Persuasions* 30 (2008): 135–148.

22. Thompson, Sense and Sensibility *Screenplay and Diaries,* 68.

23. Ibid., 85.

24. Ibid., 237. In her set diary, Thompson notes of this scene that Lee didn't call cut when expected but allowed it to go on beyond the planned blocking. She recounts, "Later Ang said that he wanted the camera to watch the *room,* sense the change in it that a man, that sex, had brought. For Ang the house is as important a character as the women." Dilley also notes of this moment that Lee "was particularly interested in the flow of energy in a film—its *qi* (breath, or spirit)—taking everything as a whole, in its widest possible context." Dilley, *Cinema of Ang Lee,* 99.

25. Burke, *On the Sublime and Beautiful,* 49.

26. If the landscape where innocent Marianne first meets Willoughby is the arche-typal garden, is he then the despoiling serpent? As Sulloway describes it in *Jane Austen and the Province of Womanhood,* he has a seductive "serpentine quality" that he shares with other Austen antiheroes such as Wickham from *Pride and Prejudice* and Frank Churchill from *Emma* (197).

27. Thompson, Sense and Sensibility *Screenplay and Diaries,* 253.

28. Ibid., 179.

29. Ibid., 184.

30. Duckworth, "Landscape," 283.

31. One major difference between the actor and the character as Austen describes him in *Sense and Sensibility* is that Edward is not meant to be good-looking: "He was not handsome, and his manners required intimacy to make them pleasing. He was too diffident to do justice to himself; but when his natural shyness was overcome he gave every indication of an open affectionate heart" (18). Hugh Grant can do a stuttering diffident shyness, but he was really much too attractive to play the part. As Thompson says, Grant is "repellently gorgeous, why did we cast him? He's much prettier than I am," even while admitting that she wrote the part for him (Sense and Sensibility *Screenplay and Diaries,* 212).

32. Thompson describes Elinor in her set diary as a "witty control freak. I like her but see how she could drive you mad. She's just the sort of person you'd want to get drunk, just to make her giggling and silly" (Sense and Sensibility *Screenplay and Diaries,* 253).

33. Quoted from Thompson, Sense and Sensibility *Screenplay and Diaries* script, and available for viewing in the bonus materials of the film DVD, along with a second scene between Edward and Elinor after the proposal when they kiss in a lovely garden landscape on a bridge.

34. Thompson, Sense and Sensibility *Screenplay and Diaries,* 199–200.

35. Ibid., 201.

36. See chapters 10, 11, and 12 in Harry M. Benshoff and Sean Griffin, *America on*

Film: Representing Race, Class, Gender, and Sexuality at the Movies (Malden, Mass.: Wiley-Blackwell, 2009), for more information about representations of masculinity and femininity in American film.

37. Jim Kitses, "Authorship and Genre: Notes on the Western," in *The Western Reader,* ed. Jim Kitses and Gregg Rickman (New York: Limelight Editions, 1998), 59.

38. Jim Kitses, "All that *Brokeback* Allows," *Film Quarterly* 60, no. 3 (2007): 25.

39. Kitses, "Authorship and Genre," 59.

40. Kitses, "All that *Brokeback* Allows," 26. For a similar description of the contrast between interior and exterior space, see Camille John-Yale, "West by Northwest: The Politics of Place in Ang Lee's *Brokeback Mountain,*" *Journal of Popular Culture* 44, no. 4 (2011): 1–15, and Judith Halberstam, "Not So Lonesome Cowboys," in *The Brokeback Book: From Story to Cultural Phenomenon,* ed. William R. Handley (Lincoln: University of Nebraska Press, 2011), 191. Halberstam explains that the western "reveals a potpourri of mutual masculine longing and homoerotic posturing" because "the genre demands that men leave their women to become men and that they spend huge amounts of time with another man in a relationship of surrogate marriage" (190, 195).

41. Benshoff and Griffin, *America on Film,* 407.

42. Larry McMurtry and Diana Ossana, "*Brokeback Mountain,* the Screenplay," in Brokeback Mountain: *Story to Screenplay,* ed. Annie Proulx, Larry McMurtry, and Diana Ossana (New York: Scribner, 2005), 70. All quotations of dialogue from the film that appear here are taken from this screenplay.

43. Roger Clarke, "Western Special: Lonesome Cowboys," *Sight and Sound Magazine,* January 2006 (http://www.bfi.org.uk/).

44. McMurtry and Ossana describe this wind as "relentless" in their screenplay (27).

45. Ara Osterweil, "Ang Lee's Lonesome Cowboys," *Film Quarterly* 60, no. 3 (2007): 38.

46. David Lusted, *The Western* (London: Pearson Longman, 2003), 181, 184.

47. Kitses, "All that *Brokeback* Allows," 24.

48. Annie Proulx, "Getting Movied," in "*Brokeback Mountain,* the Screenplay," in Proulx, McMurtry, and Ossana, Brokeback Mountain: *Story to Screenplay,* 138.

49. McMurtry and Ossana, "*Brokeback Mountain,* the Screenplay," 83.

50. For a further look at Jack and Ennis as western heroes, see Kitses, "All that *Brokeback* Allows," 26–27. Kitses claims: "The Western's liberating confrontations and duels, the resolution of personal and communal conflicts, is denied these heroes. They become impotent, repressed, oppressed."

51. Lusted, *Western,* 181.

52. Roger Ebert, "Forbidden Love: *Brokeback Mountain* Tells a Powerful Story of Two Men and an Unforgiving World," *Chicago Sun-Times,* December 16, 2005, NC 30.

53. The appearance of the song "Quizas, Quizas" in *Brokeback Mountain* as Jack wanders through a street in Mexico looking for a male prostitute seems an homage to Wong Kar-Wai's *In the Mood for Love* (2000), which prominently features Nat King Cole's version of this song to punctuate moments of isolation and romantic betrayal for the main characters.

CAN'T GET NO SATISFACTION

Desires, Rituals, and the Search for Harmony in
Eat Drink Man Woman

Carl J. Dull

From Tension to Harmony

One of the reasons *Eat Drink Man Woman* (1994) is such an exquisite film is because it seamlessly blends sumptuous spreads of traditional Chinese cuisine with a rich mixture of characters, passions, and conflict. The displays of culinary expertise are filmed with the same expert subtlety and precision given to the emotional trials of the Chu household, making the film itself a cinematic dish that is richly rewarding and worth revisiting numerous times to fully appreciate its complexity and variety. In a family with unique personalities and a complicated history, the fragile status quo is upset by new developments and old tensions, leading ultimately to a new possibility of harmony. As part of this struggle, I also appeal to the Confucian philosopher Xunzi (310–220 BCE) to discuss problems of human nature and desire.

One of the more uniquely rewarding features of *Eat Drink Man Woman* from my perspective as a teacher of Chinese philosophy is the manner in which the film provides an excellent framework to discuss several important elements of Confucianism. Each character struggles with love and family, as well as the delicate balance between satisfying emotional needs and maintaining interpersonal harmony. All of these topics are explicitly addressed by classical Confucian philosophy, and the film provides an excellent vehicle for discussing these themes.

In this chapter, I discuss the nature of harmony in a family setting, the conflicts between emotion and harmony, and how ritual and expression are both crucial elements for achieving harmony in interpersonal relationships. Using the Chu family as an example, we see how wounds from the past and old conflicts create tension between family members, and how the growth and development of the romantic relationships for the daughters breaks the delicate status quo and brings old trauma to light. This is ultimately a therapeutic experience for each of the characters, as it allows them to experience change and growth, and to reveal important points about the relationship between emotional expression, ritual, and harmony.

This leads us deeply into the thought of Confucius (551–479 BCE), Mencius (372–289 BCE), and Xunzi, all of whom were concerned with the problem of harmony and emotional well-being. Rather than asserting that any one of the three provides a superior model, I suggest that each provides a key insight into the nature of emotion and harmony: Confucius recognizes the need for allowing the unique abilities of each person in a group to contribute to group functionality; Mencius recognizes the importance of emotional expression as part of healthy human functioning; and Xunzi recognizes the importance of providing ritual frameworks that guide and direct human desires and lead them to healthy satisfaction. Conversely, we can also use the insights of these thinkers to diagnose problems in the family: Chef Chu enforces old rituals on a family that needs growth and development in order to function healthily while secretly stifling expression of his own feelings; Jia-Jen, the oldest daughter, uses ritual to hide behind emotional vulnerability; Jia-Ning, the youngest daughter, acts impulsively on her romantic feelings toward Guo Lun; and Jia-Chien, the middle daughter, presents what I think may be the most complicated case in the film: a consummate professional and secretly a virtuoso chef like her father, she is talented, passionate, and fully capable of writing her own future; however, unsure of what she really wants in life, she is left without the kinds of relationships with people who truly appreciate her talent and personality.

In terms of harmony, one of the most important questions is whether we can balance expressing particular emotional needs while still maintaining concern for the overall stability of a group. In other words, can harmony accommodate both personal and social needs? In order to answer this question, I provide several models of harmony: harmony as a culinary dish, harmony in terms of music, and harmony in terms of team sports competition. Each of these models addresses the problem of how individual elements relate to the functioning of the whole. Each of these models, I contend, can be explained in terms of a more generalized model of personal–environmental interaction, a model of personhood proposed by David Hall and Roger Ames. This model is described as the focus–field model and is based on classical Chinese cosmology and process philosophy.[1] Finally, at the end of this chapter, I augment this model to include concerns that fall under the umbrella of moral psychology: namely, how the focus–field model can function in terms of emotional needs and social harmony.

Models of Harmony

Harmony is precisely like a fine dish: each ingredient in the dish possesses unique properties, but it is the combination of ingredients that creates a unique experience. No single ingredient should overpower the other, and all the ingredients should work to accentuate the others; this creates a combination of flavors instead of a single flavor, making a dish that is both enjoyable and nourishing.[2] Roger Ames and Henry Rosemont support the analogy by describing the role of harmony in the early corpus of Chinese literature:

> Throughout the early corpus, the preparation of food is appealed to as a gloss on this sense of elegant harmony. Harmony so considered entails both the integrity of the particular ingredient and its ease of integration into some larger whole. Signatory of this harmony is the endurance of the particular ingredients and the cosmetic nature of the harmony in an order that emerges out of the collaboration of intrinsically related details to embellish the contribution of each one.[3]

Confucius himself alludes to the strong relationship between music and harmony.[4] Music is a way to teach harmony, to allow people to attune themselves to patterns of social interaction and then develop their own ability to move within those structures, develop their own voices, and effect their own creative changes in the experience of the listener:

> The Master talked to the Grand Music Master of Lu about music, and said: "Much can be realized with music if one begins by playing in unison, and then goes on to improvise with purity of tone and distinctness and flow, thereby bringing all to completion."[5]

Each instrument must be in tune with the others, but each instrument also has its own unique sound and role to play in the overall composition. If the instruments are out of tune, or if the musicians are out of rhythm with each other, then the effect is unpleasant. This is different from intentional uses of atonality and dissonance, which actually function to highlight how musical relationships work. These kinds of experiences actually require highly practiced musical skill. In the initial case of simply being out of harmony, the result of the experience is usually a disappointing sense of failure.

I also liken harmony to the manner in which a team functions together. Each member of the team has a specific role to play, but each is also in that role because of individual talents and abilities. The better someone is at performing that role, the more he gets to exercise his talents within the context of a group activity. The metaphor of a sporting event, such as a soccer game, provides an excellent representation of the kind of coordination any group must achieve in order to overcome obstacles or problems. Each member of the team has to function to the best of his abilities, but that also includes acting with goals determined by success of the group as a whole. If each member of the team tries to be an individual superstar, the coordination of the team collapses, the endeavor of the group fails, and the individual actually loses opportunities for showcasing talents or abilities.

It is tempting to think team-oriented behavior may eliminate the possibility of personal recognition, but this is a false dichotomy. It is perfectly easy to recognize the abilities of a player who plays with the success of the team in mind. In the long run, such a player will actually receive more opportunities for demonstrating his talents and therefore more recognition. The best way to practice our talents is to engage the roles we are faced with, and practice excelling at those roles in the context of the activity that keeps presenting challenges and opportunities for someone in that role to overcome. A purely individualistically minded athlete will not be presented with the same kinds of opportunities or contexts for performing well.

It is important here that *Eat Drink Man Woman* makes such a strong comparison of the culinary arts to harmony because there are multiple moments in the movie where the metaphor seems important. Chef Chu and his wife were said to constantly argue in the kitchen, particularly over the appropriate amount of ginseng in ginseng soup. What appeared to be clashing personalities was actually the expression of a shared passion. Their shared passion for cooking led to a passionate combination of personalities. By comparison, at the beginning of the film, Chu's wife has been dead for many years, and he is unable to properly express his secret feelings for Jin-Rong. His sense of taste is deteriorating, and he can only judge the quality of his dishes by the expression on Old Wen's face.

Jia-Chien, the middle daughter and a successful professional with a national airline, is also a talented chef. Her talent and passion lead her to argue constantly with her father; the family dinner barely begins before the two are presented with an opportunity for conflict. Just as her father begins to make a prepared announcement, Jia-Chien makes a face in response to the taste of his soup. She attempts to avoid conflict, but when pressed repeatedly by her father, she responds critically, both of the soup and of his taste. This causes argument between Jia-Chien and her older sister, Jia-Jen, who admonishes her not to say anything. It is worth noting that Jia-Jen long ago took responsibility for raising the younger two sisters, displacing her role as oldest sister and forcing herself into the role of surrogate mother. The tension is clearly evident between the two, just as the tension between Jia-Chien and Chu is evident.

The irony of the initial formal Sunday dinner scene should not be lost on the viewer: just as the different dishes in the Sunday dinner suffer from the imbalance of ingredients, the different members of the family are in opposition and dissatisfied as a result of their imbalanced relationships and emotional frustrations.

Focus and Field

Discussing a model of personhood that we find active in interpersonal relationships can elucidate both of these metaphors for harmony. I turn here to the focus–field model provided by David Hall and Roger Ames, who describe human activity in terms of a focal point within a field of activity.[6] Our status as persons is not fixed. Instead, our identity as persons is tied to the interaction of many different ongoing and dynamic processes. This does not mean our status as persons is trivialized, but rather it simply shows how we are constituted through a variety of processes within our environment. There is no particular limit to the number and kinds of processes involved, but they include factors such as physical, social, emotional, and cognitive. It simply means that we as persons exist within and through a field of processes, and that we have the ability to influence different elements of the field. This is similar to the analogy of harmony in the professional sports team, where each member plays on a field of activity and is able, through his abilities and talents, to create change and influence the game.

Nor does this mean that our identities or our decisions are reduced to a kind of environmental determinism. We have, within the field of activity, the ability to make choices and decisions that alter areas of the field. We have the ability to exert our energies or power (*dé,* virtue) to alter the direction of other processes within the field. Furthermore, any element in the field can act as a focus and can be understood as exerting power or influence on other areas of the field. In this respect, any *dé* can be seen as a collection of powers that can influence any other element in the field, or the overall system itself. The entire system can be seen as the process of *dào,* which gives rise to the Ten Thousand Things, bringing everything into existence through processes of growth and transformation.[7]

Perhaps one of the most important points of this model is that, as people, it means that we develop and grow through our relationships. This stands in strong contrast to many of the assumptions of Western social and political theory. Classical Western political theory, such as that of Locke or Hobbes, views the individual as existing prior to social participation, and it regards social and political involvement as a necessary evil that restricts human freedom. Confucianism, on the other hand, regards personhood as a process of becoming: we are brought into the world through our relationships, and we grow through our participation in social relationships. We learn how different social roles function, we grow into new roles, and we leave old roles behind; we even learn how to modify, alter, or reject roles. Social involvement represents the beginnings of human potential, not a restriction of freedom. Strictly speaking, one cannot exercise one's virtue (*dé*) outside of social relations, because without social relations there are no contexts in which to apply one's abilities. Thus, as persons, we need relations to become better persons.

Here I want to augment this model by adding some specificity to some of the processes. In particular, I wish to add discussion on the nature in which emotions and relations function in terms of this model. As we can see in *Eat Drink Man Woman,* the interplay of emotions and relationships forms an important part of the manner in which we are able to function as focal points within the fields of our activity: a key component of the focal energy of any person in the field is his emotional character. This includes desires (which pulls him toward other elements in the field), the capacity for expression, and the ability to create meaningful structures in the constantly changing field of relations.

Expression is a powerful element in the focus–field model. Expression is the manifestation of desires or intentions and occurs in many forms; these include language, emotion, physical motion, and performance. Expression exerts pressure on elements in the surrounding environment and presents opportunities for response from the environment. A standard Western interpretation is to assume that we must make a distinction between emotions and language. By contrast, when we look at expression as a kind of force, we see how expression exerts pressures on different elements in the field. This kind of pressure occurs whether or not the expression occurs through language or emotion. Sometimes this pressure alters the field immediately, as in the case of physical action. Other times this pressure presents possibilities of more balanced responses, as with linguistic and emotional expression.

In any case, the act of expression creates a moment whereby transformation can occur. The expression can either be received or rejected, which again alters the arrangement of elements in the field. We see this clearly in the romantic engagements of the three daughters: Jia-Jen has her moment of vulnerability and then kisses Chou Ming-Dao; Jia-Chien cooks dinner for Raymond and allows herself a moment of honesty regarding her relationship with her parents (which Raymond ignores in favor of being frivolous); and Jia-Ning's blunt and pragmatic discussions with Guo Lun lead to their rapid romantic engagement.

Desires pull us toward different elements of the field. In traditional Chinese literature, desires include a mixture of material and immaterial desires. All of the senses possess desire for certain stimuli. The eyes desire visual stimulus, the ears desire auditory stimulus, and the mouth desires pleasing tastes:

> The five colors make people's eyes go blind
> The five tones make people's ears go deaf
> The five flavors make people's mouths turn sour
> Galloping and racing, hunting and chasing,
> Makes people's minds go mad
> Goods hard to come by corrupt people's ways.[8]

In the thought of the Warring States,[9] there is an important relationship between the senses and the rest of the world. The senses do not simply convey information; instead, they function through desire. They desire certain stimuli and actively search for the objects that satisfy their needs. This creates a relationship of intentionality between the senses and the world, in which the senses are searching, making distinctions, and coming into completion as they reach satisfaction. As pointed out in the quotation above from the *Daodejing*, however, too much stimulus damages the senses. It distracts the person from what is most important to living in the world: being attentive to the ongoing changes in *dào*.

It is worth noting that classical Chinese literature does not place significant importance on whether the desire is material or immaterial. What is important is whether the desire is brought to completion (*chéng*). This includes the desires of the senses as well as desires for knowledge and fame. The senses and the mind all desire completion, in terms of having their desire satisfied. But in order for this completion to be achieved, our spirits are restless and constantly searching for objects of satisfaction. The following passage from the *Zhuangzi* perfectly demonstrates the manner in which human activity is driven by the need to achieve the completion or satisfaction of our desires, a process that pulls us headlong into dangerous circumstances without thought of how this process is slowly destroying the vital capacities that keep us functioning and healthy:

> Great understanding is broad and unhurried; little understanding is cramped and busy. Great words are clear and limpid; little words are shrill and quarrelsome. In sleep, men's spirits go visiting; in waking hours, their bodies hustle. With everything they meet they become entangled. Day after day they use their minds in strife, sometimes grandiose, sometimes sly, sometimes petty. Their little fears are mean and trembly; their great fears are stunned and overwhelming. They bound off like an arrow or a crossbow pellet, certain that they are the arbiters of right and wrong. They cling to their position as though they had sworn before the gods, sure that they are holding on to victory. They fade like fall and winter—such is the way they dwindle day by day. They drown in what they do—you cannot make them turn back. They grow dark, as though sealed with seals—such are the excesses of their old age. And when their minds draw near to death, nothing can restore them to the light.[10]

In *Eat Drink Man Woman,* basic human desires include the need for food and sex. Chu and Wen question whether there is more to life than merely satisfying these desires, and we see through the film that the manner in which we satisfy these desires is important. Furthermore, the manner in which these desires are satisfied or left unsatisfied creates narratives in the histories of the persons who struggle with the presence of these desires in their own lives. As in the case of Jia-Jen, desires can be repressed; in the case of Jia-Ning, they can be acted on impulsively; or they can be satisfied through nontraditional means, such as with Jia-Chien and her relationship with her ex-boyfriend, Raymond.

Rituals constitute structures or patterns of activity within the field that express emotion and help satisfy desires. Rituals do include explicitly formalized rituals, such as the weekly Sunday dinner at the Chu household, or Chou Ming-Dao's baptism and conversion to Christianity. However, ritual also includes structures or patterns of meaning that are less explicit but that still constitute a structuring of experience. In fact, any human activity has the capacity for being understood as a ritual when that activity becomes incorporated into the collection of symbolic meanings that constitute culture and language. The scope of ritual includes handshakes, small nods of the head, and how one walks, talks, or even enters a room. Language is a ritual that is constantly undergoing alteration and change, in some cases being preserved to maintain traditional meanings, while at other times being changed to create new meanings. Ultimately the line between traditional and new is arbitrary, as new becomes traditional, and traditional can even in some cases become new.

Ritual is possible because of the human capacity for aesthetic experience. Any element within experience can be isolated and designated as having symbolic value. These symbols then become useful in navigating experience, and especially useful in creating structures or habits that provide stability and transition in moments of uncertainty. Ritual, for Confucianism, is a process of inheriting the wisdom of the past to address the problems of the present in order to make smooth transitions into the future. Ritual is a manner of structuring experience that provides stability and consistency. Ritual is not meant to be adhered to blindly or for its own sake, but it provides certain possibilities of harmony. Ideally, rituals should be practiced that lead to nourishing human needs and organizing human desires in ways that promote harmonious relationships. This includes relationships between people and relationships within nature.

Expression, desire, and ritual all form important elements of the focus–field model. Expression and desire create pressures within the field, and ritual creates structures that help address those pressures in ways that are healthy and stabilizing. Desires are constantly searching for opportunities within the field to satisfy needs, while expression provides possibilities. As seen in Jia-Ning and Guo-Lun's relationship, their youthful expressions of desire and romantic interest lead quickly to possibilities. As in the case of Chef Chu, his inability to express or even discuss his emotional interest inhibits his ability to have the satisfying relationship he really wants. And as seen with Madam Liang, her constant expression of desire and criticism actually disrupts the possibility of satisfaction. Her constant criticism ultimately makes her an undesirable candidate for a relationship, as it becomes clear she has only her own interests in mind and not those of others.

On the negative side, ritual can become an overpowering, stifling expression or can force habits of activity that provide only a superficial continuity of experience. This kind of superficial continuity is dogmatic or rigid adherence to ritual for its own sake; it preserves superficial consistency while ignoring the problems or conditions that require attention. It also may have some degree of success, but failing to address the actual needs and concerns will result in a tragic breakdown of order. Forces in the field of activity will overpower the simple reliance on ritual for its own sake.

At this point, we have to face an important question: is it more important for our emotions to receive proper expression, or is it more important for our emotions to be structured in the context of certain relationships and socially acceptable structures? This question takes the same shape as the debate between Mencius and Xunzi, both intellectual followers of Confucius who explore the problems of emotion. Mencius claims that proper human activity is the result of the proper expression of the emotions. Xunzi, on the other hand, claims that human emotions are disfigured and lack proper direction, and that they must be structured by ritual in order to attain stability and harmony. I suggest that both provide an important insight in the manner in which emotions function, and that both expression and healthy structure contribute to harmony. To make this case, I will briefly discuss the attitudes toward emotions and harmony in both Mencius and Xunzi. Using their models of emotional well-being, we can then create a series of diagnoses and treatments for the characters in *Eat Drink Man Woman*. Chef Chu, Jia-Jen, Jia-Chien, and Jia-Ning all suffer from an imbalance of emotions and relationships in their lives, and through the film, we see each of the characters undergo a transformation that brings their emotions and relationships into healthier balance.

Mencius: Expression

Mencius' morality is based on the Four Sprouts model of expression. For Mencius, morality is internal in the sense that the seed for any moral action occurs first as an internal sprout, which then sprouts into a social response. The key issue is not any kind of conflict between idea and reality, but rather the process of feeling and expression in response to the appropriate kinds of situations:

> The heart of compassion is the germ of benevolence; the heart of shame, of dutifulness; the heart of courtesy and modesty, of observance of the rites; the heart of right and wrong, of wisdom. Man has these four germs just as he has four limbs.[11]

For Mencius, claiming that morality is internal simply means that we experience internal feelings, thoughts, or emotions in response to environmental situations. What is absolutely critical is the process of letting those feelings grow into realizations of performed activity. Regardless of the actual nature of any such feelings, our experience of them is often as if they are internal feelings, and we use language, ritual, and action to express the internal state and bring about a realization of external conditions. Thus, for Mencius, being moral is the expression of things we feel in response to situations in directions that are socially responsible.

Mencius provides two examples, the example of a child falling into a well and the example of a prince ordering the ritual sacrifice of animals. In the first example, Mencius claims that the moral person cannot but help feel an immediate emotional response to the child's plight and will act quickly in response to the situation. The point of the example, which may seem extreme, is simply to point out that we have internal feelings in response to situations and our environment. This, I suspect, is one of the reasons that Mencius expresses such concern about environment and education: it's not simply that we learn by example, but that we learn in response to our environments, and what we are learning is what kinds of feelings, emotions, and thoughts are effective in interacting with our environment.

In terms of the second example, which is of King Xuan, Mencius chastises the king for sparing an ox while being willing to sacrifice a lamb. The population deems King Xuan miserly for this action because he is willing to sacrifice a smaller, less expensive animal. Mencius, however, recognizes that what actually motivated the king's behavior was his interaction with the animals: before the sacrifice, King Xuan saw the ox but not the lamb. Consequently, he was moved by the plight of the ox but not the lamb. Mencius informs him:

Your bounty is sufficient to reach the animals, yet the benefits of your government fail to reach the people. That a feather is not lifted is because one fails to make the effort; that a cartload of firewood is not seen is because one fails to use one's eyes. Similarly, that peace is not brought to the people is because you fail to practice kindness.[12]

King Xuan does not lack the ability to feel the plight of the people; he simply has not made the effort:

In other words, all you have to do is take this very heart here and apply it to what is over there. Hence one who extends his bounty can bring peace to the Four Seas; one who does not cannot bring peace even to his own family.[13]

If King Xuan makes the effort to extend his attention to the people, and to see their plight firsthand in the same manner as he saw the plight of the ox, then according to Mencius' model, he would certainly extend his prosperity and benevolence to his people. This is an incredible testament to Mencius' belief in goodness of human beings: that when presented with suffering, we cannot but help to feel sympathy for their situation and a desire to alleviate their suffering through actions of our own.

Xunzi: Ritual

Xunzi, on the other hand, presents a model of personhood that emphasizes the role of ritual in controlling and directing the desires. According to Xunzi, human beings are by their nature creatures of desire, constantly hungering for satisfaction and acting on base feelings of need:

The nature of man is that he is born with a fondness for profit. If he indulges this fondness, it will lead him into wrangling and strife, and all sense of courtesy and humility will disappear. He is born with feelings of envy and hate, and if he indulges these, they will lead him into violence and crime, and all sense of loyalty and good faith will disappear. Man is born with the desires of the eyes and ear, with a fondness for beautiful sights and sounds. If he indulges these, they will lead him into license and wantonness, and all ritual

principles and correct forms will be lost. Hence, any man who follows his nature and indulges his emotions will become involved in
wrangling and strife.[14]

Xunzi describes human nature as evil, but this is not a metaphysical evil or
absolute evil; this is a kind of behavior that is often described as wicked,
petty, selfish, or destructive. The character for è is often translated as "evil,"
although sometimes it appears as "wicked," which I think is more appropriate than "evil" if a single term must be used. The etymology depicts a
deformed man over the character for the heart–mind, xīn. This suggests that
what the character actually means is a dysfunctional collection of emotions
and desires that result in harm, loss, and destructive behavior. The kind of
disfigurement suggested in the etymology is not physical disfigurement, but
in the sense of failing to live up to our responsibilities or grow into our various social roles. We are disfigured in the sense that we allow our emotions
to overcome the boundaries of acceptable social behavior, creating disorder
and harm to others and ourselves[15]:

> What is the origin of ritual? I reply: man is born with desires. If his
> desires are not satisfied for him, he cannot but seek some means to
> satisfy them himself. If there are no limits and degrees to his seek-
> ing, then he will inevitably fall to wrangling with other men. From
> wrangling comes disorder and from disorder comes exhaustion.
> The ancient kings hate such disorder, and therefore they established
> ritual principles in order to curb it, to train men's desires and to
> provide for their satisfaction. They saw to it that desires did not
> overextend the means for their satisfaction, and material goods did
> not fall short of what was desired. Thus both desires and goods were
> looked after and satisfied. This is the origin of rites.[16]

Xunzi shows great concern over the capacity for human desire to consume
things beyond the limit of sustainability, the point in which desire destroys
the very goods that were satisfying the needs of the desire. Xunzi's narrative
actually stands in strong contrast to the narratives of Western social regulation, which assume that scarcity of goods is what prompts conflict. Xunzi
notes that the problem is not the scarcity of goods per se, but rather that
the human desire for those goods can extend without limit. He explicitly
recognizes that human desires must be regulated in order to preserve the

healthy functioning of those desires, as well as to preserve the goods that sustain human activity.

Xunzi's prescription for the problem of desire is ritual. Ritual, in its many forms, provides the frameworks and boundaries to properly direct human desire. Ritual ensures human desires are satisfied in ways that are healthy and sustainable:

> Therefore, man must first be transformed by the instructions of a teacher and guided by ritual principles, and only then will he be able to observe the dictates of courtesy and humility, obey the forms and rules of society, and achieve order.... A warped piece of wood must wait until it has been laid against the straightening board, steamed and forced into shape before it can become straight; a piece of blunt metal must wait until it has been whetted on a grindstone before it can become sharp. Similarly, since man's nature is evil, it must wait for the instructions of a teacher before it can become upright, and for the guidance of ritual principles before it can become orderly.[17]

Although it may appear that Xunzi and Mencius possess two incompatible views on human nature, both models actually share a critical element in regard to the functioning of human emotion. Xunzi recognizes human desires as operating through need and satisfaction, while Mencius regards human emotions as operating through internal feeling in response to an environmental situation, followed by a process of allowing those feelings to become realized through expression or performance. The point that is similar between these two models is that both regard feelings as processes that have targets of intentionality and operate in response to elements with the field of activity. Xunzi focuses on the destructive capacity of desires, while Mencius focuses on the positive transformation of feelings into moral activity, but both see human nature in terms of active process in relation to objects, intentions, and the need for a kind of completion.

So although they may have different opinions on the moral character of man, their models both present strong tools for diagnosing problems related to emotions and desires. Bringing to light the manner in which desire and expression function presents opportunities for therapeutic treatment. In this sense, we can regard both their models as a kind of moral psychology: they both present models on how we should respond to our feelings, emotions, and desires. They both understand that feelings and desires are a central part of human activity. And they both understand that developing our responses to emotions and desire is a critical part of becoming a healthy, functional human being.

Diagnoses and Treatments of the Characters in the Film

In this light, I propose that we can offer some diagnoses and therapeutic recommendations for the different members of the Chu family. Nearly every character in *Eat Drink Man Woman* possesses enough personality to permit analysis, but here we will mainly address Chef Chu and his three daughters. Each character grapples with personal emotional issues that ultimately change the course of his or her life, but each transformation in the film also changes the harmony of the family as a whole. Thus, each character's emotional development is ultimately a critical part of bringing balance to the family as a whole. This allows the family unit to function properly, as a vehicle for helping each member of the family to grow, learn, and enter into new relationships. The alternative is for the family unit to remain oppressive and stifling, preventing the characters from successfully transitioning into healthy emotional relationships.

Master chef Chu is the widowed father of three single daughters, all of whom remain living at home. Since his wife died, the eldest daughter, Jia-Jen, has assumed the role of surrogate mother to Jia-Chien and Jia-Ning. In terms of Chef Chu's relationships, he secretly harbors feelings for Jin-Rong, a longtime friend of the family who is undergoing a divorce. Because the divorce is not yet final, Chu cannot reveal their relationship or his feelings, leaving him primarily preoccupied with concerns over his three daughters. As mentioned by Old Wen, he is as "repressed as a turtle"; he can't get what he wants, and he doesn't want what he has. His ability to express his feelings is completely repressed and his desires are unsatisfied. The weekly Sunday dinner is a constant source of trouble. In terms of his daughters, he is afraid Jia-Jen will never leave home, he argues constantly with Jia-Chien, and he pays the least attention to Jia-Ning. Despite this, he cares deeply for his daughters, but their coming of age and the possibility of their leaving home disrupt his roles as caregiver and authority figure.

As the film progresses, we see him turn his attention for care to Shan-Shan, Jin-Rong's daughter. Chu begins cooking small meals for Shan-Shan, thanks to Jin-Rong's own lack of cooking skill. But because his own personality demands grand audiences (as pointed out by Old Wen), he is unable to moderate his cooking. Soon he finds himself preparing lunch orders for Shan-Shan's entire class, which seems to satisfy his need for cooking and caregiving but still leaves his romantic interest unfulfilled. His relationship with Jin-Rong remains hidden until the finale of the film, when Jin-Rong's divorce is finalized and Jia-Ning and Jia-Jen have both moved out of the house, now in successful relationships of their own. It isn't until this final point that Chu finally regains his sense of taste and finds balance in his relationship with Jia-Chien. Thus, Chu's problems can be described in terms of desire, expression, and ritual, and the process of bringing those three elements into balance. And as we will see with his three daughters, their own relationships affect his own, as their growth and transformation provides him with the space necessary to make new arrangements in his own life.

Jia-Jen, the oldest daughter, suffers most immediately from an overabundance of ritual in her life. When Mrs. Chu died, Jia-Jen assumed the responsibilities of caring for her younger sisters, which produced conflict between her and Jia-Chien, and even occasionally Jia-Ning. This doesn't help the long-standing rivalry between the two: Jia-Jen was never allowed to cook, whereas Jia-Chien was allowed to learn everything in the kitchen. It's worth noting that we never actually see Jia-Jen cooking, only cleaning, which seems symbolic of the role forced on her by circumstances. Jia-Jen hides her lack of emotional development under a story of lost love and a broken heart. The story we find is false, and probably conceived as an excuse for her to avoid emotional entanglements while dealing with the difficulties of caring for her two younger sisters. She also seems to have accepted her fate as caregiver for her father as he grows older, even though Chu secretly wants her to be married and gone from the house.

The first scene with Jia-Jen shows her riding the bus while listening to tape recordings of choir music, which are embodied rituals that support religious practice. When Chou Ming-Dou appears as a romantic prospect (as surprisingly as the volleyball bouncing into her classroom), she acts guarded. She dreamily watches Chou Ming-Dao drive through the crowd on his motorcycle. When he actually stops to talk to her, she is completely taken by surprise; she stands for a moment, unable to hear him because of the music playing in her earbuds. The film's presentation of the experience from her point of view, with the viewer likewise able to hear the music but unable to hear Chou's words, expertly makes the point that Jia-Jen has allowed herself to seek emotional shelter in rituals that shield her from emotional interaction.

This shielding is not without reason. Jia-Jen's students abuse her emotions by writing false letters, suggesting the existence of a secret admirer who is too shy to admit his attraction. The letters arouse her interest, but when it appears that Chou isn't interested, she guards herself carefully. When she finally possesses the confidence to express her feelings, she undergoes a radical visual transformation, changing from her traditionally socially conservative attire to the dress of a modern professional woman. When the letters are exposed as fakes, she suffers a crisis of vulnerability, but Chou Ming-Dao resolves the crisis. When she passionately kisses him, he is first taken by surprise, which fortunately moves to happiness, and he returns the kiss. This begins the restoration of her ability to express her emotions, which then eventually comes into balance with her need for ritual and structure.

Old Wen describes Jia-Chien as the perfect blend of her father and mother: stubborn, willful, pompous, and picky. In reality, she is talented, ambitious, and passionate, and she appears to possess the ability to write her own future. She constantly outperforms her male peers but has ambivalent feelings regarding her upcoming promotion to head the Amsterdam office of her company. Her initial concern seems simply to gain space from her father while living in the same house. She attempts to buy into a developing high-rise, but when the development is exposed as a scam, she loses her savings and is forced to remain at home with her father.

She harbors resentment from being banned from her father's kitchen, and it is apparent throughout the film that she passionately enjoys cooking, making grand dishes with the same delicate complexity as her father and mother used to make. Like her mother, she is passionate, but her major relationship involves an artist who simply uses her for sex instead of providing support and structure. Her talents are wasted on Raymond, who lacks the ability to appreciate her skill and character. When she expresses regret at being banned from the kitchen and losing the happy moments of childhood, Raymond responds frivolously and without appreciation for her vulnerability.

Li-Kai appears to represent a much more compatible companion—someone talented, professional, and successful. However, when it appears that he may have been the man who broke Jia-Jen's heart in college, Jia-Chien tempers her interest to discover his true nature. When she discovers Li-Kai is innocent and Jia-Jen contrived the story, she seeks comfort at Raymond's apartment, only to discover he's sleeping with another woman. She ultimately becomes completely disgusted with Raymond when he simultaneously announces his marriage to his mistress while proposing to continue his romantic arrangements with Jia-Chien. To add insult to injury, he praises his new fiancée's cooking while completely oblivious and uncaring of Jia-Chien's previous efforts.

The mixture of family pressures and the inability to identify a clear direction for her own passions leaves her with an ongoing desire to simply flee her current life. Her real challenge is that she doesn't know what she really wants in life. Being talented and successful, she has the ability to do anything, but she needs space to discover her direction. She ultimately turns down the promotion to stay in Taipei with her family. This provides some balance between her professional ambitions and her family structure. It also gives her the time to explore her options as someone who has transcended traditional roles and has the ability to do whatever she wants.

Jia-Ning displays a curious mix of idealism, pragmatism, and sympathetic compassion. She has little patience for the dating games and manipulation by her coworker. While Guo Lun is suffering from his overwrought heartache at Rachel's machinations, she informs him directly that true love doesn't make the kinds of demands and injuries he is forced to suffer. Perhaps both suffer from inexperience and naïveté, but as they express their ideas regarding love and romance, they move closer together. Somewhat ironically, the moment that brings them together emotionally is a moment without speech, where they stand in the darkroom looking at pictures of Guo Lun's grandmother. The compassion Guo Lun feels for his grandmother is evident in his pictures, and Jia-Ning expresses her sympathy and compassion for Guo Lun by taking his hand.

Their relationship quickly grows, and soon Jia-Ning brings the news to the family that she is pregnant with Guo Lun's child. She also helps resolve the loneliness of Guo Lun, who suffers from an absent family. In fact, Guo Lun receives the benefits of the transformation as well because his own parents are absent; he moves from the role of existentially distraught and abandoned teenage son to socially engaged and responsible father. Lacking his own family, he now enjoys the company of Jia-Ning, a father-in-law, a brother-in-law, three sisters-in-law, and a mother-in-law.

Creation of Harmony in the Family: Expression, Ritual, and Transformation

The breakdown and restoration of order in *Eat Drink Man Woman* might be what we expect in a Shakespearean comedy. However, instead of the social norms of Elizabethan England dictating the nature of order, we see instead the use of ritual, expression, and transformation. A new harmony replaces the old status quo, one in which each of the characters is capable of expressing his or her desires, has a healthy structure in which to exercise these desires, and has taken on new roles and responsibilities. Jia-Jen overcomes her forced repression to discover love, passion, and companionship with Chou Ming-Dao. Jia-Ning leaps from youngest daughter to mother in her own right, but she has what appears to be a supportive and caring family to assist her in her transformation.

In response to Chu's question, "Is there more than food and sex?" I think the film itself answers in the affirmative. Wrestling with harmony and relationships presents a beauty and satisfaction that is more than the mere satisfaction of desires. Xunzi likewise thought that once desires were satisfied in the proper manner, then human activity would become elevated to function in accordance with the workings of *tiān*.[18] Allowing for one's desires to be satisfied in ways that are healthy and harmonious provides the ability to enjoy life. Harmony provides the spaces and contexts for the passions to be exercised in ways that are healthy, leading to an enrichment of experience. Near the end of the story in *Eat Drink Man Woman,* the final formal dinner scene contrasts to the opening scene. In the opening, Chef Chu prepares the entire dinner by himself, in isolation, alienated from his daughters in various ways. In the closing, Chef Chu is surrounded by a wealth of relations. Traumas of the past have been brought to light, new relationships have been formed, and all the characters have been allowed to grow into new stages of their lives.

This points toward the idea that our desires are not merely personal but are socially directed, and that by understanding the social nature of our ideas, we can live in ways that facilitate expression, structure, and satisfaction. Thus, our performance within our relationships is like the performance of musicians in symphony: structure and emotion become integrated so as to create a kind of consummating experience. This does not mean an experience that provides a final resolution to every problem, but rather an experience that combines all of the elements of a person's life in a way to create a wholeness of meaning that integrates the various strains of music into a tapestry of sound, or the mixture of various ingredients into a complex feast, or the interplay of personalities that create new possibilities for personal growth and transformation in the context of nurturing social environments.

Notes

1. David Hall and Roger Ames, *Anticipating China: Thinking through the Narratives of Chinese and Western Culture* (New York: State University of New York Press, 1995), 279.

2. Confucius, *Analects,* in *The Analects of Confucius: A Philosophical Translation,* ed. Roger T. Ames and Henry Rosemont Jr. (New York: Ballantine, 1998).

3. Ibid., 56.

4. Ibid., 17.11.

5. Ibid., 3.23.

6. Hall and Ames, *Anticipating China,* 279. For a detailed exposition of the focus–field self, see Chapter 1 of this volume.

7. It is worth noting that this process of creation is not creation ex nihilo, out of nothing, but rather the simple processes of birth, growth, and death. *Dào* is the ongoing natural processes of the world in which all things undergo change.

8. Laozi, *The Tao Te Ching (Daodejing),* trans. Stephen Mitchell (New York: Harper, 2006), chap. 11.

9. The Warring States period (Zhànguó Shídài) was an era of civil unrest that lasted from 475 BCE until the reunification of China under the Qín dynasty in 221 BCE. Many of China's greatest philosophers were writing or teaching during this time, including Confucius, Mencius, Sunzi, Laozi, Zhuangzi, and Xunzi.

10. Zhuangzi, *The Complete Works of Chuang-Tzu,* trans. Burton Watson (New York: Columbia University Press, 1968), 37.

11. Mencius, *The Four Books, The Great Learning, The Doctrine of the Mear [i.e., Mean], Confucian Analects [and] the Works of Mencius,* trans. James Leggus (New York: Napu Press, 2010), 2A6.

12. Ibid.

13. Ibid.

14. Xunzi, *Hsün Tzu: Basic Writings,* trans. Burton Watson (New York: Columbia University Press, 1996), chap. 23.

15. Ironically, this interpretation may actually bear some conceptual similarity to the understanding of evil as a term used by Jesuit missionaries in China. The understanding of evil in traditional Catholicism is the absence of good and allowing the desires to direct one toward sinful behavior instead of being guided toward goodness through surrender to God—that is, the ideal. Minus the metaphysical implications in the Catholic interpretation, both interpretations suggest that emotions and desires have the powerful capacity for misdirecting human activity in ways that harms our persons and the well-being of those around us.

16. Xunzi, *Hsün Tzu,* chap. 19.

17. Ibid., section 23.

18. Ibid., chap. 19.

PATERNALISM, VIRTUE ETHICS, AND ANG LEE

Does Father Really Know Best?

Ronda Lee Roberts

In the Father Knows Best trilogy—composed of the films *Pushing Hands* (1992), *The Wedding Banquet* (1993), and *Eat Drink Man Woman* (1994)—Ang Lee explores the role of paternalism in modern society. All of the characters in these films face the tension between traditional values and the modern, fast-paced lifestyle that drives American life. The clash between the two experiences causes friction when it comes to decision-making practices. The individual experiencing the clash then needs to determine whether or not he or she will accept the modern choices or adhere to the traditional culture. It is difficult to illustrate the clash and the tensions that push at the edges of what many of us want: to keep tradition to some extent, while allowing for the addition of novel ideas and cultural practices. Ethical theories can help resolve these tensions by guiding decisions about right and wrong. I will argue that, unlike deontology and utilitarianism, the virtue ethics of Confucius and Aristotle can best accommodate the tenuous relationship between traditional and modern morality.

Pushing Hands, Pushing Lifestyles: Confucianism and Traditional Asian Culture

Confucianism is often classified as a religion, but its complexity and sophistication make it more of a philosophical system than a religious tradition. Confucianism is a system of virtue ethics and political philosophy that was first articulated in Confucius' (551–478 BCE) *Analects*. It is grounded in the notion that we can cultivate ourselves ethically through the refinement of our actions and beliefs. There are three primary concepts at the center of Confucian social practices: *rén, yì,* and *lǐ*.[1] All three of these concepts serve as a means for guiding an individual's interactions with his or her community with the goal of striving toward and maintaining what is good.

Rén is the virtue associated with acting in an altruistic and empathetic manner toward other community members, and it is considered to be the primary social virtue in Confucianism. In order to demonstrate compassion, many Confucians will denigrate or devalue themselves in an act of humility because demonstrating pride may hurt another's feelings.[2] Another component of *rén* is the belief in the golden rule—one should do unto others what one would want for oneself. The concept of *rén* is also the justification of many social welfare systems.[3] Because we should have a strong sense of compassion for others, we should care for those who may be suffering, and we should take care to ensure that fairness is executed in our political and welfare systems.

Lǐ facilitates human interaction through a system of proper rituals and etiquette. *Lǐ,* when taken as a system of norms spelled out for a community, involves ritual actions, but it can also mean manners or decorum. In short, one can say that *lǐ* is the way in which one conducts oneself within Chinese society.[4] Ritual actions were presumed to be those where rulers could align themselves with the energies of the gods, and by extending such actions to the general community, each member could be in his or her right place.[5] Although these ritual actions began as a spiritual practice, they then broadened to the community as a way to demonstrate societal norms and intricacies in relationships among people.[6]

Yì is the virtue that grounds actions and laws in generalizable moral principles. *Yì* is difficult to translate, but it can be interpreted for the purposes of this investigation as a determination and capacity to act in a morally appropriate way.[7] Thus, by cultivating this quality, we can demonstrate a capacity to derive meaning from ritual, *lǐ,* and dedicate ourselves to *rén.* Part of this is through eradicating boundaries that exist in Western societies between self and other.[8]

Rén, lǐ, and *yì* are not the only important concepts existing in Confucian social and political thought. In addition to these three virtues, there are the filial virtues, or *xiào,* the rules for engagement with individuals in a family depending on their place in the family. There are five different relationships in Confucian ethics that are special, all of which entail specific duties of one individual to another.[9] For example, the son is supposed to take care of his parents and conduct himself in a particular way outside the home so as not to bring shame on the parents. Rebellion against parents is looked down on, and sons should strive to ensure the production of male heirs. While *rén, yì*, and *lǐ* are all important virtues, in practice, *xìao* is often considered the primary virtue.[10]

In his first feature film, *Pushing Hands,* Ang Lee plays with the tension between the paradigms of traditional Confucian values and Western values. Master Chu is thrown into the world of New York City with Martha, his daughter-in-law, and his son, Alex. Master Chu has emigrated from Beijing and is a *tàijíquán* teacher.[11] It can be difficult to adapt to living in a new country—more so when that adaptation also involves learning a new cultural paradigm. When Master Chu is thrown into the chaos of New York City, he is suddenly in a new community and must learn how to reconcile the differences between his Confucian ideals and the reality of contemporary urban America. While staying with his family in New York, Master Chu realizes that American culture is far more individualistic. After much conflict with his daughter-in-law and son, Master Chu moves out—something unheard of in Chinese culture, as multiple generations live together and the younger generations provide for the older generations. This is only the first of many things that Master Chu must deal with when it comes to adapting to New York City.

In one poignant scene, Master Chu tells the rude boss that he will leave if the boss can move him. He stands in place as the boss, the other restaurant workers, and even the police try to remove him. Not only does this scene demonstrate Chu's reluctance to be physically pushed around by others, but it also illustrates his reluctance to be moved by the New York and American culture. He wants to hold fast and strong against the pressures of society to abandon his traditional mind-set, and he refuses to bend outside of his Confucian values to do so. Thus, the thrust of the film deals with Master Chu's struggle to reconcile his traditional belief system with modern Western society.

It is difficult for Master Chu to demonstrate a commitment to *rén, lǐ, yì*, and *xìao* when he has no outlet for them. Instead, everything about New York City confronts these virtues. His daughter-in-law makes him feel out of place because she is individualistic while he is not. This conflicts with *xìao*. When he wants to conduct his *tàijíquán* rituals, he is met with frustration because they are viewed as outdated. What Master Chu needs is a reliable system for marrying together his traditional ethical system with the modern world with which he is confronted.

The Wedding Banquet—A Paternal Feast: Deontology, Utilitarianism, and Paternalism

When trying to reconcile the differences between traditional and modern cultures, it may be helpful to take a look at the two major systems of ethical decision making in modern Western philosophy. Both Immanuel Kant (1724–1804) and John Stuart Mill (1806–1873) are noted philosophers who generated moral theories that discussed—and criticized—paternalism. Paternalism is the idea that a state or individual claims the right to protect an individual by limiting his or her freedom to engage in activities that bring harm only to that individual.[12] Examples of paternalism include laws that prohibit the use of drugs, mandate helmets for motorcyclists, and regulate sexual conduct among consenting adults.

Kant and Mill were vehemently against paternalism. From the Kantian perspective, paternalism is problematic because it fails to respect individuals as persons. In the second formulation of the categorical imperative, Kant writes:

> Now, I say, man and, in general, every rational being exists as an end in himself and not merely as a means to be arbitrarily used by this or that will. In all his actions, whether they are directed toward himself or toward other rational beings, he must always be regarded at the same time as an end.[13]

When a system of actions is prescribed to an individual without regard for that individual's autonomy (the ability to make free and rational decisions), it instead regards that individual merely as a means. In other words, by prescribing actions for others, we take away their freedom to choose and regard them as individuals incapable of rationality. For example, at a university, an administrator might try to dictate what textbooks a professor should use in his courses. Obviously, the professor is rationally informed about the subject matter and what books would work best, and so for an administrator to try to control this could be seen as paternalism and would violate Kant's second formulation of the categorical imperative.

Mill also rejects paternalism. In *On Liberty* (1869), Mill offers a thorough critique of paternalistic ethical systems. He seeks to answer the questions:

> What, then, is the rightful limit to sovereignty of the individual over himself? Where does the authority of society begin? How much of

human life should be assigned to individuality, and how much to society?[14]

The answer, for Mill, is not entirely clear-cut. At first, he states that the realm of individual autonomy should only be left to individuals; society should only have authority over societal issues. The reason this is not a clear distinction is that the line between individual and society can bleed into one another because of our relationships to other individuals. Mill solves this problem with his harm principle, which states that acts endangering others or the greater good are to be avoided, which makes it permissible to create rules to prevent these. However, acts that endanger only oneself should be permissible. For example, my decision to drink alcohol or ride a motorcycle threatens only me and thus should not be restricted, while my decision to ride my motorcycle drunk threatens others and should be prohibited.[15]

Keeping this in mind, we can turn to Ang Lee's Father Knows Best trilogy. Master Chu is not the only one who has a hard time adjusting to American life in Ang Lee's films. In *The Wedding Banquet,* the characters deal with a radically different situation. This film follows Winston Chao, a gay man who lives with his partner, Simon, in Manhattan. His parents wish to see him marry and push him to date women. They sign him up for a dating service, but Winston intentionally provides unrealistic criteria for his ideal woman: a tall Chinese opera singer who holds two doctorates and is fluent in five languages. Tired of such chicanery, Winston, Simon, and a tenant in the apartment, Wei-Wei, come up with a plan. Winston will marry Wei-Wei, who needs a green card, and then his parents will stop sending him off on dates.

Naturally, this plan does not go smoothly. Winston's parents, Mr. and Mrs. Gao, fly out to New York from Taiwan with money for a beautiful ceremony. Winston marries Wei-Wei at the courthouse, and his mother is stricken by grief because they did not have a large ceremony. They have dinner at a restaurant, where an old friend of Mr. Gao suggests they have a wedding banquet. This friend insists that Winston is being incredibly insulting to his father by not having such a banquet. Naturally, this is an expression of Confucian filial piety. Winston and Wei-Wei agree, albeit reluctantly, in order to honor the wishes of Winston's parents.

Simon begins to feel left out, which creates a strain in his relationship with Winston. Winston becomes increasingly stressed out, and during the banquet, Wei-Wei seduces him, which results in a pregnancy. Winston finally confesses to his mother that he and Simon have a relationship—one that Mr. Gao has already figured out existed. The Gaos are supportive of the new, nontraditional family; by the end of the film, they have had to reconcile their traditional beliefs with modern practices and this nontraditional family.

Paternalism causes the Gaos to wish for a traditional family and causes their son Winston to feel guilt when he does not fit into the mold of his parents' wishes. Both Kant and Mill might say that the Gaos did the right thing in the end by accepting Winston and his lifestyle choices.[16] They had to dispel these traditional beliefs and take on a more individualistic worldview in order to see that their son was better off when they accepted him as he was.

Eat Drink Man Woman: Why Aristotelian Temperance is Necessary

For the Greeks, temperance was one of the most important virtues. Aristotle believed that virtue lay in the mean between two extremes. For example, foolhardiness and fear were excesses along the same continuum; courage would be located in the middle. He writes:

> It is possible, for example, to feel fear, confidence, desire, anger, pity, and pleasure and pain generally, too much or too little; and both of these are wrong. But to have these feelings at the right times on the right grounds towards the right people for the right motive and in the right way is to feel them to an intermediate that is to the best, degree; and this is the mark of virtue.[17]

In other words, rather than calling some abstraction a virtue or prescribing a specific set of actions as virtuous, Aristotle argues that virtue lies in determining the proper emotional response to a situation. As Aristotle writes, virtue "is a purposive disposition, lying in a mean that is relative to us and determined by a rational principle, and by that which a prudent man would use to determine that."[18]

Virtue ethics are not prescriptive; instead, Aristotle writes that they are instructive and consist of good habits that have been developed over time. Aristotle distinguishes between two types of virtue: intellectual and moral.[19] For intellectual virtue to grow, there needs to be experience and instruction. In this capacity, Aristotelian virtue ethics could be seen as congruent with some of the Confucian teachings about virtue. Moral virtue comes from habit. Aristotle writes, "The moral virtues, then, are engendered in us neither *by* nor *contrary to* nature; we are constituted by nature to receive them, but their full development in us is due to habit."[20] In other words, when it comes to having a good character, we can only determine the right action through experience and developing good habits.

In *Eat Drink Man Woman*,[21] Chef Chu clashes with his daughter, who works at Wendy's—after all, it's a symbol of Western culture taking over in Eastern nations. Just as Wendy's encroaches on Eastern tradition, so does Western culture impinge upon Chef Chu's three daughters. As they meet men, focus on their careers, and wrestle with emotional questions, they come to Sunday dinner at their father's home less frequently. Naturally, this concerns Chu, and we see the daughters from his perspective. The women are increasingly caught up in their own lives, and unlike in traditional culture, they are becoming increasingly independent and separated from their father. In this way, not only has Western culture colonized the way food is prepared, but it has also changed the way that individuals relate to one another.

Food, drink, and sexuality are at the heart of this film. In addition to traditional, Confucian values, Aristotelian virtue ethics play an important role. Jia-Chien, for example, is constantly walking a tightrope between her commitment to having a successful career and her traditional family upbringing. Jia-Ning has to account for her romantic whims, her employment at a fast food chain, and her role as a student. Chef Chu watches his daughters sort out their new lives and the way they balance modern culture with traditional culture. This balancing act requires that they follow the golden mean articulated by Confucius and Aristotle, which is the only way to reconcile the differences between traditional paternalist cultures and modern individualist cultures.

Paternalist Ethics versus Virtue Ethics in the Modern World

The thread between the three films is the clash between tradition and modernity, especially Western modernity. Confucian virtues must somehow be reconciled with a culture that emphasizes the individual and has little regard for the family. In order to be successful in the modern world, many of Lee's characters have to give up traditional values and practices. In *Pushing Hands*, Master Chu's family members have moved away from tradition. They are rebellious and individualistic, forcing Master Chu to move out and try to make a living in New York on his own. In *The Wedding Banquet,* the Gaos have to reconcile the fact that their son is homosexual and married to a woman whom he does not love with the traditional roles they expect him to take on. In *Eat Drink Man Woman,* Chef Chu must reconcile the fact that Western civilization and values have taken over his daughters' lives and are driving a wedge between him and his family.

Because of the inability of the application of the Confucian ethical system to cover the tension between traditional and modern, a new ethical model must be found by Master Chu, the Gaos, and Chef Chu. Deontology, an ethical system grounded in universal moral principles, does not effectively reconcile this tension. Kant suggests that they must follow a categorical imperative, a rule for guiding our actions that can be consistently universalized for all rational beings. This is contrary to Aristotle, who believes that different situations may require a different virtuous action. Kant's ideas cannot work when reconciling traditional values with modern values because deontology is focused on rules that do not allow for special situations or relationships where there might be an exception to that rule. Mill's ideas also cannot reconcile the problems in Lee's Father Knows Best film trilogy. The main reason for this is that utilitarianism cannot take into consideration special relationships. For *Pushing Hands,* it would seem that the greatest action of utility is for Master Chu to leave the home, which he ultimately does. It would be far better and more useful if there could have been a balance found between the old ways and new ways. What will work, then, is a return to virtue ethics. Centered on a cultivation of habits and right attitudes, Aristotelian and Confucian virtue ethics allow for special relationships, special situations, and complex relationships between the old and the new. For the right action to occur, it has to be the action that fits the situation. Ethics, for Aristotle, is a matter of habit, of learning what the best action is through practice.

In *Pushing Hands,* the right action for Master Chu is to leave the home of his daughter-in-law and son even though this conflicts with his traditional moral beliefs. It is the right action because the friction is harming his relationship with his family. It does not support Aristotle's idea of human flourishing—happiness. In *The Wedding Banquet,* the right action is for the Gaos to put their son's happiness ahead of their traditional values. They have no choice but to accept and love their son, regardless of his sexual orientation. In *Eat Drink Man Woman,* Chef Chu needs to adapt to his daughters' changing ways, but he also needs to help them develop and cultivate the habits necessary to lead moral lives. Part of this cultivation involves learning and practicing temperance in one's relations.

By looking at the need to reconcile tradition with modernity as one primarily driven by virtue ethics, it is easier to understand the delicate situations that arise from the various situations that the characters in Ang Lee's Father Knows Best films find themselves in. The situations and the conflict between tradition and modernity are complex, and blanket, universal theories are not robust enough to describe the kinds of decisions that need to be made and executed. By taking the time to determine what the right action is, and by carrying it out in the right way, at the right time, and with the right people, then at the end of the films, the fathers find a sort of peace with their nontraditional children. Had the fathers adhered to a different type of ethics or had they not morphed their traditional, paternalistic ethical beliefs into a virtue ethics outlook, they would have had something worse happen: they would have lost their children in the struggle. Thus, in the move from a paternalistic ethics to a virtue ethics, these men can reclaim the relationships they so desperately want while holding onto the principles of *rén, yì,* and *lǐ.*

Notes

1. The discussion here is meant to give a broad overview of Confucianism for the purposes of discussing how it is that we can reconcile Confucian beliefs with modern life. For an in-depth discussion of Confucian philosophy, see James McRae, Chapter 1, this volume.

2. Jeffrey Riegel, "Confucius," in *Stanford Encyclopedia of Philosophy* (http://plato.stanford.edu/).

3. Ibid.

4. David Hall and Roger T. Ames, *Thinking through Confucius* (Albany: State University of New York Press, 1987), 85.

5. Ibid., 86.

6. Ibid., 88.

7. Ibid., 89.

8. Ibid., 93–94.

9. These five relationships are: ruler to ruled, father to son, husband to wife, elder brother to younger brother, and friend to friend. See Chapter 1 for a detailed exposition of the five cardinal relationships.

10. James Wang, "The Confucian Filial Obligation to Care for Aged Parents," presented at the Twentieth World Congress of Philosophy, Boston, Mass., August 10–15, 1998 (http://www.bu.edu/wcp/).

11. This martial art is written as *t'ai chi ch'uan* in the Wade-Giles system of Chinese romanization and has been adopted into English as tai chi chuan.

12. Gerald Dworkin, "Paternalism," in *Stanford Encyclopedia of Philosophy.*

13. Immanuel Kant, *Foundations of the Metaphysics of Morals,* 2nd ed., trans. Lewis White Beck (Upper Saddle River, N.J.: Prentice-Hall, 1997), 45.

14. John Stuart Mill, *On Liberty* (1869), full text at Bartleby.com (http://www .bartleby.com).

15. This issue becomes more complicated when we consider the insights of modern rights theorists, who rightly point out that there really are no acts that actually only affect oneself—what I do to myself usually affects others, and indeed may violate their rights. For example, if I kill myself, someone has to clean up my mess, and unless I am known to no one, someone is likely to be emotionally affected by my act.

16. However, Kant poses arguments covering where and when sexual intercourse is appropriate in his *Metaphysics of Morals.*

17. Aristotle, *The Ethics of Aristotle: The Nicomachean Ethics,* trans. J. A. K. Thomson (New York: Penguin Books, 1976), 101.

18. Ibid.

19. Ibid., 91.

20. Ibid.

21. For a detailed exposition of the plot of *Eat Drink Man Woman,* see Carl Dull, Chapter 6, this volume.

LUST, CAUTION

A Case for Perception, Unimpeded

Basileios Kroustallis

Cognitive/Affective States

When British film critic Peter Bradshaw reviewed Ang Lee's 2007 film *Lust, Caution,* he carefully noted (even though he praised the film) that it "does not offer the same unmediated insight into the minds and hearts of its lovers that *Brokeback Mountain* [2005] did. Fundamentally, we all felt that we knew, really knew, what it felt like for the two cowboys to be in love; here the question is a little more difficult."[1] But is *Lust, Caution* really an emotional riddle to be deciphered? Or is it rather the case that affective states in the film are part of a more comprehensive cognitive network, with perception as the primary focal point of both knowing and feeling? An understanding of perception as both influencing reasoning and cognition and shaping affect in the characters and setting of *Lust, Caution* may provide insight into the film.

Lust, Caution, a psychologically intense spy drama set in World War II Hong Kong and Shanghai, is filled with innuendos and nonexplicit occurrences of cognitive and affective states. Therefore, a philosophical review of these attitudes would not proceed successfully if a sequential interpretation were applied (where empirical evidence leads to reasoning and decisions, which subsequently produce emotions and actions), because there are too many unknown factors in such a model. The power of the film lies in its unmitigated application of a perceptual process, which provides a direct connection between the subject and the world inside which he or she acts; the relevant interpretation bypasses traditional philosophical distinctions between subject and object, mind and body, without failing to secure a definite structure and content of perception.

Here I discuss three variants of the role that perception acquires in *Lust,*

Caution to construct a direct connection between the subject and the world he or she inhabits. First, the model of environmental aesthetics that Arnold Berleant (b. 1932) pursues eschews the prominent aesthetic paradigm of the disengaged observer and fine art lover to relocate aesthetic appreciation to all domains of engaged perceptual experience.[2] The developing character of Wong Chia Chi (Tang Wei) learns to throw herself into, and reappraise aesthetically, an initially hate-invested espionage environment. Second is the phenomenological emphasis on body and its inherent ambiguity as the key to cognition in Maurice Merleau-Ponty (1908–1961), which can justify not only the presence but also the overall function of the intense sex scenes in Lee's film.[3] Finally, the eerie, almost hopeless feeling of changing the world for the better that Wong Chia Chi entertains stands on firmer ground if it is viewed within Fang Dongmei's (1899–1977) grand scheme of comprehensive harmony and his key notion of creative creativity.[4] This neo-Confucian metaphysical and moral system strongly advocates that the human subject can reach the desired harmony with his or her surroundings—even if, as in *Lust, Caution*, this only takes place within the medium of cinema itself.

Switching between Environments

Wong Chia Chi is a young university student in 1938 Hong Kong during the second Sino-Japanese war (1937–1945). Abandoned by her father, she soon joins a university drama group, led by a fellow student, Kuang Yu Min (Leehom Wang), and performs in patriotic dramas with great success. When Kuang asks the rest of the group to expand its activities from theater plays to real actions and assassinate the notoriously secretive Japanese collaborator, Mr. Yee (Tony Leung Chiu-Wai), Wong agrees. She becomes the perfect bait for Mr. Yee as Mrs. Mak, the bored wife of a Hong Kong merchant. Through her initial acquaintance with Mrs. Yee (Joan Chen), Wong enters the world of Mr. Yee as his potential mistress and assassin.

Up to this point, the plot has had Wong perceive her own environment through what Arnold Berleant describes (and rejects) as the disengaged paradigm of aesthetic appreciation. According to this model, made prominent since Kant's *Critique of Judgment* (1790), for the aesthetic experience to have an objective status, the appreciating subject should be disengaged from both his personal preferences and any practical ends the watched specimen may confer, yet his feeling of pleasure toward the art object should be able to command universal validity.[5] The Platonic distinction in *Greater Hippias*[6] between higher (vision, hearing) and lower (smell, touch, taste) senses has conferred the means of this disengagement model: aesthetic appreciation is tied up with higher senses and has the fine arts assigned as its application domain, whereas practical crafts appreciation (such as cooking and shoemaking) belongs to the province of the lower senses. Berleant argues that aesthetics is founded on sense perception (*aisthēsis* in Greek), which involves the engagement of all of the sensory faculties of the human body. Human beings are active participants in and contributors to their contexts, and this interrelational process becomes the ground from which meaning and value are continually generated.[7]

In *Lust, Caution,* Wong Chia Chi is a university student turned actress who uses her theatrical, sight-only skills to play the different role of Mrs. Mak. She reflects a dualistic framework of performer and audience: she is a subject who distinguishes herself from her performing environment of upper-class Chinese collaborator officials (even though she tends to be a part of it), and she relies on already formed conceptual notions about country, love, and comradeship. This attitude should not be misconceived as a cold or even halfhearted commitment to the adopted cause. Wong Chia Chi as Mrs. Mak is convincing as no one else would be, and she believes in the part assigned to her. Yet she still thinks of her life as an inconsequential extension of her theatrical life. It is only when she realizes that the theater play has real-life consequences she did not foresee that Wong Chia Chi abandons the paradigm of the sight-only aesthetic with its emphasis on specific object evaluation (here "the Japanese horrible collaborator Mr. Yee"). The unplanned but cold-blooded murder of Mr. Yee's associate, Tsao (Kar Lok Chin), whom Wong watches through her balcony, was not on the students' agreed-upon agenda of resistance. Repulsed by this realization, Wong decides to leave the resistance group.

Some years later, though, and on a renewed invitation from the resistance group, Wong repeats her task. There is a whole new Shanghai environment, which she now directly perceives and investigates with all her senses, movements, and moral and cultural values.[8] Where previously she could not, now Wong enjoys the tactile feel of playing mah-jongg, and she holds her own against Mrs. Yee and her friends with confidence and grace. Her environment neither stands opposed to nor surrounds her, but is continuous with her activities.[9] Her past moments of being alone with Mr. Yee occurred only inside the neutral surroundings of a restaurant space, and Mr. Yee never entered Wong's rented apartment. She can now meet him in his own secret flat, smell the flowers, and sense the dust on the furniture, while at the same time she is a guest in his home and worries about the resistance-related papers she sees him burning. Wong Chia Chi perceives that Mr. Yee is not a disengaged target to be assassinated but rather a subject whose world she must enter, sense for herself, and evaluate accordingly as beautiful, horrible or even both. But she needs to abandon her ready-made conceptions, which get in her way. Wong complains repeatedly about the bulk of fake facts about her identity that the resistance leaders gave her and that she needs to memorize.

Direct engagement is the prerequisite of musical appreciation. Wong and Mr. Yee meet at a geisha house in the Japanese section of Shanghai, and Wong hears some women sing a Chinese folk song. She is not restricted to the role of a listener and decides to sing herself. Even though she claims that "she sings better than the others," her behavior does not indicate jealousy or vanity. What Wong clearly states to Mr. Yee is that she will sing a song for him; she moves deeper into his psyche, and has Mr. Yee crying as a result.

"A young girl to her man is like thread to its needle," the song lyrics suggest. Wong's gradually changing relationship with Mr. Yee has her alternating between being a lure and a predator. This situation was not part of the original conspiratorial plan, as a fearful and surprised Wong expresses in a secret resistance meeting. But this development does not come from unleashed emotions that cancel former perceptions. Even if Wong now feels what it is to be in love, she still perceives Mr. Yee as a Japanese collaborator who has to be assassinated. This perception still continues to fuel her moral valuations negatively. At the same time, it seems increasingly clear that her aesthetic appreciation of this situation colors her relationship with Mr. Yee not as ugly and distasteful, but, gradually and implicitly, as positive and beautiful.[10]

The film's stock negative coloring of prostitution and paid companions and Wong's role in it only confirms that aesthetic appreciation of an environment may permit more individual freedom than suggested without resulting in relativism; it only proposes a different, functional interaction between the subject and his environment. The initial setup of Kuang with the Japanese collaborator, Tsao, takes place inside a cabaret, and Wong watches the girls looking down from their balcony. She subsequently agrees to have her first sexual experience with a fellow student who has only bedded whores. Wong Chia Chi seems destined to sell her body for the patriotic cause, but her relationship with Mr. Yee goes further than that. When she enters the

Shanghai geisha house, the male attendants want to take advantage of her, and even Wong herself thinks (and tells Mr. Yee) that the venue for their date makes her his whore. However, the woman in charge of the geisha house (which is not necessarily a whorehouse) sets the record straight: "This is a customer, not one of our girls." Wong Chia Chi has been a part of Mr. Yee's environment, and her relationship with Mr. Yee cannot be appreciated with the physical and emotional distance a whore may have for her client. Wong redefines her position by meticulously acting and responding to the challenges of the environment she chose to be continuous with.

Sexual Ambiguity, Necessary Repetition

The three graphic (and extremely complicated) sex scenes between Tang Wei and Tony Leung Chiu-Wai caused much concern when *Lust, Caution* was released. Rated NC-17 in the United States (the commercial kiss of death), the film was edited in China with the director himself making the cuts, but it was released uncut in Hong Kong.[11] Still, Ang Lee testifies to the importance of these scenes: "This is the ultimate performance and I have to contort their bodies, the body language has to speak for the movie otherwise I couldn't go on, the rest of the story doesn't exist. So it starts from there and the execution, the nuances is something that happens on set."[12] Body language may "speak for the movie," but its language does not necessarily lead to clear-cut conclusions. The film's sex scenes do not unveil the characters' concealed emotions. The importance of sexuality in *Lust, Caution* does not lie in unlocking a system of forbidden (Freud would also say unconscious) desires and cannot be justified only by means of its functional significance for the unfolding narrative, for this alone does not explain the sheer complexity of these scenes. The answer needs to include the more generic perception of a body interacting with other bodies and the world itself in a nondeterminate, essentially ambiguous way.

Rejecting long-standing Western philosophical dualisms (subject versus object, mind versus body), Maurice Merleau-Ponty, in his *Phenomenology of Perception* (1945), connects bodily interaction with the environment and the role of sexuality within that activity in a direct chain from perception to activity. In his account of cognition, he avoids both a Kantian subject who already brings her own a priori cognitive presuppositions to the world and an empiricist view of perception as piecemeal activity complemented by associative reasoning. Cognition involves the body and its already prepared, implied, or actual movements that reach out to the external world: without being restricted to reflex movements or individual bodily sensations, bodily behavior unveils a meaningful content that engages with the environment. When a person is stung by a mosquito, Merleau-Ponty writes, he "does not need to look for the place where he has been stung. He finds it straight away, because for him there is no question of locating it in relation to axes of co-ordinates in objective space, but of reaching with his phenomenal hand a certain painful spot on his phenomenal body."[13]

This directly experienced relationship between carefully implemented hand and body movements and the environment abounds in *Lust, Caution*. Artificial objects (keys, cups of coffee) are used as the end point of a person's meaningful movement, which may or may not initiate a different movement from a different person who already perceives their significance. When Wong leaves her lipstick on her coffee cup, Mr. Yee is the first to notice the lip-shaped smudge that may invite his kiss. Mr. Yee does not watch Wong's lips (a more usual object of desire) but rather is immersed in her movements as she almost kisses the coffee cup. When they both head to the house where Wong and her fellow students stay, Wong does not conceptualize the importance of searching for and playing with the key of their rented flat in her hands (which may lead to the assassination of the unsuspecting Mr. Yee). She knows the relevant movements her hand has to make, and the close shot Ang Lee provides makes spectators feel all the sexual connotations of the foreplay that results to open an otherwise closed door. Still, the situation is ambiguous. One never knows whether Wong feels attracted or repulsed by Mr. Yee.[14]

Questions of autonomy and dependence through sexual bodily interaction fuel the intensity of the three sexual encounters of Wong Chia Chi and Mr. Yee.[15] The violent attitude of Mr. Yee toward Wong in their first sexual act is reversed in Wong's halfhearted attempt to suffocate Mr. Yee with a pillow throughout their third, almost frenetic encounter. But a comprehensive, clear-cut system of latent, unconscious representations that are fulfilled in their sexual activity cannot wholly explain this behavior, which remains inherently ambiguous. A baffled Wong describes her first meeting with Mr. Yee to her resistance collaborators with the words, "The house smelled of perfumes, jasmine flowers," only to conclude with the utterly apologetic, "I don't know." At her next resistance meeting, she reveals more ambiguous feelings, which culminate in her despairing, "He enters my heart." The ambiguous attitude of Wong Chia Chi is neither the result of her feeble character (she plays her dangerous part in a pitch-perfect way) nor a sign of her falling for Mr. Yee and abandoning her cause (she feels worn out, but she is still loyal and remains committed to what has been asked of her). It is only when Wong enters the domain of sexuality through her body that these certainties recede and an essential ambiguity takes up residence.

Sexuality is an essential link that connects perception with action, without the need for mediating cognitive representations that would help circumscribe consequent activities. This unmediated knowledge does not come at once, but rather comes through a feedback loop or an intentional arc between perception and action: perceptual situations cause personal–bodily actions, and the environmental response these actions evoke further inform any subsequent action concerning the same goal.[16] The series of sexual encounters, but also the whole repetitive narrative structure of *Lust, Caution*, works in such a way as to foster a better understanding of the characters and their environment through successive efforts and movements. The students' unsuccessful attempt to assassinate Mr. Yee is followed by a renewed effort three years later, starting the clock afresh. Specific scenes and features within that plan enhance this impression. The long hair Wong Chia Chi wore as a student before her involvement reappears in the Shanghai settlement; her first public meeting with Mr. Yee takes place through a game of mah-jongg she plays with his wife and her friends; her first intimate encounter with him occurs during rainy weather.

Yet these similarities do not fail to reveal Wong's modified response to changing situations. In 1942, her life in Shanghai has hungry people queuing for food, whereas her Hong Kong student years were accompanied by joyful soldiers going to the front. Her mah-jongg game has gotten better, and instead of waiting in the rain, she now has Mr. Yee's chauffeur to drive her to Mr. Yee's apartment. Wong herself is less innocent, as she herself confesses to Kuang, and more fearful for her life; yet she is more attracted to Mr. Yee. The more mature Wong Chia Chi now has to remember more facts about her fake identity, yet she is more tired of playing that game of deception.

The ritualistically repeated sequences highlight how cognition becomes available through previous interactions, rather than being achieved as a result of intellectual consideration. Wong Chia Chi neither reasons nor meditates about her past state in order to form her present decisions. Her renewed perception of situations already encountered makes her adopt a modified response. This is more than know-how and acquisition of a specific skill. Wong throws herself into the environment and the situations she faces; she does not act with the domain-selective attention an experienced actor has to give to his role, while at the same time hearing the audience's breath. Her own knowledge reflects the specific environment, in the same way that the always-present mirrors in *Lust, Caution* reflect a different face from oneself.

The Creative Mrs. Wong Chia Chi

The narrative of *Lust, Caution* does not unveil much of its characters' states of mind; it relies on Ang Lee's directorial technique and the actors' performances to communicate this emotional ambiguity and cognitive development.

Actress Tang Wei, as both Wong Chia Chi and Mrs. Mak, offers a subtle, intelligent, and powerfully changing performance that makes the young student singing in Hong Kong streets a different person from the mature woman emotionally involved in a relationship on the razor's edge. Still, Tang Wei's face and posture retain dignity throughout the film, even in her final and fatal moments, which seems difficult to reconcile with her role as femme fatale: she looks exotic, a sharp contrast from her wartime days.[17]

Ang Lee has explored the human soul before, having previously presented a non-Western culture with strict moral rules and traditions to be followed. His *Crouching Tiger, Hidden Dragon* (2000) borrows elements from both Confucianism and mystical Daoism to recreate a historical environment in which his characters operate.[18] However, whatever romantic innocence and positivity these values had in his previous work supports nothing but a theater of mindless massacres in *Lust, Caution*. The humanistic undertones of this film remain the sole responsibility of Wong Chia Chi, who unsuccessfully attempts to impose these values on her own environment, and who eloquently presents what Fang Dongmei has called creative creativity. The eclectic mix the Taiwanese philosopher borrows from traditional Chinese philosophies (Confucianism, Daoism, and Mòzǐ) as well as the process philosophy of Whitehead's and Bergson's vitalism builds a grand metaphysical and moral scheme of comprehensive harmony between individual and nature, a scheme far away from artificially constructed dualisms.[19] Fang Dongmei insists, in a Socratic manner, that human nature is not radically defective and that the process of continuous creativity may lead to the genesis and promotion of human values. Human creativity signals the genesis and promotion of human values, and this creativity can bring forms of value into existence.[20]

This is hardly what the university students have in mind when they plan the assassinations in *Lust, Caution* and orchestrate the cold-blooded murder of the Japanese collaborator, Tsao. Still, Wong, who is the first to leave the theater of blood and break off with her partners, learns to change her priorities and values. Wong Chia Chi develops in the way Nora emancipates herself from her husband in Ibsen's *A Doll's House* (1879). This celebrated play was to be performed by Wong's university theater group, but it was shelved in favor of a more patriotic play about China at war. However, Nora's progressive independence resonates with Wong's emancipation from ideals she does not feel altogether comfortable with.

This development accompanies the intervention of the natural environment—here, rain—as an active player in the process. Wong Chia Chi's first happy moment is realized as she enjoys the rain outside her bus window, contemplating her theatrical success and having feelings for Kuang. Wong's initially rigid behavior subsequently loosens; she is like a raindrop that falls into the river and makes it grow, but then renews itself as part of the river.[21] Her first intimate encounter with Mr. Yee occurs during heavy rain, and the aftermath of their first sexual encounter has Wong gazing on a ray of sun outside the window. Ready-made associations linking sunshine and happiness are not evident here; rather, Wong Chia Chi's environment uses rain to signal the spring of subsequent behavior.

Flowers also play a specific role. The naked Wong observes them outside her window immediately after her deflowering. Her elegant blue dresses, which assist her in her encounters with Mr. Yee, are adorned with flowers and leaves. The smell of jasmine flowers in Mr. Yee's secret apartment hints at her indecision in conspiring against him. Beauty in nature and individual moral decisions are intricately linked.[22]

Wong and Mr. Yee's troubled relationship does not rest outside this scheme. With a *yīn–yáng* proclivity, Dongmei finds a cosmological principle of intensified emotional contrast in the male–female union, which functions like the connection of opposite electric charges across a spark gap. This union has a specific polar sign for each part: "The meek finds attraction in the strong—to the strong, the meek is always lure."[23] Sympathetic love motivates this scheme, as Wong's behavior toward her lover indicates.

Still, the harmony that Wong Chia Chi seeks is not to be found in her external, theatrical environment but in the world of cinema. Watching the separation story of *Intermezzo* (Gregory Ratoff, 1939) with Leslie Howard and Ingrid Bergman (which reminds Wong of her father abandoning her) makes Wong cry for the first and last time. Cinema may intensify her current fears—a poster of Alfred Hitchcock's 1941 film *Suspicion* hangs outside the theater—but it also teaches her how two people can be in love and still hurt each other. When a showing of *Penny Serenade* (George Stevens, 1941) is interrupted with an update on the war, Wong returns to her espionage role. Theatrical play involves live actors, but the cinema is only a screen to be watched. Yet the cinema represents a spectacle that can also be entered; it is a domain of vacuity to be filled by her own character.[24]

The model of creative creativity requires continuous creation; it considers human psychology according to a scale of development, thereby permitting human creativity to subside instead of increase.[25] Even though none of the characters around Wong Chia Chi fall completely into the constructive, positive version of this scheme (Mr. Yee himself seems to be momentarily carried away, but he never practices this creativity on his own), Wong is the one who originally has a good nature. She constantly seeks to elevate herself beyond what her own predicament permits, but without abandoning that predicament altogether. Wong will not fall in love and forget her own patriotic cause; instead, she learns, through love and through constant reminders of natural beauty and creation, to relocate and elevate her own scheme of values.

Lust, Caution can be as emotionally complex and cryptic as Peter Bradshaw proposed. But it emphasizes human perception, in its various manifestations, as the attempt to connect (even in ambiguity) all cognitive processes, interrelations, and actions. As Berleant argues, aesthetics is not a matter of detachment but rather a process of directly engaging one's context in a participatory manner. This necessarily involves an emphasis on the body as the medium of engagement, which, as Merleau-Ponty claims, is essential to cognition. The sexuality of *Lust, Caution* thus becomes an aesthetic process through which the main character of Wong Chia Chi is creatively cultivated in the manner described by Fang Dongmei. Ang Lee may narrate an espionage drama, but at the same time, he meticulously paints the tight interrelations between perception and action, human and environment, on his own cinematic canvas.

Notes

1. Peter Bradshaw, review of *Lust, Caution, Guardian*, January 4, 2008 (http://www.guardian.co.uk).

2. See Arnold Berleant, *Art and Engagement* (Philadelphia: Temple University Press,

1991), *The Aesthetics of Environment* (Philadelphia: Temple University Press, 1992), and *Sensibility and Sense: The Aesthetic Transformation of the Human World* (Exeter: Imprint Academic, 2010).

3. Maurice Merleau-Ponty, *Phenomenology of Perception* (1945), trans. Colin Smith (New York: Routledge, 1995).

4. Fang Dongmei, *Creativity in Man and Nature: A Collection of Philosophical Essays* (Taipei: Linking, 1980).

5. Immanuel Kant, *Critique of the Power of Judgment*, trans. Paul Guyer and Eric Matthews (Cambridge: Cambridge University Press, 2000).

6. Plato, *Greater Hippias*, in *Plato: Complete Works*, ed. John Cooper (Indianapolis, Ind.: Hackett, 1997), 898–921.

7. Berleant, *Aesthetics*, 16–17.

8. Berleant, *Sensibility and Sense*, 195.

9. Berleant, *Aesthetics*, 20: "We begin to understand environment as the physical–cultural realm in which people engage in all the activities and responses that compose the weave of human life in its many historical and social patterns."

10. Berleant, *Sensibility and Sense*, 168–170, pays attention to the potential conflict that ensues when negative moral appreciation conflicts with positive aesthetic appreciation. Leni Riefenstahl's cinematic work to the service of the Nazi cause serves as a prominent example.

11. Robert Chi, "Exhibitionism: *Lust, Caution*," *Journal of Chinese Cinemas* 3, no. 2 (2009): 177–187, traces the history of spectator reception of different censored or uncensored versions of *Lust, Caution* in mainland China, Singapore, Taiwan, and Hong Kong, and unveils the distinct psychological versus political issues that respective U.S. and Chinese critics tended to emphasize.

12. Richard Brunton, "*Lust, Caution* Interview with Ang Lee," *Film Stalker*, January 23, 2008 (http://www.filmstalker.co.uk).

13. Merleau-Ponty, *Phenomenology*, 105. On what Merleau-Ponty calls motor intentionality, see Sean Dorrance Kelly, "Seeing Things in Merleau-Ponty," in *The Cambridge Companion to Maurice Merleau-Ponty*, ed. Taylor Carman and Mark B. N. Hansen (New York: Cambridge University Press, 2005), 102: "We experience our environment at least partly in terms of the activities it immediately leads us to perform."

14. Merleau-Ponty, *Phenomenology*, 168: "There are here blurred outlines, distinctive relationships which are in no way 'unconscious' and which, we are well aware, are ambiguous, having reference to sexuality without specifically calling it into mind."

15. Ibid., 167: "[My body] is both an object for others and a subject for myself."

16. Hubert L. Dreyfus, "Merleau-Ponty and Recent Cognitive Science," in Carman and Hansen, *Cambridge Companion*, 133: "Skills are acquired by dealing repeatedly with situations that then gradually come to show up as requiring more and more selective responses."

17. Manohla Dargis, "A Cad and a Femme Fatale Simmer," *New York Times*, Sep-

tember 28, 2007 (http://movies.nytimes.com). Dargis accuses Ang Lee specifically of the failure of Wong Chia Chi to convince as the traditional femme fatale character.

18. See Horace L. Fairlamb, "Romancing the Tao: How Ang Lee Globalized Ancient Chinese Wisdom," *Symplokē* 15, no. 1–2 (2007): 190–205.

19. Fang Dongmei is not the only Taiwanese philosopher to attempt a synthesis of different philosophies. See Vincent Shen, "Creativity as Synthesis of Contrasting Wisdoms: An Interpretation of Chinese Philosophy in Taiwan Since 1949," *Philosophy East and West* 43, no. 2 (1993): 279–287, for a review and classification of different comprehensive philosophical proposals in post–World War II Taiwan. Shu-Hsien Liu, *Essentials of Contemporary Neo-Confucian Philosophy* (Westport, Conn.: Praeger, 2003), 73–89, presents Fang Dongmei's philosophy not only as a synthesis between Greek, modern European, and Chinese philosophies, but at the same time as a reinterpretation and elimination of the moralistic and negative undertones of the respective Confucianism and Daoism philosophies, in order to foster his own philosophical–creative proposal. Chenyang Li, "Fang Dongmei: Philosophy of Life, Creativity and Inclusiveness," in *Contemporary Chinese Philosophy,* ed. Chung-Ying Cheng and Nicholas Bunnin (London: Blackwell, 2002), 271–273, argues that Fang Dongmei's emphasis on life and creativity sets him apart from other contemporary neo-Confucians.

20. Fang Dongmei, *The Chinese View of Life: The Philosophy of Comprehensive Harmony* (Taipei: Linking, 1980), 53ff., and *Creativity in Man and Nature* (Taipei: Linking, 1980).

21. Dongmei, *Chinese View of Life,* 14. The Daoist concept of *wúwéi,* usually translated as "effortless or natural action," is primarily associated with the water and its power to move, change, and transform nature by its own self-transformation.

22. Dongmei, *Creativity,* 39.

23. Dongmei, *Chinese View of Life,* 47.

24. Whitney Crothers Dilley, "Globalization and Cultural Identity in the Films of Ang Lee," *Style* 43, no. 1 (2009): 45–64. She also notices the influence of films for the main character. However, she ties them into the film noir tradition (a genre essentially defined by Western values), here enriched with an overall globalization theme that also informs the narrative structure of *Lust, Caution.* What Wong does with these films, though, is much more complex: she embraces the different kinds of creative feelings in these films. It is no wonder that the more noirish and less positively charged films—*Destry Rides Again* (George Marshall, 1939), *Suspicion* (Alfred Hitchcock, 1941), and *The Thief of Baghdad* (Ludwig Berger, Michael Powell, and Tim Whelan, 1940)—only function as film posters, not films that Wong Chia Chi actually watches.

25. Dongmei, *Creativity,* 96: "There is the dangerous tendency of devolution in the impeded and distorted process of creativity."

Part 2

THE WESTERN PHILOSOPHY OF ANG LEE

The Power to Go Beyond God's Boundaries?

Hulk, Human Nature, and Some Ethical Concerns Thereof

Adam Barkman

Judeo-Christian Themes

"We live in an upside-down world," remarks director Ang Lee. "Biblically, we lost Paradise."[1] This comment is central to Lee's vision for his 2003 movie *Hulk*, based on the Marvel comic book series *The Incredible Hulk*. In past films, Lee demonstrated an array of philosophical approaches, but in this movie, the philosophical themes and concepts are religious ones, especially Judeo-Christian ones. For example, when Bruce Banner (aka the Hulk) blows up a frog during a lab test, his longtime love, Betty Ross, jokes that they now know who they can turn to when a "plague [of] frogs start falling from the sky." The allusion to the ten biblical plagues is clear, as is the implication that Bruce is a kind of Moses figure who will be a hero in the future. Further allusions to—not to mention direct statements about—Bruce being like the biblical Isaac and being predestined to a certain life path are sown throughout, yet all serve the general theme of losing paradise.

What is paradise in this movie, such that it can be lost? Probably drawing on the general ethos of Daoist and Mahayana Buddhist sympathies with the natural world, but fleshing these out in more Judeo-Christian terms, Lee seems to suggest that paradise is the state of peace or harmony that exists when the laws of nature are discerned and respected. The heroes are those who obey objective natural laws, especially those pertaining to what is natural to humanity, and the villains are those who, in the words of Banner's father, David, aspire for the "power to go beyond God's boundaries." In the movie, Lee makes it clear that the villains are the metaphysical materialists, who reduce human nature and personal identity to mere bundles of matter and then treat them accordingly, while the heroes are those who recognize that human nature is an immaterial essence and treat it as such. In strict metaphysical terms, the vision of human nature and natural laws in *Hulk* is also at odds with most Chinese conceptions of human nature and natural laws, but I believe this is accidental to Lee's purpose in the film. Thus I argue that *Hulk* can be seen as a polemic against materialistic reductionism of human nature and ethics, and that this polemic takes place vis-à-vis the preferred vision of human nature and natural ethics that is, very roughly, Judeo-Christian.[2] Lee, of course, isn't himself a Jew or Christian, but Stan Lee, the creator of the Hulk, is Jewish with Christian sympathies, and it makes sense that, insofar as Ang Lee wanted to stay true to Stan Lee's vision, these conceptions of human nature and ethics would be apparent in the film.[3] Is Bruce Banner identical to the Hulk? If so, how? Can genetic engineering affect human nature? How does ethical behavior shape personal identity? Is all genetic modification of human nature unnatural? Here, I explore these questions, as well as other ethical ones having to do with human nature in *Hulk*.

Materialist Monsters

Hulk begins with David Banner,[4] Bruce Banner's father, working in his military lab on an experiment having to do with genetic improvement. We read notes like "Regeneration is immortality," which hints that David is a metaphysical materialist, who believes that man is nothing but a bundle of matter or a collection of accidental properties.[5] We infer this because if David believed that a human being is a rational soul, spirit, or person, which is an indivisible substance with essential properties (an essence), then he would very likely believe that human beings possess a kind of immortality already (one independent of bodily existence), and hence would not likely be so obsessed with genetic immortality.

But besides being a metaphysical materialist obsessed with bodily immortality, David is also—and not coincidentally, the movie seems to suggest—a bad man. When the military properly forbids him to experiment on human subjects, he defies them and experiments on himself. In addition to the immorality of disobeying a direct order for no good reason, David is a bad man because he fails, after having injected himself with an experimental drug, to take precautions to prevent his wife, Edith, from getting pregnant, ultimately resulting in her conceiving a child with altered DNA. (I take it that, all things being equal, it's immoral, and not genetic discrimination, for a person to intentionally try to conceive when the risk of the child having a serious defect is high.) Furthermore, when the military discovers that David experimented on himself, they shut him down, and in a fit of rage (take note), he kills Edith while trying to dispose of his experiment—his son, Bruce.

Later on, when David is finally released from prison, he kidnaps Betty Ross, Bruce's girlfriend, and expresses his extreme annoyance that she wants to "cure [Bruce], fix him." To David the materialist, social Darwinism, the ethics endorsing survival of the fittest, is most logical. Thus, he sees the powerful but out-of-control Hulk to be the true person, and Bruce to be "a weak little speck of human trash." In his Hulk state—internally, a state of foggy rationality—Bruce actually agrees, calling his normal state "a puny human." That David agrees with the fairly dull-witted Hulk is important because both largely act subhuman rather than superhuman, all the while imagining it to be the other way around. Thus, Ang Lee tellingly admits, "Sometimes I think the father is the real Hulk." That is, the materialist is the monster.

David's argument, then, assumes, in true materialistic fashion, that there is no natural, proper, essential, or designed pattern for how things—the world around him and his own person—should be, and so there is really no reason for him not to do as he pleases. And since what pleases him is to experiment on himself and his child, there is no reason for him not to do so; thus, he says, "It's the only path to the truth that gives men the power to go beyond God's boundaries!" David obviously doesn't believe in a literal God, but rather uses God as a metaphor for the notion of indivisible essences and the proper functioning of such. Moreover, because unchanging wholes and the proper functioning of such wholes have a normative or ethical dimension that forbids man from doing whatever he likes, David rails against this ethical dimension as well, speaking with admiration for "a hero of the kind that walked the earth long before the pale religions of civilization infected humanity's soul!" Savage, amoral "heroes" of the social Darwinist kind are what David the metaphysical materialist clamors for.

But David isn't the only metaphysical materialist monster in the movie. Major Glenn Talbot, a former solider now working in the private sector, is the other materialist in the movie, and—again not coincidentally—he is also the secondary villain. Talbot has a keen interest in the genetic experiments that Bruce and Betty are working on, but while Bruce and Betty want to use their experiments to find cures to benefit humanity, Talbot wants to privatize their research and use it for military purposes—ultimately, to make money. This is the first suggestion that he is a villain. He later becomes clearly so when he's not opposed to killing Bruce in order to get his sample of Hulk DNA: "I'm going to carve off a piece of the real you," he says. Talbot's social Darwinian ethics ("I'm stronger, so I can take what I like") suggests he's a metaphysical materialist because he appears willing to reduce Bruce/Hulk to his DNA (a part of his physical makeup), rather than seeing him as a rational soul, spirit, or indivisible essence with inherent personhood and inherent rights. Bruce/Hulk is matter to be exploited.

Soul and Body

Against the metaphysical materialists are those who respect God's boundaries of stable essences and natural laws. Bruce and Betty are the foremost proponents.

We know that Bruce was born with an altered genetic code that boosts his immune system. Thus, when his experiment with gamma-infused nanomeds (nanobots that help repair the body from the inside) goes wrong, he (risking his life to save his assistant's) miraculously survives. However, the experiment gone wrong further alters his biochemistry. Does Bruce's altered DNA mean that he is no longer himself?

To begin with, it's the metaphysical materialists—the villains in Lee's movie—who imagine that one's personal identity is one's DNA (on account of DNA being biochemistry, which is, in turn, matter). Against them the movie makes it clear that if a person were identical to his DNA, then any alternation to his DNA would imply the literal loss of self, which is implausible and certainly not true of our hero, Bruce.

To elaborate, consider gene therapy. We are all born with so-called junk DNA, much of which disposes us to an array of diseases, in particular cancer. If we were able to remove the junk DNA, or even fix the junk DNA (discover a drug to cure cancer), then we would, in fact, not be curing the same person, but creating a new one. The drug wouldn't save me but would in fact kill me and create a new man. Moreover, imagine that in the course of this treatment I suffered traumatic brain damage such that I lost many or most of my memories. If I am identical to my memories qua biochemistry (organized by my DNA), then in losing memories, I would, again, literally cease to be me. The improbability of this is expressed in our ordinary language—"I forgot something," not "I died." As we shall see, when Bruce's DNA is radically altered, not once but twice, he is still clearly shown to be himself.

True to the spirit of the early comics,[6] Ang Lee makes it no secret that although Bruce's body has undergone an alteration, it's still his body, and he is still himself. But what holds the unity of the body together through change, and what constitutes Bruce's personal identity? The answer to both of these questions is the human soul or spirit as roughly conceived in Judeo-Christian terms.

When Bruce becomes the Hulk, Betty, who knows Bruce "better than anyone," immediately recognizes the green monster to be Bruce vis-à-vis his eyes, the window to the soul. Or again, when Bruce as the Hulk later goes on a rampage, Betty tries to calm him down:

BRUCE: You found me.
BETTY: You weren't hard to find.
BRUCE: Yes, I was.

Betty could see, where others could not, the truth of the matter, namely, as she later explicitly says, that Bruce as the Hulk is "a human being." She can recognize the indivisible soul or spirit inside the green monster, and we, the audience, were meant to see this as well. In his director commentary, Lee says his obsession with CGI in the movie (including being the principal actor in the Hulk motion-capture suit) wasn't so much to make a spectacular smashfest, but rather was to unify that which was previously separated. This is to say that while in the comic books and TV shows the Hulk always looked radically different than Bruce, in *Hulk*, Lee intentionally tried to let Bruce's soul or spirit shine through the green body by mapping actor Eric Bana's eyes and facial features onto the CGI Hulk: "The challenge was could I make Bruce Banner and the Hulk one person, instead of like in the comics or TV series where there are two actors or two different entities."[7]

Lee's brilliant and unique effort to show the unity of Bruce through CGI is a strong metaphysical comment on the nature of the soul and spirit, and it is consistent with the general Judeo-Christian theme throughout—namely, that the human soul or spirit is best conceived as a substance with both essential and accidental properties.

Central to this is the notion that some essential properties in the human substance are nondegreed, meaning they are either 100 percent present or 100 percent not. The essential properties of "being human," "having the ultimate capacity for rationality," "having the ultimate capacity for language," and so on are such properties, and if these properties aren't present, then the substance isn't a human substance or soul.[8]

Of course, based on the behavior of Bruce as the Hulk, it might not seem as though the Hulk has all of these; indeed, he himself even spoke of "that mindless Hulk," and certainly, if taken literally, being mindless would disqualify the Hulk from being human. However, this language is rhetorical rather than metaphysical, and more importantly, this confusion stems from a misunderstanding between ultimate capacities and lower capacities.

The human person—in our case, Bruce—is a soul or spirit. This means, among other things, he can still be himself or a human person without a body (the ancient Chinese just as much as Jews and Christians talk about the possibility of such disembodied ghosts). Because Bruce's Hulk body, brain, and biochemistry are different from his human body, brain, and biochemistry, Bruce, as a soul, cannot (or at least not optimally) actualize his ultimate capacity for rationality, language, and free will in his Hulk body. His Hulk body, in other words, doesn't have the lower capacity that Bruce's human body does for rationality, language, and free will. Nevertheless, the absence or near absence of demonstrable, empirical evidence of these ultimate capacities doesn't mean that such ultimate capacities are absent. All it means is that the lower capacity—bodily capacity—isn't there.

To clarify, take a human fetus, an infant, a mentally handicapped person, or someone who is brain dead. If we have reason to believe that the soul or spirit is that which animates the body (we will discuss this in a moment), then the beating heart of a human fetus makes it extremely likely that a human soul or spirit is present. However, the fetus can't demonstrate its ultimate capacity for rationality, language, and so on because its lower capacities aren't developed yet; nevertheless, insofar as it's a human soul, it must necessarily possess these ultimate capacities in a nondegreed way. If we think the fetus is ensouled, then it is 100 percent human, not 40 percent or even 99 percent.[9] Ditto for the infant who can't demonstrate much or any rationality early on, the mentally handicapped person, and the brain-dead person. The same reason that Talbot is immoral for wanting to kill the Hulk (he does not consider the Hulk to be a human person) is the same reason it's likely immoral, all things being equal, to engage in abortion, infanticide, and eugenics.

In the course of this, I've assumed that the soul doesn't merely have a body in the same way that a captain has a ship.[10] Judaism and Christianity (and Chinese religion in its own way) have long insisted that the soul's connection to the body is more intimate than this, and this intimacy is what Lee tries to demonstrate through the soul-in-the-body CGI depiction of Bruce in the Hulk. The general idea is this: the soul is prior to the body, but it also gives rise to and guides the development of the body via the body's DNA. The ultimate capacity for the soul to develop or form a body with both general human features like arms and legs, and also specific ones like facial features and fingerprints, means that it's likely that even if the material the soul has to work with has been altered, the body's form will likely still both be humanoid and demonstrate unique features determined by the particular soul's "this-ness," or the essential property that differentiates one human soul from another. This is why Christianity depicts our new bodies in Heaven as ones still visibly similar to our current ones, why the Hebrews (and Chinese) tend to depict human ghosts as observably similar to their embodied forms, and why the Hulk is both humanoid and has Bruce's facial features.

In terms of controlling the formed body, the soul and its faculties direct the brain, which in turn controls the actions of the body. The soul affects the body, but crucially, the body also affects the soul. When DNA is altered, biochemistry changes, including the biochemistry in the brain (scientists have only recently discovered that our actions literally alter our brains). The result is that the soul can no longer move the body as it previously could, but must now move it in accordance with the new biological makeup (its different lower capacities). The body and soul are intimately related (as Jews, Christians, and the ancient Chinese insist), but not, as with the materialists, reducible to each other.

The Hulk Event

So what exactly is the Hulk? Lee has called *Hulk* a psychodrama,[11] which suggests that it's primarily about the *psyche* (soul) and its faculties, such as the conscious mind, the subconscious mind, free will, memory, and emotions. "The Hulk," of course, can refer to the large, green-skinned body that Bruce takes on, but in terms of psychology and metaphysics, it's best thought of as an event, such as a flash of lighting, the dropping of a ball, or an explosion of anger.

When Betty first encounters Bruce as the Hulk, she hypothesizes that Bruce's "anger is triggering the nanomeds," which in turn changes Bruce's human body into the Hulk. In other words, the Hulk is an event triggered by rage. But this is still just Hulk 101, and Lee would take us further.

Discussing his 2000 movie *Crouching Tiger, Hidden Dragon,* Lee says that "crouching tigers" and "hidden dragons" have to do with what lies below the surface, in particular the hidden "passions, emotions, desires—the dragons hidden inside all of us."[12] In his commentary on *Hulk,* Lee says that a common theme in all of his movies, and especially *Hulk,* is that of repression or what the human spirit holds back or hides; to say that we have dragons hidden inside all of us is, in more particular terms, a way of saying we all have a Hulk inside us.[13]

The Hulk event is triggered by anger, but not only anger flowing from conscious understanding (which we will return to), but also from subconscious—repressed—thoughts and memories, which Lee especially identifies with anxiety and fear (and in Bruce's case, the anxiety of having watched his father murder his mother). Thus, it's not accidental that our first glimpse of the Hulk is while Bruce is dreaming (an uncontrollable, often fear-inducing event), and that the Hulk is also first introduced to the external world by stepping from the shadows (often associated with fear of the unknown) into the light. Bruce describes the Hulk event as "being born or coming up for air" or as "a vivid dream . . . [of] rage, power and freedom," to which he adds, "And you know what scares me the most? When it happens, when it comes over me, when I totally lose control . . . I like it."

Bruce likes losing control vis-à-vis irrational fear, not because he knows that this is proper, right, or good, but because he likes the numbing feeling that rage brings about. Strong hate often overcomes strong fear.

But this is the perverse, subconscious Hulk event (known in the comics as the Devil Hulk[14]). The hate, anger, or rage that drowns out the anxiety brought on by repressed memories is no long-term or healthy solution to the problem. What is repressed must be brought to light and dealt with, or else all sorts of disorders, including multiple personality disorders, can result; unexercised ghosts hinder the natural harmony of the soul, body, and external world and so mustn't be allowed to manifest in irrational spurts of anger.[15] Unbridled power is what David Banner dreams of, but he is, we recall, the villain.

If fifty years of the incredible Hulk has taught us one thing, it's that the solution isn't to label all anger as bad, but rather to recognize that anger is good in and of itself, and must be naturally or properly manifested, which is to say manifested in the service of rational deliberation aimed at truth. This is no easy task for human beings, much less one with the Hulk's biochemistry; however, it can be done.[16] For example, when the three genetically altered dogs attack Betty, Bruce as the Hulk knows that he has a moral duty to protect the weak, and with this rational, moral consideration in mind, he summons his anger to fuel his body to proper action: to defend the weak. He does this again when he prevents the F-22 from crashing into a crowd of people on the Golden Gate Bridge. These acts are the actualization of the human essential property "to have the ultimate capacity to act morally," and so we can say that by acting morally and heroically, Bruce as the Hulk becomes a more actualized human person. The Hulk body might be harder to control than the human body, and so moral praise and blame will be a bit different[17]; however, the way they need to be controlled is the same: with the higher faculties in the soul controlling the lower ones.

A Parable about Paradise

I've said that Bruce and Betty are those who respect God's boundaries of stable essences and natural laws, while metaphysical materialists like David Banner and Glenn Talbot are those who don't. I've argued that Bruce and Betty correctly understand human nature to be a substance with a number of essential properties, and that giving these properties full consideration and acting in accordance with them (in particular, the ultimate capacity for morality) is natural and right. It's natural and right to consider the Hulk to be a person and to treat him as such, and it's unnatural and immoral not to; it's natural and right for Bruce to try and protect Betty from the dogs (especially because he himself was in no danger of dying), and it would be unnatural or immoral if he hadn't. The materialists are the real monsters in *Hulk* because they have an unnatural conception of human nature, and on the basis of this unnatural conception, they treat humans unnaturally.

What I've assumed throughout, however, is that part of what's natural to humans is to have the ultimate capacity not just for rational thought in general, but scientific thought in particular. It's natural for humans to want to study the physical world, and it's natural, all things being equal, for them to want to test, experiment, and discover. Our heroes, Bruce and Betty, understand this well.

Nevertheless, as with most aspects of life, there are tremendous complexities involved in this. For example, gene therapy, which has to do with restoring a broken original state, seems natural enough, but is it also natural to experiment with genes that aren't obviously broken? Even if we have some conception of what is natural to the human body, do we understand this perfectly? Could our bodies, at one time in the past—perhaps in Paradise— have been like the Hulk's in that they could grow larger and heal faster? Is our current "normal" really natural or is it still somewhat unnatural? What are the precise limits of human nature and the human body such that if crossed, they would no longer be themselves?

Lee's proposal in *Hulk* is that we lost Paradise by defying God's boundaries of real wholes and stable natural laws, which, although not always obvious to us, nevertheless need to be sought out as best we can. If we don't do this, we will be like Adam and Eve, who rebelled against God's natural laws, or like the metaphysical materialists in *Hulk* who manipulate human nature in ways that are unnatural and unjust, seeing Bruce as an animal to be experimented on, not a human person, a soul, with inherent rights, dignity, and worth beyond any animal. I conclude by saying, then, that Lee's *Hulk* is a parable about Paradise, an incredible film about human nature and the countless ethical issues pertaining to it.

Notes

1. Ang Lee, "Commentary on *Hulk*," in *Hulk* DVD, disc 1, dir. Ang Lee (Universal, 2003).

2. Judeo-Christian conceptions of human nature and ethics owe a great deal to Greek philosophy, in particular Aristotle, who was the first to speak philosophically about substances, properties, accidents, and essences.

3. Lee apparently loves Western superhero comics, especially Stan Lee's Marvel heroes. Thus, even in *The Ice Storm* (1997), Stan Lee's Fantastic Four play an important metaphorical role in the film, and in *Hulk,* Ang Lee says plainly, "I'm a translator of that comic world." Ang Lee, "The Unique Style of Editing *Hulk*," in *Hulk* DVD, disc 2. In the Marvel universe, the chain of being starts with a Judeo-Christian God, followed by a host of lesser entities, including the Living Tribunal, the primordials, the elders, sky fathers, lower gods, and so on. For more on this, see Adam Barkman, "'No Other Gods before Me': God, Ontology and Ethics in the *Avengers'* Universe," in *Avengers and Philosophy,* ed. Mark White (Oxford: Wiley, 2012).

4. In the comic books, it's Brian Banner, not David Banner.

5. For more on materialism, see Paul K. Moser and J. D. Trout, eds., *Contemporary Materialism: A Reader* (London: Routledge, 1995).

6. In *Incredible Hulk* #3 (1962), we are told that the Hulk "isn't really just an inhuman monster to be destroyed. . . . He's Bruce Banner!"

7. Ang Lee, "Evolution of the Hulk," in *Hulk* DVD, disc 2. In addition, we are told that Lee was chosen to the direct the movie because what comes through in all his films is humanity—here, the humanity of the Hulk.

8. The Judeo-Christian tradition typically asserts that essential to all human persons is the ultimate capacity for rationality, the ultimate capacity for free will, the ultimate capacity for emotions, and perhaps a few other essential properties. More controversially, many in this tradition would say that gender is an essential property to the human soul, such that human souls have either the essential property of being masculine or the essential property of being feminine. Even God, in terms of this tradition, is more properly understood to be "God" rather than "Goddess," and the Hebrew scriptures record instances of both masculine and feminine angels. Far from being a mere social construction, then, the gender of the soul would be formative in determining and hard-wiring (not always perfectly) the sex of the body. Nevertheless, my purpose here isn't to provide an exhaustive list of essential human properties, but rather to emphasize that to be human doesn't require demonstrating via the lower bodily capacities the soul's ultimate capacities.

9. This is why the Christian creeds declare Jesus fully God and fully man, because it's a logical contradiction for Jesus to be half man or possessing half a human soul. Of course, although this statement (like the one declaring God "three persons in one substance") isn't a logical contradiction, it also isn't very clear as to its meaning.

10. Issues of mind, body, soul, and personhood are discussed in the philosophy of mind and philosophy of the person. For more on these issues, see William Jaworski, *Philosophy of Mind: A Comprehensive Introduction* (Malden, Mass.: Wiley-Blackwell, 2011); the relevant chapters in Michael Loux and Dean Zimmerman, eds., *The Oxford Handbook of Metaphysics* (Oxford: Oxford University Press, 2003); and the entries on "Identity" and "Personal Identity" in the *Stanford Encyclopedia of Philosophy* (http://plato.stanford.edu/).

11. Ang Lee, "The Incredible Ang Lee," in *Hulk* DVD, disc 2.

12. Ang Lee et al., Crouching Tiger, Hidden Dragon: *A Portrait of the Ang Lee Film Including the Complete Screenplay* (New York: Newmarket, 2001), 76.

13. Lee, "Commentary on *Hulk*." This idea is also very true to the comic books, where in a dreamlike sequence, the Hulk tells Bruce, "Hulk is your own dark thoughts, your own anger, your rage!" *Incredible Hulk* #315 (1986).

14. Tom DeFalco and Matthew Manning, *Hulk: The Incredible Guide* (Toronto: DK, 2008), 129.

15. In *Incredible Hulk* #377 (1990), we are told that Bruce suffers from a multiple personality disorder, but in this very issue, his personality is unified through the work of the psychiatrist to the superheroes, Dr. Samson.

16. For the first 270 issues of *The Incredible Hulk*, Bruce as the Hulk couldn't rationally cause himself to become the Hulk, even though as the Hulk he had enough rational control to occasionally do heroic deeds; however, in *Incredible Hulk* #272 (June

1982), Bruce was eventually able to improve on this to the point where he could even rationally cause his transformation into the Hulk. Needless to say, this is the ideal way to control anger. However, when new writers took over *The Incredible Hulk,* this was undone to some extent.

17. "I should have known that Bruce Banner isn't always responsible for what the Hulk says and does," says Bruce's pal, Rick Jones. *Incredible Hulk* #6 (1963).

DISPLACEMENT, DECEPTION, AND DISORDER

Ang Lee's Discourse of Identity

Timothy M. Dale and Joseph J. Foy

Authentically Being Oneself

Ang Lee is a director known for adapting complex and sophisticated narratives into traditional film genres. Through a distinct filmmaking style, Lee's movies simultaneously take advantage of the tools available in each genre while also challenging, expanding, and transcending the genres themselves. This chapter examines three of Lee's notable contributions to genre films, *Crouching Tiger, Hidden Dragon* (2000, martial arts), *Hulk* (2003, superhero-action), and *Brokeback Mountain* (2005, western), arguing that Lee transcends the genres in part by presenting a consistent philosophy of identity across the films.[1] Specifically, through these movies a philosophy of identity emerges that is skeptical of the social implications of authentic identity. In each film, the primary characters hide significant parts of their identities, which leads them to a dislocation from society, and, when exposed, their identities produce disorder and tragedy. Lee's heroes are limited by context, the social and political world unable to incorporate their distinct ways of being. His depiction of identity is a pessimistic one, suggesting that authentic identity is ultimately irreconcilable in the social and political world.

In *Crouching Tiger, Hidden Dragon,* Lee's warrior character, Yu Shu Lien, gives familiar advice to Jen, another young female warrior, when she recommends, "Whatever path you take in life, be true to yourself." This advice echoes a common ethical refrain that personal integrity is an essential element of happiness and fulfillment. Being true to ourselves implies that acting in accordance with our true nature is the best way to interact with others and represent ourselves in the world. It also means that there is an authentic identity at the core of every human being, and that our obligation is to discover this identity and act according to its precepts. Being true to ourselves also requires trust that others will respect our authenticity.

There is a great deal of dissonance, however, between this understanding of individual identity and the realities of the social world. Moral norms exist that tell us which identities are acceptable and which are not, and revealing identities that are unacceptable in a society can lead to tragic consequences.[2] Authentically being oneself, then, is more complicated in practice than merely expressing the essence of one's identity to an accepting social world. The social world can be a hostile place for authenticity, and being oneself is usually a negotiation between self-understanding and the external pressures of social expectations.

Who Am I? I Am the Invincible Sword Goddess

In terms of Western philosophy, identity typically refers to the essence of the self that subsists over time and experiences the world. The modern notion of identity is rooted in an individualistic conception of the self and is captured by Descartes' observation, "I think, therefore I am." Here, the individual experience of reason is asserted as the core of identity. The condition of authenticity pushes a notion of identity even further to suggest that there is substance to the self that is a way of being all its own, and implies that the self exists in a binary where it must choose either to be authentic (what it is) or inauthentic (what it is not). This notion of choice at the center of the experience of identity is noted by Søren Kierkegaard (1813–1855), who believed that the individual subject always chooses for itself what it wants to be and how it interprets the world. The most important choices for the subject, according to Kierkegaard, are acts of faith (religious belief or romantic love) that connect the individual to the world. Authenticity in this view is thus a consequence of choice and results in a kind of relationship between the self and the world.[3]

Martin Heidegger (1889–1976) is another philosopher who offers a detailed depiction of authentic identity. In *Being and Time* (1927), Heidegger refers to the human being as *dasein,* the being with experience of itself that is located at a finite point in time. In contrast with Kierkegaard, Heidegger's *dasein* has an identity that is an articulation in the present of a connection between our history and where we choose to project ourselves into the future.

An authentic existence is one in which identity chooses things for itself, free from the determination of external forces. For Heidegger, however, authenticity is not a requirement for existence because humans are free beings who are also determined and limited in a world of others. Identity thus constantly slips between inauthentic and authentic ways of being.[4]

Jean-Paul Sartre (1905–1980), influenced by Kierkegaard and Heidegger, proposes that an authentic identity is that which chooses things for itself.[5] According to Sartre, identity means that an individual creates a framework for understanding the world through her own actions. The ultimate freedom characterizing the human experience is one in which every choice is an expression of identity. Inauthentic actions involve making excuses, or blaming choices on external pressures or moral systems. Sartre also notices, however, that the expression of authentic identity will always be limited because we do not ultimately have control over the world or others within it. Thus, Sartre describes the fundamental human experience as one of nausea and anguish, having to make choices in a world where the pressure of every choice creates morality but ultimately can have no effect on others.

Kierkegaard, Heidegger, and Sartre each provide views of the authentic as having a complex relationship between given identities, individual choice, and the social world. As a filmmaker, however, Ang Lee never offers a sophisticated or coherent view as to how one comes to possess an authentic identity, or what such an identity entails. His movies simply take identity as a given—often depicted as an internal truth about one's self that has been hidden, or a desire that goes unsought or unfulfilled—but do not elucidate how one comes to possess such an identity or how to distinguish between the authentic and the inauthentic. Lee's narratives seem to presume, although they do not elaborate on, an existentialist view of identity, reflecting the ideas of Kierkegaard, Heidegger, and Sartre, as evidenced in the analyses of the films that follow.

Although there is not an internally consistent account of what is authentic, what Lee considers to be inauthentic behavior coincides most strongly with the Sartrean deception that hides the true self or desires from an intolerant society. As illustrated by his central protagonists, Lee suggests that the hidden self earns scorn or vilification if it is exposed. Whether those are desires to break with traditional norms and assumptions ascribed to gender or racial identity, sexual desires that are deemed as deviant or abnormal, or a host of other possibilities, these urges are suppressed and hidden from the ever-present surveillance of society. And, following Sartre, the hiding of the true self from the world creates in Lee's characters nausea and anguish. Rather than focusing on the distinction about the authentic or inauthentic self, however, Lee chooses to focus on the suffering of individuals who are trying to negotiate between social acceptance and their genuine selves.

Adding to the identity philosophical account of authenticity, Lee addresses the disruption and destruction that occur when an individual presents an authentic identity to society that does not conform to established norms. Lee's discourse on identity calls to mind the philosophical criticisms of postmodern society by French social theorist Michel Foucault (1926–1984). In *Discipline and Punish* (1975), Foucault argues that society eliminates free will and genuine action on the part of citizens through the establishment of collective norms and values that are socially and politically enforced in order to categorize and control individuals.[6] The social and cultural institutions that establish normativity effectively shape the identity of the masses into conformity with a prescribed social order. When one steps outside of this normalized prescription for behavior, one is classified as deviant, and society moves to correct that behavior. Such deviance is either met with isolation from society (for example, incarceration within a prison system designed to maximize surveillance and impose rigid discipline in order to "rehabilitate" the offender), or destruction through various forms of diagnosis and treatment of that behavior through psychology and medicine.[7] Therefore, the presentation of behaviors that have been socially classified as deviant or dangerous creates a form of disorder that can only be rectified through displacement of the individual or by destruction of the authentic self.

Like the writings of Foucault, Ang Lee's films frequently highlight the tension between identity and social normativity. His protagonists are often forced to hide their identities in the face of antagonistic external pressures. These same protagonists are also motivated by a desire to explore and express their identities, however, and the story lines of the films depict the struggles and suffering (the Sartrean angst) that result from these tensions surrounding authenticity. In particular, Lee's films *Crouching Tiger, Hidden Dragon, Hulk,* and *Brokeback Mountain* portray a dislocation of their main characters, the deception that these characters' identities require, and the disorder that results from the exposure of their identities. In each of these films a central deception involving true identity forces the main character or characters into exile, displacing and alienating them from society. The hostility this generates between characters forces further fragmentation and conflict, and each of the films ends in the annihilation of a character whose authenticity was ultimately irreconcilable with the moral order of the world in which he or she lived.

No Action without Reaction . . . No Desire without Restraint

The visually impressive martial arts film *Crouching Tiger, Hidden Dragon* is concerned with identity at many levels. The title of the film itself is a reference to a Chinese proverb, *"Cáng lóng wò hǔ"* (hidden dragon, crouching tiger), which expresses a caution to not ignore that which lies beneath the surface. The title is appropriate because all of the characters in the film have had to hide their identity or defer their emotions toward each other as a result of external social pressures—they are denied, or rather deny themselves, the existential possibility of identity choice. The multilayered story produces a narrative in which Lee explores struggles with gender identity, individual relationships, and cultural authenticity. The film's stunning visuals and heroic fight scenes provide the backdrop for painful stories about characters who are unable to exist as their complete selves or achieve their heartfelt destiny.[8]

The story for the film is borrowed from a five-volume novel written by Wang Du Lu set in the nineteenth-century Qing dynasty. At the center of the story are friends Li Mu Bai (Chow Yun-Fat) and Yu Shu Lien (Michelle Yeoh), aging expert warriors who have never dared pursue their love for each other. Li is the owner of a powerful sword called the Green Destiny, which was given to him by his master. At the end of his career, Li decides that he no longer should have the sword, and he gives it to Yu with the request that she give it to their friend Sir Te (Sihung Lung). The sword is stolen, however, and is traced to the compound of an aristocratic young woman named Jen Yu (Ziyi Zhang). Li and Yu soon discover not only that Jen's servant is the elusive villain, Jade Fox (Pei-pei Cheng), who killed Li Mu Bai's master many years before, but also that Jen has become a skilled warrior herself by studying the Wudang warrior manual. Although she lives a life of privilege, Jen is unhappy with her arranged marriage, and she longs for a life of adventure and Sartrean self-creation. Her longing is connected to a secret love she has for the desert thief, Lo (Chen Chang). When Lo returns for Jen, she refuses him, but she also runs away from her marriage to steal the Green Destiny again. This time, pursued by Li, Yu, and Jade Fox, Jen battles Yu and Li before finally being captured by Jade Fox. In the final fight to free Jen, Jade Fox is killed and Li is mortally wounded.

Gender roles and identity are at the center of this story. Jen does not want the life that has been chosen for her as the daughter of an aristocrat, and the way she empowers herself is to wear a disguise and use her self-taught warrior skills as a thief. We learn that her servant, Jade Fox, became a villain and killed Li Mu Bai's master because she was rejected for being a woman by the Wudang. Thus, the violence in the film comes about as a reaction to the limits that social norms have placed on these women characters.[9] Yu is also unable to have what she ultimately desires—a relationship with Li. Freedom and power are unavailable to the women in the film, and Jen's apparent suicide at the end of the film represents the only way to escape from the limitations imposed by society and the disorder caused by the violent reaction to it.[10]

In addition to these restrictions of gender identity, all feelings of love go unfulfilled for each of the characters in the film. As the central relationships in the film, neither Li Mu Bai and Yu Shu Lien nor Jen and Lo are able to pursue an authentic relationship because of the external limitations of codes of honor and social class. The existential pursuit of true—authentic—feelings is impossible in this context, and the only possibilities for the self in relation to others are dependence, restraint, and self-surrender. As Li explains to Jen: "No growth without assistance. No action without reaction. No desire without restraint. Now give yourself up and find yourself again." Li has only known a life of restraint, and while he has achieved a high level within his warrior class, he is ultimately unable to attain the happiness he would find in a relationship with Yu Shu Lien. Jen finds herself in a similar struggle in her love for Lo. For Jen, however, her violent reaction to the limits placed on her identity cause her to seek self-destruction rather than fulfillment. Li Mu Bai reflects on this subversion of authentic human relationships when he declares to Yu, "Crouching tigers and hidden dragons are in the underworld . . . but so are human feelings."

Through *Crouching Tiger, Hidden Dragon,* as with other of Ang Lee's genre films, Lee is intentionally confronting us with a skeptical view of the relationship between individual identity and social obligation. This film uniquely allows Lee to do this while also exploring tensions between the Chinese and American cultures that intersect in the martial arts genre. The film itself is a product of Lee's divided cultural identity.[11] The tension between cultures is unresolved, however, just as the tension between individual and society is unresolved in the narrative. Lee does not provide a way to escape from the limits of tradition except through death, and the individual is essentially trapped between social structures and individual desires. The destruction of the heroes in the film reveals Lee's pessimism and shows that his story is more about the tension than it is about the resolution.[12] As Lee himself described the film, "My reflection on the material is my creative output into the film. That's my authorship. Unless I feel emotionally and personally in touch with the material, I don't want to do it. I use the language of genre to tell something that's internal; I'm making a martial-arts picture, but what I'm really dealing with is the hidden dragon."[13]

You Wouldn't Like Me When I'm Angry

Coming off the major box office and critical success of *Crouching Tiger, Hidden Dragon,* Lee was given the opportunity to direct his first big-budget film, *Hulk.* Despite the high expectations surrounding the film, *Hulk* was met with mixed reviews, with critics both praising and attacking Lee for his intellectual foray into the deep psychology of Dr. Bruce Banner (Eric Bana) and his alter ego, the Hulk. Lee, who envisioned the Hulk as a "very sad monster, and a superhero at the same time," used the film as an opportunity to further explore the relationship between identity and society.[14] In doing so, he created a transcendent depiction of the Hulk that parted from traditional formulas applied to the superhero and action genres.[15]

The attempt to provide a rich insight into Banner reveals much about Lee's use of film to provide commentary about identity in contemporary society. Banner is born with a mutated DNA structure that was passed onto him by his father, a fact kept from him throughout his childhood. Bruce's father, David (Paul Kersey and Nick Nolte), had been performing experiments on himself in an attempt to improve the human genome. When his experiments are shut down by military officer Thaddeus Ross (Todd Tesen and Sam Elliot), David Banner goes berserk, destroying his lab and accidentally killing his wife (Cara Buono) in the process. With his mother dead and his father in a mental institution, a very young Bruce is sent to a foster care facility and is later adopted. He retains no conscious memories of what happened to his biological parents; he only has flashes of his former life in dreams.

The film jumps to a newly graduated Banner working as a researcher in the same field as his father, developing nanomeds that would give human beings incredible regenerative abilities. He quickly becomes the focus of attention by Ross, as well as Ross's estranged daughter, Betty (Jennifer Connelly), Major Glenn Talbot (Josh Lucas), and his father, who has covertly made his way back into Bruce's life. All of these principals, with the exception of Betty, who truly cares for Bruce for the person he is and not for some other instrumental or suspicious reason, begin to try and force their own separate agendas onto Bruce. David Banner wants to use Bruce to continue his now perverse genetic experiments, Talbot wants to use the nanomeds to further the interests of the military-industrial complex, and Ross becomes extremely distrustful of Bruce's true nature, hoping to divert him from ending up like his father. Only Betty establishes what might be considered an authentic relationship with Bruce, accepting him for all that he is, which is why she is able to connect with him and help him to control his rage and transformations.

It is through the relationships that Bruce experiences that we gain insight into Ang Lee's perspectives on the individual and identity within society. Bruce Banner is, from his very birth, a unique individual. At first, society seeks to keep him from knowing his own origins, causing him to unknowingly suppress that part of himself. He is unwittingly cut off from his own history, which someone like Heidegger would suggest is essential to formulating a true sense of what we wish to project of ourselves into the future, and is therefore unaware of what his authentic self might entail. When he graduates and begins pursuing the career, love, and life he believes he has chosen for himself, though by all accounts it is a life that fully conforms with the dominant social narrative in which he has been socialized without knowing his own past or self, social forces continue to collude to dislocate him from the autonomous selection of his own unique nature. This causes an intense rage to build within him—the Sartrean angst that precedes critical self-reflection in an attempt to discover one's authentic self. His rage stimulates his mutated DNA, resulting in the creation of the Hulk, whose strength and wrath causes disruption and destruction.

As opposed to the other forces working to mold Bruce's identity into conformity with society, Betty, out of her pure love for Bruce, wants to help him negotiate between his authentic nature and social order. However, in the end, the only way to maintain society and allow Banner to be who he truly is comes from dislocating him from society, removing him to an isolated area of the Amazon rain forest. Society cannot incorporate Bruce's authentic nature because of its disruptive nature, and so Banner and the Hulk are banished.

Because it is a film based on an iconic comic book hero, it is easy to make the mistaken assumption that Lee, as a director, is not responsible for communicating a philosophy as much as he is merely giving a cinematic re-creation of someone else's vision. However, such a perspective overlooks the intentional way that Lee sought to transform the original conception of the Hulk into a philosophical reflection on identity in his film.[16] After all, it was Lee who, disappointed with the script he received, brought James Schamus onto the project to rework the story and various characters. Schamus, who coproduced and cowrote with Lee on many other film projects, including *Crouching Tiger, Hidden Dragon*, helped Lee rework Hulk's origin story into an epic narrative that explores the dynamics of the relationship between fathers and sons. However, as a more expansive vision, this relationship became expressed as the paternalistic nature of the forces of society working to either force suppression or conformity of identity or isolate and marginalize it to the fringe. Rather than merely fulfilling the original vision of the Stan Lee and Jack Kirby comic books, Ang Lee's *Hulk* transcends the cinematic genre and provides a philosophical expression about society's treatment of authentic expressions of the self.

I Can't Stand Being Like This No More, Jack

No film propelled Ang Lee into the upper echelon of filmmaking quite like *Brokeback Mountain*, which provides an interesting recasting of the traditional western to comment on the tension between authenticity and society. *Brokeback Mountain*, set in Wyoming, uses the incredible cinematography provided by naturalist shots of the American West and the western motif as the setting of the homosexual relationship between Jack Twist (Jake Gyllenhaal) and Ennis Del Mar (Heath Ledger). The setting of the film works to demonstrate the oppressive nature of an intolerant society when juxtaposed against the liberating backdrop of the frontier. As Jack and Ennis try to escape society and flee into the frontier to find temporary interludes of authentic expression, Ang Lee's western exposes a larger dismantling of that personal sphere of individual identity by the oppressive forces of society.[17]

Brokeback Mountain, a film adapted from a novella by Annie Proulx (1997, 1999), begins in the early 1960s with Twist and Del Mar meeting when they are hired to tend sheep for a rancher, Joe Aguirre (Randy Quaid). Their isolation develops into a friendship over the course of the summer. One night, as Ennis lies shivering outside, Jack invites him to share the tent and keep warm. As they lie down together, Jack reaches under the blanket to caress Ennis, who wakes with a start. At first Ennis holds Jack back, but he quickly surrenders to his desire, pushing Jack to the ground and having sex with him for the first time. This scene is both intense and quick, and the sexual encounter aggressive and rough. The next day Ennis warns Jack that what happened was a one-time thing, but their feelings for one another are strong. When the two are to leave Brokeback Mountain and return to society, what starts as a playful good-bye turns aggressive, with Jack bloodying Ennis's nose and Ennis putting Jack down with a hard blow to the head. The tension they feel about having to leave the frontier isolation and reenter society manifests in destructive behavior; Jack and Ennis have no other outlet for the conflict that their feelings for each other poses when set against the prevailing social and cultural expectations.

Despite their love for one another, Ennis and Jack attempt to suppress their authentic identities by conforming to social expectation. They both get married. Ennis and his wife, Alma (Michelle Williams), have children. Jack goes to work for his wife Lureen's (Anne Hathaway) father. The only time they are able to be who they truly are comes once a year, when they seek isolation away from the intrusion of society with an annual fishing trip in which they are able to express their love for one another. Jack tries to convince Ennis that they could permanently escape society by establishing a life together on a small plot the Twist family owns. However, Ennis recalls a story his dad told him in his youth about a man who was tortured and beaten to death after a group of men began to suspect he was gay. Unable to suppress or change his homosexuality, society destroyed the man so that it could maintain its conventions and expectations without challenge.

Like the writings of Foucault suggest, this identification and categorization of deviance by society led to a situation in which one is unable to escape from constant surveillance and the corrective measures of society. In this case, the man in Ennis's father's story was monitored by society and was beaten to death for stepping out of conformity in pursuit of his authentic identity. Moreover, the relaying of that story from father to son created in Ennis a perpetual paranoia that he is always being watched, that he will be discovered for his true feelings. He forces his life and actions to conform to the dominant social order and normative expectations out of fear that he too will meet with such a fate.

Jack and Ennis attempt to continue deceiving others by suppressing their authentic selves when in society, only to remove themselves temporarily for their yearly fishing trips to express the true feelings that lie buried and hidden. Jack escapes to Mexico in order to have encounters with men there before returning back to his inauthentic life with Lureen. Ennis tries to be the husband and father he is expected to be, but his feelings often surface in moments of rage and aggression, like the evening he brutally beats two bikers who make lewd comments about his sex life with his wife during a community fireworks display. Eventually, Ennis's marriage falls apart after he is unable to reconcile with Alma after she discovers his and Jack's secret relationship. Jack carries on a discreet affair with another married man, Randall Malone (David Harbour), in an attempt to create a life parallel to the one he wanted with Ennis. Neither is satisfied. Both are displaced from themselves and their true, authentic identities.

The pain both Jack and Ennis experience from not being able to be authentic weighs heavily on them. Jack, after admitting to his rendezvous in Mexico to Ennis, who then threatens Jack, blames Ennis's unwillingness to completely displace themselves from society for their ongoing pain. Jack yells, "We coulda had a good life together. A fuckin' real good life. Had us a place of our own. But you didn't want it, Ennis. So what we got now is Brokeback Mountain. Everything is built on that. That's all we got, boy." Ennis, who has always been terrified of how society would react to their relationship, reveals his Sartrean anguish as he painfully summarizes his own suffering that comes in the simultaneous disconnection from himself and displacement from society: "It's 'cause of you, Jack, that I'm like this. I'm nothin.' I'm nowhere."

When he gets a postcard he sent to Jack back with a note that Jack is dead, Ennis calls Lureen to find out what happened. She detachedly tells Ennis a story about how Jack was killed while trying to pump up a tire on his truck; it exploded, and the rim hit him in the face. By the time someone found him, he had drowned in his own blood. However, as she relates the story, it is juxtaposed with a Foucauldian turn; Ennis has flashes of Jack being attacked by a group of men who identified Jack as being gay, destroying that authenticity by beating him to death.[18] Lureen continues to recite what seems like a memorized narrative that she has given to several people as a last act of deception to meet with social expectations and values. The penultimate conclusion of the movie has Ennis visiting Jack's parents as an old buddy paying his respects after Jack's death. There he finds the bloodied blue shirt Jack wore on the last day they were at Brokeback Mountain together when they first fell in love. Jack's mother lets Ennis keep the shirt, which he hangs in his closet in the small place where he lives alone.

Lureen and Jack's mother both seem to know that there is more to Jack and Ennis's relationship than a mere friendship from herding sheep together and going fishing. However, no one is willing to confront or speak about what that relationship might have been or the pain they all share from Jack's death. Jack, unable to fully suppress his authentic nature, is destroyed. Ennis, however, is forced to continue his life of deception and dislocation from his own authentic self, continuing to try and be a good and loving father, all the while longing in silence and in secret for his lost friend and lover.

I Wish I Knew How to Quit You

When Jack utters those now immortal words to Ennis—"I wish I knew how to quit you"—he expresses the deep-rooted philosophical perspective of Ang Lee's artistry as it relates to the tensions created between authenticity and social conformity. It would be so much easier if individuals could just cut themselves off from their authentic feelings so as to more easily fit into social norms and conventions—less painful and less harmful. Yet our authentic natures are not so easily governable or displaced. It is a process that is equally, if not more, painful, and we are left with trying to negotiate who we are in relation to what society expects.

Social order creates an oppressive set of expectations that ultimately forces the individual to either conform through suppression and deception, or be cut off through dislocation from community. The disruption of the authentic in relation to social convention becomes something that society does not otherwise tolerate, and so the individual is suppressed, isolated, or destroyed. Lee's films force us to examine the tensions that exist in a liberal society, one in which the rights of the individual are to be protected and preserved against collective repression, and communities of people who construct normativity that works against the authentic expression of the individual that liberalism seeks to allow. Ultimately, we are called to reconsider our notions of justice and authenticity as it relates to social arrangements and personal identity. Lee's films offer a bleak conclusion in which disorder is only overcome through displacement or destruction of the authentic.

Ang Lee does not solve the problem of disorder in his films; nor does he provide a way to rescue authentic identity. This is because he is not making films about a possible future utopia. Instead, he is presenting narratives about our world and the people who are suffering within it. In *Crouching Tiger, Hidden Dragon, Hulk,* and *Brokeback Mountain,* Lee interprets genres that are already about displacement, deception, and disorder, but he brings these features of the genres to the fore, consistently telling us that heroes do not emerge intact from these contexts. Rather, his films intend to show us the hidden dragon. These films offer a social commentary on our world and the difficulty involved in being authentic within it. Lee expects us to come away from these movies with an experience of the threat that social norms and structures pose to individual identity. Lee's discourses of identity leave us with a question as to whether our society can peacefully and honestly tolerate a range of identities and personal relationships.

Notes

1. The martial arts genre includes the common motif of a hero who is isolated or displaced, and who often takes on a disguise while fighting against the forces of oppression. The superhero action film similarly includes a prototypical hero who hides a true identity, and who is isolated to some degree from the rest of society. Isolation and displacement are also common to the genre of the western, where the frontier serves as a liberating location for a hero with a complicated past. Common to these genres, and unlike Lee's appropriations, the heroes are ultimately successful at combating the evil they find in the world, and they are able to overcome the dislocation and disorder through heroically individualistic actions.

2. Amartya Sen criticizes the social expectations and performance of single-dimensional identity as the root of violence in the modern world. He describes the "solitarist" view of identity as one in which individuals are exclusively understood as belonging to a single group. Sen argues that individuals are a collection of identities, and cruelty and brutality exist when individuals or societies expect identity to be understood in isolation. See Amartya Sen, *Identity and Violence: The Illusion of Destiny* (New York: Norton, 2006).

3. Søren Kierkegaard, *Concluding Unscientific Postscript,* trans. David F. Swenson and Walter Lowrie (Princeton, N.J.: Princeton University Press, 1971); and Søren Kierkegaard, *Fear and Trembling,* trans. Howard V. Hong and Edna H. Hong (Princeton, N.J.: Princeton University Press, 1983).

4. Marin Heidegger, *Being and Time,* trans. John Macquarrie and Edward Robinson (London: Blackwell, 1962), 150–157.

5. Jean-Paul Sartre, "Existentialism Is a Humanism," trans. Philip Maret, in *Existentialism from Dostoevsky to Sartre,* ed. Walter Kaufmann (New York: New American Library, 1956), 345–368.

6. Michel Foucault, *Discipline and Punish: The Birth of the Prison,* trans. Alan Sheridan (New York: Pantheon Books, 1977).

7. For more on Foucault's views on social classification and mechanisms of enforcing conformity, see Michel Foucault, *Madness and Civilization,* trans. Richard Howard (New York: Random House, 1965); Michel Foucault, *The Order of Things: An Archaeology of the Human Sciences,* trans. Alan Sherdan-Smith (New York: Random House, 1970); and Michel Foucault, *The History of Sexuality, Volume 1: An Introduction,* trans. Robert Hurley (New York: Random House, 1978).

8. Symbolizing the film's elusive and tragic vision of fate is the sword, the Green Destiny, which is constantly being stolen and changing hands. As desirable as it is, it only brings tragedy to its possessor. As Li Mu Bai describes it, "Too many men have died at its edge. It may look pure, but only because blood washes so easily from its blade."

9. For further discussion of the feminist messages in the film, see Kenneth Chan, "The Global Return of the Wu Xia Pian (Chinese Sword-Fighting Movie): Ang Lee's *Crouching Tiger, Hidden Dragon,*" *Cinema Journal Volume* 43, no. 4 (2004): 3–17.

10. The authentic desires of all of the female characters are determined by society to be illegitimate, and there is ultimately no peaceful or plausible way to assert these desires. See Rong Cai, "Gender Imaginations in *Crouching Tiger, Hidden Dragon* and the Wuxia World," *Positions: East Asia Cultures Critique* 13, no. 2 (2005): 441–471.

11. Christina Klein, "*Crouching Tiger, Hidden Dragon:* A Diasporic Reading," *Cinema Journal* 43, no. 4 (2004): 18–42.

12. Kenneth Chan argues that Lee's critique of patriarchy and traditional Chinese culture is inflicted and incomplete because he does not offer an overall alternative to cultural centrism and patriarchal hegemony. See Chan, "Global Return," 3–17.

13. Philip Kemp, "Stealth and Duty," *Sight and Sound,* December 2000 (http://www.bfi.org.uk).

14. Andy Seiler, "Ang Lee Gets inside Hulk's Head," *USA Today,* April 13, 2001 (http://www.usatoday.com).

15. It is worth noting that the break from expectations often applied to big-budget action movies is, at least in part, an explanation for the mixed reception of the film. Although notable critics like Paul Travers at *Rolling Stone* praised the action sequences and effects, criticizing the length and psychodrama surrounding Banner and the Hulk, others, like Roger Ebert, found the personal identity aspects of the film a welcome and refreshing take on the blockbuster superhero genre. Lee's efforts to create a transcendent film are reflected in these countervailing critiques.

16. In an interview with a reporter, Lee claims that he wanted to use *Hulk,* a big-budget action film, to create a modern myth narrative that incorporated elements from King Kong, Faust, Frankenstein, and Greek mythology. Scott B., "An Interview with Ang Lee," *IGN Movies,* June 17, 2003 (http://uk.movies.ign.com).

17. This argument was original conceived in Joseph J. Foy, "Tuning in to Democratic Dissent: Oppositional Messaging in Popular Culture," in *Homer Simpson Marches on Washington: Dissent through American Popular Culture,* ed. Timothy M. Dale and Joseph J. Foy (Lexington: University Press of Kentucky, 2010), 1–17.

18. The death of Jack Twist mixed with the Wyoming backdrop evokes images of the brutal beating death of Matthew Shepard, a gay college student, in Laramie, Wyoming. Shepard was taken from a bar by two men and driven into the countryside, where he was severely beaten and his shoes and wallet taken. He was then hung on a snow fence and left for dead. By the time he was spotted by motorcyclists in the early morning (they said they initially thought Shepard was a scarecrow) and rushed to a hospital, Shepard died as a result of the combination of the beating and exposure. See James Brook, "Witnesses Trace Brutal Killing of Gay Student," *New York Times*, November 21, 1998 (http://www.nytimes.com).

SUBVERTING HEROIC VIOLENCE

Ang Lee's *Taking Woodstock* and *Hulk* as Antiwar Narratives

David Zietsma

Culture of Violence

Popular culture is replete with images of violence. The use of violence is especially widespread on entertainment screens, as evidenced in video games such as *Call of Duty* (Activision, 2003) and *Assassin's Creed* (Ubisoft, 2007), television shows such as *The Shield* (2002–2008), *Oz* (1997–2003), and *Criminal Minds* (2005–present), and films such as *The Departed* (Martin Scorsese, 2006), *300* (Zack Snyder, 2006), and *Righteous Kill* (Jon Avnet, 2008). This culture of violence is enmeshed in a broader culture of nationalistic militarism that celebrates violence as a heroic means to moral ends. A multitude of war films depict American war experiences through images of heroic violence. Films with a range of perspectives on war such as *Saving Private Ryan* (Steven Spielberg, 1998), *First Blood* (Ted Kotcheff, 1982), *Platoon* (Oliver Stone, 1986), and *Windtalkers* (John Woo, 2002) are united in extolling violence as a noble avenue for overcoming evil and saving others.[1]

How is this hegemonic discourse of violence constructed? What individual and collective identities does such cinematic violence perform? How are images of violence connected to real-world violence? Slavoj Žižek has suggested that looking directly at real-world violence precludes understanding because "the overpowering horror of violent acts and empathy with the victims inexorably function as a lure which prevents us from thinking." Žižek's answer to this problem is to cast sideways glances, to look awry at real-world violence. In doing so, Žižek utilizes numerous cinematic representations of violence, such as *Fight Club* (David Fincher, 1999), *A Few Good Men* (Rob Reiner, 1992), and *North by Northwest* (Alfred Hitchcock,

1959). Although he does not probe these linkages, Žižek's sideways glance implies that the cultural horror of violence is enmeshed with an indulgence in cinematic depictions of heroic violence.[2]

This chapter looks doubly awry at real-world violence by exploring Ang Lee's *Hulk* (2003) and *Taking Woodstock* (2009) as films that subvert heroic violence. In other words, I do not survey heroic violence films discovered in looking awry at real-world violence, but instead attempt to look awry at such films and thereby catch a glimpse of their internal symbolic structures by exploring two films that negate heroic violence. I argue that Lee opens up the discursive space to critique the hegemonic narrative of heroic violence by creating two films that do not fit their anticipated narrative form. In turn, this narrative disturbance allows Lee to present a demasculinized and nonviolent heroism. Finally, by framing both films in the context of American wars, especially the Vietnam War, Lee's subversion of individual heroic violence emerges as a critique of American patriotic militarism.

In these two films, then, violence functions as an obstacle to self-realization, meaningful relationships, and a hopeful future. Lee philosophizes that nonviolence is a more human and more effective path to personal and national redemption. From the perspective of a philosophy of nonviolence, *Hulk* and *Taking Woodstock* fit philosopher Douglas Lackey's categorization of universal pacifism, which prohibits all violence in both its radical early Christian and later Gandhian forms. In this category of universal pacifism, all violence is ultimately destructive and therefore should be avoided. Lee's philosophy of nonviolence tends toward these radical Christian and Gandhian forms of universal pacifism, forms that might "transform the souls" of one's opponents and afford "personal redemption" through "nonviolent resistance to evil."[3]

Disturbing the Narrative Form

Both *Taking Woodstock* and *Hulk* defy the expected narrative form of their respective genres. At the outset, *Taking Woodstock* suggests a story about the sexual coming of age of Elliot Tiber (born Elliot Teichberg). A phone call early in the film from a boyfriend leaves Elliot feeling jaded. Will Elliot be able to overcome this rejection as well as his fear of what his parents and the community might think about his sexuality? Later, an obvious sexual attraction between Elliot and a muscular construction worker on the motel site results in a passionate kiss on the dance floor. But despite these teases, the film sets aside the sexual identity question, first by virtually abandoning the construction worker story line as a significant plotline, and second, by imaging Elliot's LSD experiment as rife with both homo- and heterosexual overtones toward which Elliot appears completely neutral and unaffected. Unlike sexual identity films such as *Philadelphia* (Jonathan Demme, 1993), no heterosexual characters rescue Elliot and propel him to self-liberation. Instead, *Taking Woodstock* depicts Elliot's supposed turmoil over his sexuality as immaterial to his ultimate heroism in propelling others on to liberation and self-realization.

Hulk anticipates a traditional heroic narrative of a confident male hero who embraces his supernatural gifts to accomplish feats of violence that overcome evil and rescue the innocent. As scholars such as Susan Jeffords and Christina Jarvis have demonstrated, American culture routinely imagines manhood through the image of muscular, agile, quick-thinking men who excel in combat against evil enemies.[4] This is, after all, the standard motif in films that feature comic book superheroes such as Batman, Superman, and Spider-Man, all of which participate in a cultural celebration of extraordinary masculinity. Within such films, heroes with superhuman abilities overcome evil villains through drawn-out fight scenes replete with superfluous destruction and special effects–enhanced brutality.[5] Such moral violence is simply a gift that must be exercised, a duty and responsibility to be carried out, whether the hero wants to or not. As Peter Parker puts it at the end of *Spider-Man* (Sam Raimi, 2002), "I will never forget these words: 'With great power comes great responsibility.' This is my gift, my curse."

In *Hulk*, the expected heroic violence of a comic book superhero story never really takes place. To ensure that this absence does not go unfelt, the film indicates that such a heroic story might take place. For example, before Bruce Banner leaves for college, Banner's foster mother tells him, "There's something inside you . . . so special. Some kind of greatness. I'm sure someday you're gonna share it with the whole world." But these hopes for greatness are never realized. Instead, the film offers a portrait of an introspective, emotional man who resists his gift of superhuman strength throughout the story. Indeed, the only time that Bruce seems to relish being the Hulk is during the military chase in the desert, when he discovers his ability to jump great distances; the Hulk embraces the feeling of the wind and sun on his face in what appears to be some sort of New Age existential moment, something only emphasized by the musical score. In a further rejection of the typical superhero story, the Hulk neither confronts nor battles the villain—David Banner, his father—until the final scenes, nearly two hours into the film. And when he finally does confront David Banner, the Hulk foregoes the use of his superhuman gifts, depriving the viewer of the much-anticipated heroic violence that will save innocent people from David Banner's evil desire for power.

In both films, split screens function as a filmic form that symbolizes the content, namely the undoing of anticipated narratives. Patterned after the split screens in the first Woodstock documentary in 1970, *Woodstock*, as well as after the panels in *The Incredible Hulk* comic books, Lee's split screens add little to the story line. In some cases, the split screens even jar and disorient, challenging the viewer to follow the story from two or more vantage points or even to follow two different scenes at the same time. The form here is the content: the expected uniform film action is disturbed and the viewer is disoriented, as is the case with the narratives themselves.

Regendering Heroism

By interrupting and even inverting expected narratives forms, *Taking Woodstock* and *Hulk* open up the discursive space for reimagining heroism. The most significant way that the two films do this is through the demasculinization of the heroic ideal. The typical gendering of heroism in Hollywood films, especially in films with war themes, rests on the image of a muscular, quick-thinking male warrior whose prowess in the use of destructive weaponry and physical combat saves the day from evil. Both comic book superhero films and war combat films imagine their heroes as physically strong and confident of their righteous cause. These genres are blended perfectly in the commercially successful *Captain America: The First Avenger* (Joe Johnston, 2011). Based on the Marvel comic that appeared a few months before World War II, the film tells the story of a small, sickly soldier who is transformed into a muscular hero, Captain America. With righteous violence, Captain America battles America's evil enemy, Nazi Germany. Amid an explosion of patriotic militaristic violence in which Captain America blows up buildings and knocks evil enemies around, the film's trailer reminds us that "heroes are made in America."[6]

Taking Woodstock inverts the standard masculine hero in a number of ways, including through Elliot's aging parents, who chase off two mobsters who are demanding a share of the motel's now booming business in exchange for protection. In this scene, Elliot's mother kicks the tough enforcer in the genitals while Elliot's arthritic, stooped, and half-deaf father takes a baseball bat to the other mobster's knees and then his fleeing car. The violence is comedic rather than bloody, but his parents return to the office to the applause of the crowd. "Dad, Ma, you're superheroes!" Elliot declares.

The film also inverts masculine heroism through the character of Vetty Von Vilma, a transgendered Korean War veteran. Vilma arrives at the motel offering "real security" protection to Elliot. Vilma tells Elliot that while he was a Marine Corps sergeant serving in Korea, he fell in love with another soldier who was killed: "I went out on patrol, found the Chinese pissant who did it, and broke his neck with my own hands." But upending this narrative of heroic violence, Vilma quickly smiles and says he made up the part about killing the Chinese soldier.

The most poignant regendering of heroism through Vilma comes in a late-night chat between Vilma and Elliot. Vilma, wrapped in a pink blanket, blond, curly hair hanging down, fingernails painted with bright red nail polish, is calmly confident despite Elliot's pessimism about his own father. Throughout the chat, Vilma displays all the hallmarks of the in-charge war combat hero. He talks about ascertaining the lay of the land and getting the bat to go out with Elliot's father on dawn patrol. The film also locates Vilma in the quintessential comic book superhero unmasking moment. As Vilma gets up to leave, Elliot asks him, "Does my dad know what you are?" Like a departing superhero still in caped disguise who is suddenly asked whether others know his true identity, Vilma turns back coolly and says, "I know what I am—that does make it easier for everyone else, doesn't it?" Vilma then turns and walks quietly away, the pink blanket wrapped around his shoulders flowing like the cape of a Superman or Batman.

Of course, the ultimate hero of *Taking Woodstock* is Elliot, who not only rescues the Woodstock festival from possible cancellation at the hands of conservative forces, but also rescues his parent's motel from bankruptcy and his parents from old-age lethargy. But Elliot is hardly the picture of confident, masculine strength. Most problematic for the heroic ideal is the fact that he is gay. In addition, after the festival planners dismiss Elliot's land as unusable, Elliot—unlike the soldier or superhero who in the heat of battle immediately sees the most advantageous geographic space—is confused and uncertain how to respond. Finally, as the planners are about to leave, he remembers Max Yasgur's dairy fields down the road. But when tense negotiations with Max threaten to collapse, Elliot is nervous and anxious; he awkwardly paces around, exhibiting none of the heroic cool necessary during battle.

Despite his obvious nonmasculine shortcomings, Elliot is still the hero, responsible for not only saving the festival, but also, and especially, for rescuing his parents from lethargy and boredom. His father is revivified, smiling and telling stories, and his mother, supplied with new energy, distributes blankets. The film clarifies Elliot's role in this rebirth through the ostensibly angry voice of Elliot's mother: "It's you who brought this!" His father repeats this conclusion at the end of the film, when he tells Elliot that he was a dying man, but "now I'm alive." When Elliot doesn't seem to understand, his father spells it out: "It's because of you. It's because of you I'm alive." Elliot is the hero.

Whereas *Taking Woodstock* offers three nonmasculine characters as heroes, *Hulk* demasculinizes heroism by taking the hypermasculine hero of the Hulk and stripping him of his heroism. As Betty Ross tells Bruce's father, David, "All you've given Bruce is fear. Fear of life." If Bruce is afraid, he is also emotionally unstable and unable to come to grips with his newfound physical powers.

The Hulk's heroic battle against superdogs begins the film's delinking of masculinity and heroism. The scene is set up for the heroic rescue of the damsel in distress: Betty is alone in the cabin; the dogs have been loosed to track her down and kill her; Bruce has transformed into the Hulk and is on his way to save Betty. Initially, the Hulk arrives just in time and begins deploying his overwhelming strength to bash the dogs against trees, the ground, and each other. In one instance, the Hulk even performs the archetypal superhero move of leaping out of the way to cause two enemies to crash into each other. The dogs also appear to be winning at one point—a crucial test for all superheroes. It seems that the scene will play out as expected: a few more heroic physical moves to eliminate the dogs, then a celebratory rescue of Betty. But soon things turn particularly brutal. Rather than using well-timed, clever, and artful violence, the Hulk begins ripping the dogs apart, shredding them to pieces like an out-of-control barbarian.

The resolution of the dog battle scene begins the process of negating the Hulk's heroism by painting him as emotional and unstable—hardly the masculine image of a calm, self-assured hero. At the end of the battle, the Hulk appears almost as defeated as the dogs. Foregoing a triumphant reunion with the damsel in distress, the film shows the Hulk wandering to a nearby pond, where he collapses. Peering at his image in the water, a single tear falls from his eye and disturbs his reflection. As Betty watches from the truck, the Hulk turns back into Bruce, a bowed and hurt wreck, who stumbles back to the truck only to collapse in Betty's lap. "He sent these dogs, didn't he," he tells Betty before crying out, "But I killed them!" With disturbing growling noises, he grabs Betty's throat in a choking gesture before being startled by what he is doing and falling back into despair. Betty must now help Bruce into the cabin and cover his shivering body in a blanket.

Hulk ultimately imagines its male protagonist as a despairing and tragic figure rather than as a physical warrior using his hypermasculine Hulk ability to rescue the innocent from evil. For example, near the end of the film, a shackled Bruce is overcome with hopelessness and misery when finally he faces his evil father. A dejected Bruce says he wished his father had killed him. He confesses that he can remember his mother, that he has seen her face, her brown hair. In a helpless, depressed outburst, he cries out, "It's my mother, and I don't even know her name." Bruce then breaks down sobbing while his father looks on, ashamed.

Instead of doing the rescuing, the masculine superhero is rescued by the female protagonist, Betty Ross. Betty persuades her father to halt the military's effort to kill the Hulk. At the end of a chase scene, the Hulk finds himself facing Betty while surrounded by the popular image of heroism in America: police, firefighters, and members of the military. In this scene, *Hulk* inverts the typical heroic narrative in which, after the violent defeat of evil, the hero embraces and kisses the female protagonist as her rescuer to the applause of the crowd. Instead, the Hulk approaches Betty and begins to shrink back into Bruce. With moist eyes and sagging shoulders, he finally reaches her and sinks weakly to his knees. "You found me," Bruce tells her feebly. She responds, "You weren't hard to find." Implying a deeper finding, one beyond physically locating something, Bruce replies, "Yes, I was." As they hug each other tightly, it is apparent that Bruce is not the rescuing hero but the one who needed rescuing.

Nonviolent Heroism

Having disturbed the narrative form and demasculinized heroism within that disturbance, Lee suggests that violence precludes the possibility of redeeming people, restoring relationships, and securing a hopeful future. Lee's philosophy of violence in these films counters Lackey's suggestion that absolute forms of pacifism are illogical because they are either based on improvable supernatural deities or are internally contradictory because sometimes not killing leads to more lives being lost (and therefore amounts to killing indirectly). Lackey argues that there are four types of pacifism: a pacifism that forbids killing but not violence; a universal pacifism that prohibits all violence as destructive; a private pacifism in which one's own choices must be nonviolent but one might commit violence on behalf of a larger community, such as the state; and an antiwar pacifism that maintains that self-defense is justified, but not war. In Lackey's view, the only form of pacifism that makes sense is an antiwar pacifism that allows for personal violence in self-defense. *Taking Woodstock* and *Hulk,* however, present a philosophy of nonviolence that fits into Lackey's second category of universal pacifism—one that prohibits all violence.[7]

In Lee's films, violence simply begets more violence, and therefore violence itself as a mode of operation is inherently destructive. This is certainly the case in *Hulk,* wherein the more the Hulk fights back against the military, the greater the destructive force the military brings to bear. From the opposite perspective, in *Taking Woodstock,* it is the nonviolence of both Elliot and the peace movement that brings true hope. In both of these films, nonviolence offers the path to redemption and restoration, a form of universal pacifism that, as Lackey notes, is rooted in the objectives of early Christian and Gandhian nonviolence. In *Taking Woodstock,* Elliot repeatedly refuses to resolve problems through violence. From the chamber of commerce to the bogus citations from the motel inspectors, Elliot's efforts center on nonviolent solutions. When the motel is vandalized with the slogan "Burn Faggot Jews" painted on the wall, Elliot dismisses his father's angry desire to break heads and burn the perpetrators in tar. Elliot simply paints over the offensive images. In another instance, when the townspeople show up determined to put a stop to the concert, Elliot just shrugs them off, seemingly accepting their nonacceptance.

Elliot's nonviolence allows his actions to produce heroic results. In the scene when the mobsters arrive, Elliot's nonviolence effectively allows his parents to claim responsibility for the motel once more—a motel they had previously neglected and let fall into disrepair. The film's only violence also takes place in this scene, where Elliot's parents fend off the mobsters with well-placed kicks and a swing of the baseball bat. Rather than an endorsement of violence, this scene opens up the specter of future violence. Won't the mobsters come back with more firepower? Won't they truly mean business next time? Elliot himself is ultimately heroic as a result of his refusal to engage in violence. This is perhaps best captured at the end of the film, when Elliot is visibly angry at discovering his mother's secret stash of tens

of thousands of dollars. Yet he refrains from either verbal or physical violence; no chairs are thrown, no abusive phrases are spoken. Instead, after
a brief look away, he turns back to his mother and helps her up from the
floor, restoring the relationship.

In *Hulk*, violence is an impediment to heroism because violence only
begets more violence. In the film's final scenes, we see the corruption of
David Banner; his only desire is ever greater power and immortality. Having achieved a mutation where he draws his power from everything around
him, David grows large and powerful by becoming one with the high-voltage
electrical line. In anger, Bruce transforms into the Hulk and shatters his
restraints. The viewer may be forgiven for anticipating that at long last a
violent destruction of evil by the superhero is about to ensue; this must be
the moment that the Hulk uses his muscular strength to defeat this threat
to humankind—to defeat this villain who wishes to make all nations "disappear in a flash."

Lee subverts the anticipated climax of *Hulk* to offer a narrative of nonviolent heroism. The two superhumans, the Hulk and David Banner, race
into the sky in an unclear, formless struggle. Odd lightning flashes make the
grappled forms of the Hulk and David clear in momentary static images that
deny the violent action typical of the climactic battle scene. It is difficult to
discern what is happening until the two combatants land near a small lake,
where David quickly takes on the essence of the surrounding rocks. Even
though the Hulk smashes the David Banner rock beast repeatedly, the rocky
background and David's effort to absorb the Hulk into his essence continue
to confuse the action. Finally, the Hulk throws David into the water, where
the fight is just as murky and indistinct.

Through the final battle, however, one thing is clear: the more the Hulk
fights, the stronger David Banner becomes because he absorbs the essence
of what he touches. "That's right, keep fighting," David screams at one
point: "The more you fight, the more of you I take." As the fighting absorbs
energy from the Hulk and from the lake, the water begins to freeze. David
tells a fading Hulk, "Struggle no more . . . and give me all of your power."
At this point, Lee avoids a last-minute heroic recovery by the Hulk. Rather,
the Hulk simply gives up. "You think you can live with it?" he cries back:
"Take it! Take it all!" The Hulk abandons the violent struggle. His power
surges into David with such force that David expands into a gigantic, self-
destructing force. Before he implodes, however, the military nukes the lake,
apparently destroying David Banner for good. Although the Hulk outlasts

David Banner's evil, if the Hulk is heroic, it is only by giving up on violence and sacrificing his power.

Framed in War

Taking Woodstock and *Hulk* link the subversion of individualistic heroic violence to America's collective war violence, particularly the U.S. intervention in Vietnam. The historical memory of the Vietnam War has been fertile ground for creating narratives revitalizing a hypermasculinized patriotic American militarism as well as for staging antiwar narratives.[8] By locating his films in Vietnam War memory, Lee's philosophy of nonviolence operates at both the individual and collective level, the collective in this case being the nation-state of the United States.

As one might expect, given that Woodstock was part of a broader cultural protest movement against U.S. intervention in Vietnam, the Vietnam War pervades *Taking Woodstock*'s backdrop. In the film's opening scenes, a television newscast alerts viewers that U.S. soldiers continue to die in Vietnam. The TV then brings attention to the Arab–Israeli conflict, a move that reminds viewers in the present of the troubled Middle East, including current U.S. military activities there.

Taking Woodstock brings the war home to White Lake in the form of Billy, a returned Vietnam War veteran. Initially Billy has difficulty readjusting to civilian life; his family appears unable to understand him, and he has difficulty relating to his former friends and neighbors. The film follows his slow regeneration through the peace-centered Woodstock experience orchestrated by Elliot. At other places, too, the film points out the profound difference between war and peace on the possibility of human relationships. War reduces and threatens to destroy relationships, whereas peace offers a vista of new experiences. This is made clear in a background scene where a worker being interviewed by the press indicates that he has a son in Vietnam and a son at Woodstock; he tells the news camera that he wishes that his son in Vietnam was also at Woodstock. This scene is a filmic double entendre; it is a part of the story of Elliot's efforts, but the use of an obvious camera and interview might also be read as Lee's attempt to alert the viewer that the film itself is meant as an interview of the historical moment of Woodstock and the Vietnam War: what does this moment have to say to our present moment with its wars in the Middle East? The obvious contrast between the potential death of one son and the active living of the other son makes the human costs of war instead of peace, both then and now, palpable to the viewer.

If *Taking Woodstock* is obviously framed in the Vietnam War experience, *Hulk* subtly links both the Vietnam War and the war on terror to a narrative of superhero violence. Throughout *Hulk,* Lee keeps in view a wartime context that goes beyond the comic book's military pursuit plot. Unlike the comic book, where the Hulk emerges from Bruce Banner's own scientific accident, the film traces Bruce's inner Hulk to the years 1966–1967, when more than a half million U.S. troops were in Vietnam at the height of the Vietnam War. A young David Banner works on the military base as part of a scientific effort to enhance the physical abilities of American troops. Even though he is forbidden to test on human subjects—the apparent moral boundary—he tests on himself, an example of Lee's theme that American military culture encourages a zealousness that it cannot contain. Rooted in the Vietnam War, the biological and intellectual child of this out-of-control military effort is the Hulk.

As Lee moves the viewer into the present, glimpses of the post-9/11 war on terror and the fear of terrorism emerge. To remind the viewer of terror alerts and pervasive threats, when a mature Bruce, now a scientist, enters the nuclear research lab at Berkley, two security personnel[9] exit the building as one says to the other, "But as far as I'm concerned, security oughta be beefed up a lot more. In a place like this you can't be too careful." Both war and the corporate business of war are placed front and center as part of the problem in the form of the military contractor, Atheon Corporation. Glen, the former military man turned Atheon big shot, shows up at the Berkley lab dreaming about "GIs embedded with technology that makes them instantly repairable on the battlefield in our sole possession. That's a hell of a business."

Lee also uses striking military imagery to invoke both the war on terror and the Vietnam War. The use of helicopters over desert space, the scene of the soldiers shadowing Bruce and Betty in the abandoned base town, and the tank pursuit in the dunes all evoke images of the wars in Iraq and Afghanistan. But Lee also throws in some distinctive Vietnam War imagery, such as low-flying helicopters whipping up green, marshy waters in pursuit of the Hulk. Furthermore, the entire military chase sequence is patterned on U.S. military entry and escalation in Vietnam. If Vietnam can be summarized as advisors, ground troops, helicopter cavalry, bombing, and withdrawal, then the pursuit of the Hulk begins with the special agents who tranquilize the Hulk, the ground troops in the form of tanks who initially pursue him, the helicopter chase that seeks to destroy him, and finally the bombing of the rock towers. Lee even uses a striking Vietnam War reference when the Hulk is hiding among the rock towers. In a nod to Ronald Reagan's infamous 1965 comment that the United States could use bombing to turn Vietnam into a parking lot, Betty's father, a general, gives the command to destroy the rock towers, and the Hulk with them, by saying, "Turn it into a parking lot."[10]

Antiwar Narratives

By undermining individualistic heroic violence as a moral good in the context of American wars, Lee philosophizes that American military violence is a barrier to national self-realization that also contradicts the nation's professed righteous use of violence.[11] War is the problem rather than the solution, and it is in the antithesis of war—peace and nonviolence—that the potential lies for personal and national redemption.

Taking Woodstock uses Elliot's demasculinized and nonviolent heroism as the representation of the heroism of the antiwar protest movement. The linkage between the two revolves around the character of Billy, a Vietnam veteran. As Elliot saves the festival, the motel, and ultimately his parents, he also facilitates the saving of Billy by the antiwar protestors. This is best symbolized through the Earthlight Players theater troupe. At a play set up as part of a town's involvement in the Woodstock festival, the narrator suddenly informs the audience that the theater actors "are the judges now. Your revelry must end, and your souls will be bared for all to see. Christ who died for you, but not for me! Now we are Christ! Our nakedness will reveal your own." At this point, the troupe disrobes to nakedness, and all the members chant, "Indecent legions of decency! Fascist pornographers! Fascist pornographers! Racist warmongers! Racist warmongers! Republican cocksuckers! Republican cocksuckers!"

What is happening here? Through the Earthlight Players, the antiwar movement declares its own heroism in opposition to the heroism claimed for the war effort. The actors' easy nakedness represents the absence of both shame and gender preoccupation. At the same time, it shames the audience because as supporters of the war, the audience members wear the mask of humanity (symbolized through their decent clothing) but in reality are indecent legions because of their inability to understand the true humanity (symbolized by nakedness) of American soldiers and the Vietnamese people. In this sense, the supporters of the war are not actually bringing salvation anywhere (they are not Christ), although they proclaim to be fighting for just that. By pointing out the truth of the war—racist, undemocratic, and politically homosexual—the antiwar movement offers the townspeople a path to salvation (symbolized through the claim of being Christ). In trying to end an inhuman violence in Southeast Asia, less than 2,000 kilometers from where Lee was born, the antiwar movement represents a heroic, non-violent, and demasculinized heroism.

The antiwar movement's heroism is effectively represented through Billy, who, unlike the shamed townspeople, jumps up to join the actors, shedding himself of the imperial adventure in Vietnam by removing his fatigues and getting naked—that is, becoming human again. From this point onward, Billy is revivified; he remembers past relationships and ultimately joins in the mud slide contest with Elliot at the end of the film. Thus, as Elliot's non-violent efforts restore his parents, so too does the pacifist antiwar movement restore the humanity destroyed by American militarism. At the end of the scene, Billy, covered in mud, looks up and raises his arms in triumph toward the sky, screaming, "I love this hill!" But Elliot quickly emerges behind him and also raises his arms in triumph, screaming, "We love this hill!" The two embrace in laughter and pure friendship. The strained relationship between Elliot and Billy caused by Billy's post-traumatic stress disorder has been restored through the antiwar festival experience, a symbolic representation of the antiwar movement's heroism.

Compare the mud slide restoration scene to the scene in Oliver Stone's 1986 film *Platoon*, where Willem Dafoe's character is surrounded by the Vietnamese enemy as the result of deliberate abandonment by a fellow soldier. Covered with dirt and riddled by bullets, Dafoe's character runs until he can run no more, falling to the ground and looking at the sky with his arms raised high in defeat and death. Unlike *Platoon*, which suggests that masculine, violent heroism within the platoon can exist even when the war might be wrong, Lee philosophizes that the nonviolent, demasculinized heroism of the war protest movement is the only true salvation for an America bogged down and dying in Vietnam.

Lee also uses the subversion of heroic violence in *Hulk* to represent an antiwar ethic that critiques American militarism. The Hulk's violence is either barbaric (the battle against the dogs), is directed against the popular image of righteous violence (the military), or is abandoned altogether (he gives up against David Banner).

As the Hulk's violence corrupts Bruce's humanity, so too does patriotic militarism destroy America's humanity. The most poignant scene of the film, I suggest, is the bathroom mirror scene. Deliberately disturbing the typical chase action, Lee plants this scene in the middle of the military's pursuit of the Hulk, who has just fallen off the back of a fighter jet and is plummeting to earth when he loses consciousness. The viewer is then transposed to Bruce Banner's unconscious. The portentousness of the moment is signified by the opening shot of a razor blade sliding up Bruce's throat as he shaves in a bathroom. Suddenly, through the fog of the bathroom mirror, Bruce glimpses the Hulk staring back at him. Bruce reaches out to clean the mirror, and the Hulk's hand moves correspondingly. As Bruce pauses to stare at the image, the Hulk's hand suddenly smashes through the mirror and lunges for Bruce's throat. As he lunges, the Hulk declares in a foreboding and guttural voice, "Puny human." The violence born of military imperialism thus not only dwarfs humanity, but also seeks to choke it.

The bathroom scene perfectly inverts the Lacanian mirror stage of identity formation, in which the individuals make sense of their own fragmented experience by identifying with the whole image that they first perceive of themselves in the mirror. In Lee's view, American militarism is slowly destroying America, and he therefore inverts the mirror stage. If Americans could truly see the image with which they seek to identity—righteous heroic violence—they would be horrified. The wiping away of the fog represents the true unmasking of America, an unmasking that can only occur in the unconscious, where the symbolic order structures our imaginary. The bathroom scene unmasks America's self-image of heroic humanitarian militarism and exposes the incomplete (fragmented) collective self—the inhuman Hulk shorn of Bruce—that amounts to a violent military imperialism and its humanity-choking results.[12]

Hulk further suggests that even if the nation could recognize it, America's out-of-control violent militarism has long since elided its human costs. This is made clear when Betty protests Bruce's sedation because "he is a human being." Her father, the general, simply responds, "He is also something else"—namely a threat to American power. Lee uses the villain David Banner to even more directly critique American militarism. David is hired to help further U.S. military goals by altering genetic codes to create better soldiers. Soon his participation in military culture leads ultimately to his desire to kill his own son because he has passed on a genetic mutation. At the same time, as Judith Butler suggests, "violence is, always, an exploitation of that primary tie, that primary way in which we are, as bodies, outside of ourselves and for one another."[13] In that sense, the violent militarism of the Vietnam War enacted on both the Vietnamese people as well as on American soldiers destroys not only the most basic human relationship of parent and child, but also ruptures collective community within the nation-state.

The film's climax uses David Banner to critique American militarism directly as well as to illustrate militarism's insatiable demand for greater power. Surrounded by a military force, David screams at Bruce, "Think about all those men out there in their uniforms barking and swallowing orders, inflicting their petty rule over the entire globe! Think of all the harm they've done! To you! To me! To humanity!" After tempting Bruce to be "a hero" by overthrowing this "petty rule," Bruce screams in agony, "Go!" But David, once the hope of the military, now represents the out-of-control trajectory of American military imperialism and therefore cannot even see the humanity of his own son. "Stop your bawling, you weak little speck of human trash," he tells Bruce. America's militaristic heroic violence thus begets more violence (David Banner during Vietnam; the Atheon Corporation during the war on terror), and the humanity the United States claims to protect is viewed as collateral damage—the very term Betty's father, the military general, uses to refer to the Hulk earlier in the film, and which, really, amounts to a euphemism for human trash.

Vicious Cycles of Violence

Taking Woodstock and *Hulk* were not popular films. I would suggest that this is the case in part because the hegemonic discourse of redemptive violence is not accessible through these films. In *Taking Woodstock,* redemption occurs as the result of a nonviolent peace movement. In *Hulk,* the violent destruction of David Banner never takes place, and so the penalty for Bruce Banner's own genetic mutation and his mother's death is never satisfactorily paid. Further, the Hulk rejects the opportunity to exact justified vengeance at the moment that it becomes possible, and he instead gives up his power. Thus, both films suggest a nonviolent alternative that fails to resonate with the desire to self-identify through violent heroism. Looking at two films centered on nonviolent heroism makes it possible to suggest that real-world violence is implicated in performances of individual identities structured by hegemonic conceptions of heroic violence. Such performances make no sense when removed from individuated, localized contexts (or subjects) and therefore are incomprehensible to the broader community. The result, as Žižek notes, is collective horror and empathy for the victims, a position that renders explorations of the roots of such violence difficult if not impossible. I would suggest that looking doubly awry at real-world violence by exploring these two films that reject violent heroism enables a sharper view of the identity-driven desire at the root of the hegemonic culture of violence, a view that in no way seeks to justify such real-world violence.

Rather than reinscribing the culture of heroic violence, then, *Taking Woodstock* and *Hulk* illustrate a form of universal pacifism that rejects all violence and that offers nonviolence as a potential avenue to end cycles of violence and to open up opportunities for redemption and restoration. Why would audiences want to reject such a philosophy? Perhaps because, as philosopher Robert Brimlow suggests, such a philosophy of nonviolence, rooted in the teachings of Jesus and later echoed by Gandhi, amounts to an invitation to die. In other words, watching the Hulk willingly give up his power and face death is uncomfortable because it asks the viewer to identify with mortality. And death is an aspect of living that our culture seeks to erase, as is evidenced through the vast array of antiaging products and strategies, a fascination with medical technology that might make life last forever, and the segregation of death to special homes and wards outside the normal purview of the living.[14]

But if nonviolence invites the contemplation of death, in Lee's view, the trajectory of heroic militarism means the reality of death. Having subverted heroic violence to demonstrate the possibility of nonviolent heroism, Lee remains skeptical that the heroic violence of U.S. militarism can be arrested. *Taking Woodstock* ends against a backdrop that evokes scenes after battles from the U.S. Civil War. Elliot moves into the shot against a background of a muddy field, littered with waste, sporadic columns of smoke rising from random places, the remains of tents silhouetted against the sky, and dilapidated American flags still on poles scattered throughout. Festival producer Michael Lang rides up on a white horse, and the two are framed against the Civil War–like backdrop, wondering what to do next. The antiwar protest movement may be heroic, but the Civil War backdrop implies its forward movement will be met with violent resistance.

Hulk ends on a superficially positive note, but it is actually laden with portentous symbolism. Bruce is hiding out in a Latin American jungle, where he heroically distributes medicine to suffering people. When bad guys show up to confiscate the supplies, the threat of the Hulk emerges, and a roar is heard above the jungle canopy before the credits roll. But here, too, an ominous future is heralded. After all, as the offspring of U.S. militarism Bruce seeks to bring liberation to an underdeveloped Latin American people, a task that requires heroic violence to eliminate the evil forces that prevent the people from self-realization. This is, of course, the same rationale for U.S. violence in Vietnam, Iraq, and dozens of other nations, including those in Latin America. Lee thus subtly suggests that the cycle of heroic violent militarism continues unchecked.

Notes

1. Carl Boggs and Tom Pollard, *The Hollywood War Machine: U.S. Militarism and Popular Culture* (Boulder, Colo.: Paradigm, 2007).

2. Slavoj Žižek, *Violence: Six Sideways Reflections* (New York: Picador, 2008), 3–4, 126, 174–177, 181.

3. Douglas P. Lackey, "Pacifism," in *Contemporary Moral Problems,* ed. James E. White (New York: Thomson Wadsworth, 2009), 409–413.

4. Christina S. Jarvis, *The Male Body at War: American Masculinity during World War II* (Dekalb: Northern Illinois University Press, 2002); Susan Jeffords, *Hard Bodies: Hollywood Masculinity in the Reagan Era* (New Brunswick, N.J.: Rutgers University Press, 2002), and *The Remasculinization of America: Gender and the Vietnam War* (Bloomington: Indiana University Press, 1989).

5. Nicola Rehling points out the extraordinary nature of this image as well as its link to virile heterosexuality. See Rehling, *Extra-Ordinary Men: White Heterosexual Masculinity in Contemporary Popular Cinema* (Lanham, Md.: Lexington Books, 2009).

6. Boggs and Pollard, *Hollywood War Machine*, 37–41; Cem Kılıçarslan, "The Masculinist Ideology and War-Combat Films: Reassertion of Masculinity in Hollywood," *Journal of Faculty of Letters* 26 (2009): 101–120.

7. Lackey, "Pacifism," 406–418.

8. Jeffords, *Hard Bodies* and *Remasculinization;* Robert D. Schulzinger, *A Time for Peace: The Legacy of the Vietnam War* (New York: Oxford University Press, 2006), 162–164; H. Bruce Franklin, *Vietnam and Other American Fantasies* (Amherst: University of Massachusetts Press, 2000) 14–17, 173–201; Tania Modleski, "Do We Get to Lose This Time? Revising the Vietnam War Film," in *The War Film,* ed. Robert Eberwein (New Brunswick, N.J.: Rutgers University Press, 2006), 155–171; David Grosser, "We Aren't on the Wrong Side, We Are the Wrong Side: Peter Davis Targets (American) Hearts and Minds," in *From Hanoi to Hollywood: The Vietnam War in American Film,* ed. Linda Dittmar and Gene Michaud (New Brunswick, N.J.: Rutgers University Press, 2000), 269–282.

9. The security personnel are played by Stan Lee, creator of the Hulk, and Lou Fer-

rigno, the actor who played the Hulk in the CBS television series, *The Incredible Hulk* (1978–1982).

10. Reagan quoted in *Fresno Bee,* October 10, 1965; editorial, "Vietnam: A Dangerous Silence," *Harvard Crimson,* October 5, 1967.

11. On the origins of America's righteous nation identity in the later twentieth century, see David Zietsma, "Building the Kingdom of God: Religious Discourse, National Identity, and the Good Neighbor Policy, 1930–1938," *Rhetoric and Public Affairs* 11 (2008): 179–214; David Zietsma, "'Sin Has No History': Religion, National Identity, and U.S. Intervention, 1937–1941," *Diplomatic History* 31 (2007): 531–565.

12. Jacques Lacan, *Ecrits,* trans. Bruce Fink (New York: Norton, 2005), 75–81.

13. Judith Butler, *Precarious Life: The Powers of Mourning and Violence* (New York: Verso, 2006), 27.

14. Robert W. Brimlow, *What about Hitler? Wrestling with Jesus's Call to Nonviolence in an Evil World* (Grand Rapids, Mich.: Brazos, 2006), 160–170.

HOMO MIGRANS

Desexualization in Ang Lee's *Taking Woodstock*

Nancy Kang

Heterosexualizing Tiber's Character

Ang Lee's *Taking Woodstock* (2009) is a problematic adaptation of Elliot Tiber's eponymous 2007 memoir because it dilutes and subverts the gay liberationist ideology that is the nucleus of Tiber's work. What should have been a coming-out story veers off into a discourse weighing filial duty against duty to self. The desexualization process, which is Lee's way of rhetorically recloseting (that is, camouflaging) gay identity, is the central theme of this discussion. Desexualization is a strategic approach to the work's plot and characterization that renders peripheral what was originally central, namely homosexual identity formation. The film accommodates queerness (broadly conceived, an investment in sexual fluidity) but does not uphold Tiber's unequivocal agenda: coming out as a sexually self-aware individual. Although most of Lee's film is closely aligned with the exploratory and countercultural ethos of the autobiography, it reconfigures the original text by making homosexual identity a product of Woodstock's freewheeling historical moment rather than the result of a long process of soul searching and political coming of age.

Here I critique the ethics, motivations, and outcomes of this depoliticized approach to Tiber's text, arguing that Lee limits the democratic (read LGBT inclusive) potential of the film by taking the gay away and settling for mere queer. By toning down and arguably heterosexualizing Tiber's character, the filmmaker attempts to partially acknowledge the protagonist's identity issues while simultaneously shying away from any robust confrontation with the problems that were most formative to Tiber's personhood.

A Tie-Dyed Burst in a Queer Cosmos

Gender theorist Eve Sedgwick memorably argued that the overarching notion of queer may be defined as a "near inexhaustible source of transformational energy" despite its initial genesis in personal shame and humiliation. By that token, we might expect Lee's *Taking Woodstock* to be the cinematic equivalent of an ontological firecracker, a colorful, tie-dyed burst in a queer cosmos. Its plot would launch the gay protagonist on a spiritually uplifting (if not also drug-fueled) trip to the nirvana of sexual self-awareness and acceptance. After all, the three-day concert in White Lake, New York, plunged its revelers into a matrix of joyful nonconformity. The diversity of Woodstock's attendees, their unapologetic political activism, and their swirl of liberationist ideologies made Tiber feel at home in the world for the first time. Stifled by the small town's socially conservative values, as well as its ever-ready homophobia and anti-Semitism, he reflects, "For the first time in my life, I felt that people understood me. They saw who I was . . . they related to feelings of being misunderstood."[1]

Lee's adaptation of Tiber's memoir deconstructs what is normal through the continual ontological interplay between a heterosexual center and homosexual periphery. The memoir, in contrast, assumes a homocentrist worldview, one that desperately fights for legitimacy amid the encroachments of heterosexist privilege. These dualities are best exemplified by the split consciousness of the main character, born Eliyahu Teichberg, who oscillates between a straight-acting, sacrificial good son persona while in the rural hamlet of White Lake and the troubled, hedonistic gay man in the artistic and sexual mecca of New York City. Although audience expectation might favor an eventual repudiation of the latter life, Elliot realizes that the synthesis must be self-serving and filial at the same time. It is thus possible to be a good gay son to his working-class immigrant parents without forfeiting his individuality and right to sexual difference. According to the memoir, Woodstock's endorsement of sexual diversity presented the ideal environment in which to realize what was at the time a revolutionary possibility: an emotionally fulfilled, self-certain gay identity. Nourished by Buddhist philosophy, Elliot approximates a state of ordinary transcendence—a sense of the larger picture—catalyzed by ameliorative social forces infiltrating his narrow and anxiety-ridden personal sphere.

The film, more intent on liberating Elliot from his avaricious mother and spiritually defeated father than from his sexual secret, distorts the fun-

damental ontological premise of the text. This is the movement from closeted to uncloseted homosexual, and from abject other to actualized self.
Although the trailers add a disclaimer to the film to indicate that it was
merely inspired by the memoir, the overall fidelity to the text, from title to
characters to plot, is undeniable. Lee instead offers a cross-generic biopic
cum road trip movie, one that literally occurs in Tiber's own backyard. In
order to distance the project from charges that it endorses the so-called gay
agenda (broadly conceived, the quest for social equality and acceptance for
LBGT-identified people), *Taking Woodstock* largely desexualizes the political
and personal empowerment premise of the memoir. Lee and James Schamus, his longtime collaborator and screenwriting partner, also reconfigure
the expectation that a historically adept meditation on Woodstock need
focus on the music rather than on the lives that were changed in the midst
of—or because of—the event.

As Tiber gazes on the crowds leisurely bathing in the lake, he finds himself treated to "every kind of human being . . . husbands, wives, straights,
gays, celibates, bi- and tri-sexuals, and cross-dressers," a sight that leaves him
with "a feeling of comfort and even a little peace."[2] Although Lee acknowledges and recreates Tiber's homosexuality in a sensitive manner, he both
downplays and strategically dilutes the rhetorical imperatives of the original
memoir. These were to narrate a unique and honest life story, raise awareness and compassion for LGBT rights, and critique conservative values
inimical to Tiber's now lifelong commitment to sexual and social equality.
In the writer's words, Woodstock was a symbolic enactment of the quintes-
sentially American motto, *E pluribus unum*: "Spread across the entire field
were five hundred thousand people, all of them bound together like multi-
colored threads in a vast and elaborate carpet. . . . This is what [organizer]
Mike Lang was seeing out here—the generation that opposed war and gave
rise to the civil rights movement. These were the faces that had inspired him
to name this generation Woodstock Nation."[3]

The imagery of rainbows and woven threads is not accidental; the former suggests LGBT activism and diversity awareness, and the latter con-
notes unity, inheritance, familial warmth, and, as far as fairy tales and
mind-altering substances go, a magic carpet ride. The juxtaposition testifies to intersecting political and personal ideals, forming what is essentially
Tiber's personal welcome mat. Instead of focusing on this central trajectory
of the memoir, the coming-out story, Lee consolidates nonsexual themes
from two of his previous films featuring gay main characters. As summa-

rized by Whitney Crothers Dilley, these are *The Wedding Banquet*'s (1993) "heart-wrenching yearning for parental acceptance" and *Brokeback Mountain*'s (2005) "emphasis on human affection, human attraction, and love . . . a universal take on humanity."[4] Issues related to sexuality are relegated to the periphery as idiosyncratic personal matters that distract from larger philosophical abstractions like peace and love. These are certainly worthy ideals, but social resistance to sex and sexuality constitutes the brook of fire that must be crossed in order to understand the real work of achieving peace and love. For certain segments of the population globally, these are not universals. When Elliot attempts to wave off his family issues as trivial and as a matter of perspective when chatting with Tisha, Mike Lang's assistant in the film version, she responds that it may be narrowness and personalized thinking that "shuts out the universe. Everyone with their little perspective. It keeps the love out." Ironically, one statement earlier, she insists that Elliot's family issues might be "the most important thing happening in the universe. How do[es one] know?" This oscillation encompasses Lee's dilemma as a politically conscious director: is Elliot's personal story too short on perspective to prompt larger lessons about human experience? Should it even have to in order to be legitimate?

Queer Representation

The film adaptation envisions its protagonist's homosexuality as an interesting if incidental fact. Tiber's memoir celebrates Woodstock as a time when everyone became sexually redefined as queer. He explains, "These people weren't trapped in the duality of straight versus gay. They were free in ways that I hadn't even considered possible. This is not to say that they weren't straight or gay or bisexual, but whatever they might be, or whatever I might be, it was cool." This atmosphere also allows for variations in the expression of sexual difference, opening one's eyes to the spectrum of nonstraight identities and furnishing the notion of a safe space. As Tiber elaborates, "If a man or woman was gay, he or she was openly gay. And to my eyes, the gays were everywhere."[5] Queerness as a philosophical concept encompasses those people, contexts, disciplines, modes of production, and diverse cultural practices that contest the normative supremacy of heterosexuality. According to Henry Benshoff, individuals who may even identify as straight (like Lee) can work to conceptualize—and hence legitimize—"more inclusive, amorphous, and ambiguous" ways of sexually being in the world. This group includes people who resist ontological absolutism, identifying variously as "gay and/or lesbian, bisexual, transsexual, transvestite, drag queen, leather daddy, lipstick lesbian, pansy, fairy, dyke, butch, femme, feminist, asexual, and so on."[6]

Historically, queer has migrated from an adjective denoting the strange, the unsavory, or the unexplainable to an epithet denigrating those identified as homosexual. With the multivalent rise of queer studies in the late twentieth century, the idea of being contraheterosexual took on new meanings: queerness "emerged from the confluence of identity politics (e.g., the study of race, class, gender, and sexuality) and currents in post-structuralist and postmodern thinking—currents that questioned the stability of signification and the desirability of categorization."[7] Instead of the binary paradigm of heterosexual versus homosexual, a spectrum of sexual identities emerged, prompting panic over the cultural intelligibility of these new ways of being. Many of them were pathologized as mental disorders and relegated to spaces of sin and deviance. In the United States alone, reactions to same-sex desire have been far from uniform or universally accepting.

Although Lee has taken risks with his previous cinematic choices (*Brokeback Mountain,* for instance, was banned in China, his country of primary personal identification), he backtracks on depictions of homosexuality with *Taking Woodstock.* Although he endorsed sexual transparency in *The Wedding Banquet* with an emphatic "Honesty is the best policy. It's just the best way I've found to live my life and go about my career, and hopefully be able to sleep at night," he moves away from driving home that ethical message as vigorously in Tiber's case.[8] Much of the hesitation may have to do with the values he associates with Chinese culture, namely emotional—and by extension, sexual—repression for a greater good. This is usually in the form of a personal duty to one's parents, strongly evident in Tiber's memoir but virtually absent in *Brokeback Mountain.* Neither Jake's nor Ennis's parents play a major role in their adult lives, so no such sacrifice is necessary. The opposite is true for Elliot. Lee revealed in conversation with the *New York Times* that the "great Chinese theme" is hiding one's feelings as a form of noble sacrifice. Although speaking specifically about unrequited love in *Crouching Tiger, Hidden Dragon* (2000), Lee gestured more broadly to the creative possibilities of personal denial; by channeling such angst into more socially acceptable forms of expression, especially artistic and figurative modes, characters laid bare an array of feelings ripe for the screen and canvas.[9] Whether this combined aesthetic/ethnocultural approach carries over well into a thoroughly American story—Woodstock's summer of love—is a moot point.

As Lee outlined in a companion documentary to the video release, *Taking Woodstock* asks viewers to reevaluate "how we live in our environment [with] other fellow races and countries and cultures."[10] Such expansiveness was definitely a value that fueled the three-day event. Colliding with that which is strange or other and assimilating the foreignness into one's own sphere of comfort and normalcy are arguably premises for small-scale as well as grand-scale social revolutions. It is, however, also a decentering and often psychologically—if not also physically—violent process. The Woodstock concert was meant to serve as a catalytic moment, a ritual induction into a new age of fluidity, openness, and spiritual transcendence. As early publicity suggested, it was to be a true "Aquarian Exposition," aiming to make people "flow with the Tao" but also remain grounded in the realities of social injustice, war, and intolerance. The youthful exuberance behind the historical event, its attractiveness for profit seekers and social misfits, as well as its significant entertainment value were undergirded by weightier concerns for third world liberation, antiwar, anti-Establishment, anticolonial, antiracist, pro–civil rights, feminist, and LGBT-positive platforms. The event was thus a fundamentally contradictory and complex social phenomenon— intensely personal for revelers but always tethered to a larger social fabric pulled taut by those who resisted changing the status quo. In the memoir, this reactionary element is the townspeople of White Lake and surrounding areas like Bethel, New York.

For Lee, the problem of representation was formal as well as thematic: how to create a film that pays homage to the peace-loving, inclusive, democratic, and carefree philosophy of Woodstock without a potentially damaging fidelity to the source text. Although it is comedic by turns, Tiber's work is first and foremost a memoir of gay coming of age. Its genre is autobiography and historiography catalyzed by the spirit of the Künstlerroman, a fictional narrative tracing the genesis of an artist. Tiber's text emphasizes how coming out means coming in, specifically into the psyche of a man desiring family harmony to the point of endangering his professional and emotional stability. Tiber is obsessed with winning the approval of Jake Teichberg, his initially distant father; Lee's investment in redemptive patriarchy as a theme is clearly evident in such works as *Pushing Hands* (1992) and *Eat Drink Man Woman* (1994). Largely masking the preoccupation with filial commitment, Schamus outlined the project for *Rolling Stone* as being "about play and fun," with an overall spirit that is fundamentally "hopeful." He does not specify what the target of that hope is, but LGBT equality it is not. The major cast members include comedians like newcomer Demetri Martin as the slender and mild-mannered lead, a sharp deviation from Tiber's self-description as an overweight, unattractive Jew with a yen for bondage gear and dimly lit gay clubs.[11] Fans of such humorous fare as *Bringing Down the House* (Adam Shankman, 2003) and *American Pie* (Chris Weitz and Paul Weitz, 1999) will recognize actor Eugene Levy as good-natured Max Yasgur, whose farm was the site of the concert. Schamus titillated prospective (straight) filmgoers by divulging that Martin's character "gets waylaid by an acid trip and a three way," thereby never making it to the actual music concert. This description privileges youthful high jinks over emotional soul-searching, nascent political activism, and the often overt intimacies of Tiber's confessional mode.[12] Basing a film project on fun might be the profitable choice, but filmgoers might be prompted to ask whether the end product might not turn out to resemble an acid trip as well—momentarily uplifting but fundamentally devoid of lasting meaning.

Pink Triangle

When sexuality emerged as an increasingly prominent feature of identity formation discourses in late nineteenth-century Europe, the question arose as to whether this one factor detracted from more comprehensive assessments of a person's value.[13] The late 1960s—Woodstock's historical moment—were seminal in the United States not only because of the Stonewall riots and the ferment of civil rights, but also because gay characters could emerge more explicitly on screen, thanks to the dissolution of Hollywood's production code.[14] Of course, explicit does not mean with abandon; that was hardly the case in the court of public opinion or the minds of studio censors. Given this uphill historical trajectory, the symbolism of Elliot's self-disclosure during this time would have been doubly significant had it been featured on screen as the film's central conflict. Although Tiber has expressed unequivocal admiration and pleasure at the finished product, his statement "It's not mine anymore" has powerful significance.[15]

The Wedding Banquet, Brokeback Mountain, and *Taking Woodstock* comprise Lee's cinematic pink triangle: they differ in genre, depth of political engagement, and resonance with the director's Asian roots, but all three films offer insights into the ethics of homosexual self-disclosure. Just as the earlier films *Pushing Hands, The Wedding Banquet,* and *Eat Drink Man Woman* are popularly grouped as the Father Knows Best trilogy because they underscore the deep-seated wisdom of traditional Chinese fathers, this more recent trio tackles coming out as an inherently risky social choice. The choice that would appear the most ethically sound for the individual—that is, personal honesty—has some of the most serious social repercussions, including possible loss of friendships, familial disapproval, professional prejudice, diminished social standing, compromised sense of safety, and corroded self-respect. The last point is especially the case should internalized homophobia take over, leading to depression or other forms of potentially debilitating, if not fatal, disorders. Each film in Lee's pink triangle asks audiences to understand that honesty about sexuality—really a synecdoche for the dynamics of identity formation itself—may mean a decision between life and death. This danger is literal if we recall the specter of homophobic violence in *Brokeback Mountain* that drives protagonists Ennis and Jack increasingly deeper into the closet despite their adherence to the typical rituals of heternormality (marriage and children). The tragic conclusion, alongside the suggested scenario of Jack being beaten to death, is very much in step with early Hollywood depictions of homosexual characters. These films were often punctuated by violence by or against gays and included the death or symbolic erasure of the homosexual threat in order for an implied—if not actual—return to the hetero status quo. Even *Brokeback Mountain,* perhaps inadvertently, features aspects of this thematic reversal.[16]

Whence They Came: LGBT Struggle and the Woodstock Moment

Along with the rise of the AIDS epidemic in the 1980s and the activist bodies that advocated for acknowledgment, research funding, and social action (among them Queer Nation and ACT UP) on the part of the government and society at large, an atmosphere of vulnerability and melancholy has persisted among members of U.S. LGBT communities. This cautious sensibility has often emerged in art, very much the cornerstone of Tiber's early life as a student and interior designer during the early 1960s. Having built a reputation for his summer festivals in the Catskills region, he challenges readers to separate sexuality from creativity: "Name any artistic field—novels, plays, poetry, painting, acting, design—and you will find gay artists among those making revolutionary contributions."[17] How much has changed for gay Americans since that time? A sobering report released by the National

Coalition of Anti-Violence Programs (NCAVP) in July 2011 noted a 13 percent increase in violent antigay crimes across the country in 2010.[18] That same month, however, California became the first state to legally mandate the inclusion of LGBT history in public school (K–12) social studies classes. One month before, during the anniversary month of the Stonewall riots, the state of New York legitimized same-sex marriage, the U.S. military's "don't ask, don't tell" policy was moving toward being fully repealed, and Larry Kramer's AIDS-themed, Tony Award–winning play *The Normal Heart* (1985) received hearty reviews for its Broadway revival. Yet that month was also marred by homophobic firestorms like actor-comedian Tracy Morgan threatening on stage to stab his son if the child ever came out as gay. This invective spurred recollections of a spate of suicides in the past two years by homosexual youth, notably by Rutgers University student Tyler Clementi, who jumped off the George Washington Bridge in 2010 after being invasively cyberbullied over his sexuality. This incident is eerily similar to Tiber's reflections on the "gigantic lie" of his early existence: "I was ripped apart by my two identities, unable to resolve the conflict I faced. If I chose my own life, I would flee White Lake like a man released from a Turkish prison, but then my parents would be destitute. Then again, if I didn't choose my own life, I might drive my car off the George Washington Bridge."[19] These suicidal ideations highlight the speaker's intense filial commitment but give equal credence to his desire to be a sexual free agent, someone able to choose his own partners and lifestyle without existential crisis.

Unlike *Brokeback Mountain*, *The Wedding Banquet* and *Taking Woodstock* focus less on direct threats of physical violence than the complex dimensions of social death, or what the teenage Clementi may have feared once his sexuality became fodder for gossip and possible censure by the college dorm community. Wai-Tung's paralyzing fear of disappointing his conservative family's Confucian values in the earlier film echoes Ennis's decision to reject Jack's offer of making a life together. These men, like Tiber, inhabit a position of radical ambivalence toward their sexual identities, where acceptance and development of an assertive gay persona in a dangerously heterosexist society can result in an emotionally suffocating, deceptively choreographed half-life. Explains Tiber, "For those who choose to stay alive, many try to go straight. . . . Indeed, denial often leads to aberrant behaviors and even greater pain, not just for them but for others too."[20] Only when he meets concertgoer Georgette, a "great mother figure, an earth goddess, a woman . . . as conversant in Buddhism and the healing arts as she was in the importance of being yourself," does Tiber lose his long-held curse of homophobic self-hatred. He reveals, "[Georgette and her friends] didn't see me as Jewish, or fat, or ugly, or gay—all things for which I had been routinely rejected over the years. They saw me as some kind of hero in this great, swirling, out-of-control miracle that was Woodstock."[21] Such a catalytic figure in Tiber's quest for self-actualization—one who is also gay and espouses a philosophy of unconditional love—is problematically absent in Lee's film.

Stonewalling

Taking Woodstock embraces queerness but downplays gayness, resulting in an authorial position that lacks political commitment and diminishes both the biographical acuity and ideological integrity of the entire project. Granted, *Woodstock*'s strategic desexualization of its protagonist does not categorically efface Elliot's homosexuality, a decision that some film executives might have supported had they believed that a film with a gay protagonist would be unprofitable or too narrowly appealing. (*Brokeback Mountain*'s critical and commercial success proved that this need not be the case, but the risks were certainly present.) Lee's film camouflages and subtly straightens Tiber's gay persona, interpreting his sexuality at best as part of a larger mass culture philosophy of queer cool. Like the experimental sexualities suggested by films like *Kissing Jessica Stein* (Charles Herman-Wurmfeld, 2001), queerness becomes synonymous with sexual openness that includes but is not necessarily driven by LGBT history or politics. Queer philosophy in Lee's film generally involves being aware of sexual diversity and having an awakened (if not necessarily cause-specific) political consciousness, an investment in the fluidity and nonstandardization of identities, a marked attraction to democratic change, and a welcoming attitude toward ambiguity and difference in all its forms. Reflecting on Woodstock's queerness, which he doesn't actually name as such, Tiber reveals that one of the "greatest benefits" psychologically and sociologically was its diversity: "People of all sexual orientations were present at the concert in enormous numbers. And more important to me, many showed up at the El Monaco [the family's hotel]."[22]

Such community-building opportunities were vital, not just for gays and lesbians but for cause-minded individuals everywhere. By taking Woodstock, the memoirist does not just pun on the idea of becoming aware of the event's implications (that is, taking stock of them); he also gestures to the more practical sense of the world, as in claiming for himself—as facilitator and participant—one of self-assuredly straight America's greatest historical milestones. Ironically, when Lee's camera pans along "Happy Avenue" and "Groovy Way" to encompass nuns, antiwar protesters, environmentalists, feminists, activists from Students for a Democratic Society, and spiritual explorers embracing tai chi and yogic teachings, the impression is that these revelers are just people caring for a cause, a microcosm of what American society could be with the right motivation and venues. Gay rights advocates are, however, absent from this group. There are lesbians briefly kissing at the motel bar, but this image emphasizes physicality rather than intellectual or personal engagement.

This impression deepens when Elliot encounters prejudice: there is a clumsy conflation between anti-Semitism, homophobia, and hippie phobia, with an emphasis on the first and last aversions. The entire film downplays the memoir's undeniable conflict with the townspeople, portraying them as pesky curmudgeons, cranks, and prudes rather than the serious threat to the event and the Teichberg family that the author reveals. In the film, their graffiti jeers "Burn Faggot Jews" alongside an image of a swastika and lynched Star of David. At the neighborhood diner, Elliot has "Hippie!" "Disgusting!" and "We ought to run you Jews out of town" hurled at him, but no explicit mention of sexuality is ever made. By having the epithet "faggot Jews" directed at Elliot and his father, the full extent of the homophobia does not register, especially given that Jake Teichberg's declaration of love for his wife is part of the emotional climax of the film. Just as gayness was subsumed into queerness, the film neutralizes the specificity and severity of the homophobia, making it just another species of hate.

This effect resurfaces at the level of narrative structure. Woodstock's sexual diversity had precedents, among them the Stonewall riots, the lesser-known lavender scare that targeted thousands of gays and lesbians working for the government during the McCarthy era, and even the Holocaust's subjugation of homosexuals (from which the world inherited the pink triangle symbol). This latter point is significant because Tiber's mother repeatedly, if too glibly, evokes wartime atrocities against Jews to emotionally manipulate the people around her. Tiber was part of the Stonewall Inn crowd in Greenwich Village; before the riots, he was harassed by the police specifically as a result of his sexual proclivities, including a violent episode with an undercover officer that made him fear for his life. In the film, Stonewall is never named; we only have a veiled reference when Elliot receives a phone call from Steven, a friend heading from New York over to San Francisco. Steven mentions police raids and a riot, but neither details nor any clear intimation that Elliot even participated emerge. This rhetorical suppression is a major deviation from the memoir, which features an entire chapter entitled "Stonewall and the Seeds of Liberation." Tiber himself is unequivocal in his assessment of Woodstock as Gaystock, gushing that when "the Woodstockers arrived, everyone was flirting and coming on to everyone else, including the gays—even in broad daylight." He brags, "The summer of '69 turned run-down, humble shack number two [in the El Monaco] into a love palace."[23] Tiber is in no way the neophyte portrayed by Martin, who makes an awkwardly rustic pass at Mike Lang while high on marijuana. ("You smell good, Mike. Like an apple fritter.") Waving away drugs on three other occasions, Elliot's film persona stumbles through the unfolding terrain of his moral and sexual identity. His tentativeness is far from the experienced, desperate, and wary adult of the book, one struggling to ease his passage from self-loathing to self-acceptance.

Desexualization/Heterosexualization

Although most book-to-screen adaptations reveal some form of undesirable omission, addition, or substitution, reviewers have noted the marked shift in ideological focus demonstrated by Lee's film. Glenn C. Altschuler and Robert O. Summers complain, "The film, alas, does not really illuminate Elliot's struggle for identity or the greed that animates just about everyone around him." In *Sight and Sound*, Ryan Gilbey criticizes the tepidness of the "forbidden love" that manifests onscreen. Elliot's shy flirtation and public kiss with a construction worker named Paul, and later a morning glance at a sleeping Paul as Elliot rises, clad only in boxer shorts and a slight smile—cannot compare with *Brokeback Mountain*'s pangs of frustrated desire. Gilbey even reads the "chaste orgy" (Schamus's aforementioned threesome, inexplicably devoid of nudity) as Lee's apology for the explicitness of the NC-17-rated spy thriller *Lust, Caution* (2007). This kind of interfilmic moral conscience renders *Taking Woodstock*, in his view, "uncharacteristically reticent . . . [with] Lee lacking his customary confidence."[24] Rather than praising Elliot, Gilbey singles out Vilma, the transvestite ex-Marine and Korean War vet played by Liev Schreiber, as having greater complexity than the film's star. For any director, it is worrisome to see a supporting character outshine the lead; yet with an avuncular demeanor and a deficit of campy exuberance, Schreiber is more reminiscent of the television series *M*A*S*H*'s (1972–1983) straight cross-dresser, Maxwell Klinger, than the commanding, larger-than-life dominatrix of the memoir. After all, Vilma even offers Elliot sexual services prior to being hired as motel security.[25]

One way in which the de(homo)sexualization occurs is through a balancing process that, often subtly, suggests that Elliot's gayness is negotiable, or if not that, then always submerged in a heteronormative context. For instance, Elliot only has a same-sex kiss in the motel bar *after* locking lips with an attractive woman. While Jake is serving lesbians and other revelers (whom he compares to animals) at the bar, his son finds himself pulled into a playful crowd. A girl grabs Elliot and kisses him passionately; although he looks surprised, he doesn't pull away or show any sense of insult or violation. This kissing recalls an earlier episode when an attractive white hippie, part of a daring interracial couple (white woman, black man), screams in delight and kisses Elliot's father after receiving tickets for the event. Kissing emerges as an expression of glee or excitement, something superficial rather than serious. Paul steps in for his turn with Elliot; after a pause, the latter kisses him back with some enthusiasm, but nothing compared to that of *Brokeback Mountain*'s mauling embraces. Onlookers cheer at both instances, suggesting on the one hand that there is some equality in terms of these experiences, or on the other hand that they are equally inconsequential, playful experiments lubricated by alcohol and mindless fun.

Even the threesome that Schamus invoked earlier has Elliot accept LSD from the attractive woman of the couple, who cradles his face affectionately, just as she does her male partner's. Inside the van, the camera focuses on her seductively bare torso and doelike eyes. When Elliot first feels the effects of the drug, she comforts and clings to him while the unnamed man is in a corner enjoying his own trip; clearly the cinematic gaze here is heterosexual, with the woman as the object of desire. The initial shots of the interior of the van prominently feature nude women, and during the tryst, the young woman's face, loosely fitting peasant blouse, and exhortation—"just breathe"—take precedence over the man's perfunctory pats on Elliot's knee and chest. His only suggestive move is raking a toe up and down Elliot's leg, a gesture that appears to confuse rather than stimulate the seemingly naive visitor. After the twisting communion of the bodies, Elliot emerges from the van with the ethereal woman; her partner is conspicuously absent, save for a motionless foot in the van's entrance. They dance together like a couple, ecstatically swimming in the ocean of the crowd. In each of these examples, Elliot's homosexuality takes a subordinate position; he is situationally straight, and hetero-identified audience members will find that any sense of homoerotic tension is largely neutralized by the presence of the attractive woman. Whatever gay behavior Elliot attempts can be explained away as part of the drug trip, a "what happens in Woodstock stays in Woodstock" type of flippancy that condones any exploratory deviance. Little or no attempts are made to emphasize the protagonist's growing gay pride or desire for solidarity.

Billy, Elliot: Alike, but Not Quite

These authorial choices to tone down, straighten, and desexualize Tiber are not blatantly homophobic, but they do endorse a questionable paradigm: that queerness (as sexual fluidity) and gayness (same-sex desire) are interchangeable. Same-sex attraction thus appears more optional than innate, more a product of the counterculture milieu than a premise for lifelong awareness and self-fashioning. Lee's reluctance to portray Tiber's identity transparently and robustly can be viewed as fear of homosexual closeness, and thus as unaware or neglectful of the array of positions that gay people take toward their sexualities, whether loud and proud (like the memoir's Vilma) or quiet and subdued (like the film's Elliot). An intriguing point of contrast is Elliot's character foil in the film, a young man with psychological difficulties named Billy (Emile Hirsch). Fabricated for the film, he is a Vietnam vet who returns to White Lake traumatized, prone to shouting expletives, and bursting with rebellious mischief against his staid, conservative relatives. He, like Jake Teichberg and Elliot, finds an almost miraculous liberation in the joie de vivre of Woodstock. This healing comes while both young men slide down a mud hill and Billy waxes nostalgic about his experiences there before his deployment. The mud scene is significant because the dirt that covers them effaces the ontological specificity of the sliders; they return to the earth (literally) in order to find a part of themselves unthwarted by a judgmental, uncomprehending society. Both Billy and Elliot are misfits, but the script is quick to differentiate the two sexually. Billy's implied sex with a girl named Shirley Livingstone on that hill is inflected by his admission that he was engaged to her before leaving for war. The fact that he assisted in three football touchdowns, tipped cows, and had a high school sweetheart normalizes him as a small-town boy overwhelmed by the rigors of global conflict. The war chose him, not the other way around. He is understandably penniless after succumbing to the cheap and corrupting thrills of "fucking Bangkok." To viewers, he is more America's "prodigal son" (to use Vilma's phrase for Elliot) than Elliot himself.

To the screenwriter's credit, Billy's troubling presence bears witness to the ongoing mental traumas of war and alludes tangentially to the traditional barring of gays from the military. One exchange between them signifies upon LGBT struggle but never goes far enough to make the connection explicit. This occurs when Elliot attempts to humor the hallucinating, wild-eyed, weed-smoking Billy while waving off the drug himself. Such abstinence is something that Tiber—a prodigious recreational drug user in the text—would find absurd. After Billy blurts, "I'm fucked up!" Elliot responds, "[The army] wouldn't take me even if I wanted. Flat feet." His interlocutor scoffs, "Right . . . feet. Ha ha. Fuck. Yeah, you're not fucking normal, Elliot." To which the hero, with his typically genial, calm demeanor, remarks, "Guess not." The allegation is poignant given the social stigma against gays, but Elliot's easygoing smile reveals nothing of his inner struggle or his appreciation of Billy's signifying commentary. With his mother an overbearing shrew, his father a silent sufferer, and Elliot a repressed and unhappy artist, Billy's utterance begs the question: what is normal? Tisha remarks to Elliot early on when the issue of free tickets arises, "Who wants a hundred thousand freaks coming after them for refunds?" If freakery is the new normal for Woodstock, Elliot's trajectory toward individualized consciousness building as a gay man has but secondary value. Like the image of the Woodstock crowd as a churning sea, his identity is not unique but rather one drop among a hundred thousand—or more specifically, hundreds of thousands—of not-normal freaks. This homogenization may be welcome by some who endorse universalist ideals, but it is stifling for others who believe that differentiated identities create a more diverse world.

Habeas Corpus: The Lost and the Found

Lee's rhetorical strategy when dealing with Elliot's homosexuality is essentially soft inclusion, which invites comparison to Gilbey's observation about *Woodstock*'s overall historiographical approach: "The film resembles a crash course in how to 'do' history without belaboring its significance."[26] Lee's work "does" (works over, sanitizes, plays down) Tiber's overt homosexuality to the comfortably queer level. Although it may be a minor coup to have an LGBT character as the lead in the first place, the desexualization of Elliot is a loaded act because Lee and Schamus acutally take the sex out of homosexuality. The film avoids any deep development of its protagonist's life story by redacting his entire sexual history. *Taking Woodstock*'s definition of gay identity hinges largely on stereotypes—Steven's mention of a doll-collecting art dealer and Vilma's description of Steven as being "off to San Francisco with a flower in his hair on his sugar daddy's lap." In a work that features amorous couples fornicating in bushes, a co-ed theater troupe naked (not once but twice, with full frontal exposure), as well as a scene of communal bathing in the lake, the sexual and desirous gay body remains glaringly absent. The openness and inclusion that informed the Woodstock concert and ostensibly the film evidently do not apply to all groups.

Tiber is vigorously sexual in his memoir, even having his own S&M-themed quarters on the motel property; in the film, his New York life is merely distilled into an early conversation with his sister about moving to California and Steven's perfunctory comment that the city isn't as fun without him. Had Lee and Schamus wished to capture the rebelliousness of his protagonist and the Woodstock "nation," they might have included these racier aspects. Steven's comment is puzzling to the viewer, given that Martin's depiction of Tiber appears too quiet, calm, and controlled to have been picked up in a leather bar by photographer Robert Mapplethorpe or engaged in drug-fueled sex with writers Tennessee Williams and Truman Capote. He introduces readers early on to his lonely but habitual encounters in the clandestine world of all-night porn theaters, seedy pickup joints, and bondage clubs. Tiber is not a wallflower who stumbles good-naturedly into his attractions and affairs; hedonistic sex—and a lot of it—is the sine qua non of his pre-Woodstock days.

During the event, the book tells us, he sleeps with a volunteer stage-hand and with twin Broadway dancers, one of whom he is kissing when he accidentally outs himself to his mother. It is with this dancer, not the film's construction worker, Paul, that he experiences a life-changing epiphany: "But in that moment, two worlds suddenly joined—White Lake and Manhattan—and something in the pit of my stomach told me it was okay." Tiber is also delighted when sex tourists from out of town recognize the gay allusions in his motel signs and keep him "busy—in more ways than one."[27] Although he enjoys his trysts, the author construes his early promiscuity as a coping mechanism for social disenfranchisement: "Being desired becomes a reason to go on living. Sexual touch, however one defines it, becomes an antidote to the existential isolation that settles in the bones and blood of so many gay men." He reasons that because sexual behavior is the basis for rejecting the legitimacy of LGBT-identified people, "sex becomes a revolutionary act and for many, an act of anger. It is a raised middle finger, a thumb in the eye to all those who despise you. It confirms difference. It insists on the right to life."[28] This kind of liberating otherness was precisely the fuel for Woodstock's dancing, singing, protesting, chanting, and (to use Mrs. Teichberg's word) shtupping masses, whatever their sexual orientation. Lee's film version, however, has ample room for only one kind of liberated coupling, and it remains stubbornly heterosexual.

One final manifestation of *Taking Woodstock*'s desexualizing process is the omission of Georgette, one of the memoir's seminal characters. Much of Tiber's homosexual self-acceptance (as opposed to mere awareness) derives not from the concert's music or the drug and money issues that create the dramatic and comedic tensions by turn, but from an encounter with this Buddhist philosopher and fellow homosexual. Georgette rides in a painted school bus with three female disciples, a foil to the bus that hosts Elliot's acid-tripping young companions.[29] Her removal and yet partial funneling into Vilma's character are hermeneutic losses. Because Georgette is so closely aligned with Buddhism at a time when "there weren't many American Buddhists driving around in their own psychedelic–meditation–healing temples," her absence means neglecting an angle of vision (namely non-Christian religions) that could have clarified many of the issues causing strife and heartache in the film.[30] Georgette embodies Zen Buddhism's broad paradigm of compatible contradictions: she is an inertia-inducing 300 pounds but is in constant motion; she works in peripheral spaces (parking lots and swamps) but becomes a central presence; she is a foreigner who has felt at home in the United States for more than twenty years; she speaks openly about lesbianism and plural spiritualities at a time when closeted secrecy and religious fundamentalism (at least during the 1950s) were the norm. Vilma of the film and Georgette are similar in being transparent about their gay identities, but the former is gruff and solitary while the latter acts "nice to everyone." Tiber writes, "People gathered around her in large part because they could freely be themselves. . . . She was so honest, so open, and so relaxed, that she made you act the same way."[31] She is the one who informs Elliot, a self-proclaimed atheist, that Buddhism is not premised on a hierarchal organization of divine leadership but rather on personal accountability in the form of *karma*. Instead of focusing on his failings, like his mother does, she praises him, suggesting that he has created goodness through the concert and amplified the lives of those around him. He is thus much more than the sum of his sexual urges and filial intentions.

Health and Mental Balance

According to Buddhist tenets, Elliot's self-esteem problems, like the towns-people's narrow-mindedness, are forms of *dukkha,* or suffering, fueled by the evils of greed, ignorance, and hatred, all of which are amply in view during the film. He, like all the concertgoers at Woodstock, is part of the cycle of life, death, and endless flow of passing events known as *samsara.* The *homo migrans* of this chapter's title refers to the movement of the con-sciousness—and the body—through the karmic circle, an infinite conglom-eration of life lessons. Georgette preaches love and acceptance that to him are healing, allowing him to come out formally to his parents. She is the personification of Woodstock's ideal philosophy of unconditional love. Tiber eventually distances himself from promiscuity because he realizes that Bud-dhism encourages moderation, balance, and equanimity in all aspects of life, including sex. Zen Buddhism suggests that sexualities are not necessarily good or bad because categories are provisional (that is, empty) in the first place. The hedonism of free love culture would likely be discouraged because its excesses (and attendant risks to health and mental balance) may distract from more important matters of self-cultivation and edifying detachment. Similarly, conventional categorizations of identity (race, class, gender, and sexuality, among others) are reductions of larger wholes that may not be consequential or meaningful. As the Earthlight Players intimate, "Maybe we only think we exist when really, we don't." Sexual choices demonstrate but one limited aspect of character and may take a person only so far in terms of overall enlightenment.[32]

By desexualizing the gay main character, Lee's film reconfigures same-sex attraction as less a personal issue than a social metaphor for the real-ity of difference in the world today. The film simultaneously acknowledges yet diminishes this difference; the end result is to proclaim that Elliot is an Everyman who just happens to be gay. Such an ontological-accident prem-ise would likely be rejected by Tiber. He cannot be an Everyman precisely because he is gay, a clear impediment to equality in a starkly and unequivo-cally homophobic society. Tiber's evolution of consciousness is predicated on a mindful awareness of the present, with mindfulness denoting the joyous intensity of the moment as a template for appreciative, positive, reciprocal living. A mindful approach allows Tiber to take Woodstock, understand its implications culturally and personally, and receive credit for its success. Lee's film definitely *takes away* from Tiber's memoir through its politics of desexualization, but it gives back a personalized image of an event too often viewed with uncritical nostalgia. Ironically and yet aptly, Ang Lee's *Taking Woodstock* is—and yet is not—Elliot Tiber's story.

Notes

1. Eve Kosofsky Sedgwick, "Queer Performativity: Henry James's *The Art of the Novel*," *GLQ: A Journal of Lesbian and Gay Studies* 1, no. 1 (1993): 1–16; Elliot Tiber and Tom Monte, *Taking Woodstock: A True Story of a Riot, a Concert, and a Life* (New York: Square One, 2007), 122.

2. Tiber and Monte, *Taking Woodstock*, 123.

3. Ibid., 191. I will use "Elliot" to refer to the film character and "Tiber" to refer to the author. For an earlier version of the Woodstock story, see Elliot Tiber, *Knock on Woodstock: The Uproarious, Uncensored Story of the Woodstock Festival, the Gay Man Who Made It Happen, and How He Earned His Ticket to Freedom* (New York: Festival Books, 1994).

4. Whitney Crothers Dilley, *The Cinema of Ang Lee: The Other Side of the Screen* (London: Wallflower Press, 2007), 70, 160.

5. Tiber and Monte, *Taking Woodstock*, 116–117.

6. Harry Benshoff, "The Monster and the Homosexual," in *Queer Cinema: The Film Reader*, ed. Harry Benshoff and Sean Griffin (New York: Routledge, 2004), 64–74. For a broad cross section of criticism on queerness, see Michelle Aron, ed., *New Queer Cinema: A Critical Reader* (New Brunswick, N.J.: Rutgers University Press, 2004); Richard Dyer, *The Culture of Queers* (London: Routledge, 2002); Judith Butler, *Bodies That Matter: On the Discursive Limits of "Sex"* (New York: Routledge, 1993); and Alexander Doty, *Making Things Perfectly Queer: Interpreting Mass Culture* (Minneapolis: University of Minnesota Press, 1993).

7. Benshoff and Griffin, introduction to *Queer Cinema*, 1–14.

8. "A Forbidden Passion," Ang Lee interview, on *The Wedding Banquet* (1993) DVD, dir. Ang Lee (MGM, 2004).

9. Rick Lyman, "Watching Movies with Ang Lee: Crouching Memory, Hidden Heart," *New York Times*, March 9, 2001, E27.

10. "Peace, Love and Cinema," on *Taking Woodstock* (2007) DVD, dir. Ang Lee (Universal, 2010).

11. Tiber and Monte, *Taking Woodstock*, 165.

12. John Clarke Jr., "Producer James Schamus Says Ang Lee's *Taking Woodstock* Will Capture 'Hopeful Spirit,'" *Rolling Stone*, August 26, 2008 (http://www.rollingstone.com).

13. See vol. 1 of Michel Foucault, *The History of Sexuality*, trans. Robert Hurley (New York: Vintage, 1990).

14. Benshoff, "Monster," 67. The production code was replaced by the MPAA rating system.

15. *"Taking Woodstock* Interview," video embedded in "Elliot Tiber: Giver of Woodstock History," Woodstockstory.com (http://www.woodstockstory.com).

16. See Vito Russo, *The Celluloid Closet: Homosexuality in the Movies* (New York: Harper & Row, 1981), and the 1995 documentary of the same name directed by Rob Epstein and Jeffrey Friedman.

17. Tiber and Monte, *Taking Woodstock,* 65.

18. National Coalition of Anti-Violence Programs, "Hate Violence against Lesbian, Gay, Bisexual, Transgender, Queer and HIV-Affected Communities in the United States in 2010," Anti-Violence Project, 2011 (http://www.avp.org/documents/NCAVPHate ViolenceReport2011Finaledjlfinaledits_000.pdf).

19. Tiber and Monte, *Taking Woodstock,* 44.

20. Ibid., 67.

21. Ibid., 164–165.

22. Ibid., 163.

23. Ibid., 119–120. See David K. Johnson, *The Lavender Scare: The Cold War Persecution of Gays and Lesbians in the Federal Government* (Chicago: University of Chicago Press, 2004). Tiber's activism is centered around his Gaystock foundation (http://gaystock.com/), which aims to organize LGBT-related events.

24. Glenn C. Altschuler and Robert O. Summers, review of *Taking Woodstock, Journal of American History* 97, no. 1 (2010): 279–281; Ryan Gilbey, review of *Taking Woodstock, Sight and Sound* 19, no. 12 (2009): 76.

25. Ryan Gilbey, "Synthetic Sixties," *New Statesman* 2 (2009): 46. In the memoir, Vilma is a World War II veteran, not a Korean War veteran. His status as grandfather does not coincide easily with Schreiber's casting.

26. Ibid.

27. Tiber and Monte, *Taking Woodstock,* 118, 52–53.

28. Ibid., 71.

29. For instance, the memoir does not focus on Mrs. Teichberg's hoarding of the scandalous $97,000, mentioning it only at the end of the text as an example of how ironically prepared she was for retirement. In the film, this revelation is the climax, prompting Elliot to feel justified in leaving his parents and the property. Another important deviation: Tiber estimates that Woodstock ticket sales generated approximately $30,000 in revenue; the text does not feature him falling into a marijuana stupor and proclaiming (in a comical misrepresentation by local media) that entry into the concert would be free. See Tiber and Monte, *Taking Woodstock,* 210.

30. Ibid., 163.

31. Ibid., 163–164.

32. For more on homosexuality's place in Buddhism, see Brad Warner, *Sex, Sin, and Zen: A Buddhist Exploration of Sex from Celibacy to Polyamory and Everything in Between* (Novato, Calif.: New World Library, 2010), esp. 196–198.

Because of the Molecules

The Ice Storm and the Philosophy of Love and Recognition

Susanne Schmetkamp

The Place You Return To

For a moment, *The Ice Storm* (1997) brings everything to a standstill. Everything falls silent. As the audience will learn to appreciate, this is a time for self-reflection and for the contemplation of others. It is a condition that has not existed until this juncture because the respective protagonists have been leading parallel lives instead of recognizing each other as family members, friends, and partners. Up until now, they have been focusing their passion and desire on something that has either led them in the wrong direction or toward something they were not prepared to take responsibility for. This existential silence and stagnation constitutes the starting point of Ang Lee's film. A train breaks down in the middle of the night, icicles dangling from its wheels. The scene is dominated by ice blue and inky darkness. The camera shows a distance shot of the train, which appears to be lifeless, frozen. The audience is yet unaware of the significance of this image with regard to the film's tragic narrative climax.

In the next scene, we find ourselves staring at a comic book. A boy is sitting in the darkened train compartment reading *The Fantastic Four*. Suddenly, the light comes back on and the train jolts into life again, slowly and creakingly continuing on its journey. Paul, the boy, then offers us the following insight, which, particularly in view of the film's tragic finale, could be construed as an exposé of the film's common philosophical thread:

> In issue no. 141 of *The Fantastic Four*, published in November 1973, Reed Richards has to use his anti-matter weapon on his own son, who Annihilus has turned into a human atom bomb. It was a typical

predicament for *The Fantastic Four* because they weren't like other superheroes. They were more like a family. And the more power they had the more harm they could do to each other without even knowing it. That was the meaning of *The Fantastic Four*, that a family is like your own personal anti-matter. Your family is the void you emerge from and the place you return to when you die.

This passage is followed by more colorful images of the train pulling into a station. It is daylight: "And that's the paradox: the more you're drawn back in, the deeper you descend into the void." The boy's family—his father, mother, and sister—stand on the platform looking browbeaten and humiliated, but relieved all the same.

Lee's film *The Ice Storm* is an exhilarating, critical portrait of the 1970s, an era that featured the Vietnam War, the Watergate scandal, and the sexual revolution. The film boasts an outstanding cast, which includes Sigourney Weaver, Tobey Maguire, Kevin Kline, Joan Allen, Christina Ricci, and Elijah Wood. Above all, however, *The Ice Storm*—which is an adaptation of a 1994 book by Rick Moody—presents a bountiful source for philosophers. Existential, metaphysical, ontological, psychoanalytic, ethical, and aesthetic issues can all be discussed on the basis of the film's dramatic and formal narrative. Topics raised by the film include being, nothingness, death, alienation, loneliness, boredom, fear, puberty, sexuality, physicality, love, emotions, family, recognition, sympathy, empathy, shame, space, time, and suchlike.

In this chapter, I concentrate on a few ethical issues while acknowledging some broader existential concerns. The philosophy of love and the theory of recognition serve as central reference points for my investigation, though I hasten to add that these are fields about which there has been relatively little systematic philosophical thought and thus much of what will be said will be me engaging with the film per se. I will illustrate that the unfulfilled desire expressed in the film can be defined in terms of dialogical love, the recognition of oneself in others, the facilitation of freedom, and self-awareness through mutual recognition, as well as the transcendence of solipsism and the initiation of empathy with other people's pain. My methodology is based on a combination of analytical and phenomenological investigation.

I focus on three points, which I consider to be important for the philosophical comprehension of the film. First, I introduce a particular concept of love, one that I hold the most plausible in view of current tendencies in the philosophy of love: the dialogical concept of love, which presents love as a shared practice between two autonomous individuals who recognize and value each other's unique characteristics. Second, I invoke another important concept in contemporary philosophy, which considers social practices such as love, the family, and friendship as being successful when a condition of mutual recognition is fulfilled. This mutual recognition is constitutive of freedom and a successful self-understanding of the respective individuals. This includes the argument that humans comprehend their own selves in relation to the recognition of others, namely, by being thrown back upon themselves by the gaze of others. Third, I show that it is a certain kind of empathy and sympathy that causes the ice to break, quite literally, at the end of the film. In addition, I illustrate how the subject matter can reveal a more successful way of creating a relationship with the other and with the self.

I presuppose the fundamental premise that *The Ice Storm* offers an aesthetic experience that is capable of conveying these three facets in a unique way—both in form and content—and that the film itself therefore becomes a philosophical treatise, enabling Lee to formulate philosophical ideas and theses based on images and atmospheres, in a complex, multileveled manner.

Ben Has Decided: The Dialogical Concept of Love

In my presentation of a philosophical concept of love, I focus on so-called romantic or erotic love between adults, ignoring other forms of love, because Ang Lee focuses primarily on the subject of erotic love during the film. Initially, one has to distinguish between love as an emotion and love as a social practice. The specific feeling of love is probably more difficult to describe, and subject to more controversial debate, than the form of the framework required for a relationship based on love as a social practice. I can only treat both in relation to *The Ice Storm* insofar as they both might help to gain purchase on the film.

Among the feelings that constitute the emotional attitude of love—which should be differentiated from the mere state of being infatuated—is a deep and relatively well-established form of emotional attachment to another. Those who love emotionally do so over a duration of time and not merely for a brief moment. The practice involves the mutual expression of physical affection and sexuality with the particular other, as well as certain shared everyday practices such as cohabitation or the desire to be together: "Love is primarily a pleasurable emotion, which seems to depend upon a certain sense of union with another person, and it includes . . . a desire for the society of the beloved."[1] Furthermore, a love relationship also involves other feelings, including moral emotions such as respect, appreciation, recognition, empathy, and sympathy. We will consider these in more detail later in the chapter.

Both emotion and practice mutually permeate each other: the practice is allied to the emotion, and the emotion is dependent on the practical realization. Those who love want to be loved back, and they want that love to be embodied by some form of relationship. They want to experience a "we." Nevertheless, several objections to this argument could already be raised, including one that argues that a love affair may also be associated with feelings of love, even if the practice is left wanting—at least to a certain degree. Conversely, there are couples who insist that they love each other, even though the relationship is no longer associated with sexual gratification and the bond is more like a friendship. If our normative conception of love is too strict, we run the risk of denying both the affair and the partnership based on the friendship attribute of love. However, if the definition is too broad, we might end up including various manifestations of love that do not really deserve consideration. Among other things, the question arises as to what the "we" consists of. Is it a new being, as Robert Nozick describes it,[2] or is it a unit consisting of two individuals who share certain things but who do not merge with each other? At this juncture, it should already be apparent that my espousal of a dialogical approach means that I am opposed to stark union model concepts. Our considerations suggest that we should at least establish some normative criteria for love, which can be illustrated with examples from *The Ice Storm*.

All the various approaches to the philosophy of love agree on the premise that the beloved has an irreplaceable value for the partner, so that he or she is treasured for being special, and the two have a desire to be together.[3] Moreover, there appears to be agreement with regard to the normative idea that the partner is particularly concerned with supporting the interests of the beloved. Iris Murdoch propounds the concept of attention, which describes how the lover sees and recognizes the partner's particularity but also respects his or her autonomy. Accordingly, love is seen as "an exercise of detachment,"[4] implying that the love relationship incorporates a form of moral respect. David Velleman cultivated this idea for use in his own moral approach, in which he describes love in terms of "being emotionally affected" and as reciprocal respect for the other as an end in itself. Velleman formulated some interesting ideas, particularly with regard to the concept of being emotionally affected, insofar as he suggests that people surrender their emotional self-projection in love: "Love disarms our emotional defences; it makes us vulnerable to the other."[5]

Before we define love further, let us turn our attention to *The Ice Storm*. In view of the protagonists' behavior, it is already difficult to define any of the relationships in terms of love. Lee manages to express this in an extraordinary manner, relying on his fine satirical flair and eye for detail: Ben Hood (Kevin Kline) is having an affair with a friendly neighbor (Sigourney Weaver). His wife, Elena (Joan Allen), suspects something but does not dare talk about it. On the outside, the couple maintain a harmonious façade, both for themselves and for others: "The only big fight we've had in years was about whether or not to go into couple's therapy." Elena is remarkably thin, stiff, pinched, and anxious. She seems to want to open herself emotionally to her husband in the Velleman sense. Her resultant vulnerability appears to be so compelling that she is prepared to relinquish her own personality. The explanation for this might be found in the lack of reciprocity. Ben does not give Elena what she requires: emotional and physical affection, security, trust, and recognition.

However, the affair between Ben and Janey is not a love relationship but rather a purely physical union based on mutual gratification, at least according to Janey. She is bored when Ben starts to talk about his daily life after having sex with her. When he talks about a golf partner whom he suspects is taking secret lessons, a set of circumstances one would expect to share with a spouse but not with a fleeting sexual partner, Janey exclaims, "Ben! You're boring me. I have a husband. I don't particularly feel the need for another." Ben responds with, "You have a point there," and continues, "That's a very good point. We're having an affair. Right. An explicitly sexual relationship. Your needs, my needs." There is no room for shared interests, wishes, and practices—unless they are coupled with the sex act. The whole structure of the affair is based on the mutual satisfaction of egoistical needs, even though one can tell by the way Ben expresses himself that he would, in fact, prefer something else. Janey, however, takes the next opportunity to reject him mercilessly, culminating in a scene where she goes home from a key party with a much younger man. With this behavior, Janey signifies that her relationship to Ben is not a love relationship, thus implicitly confirming the conditions we set out above for defining a love relationship. Janey feels no particular affection for Ben; she does not believe he is irreplaceable, and she does not have his particular welfare at heart. Janey maintains her self-protection; for example, when Ben starts to tell her that his wife, Elena, has started to become suspicious, Janey simply abandons him. At that moment, the affair becomes too serious. (Weaver plays the role correspondingly frosty and tough.) Janey does not want to overcome her egoism and enter into a shared practical experience of collective action and feeling. This allows us to formulate a more precise definition of how love is to be understood as an emotional attitude and as a practice.

There are several different approaches to the philosophy of love: the union model, the care model, which has already been mentioned, and the dialogical model.[6] The union model describes love as a fusion of two people into one unit; Plato is the classic advocate of such a model, although contemporary philosophers such as Robert Solomon and Robert Nozick also support versions of this concept. In the care model, love is presented as selfless care for another person. The roots of the care model can be traced to Aristotle, but the model also boasts prominent contemporary supporters, such as Harry Frankfurt. Finally, the third model describes love as a dialogue between individuals. This model also has its roots in Aristotelian philosophy, but it does not correspond to Frankfurt's selfless approach. The German philosopher Angelika Krebs is a prominent contemporary supporter of this approach, while Amélie Oksenberg Rorty, Roger Scruton, and Bennett Helm also subscribe to a similar model.[7]

All three models introduce persuasive arguments and share interesting common intersections; they share the premises listed above but differ in fundamental ways. However, in my opinion, the dialogical model appears to be the most plausible. The union model presents the romantic unification of two loving individuals who work together to create a common single unit, which is confirmed in the performative act of saying, "I love you." "To say 'I love you' is not to report a feeling. . . . It is an aggressive, creative, socially definitive act."[8] The idea of fusion—especially in the physical sense—is also found in the other models, at least to a certain degree. In the union model, however, the lovers' union goes so far as to create a new, mutual entity, a new being or self: "Love is the concentration and the intensive focus of mutual definition on a single individual, subjecting virtually every personal aspect of one's self to this process."[9] The notion that one can no longer tell where one person starts and the other one ends is typical for this condition. An obvious objection would be that the model causes friction between love on the one hand and autonomy on the other, where the autonomy of the individual appears to be abandoned in favor of a (somewhat difficult to imagine) new entity and identity. But why should love stand in opposition to respect for individual autonomy? Moreover, should the recognition and protection of autonomy not be a moral implication of love?

Elena Hood seems to harbor the desire to recognize a "we" relationship with her husband, even if this means the surrender of her autonomy. In the above-described scene, where they talk about couples therapy, Elena slips up when she says: "Actually Ben decided that . . . well I mean we both decided that. . . ." She does not end the sentence because Ben interrupts and finishes the story. Perhaps it would make a difference if Ben would only return her love in the same measure and commit himself to a "we." However, a "we" does not necessarily mean the capitulation of the "I." We will see later that freedom and autonomy are guaranteed through recognition in successful relationships. Elena seeks confirmation of herself and her freedom in other strange or pathological ways: she rides a bicycle—as free as a child would— and steals lipsticks from the drugstore.

In the second love model, the care model, love is defined by caring for the beloved person. The welfare of the other is of utmost importance to the partner; his or her own interests correspond to the interests of the other. This model does not require reciprocity for its fulfilment. Selflessness is a part of the realization of the self in this definition of love. Strictly speaking (although not all care models are so constrictive), autonomy and individuality are replaced by the pursuit of the beloved person's interests, provided that "the lover invests him- or herself in what he or she loves, and in that way identifies with it, the interests of the beloved are identical with their own."[10]

We can use the example of Elena again, but at the same time illustrate that she is not being fulfilled. Is someone who loves really happy, even when she is not loved in return? Is it enough to satisfy the interests of the other? In my opinion, this model does not fulfill the criteria necessary for the constitution of a love relationship between adults, namely dialogue and mutual recognition.

We do not encounter real love based on reciprocity in *The Ice Storm*, but frustrated love. The pubescent and somewhat strange Mikey Carver (Elijah Wood) is infatuated with Wendy (Christina Ricci), who is approximately the same age. Wendy experiments with him but she, in turn, is more interested in the relatively childlike Sandy (Adam Hann-Byrd), who is full of coy admiration for her. Paul Hood (Tobey Maguire) is in love with Libbets Casey (Katie Holmes). However, Libbets loves Paul like a brother. Finally, Jim Carver (Jamey Sheridan), Janey's husband, remains very much in the shadows until near the end of the film. He appears to be in a similar situation to Elena, but he is, at least, capable of securing a certain amount of recognition from his work.

The third model defines love as a dialogue, which is enacted on both a mental and a physical level. According to that conception, sexuality is a bodily dialogue: sexuality is the mutual exploration and revelation of each other's incarnation, without regard for, or independent of, sexual gratification.[11] On a mental level, the dialogue of love can further be defined in terms of an attitude of respect and recognition, as well as shared practice in the form of collective action and shared lives, in addition to the emotional attitude.

The "we" notion, a togetherness that serves to define the dialogical model in relation to the joint action theory, also exists as part of this model. However, in this case, the "I" is not surrendered to accommodate a joint entity, even though the entity does exist as such in the phenomenon of shared feelings, which is why the dialogue theorists speak of love as sharing.[12] The central category of shared feelings or emotional sharing was established by the phenomenologist Max Scheler. According to Scheler, shared feelings belong to the so-called fellow feelings—the feelings we can share with other people.[13] Moreover, the phenomenon of shared feelings is not just limited to those sharing a love relationship; it can also occur between friends, family members, team partners, or complete strangers when they are subjected to a mutual experience.

One can clearly see that the protagonists in the film have lost the capacity for dialogical, autonomy-granting love as shared feeling and collective action. They have been alienated from each other both as lovers and as a family. They neither encounter each other in dialogue nor act nor feel together. Instead, they talk and live at cross-purposes. Maybe it is precisely this state of affairs that makes the molecules so attractive for Mikey, so that he longs to experience them during the ice storm: "When it freezes, because that means the molecules are not moving. It's when you breathe: It's nothing in the air, you know? The molecules have stopped. It's clean." Otherwise you always have to inhale all the bad stuff, as he previously stated in a school essay: the entire stench, the feces, and all the waste humans leave behind.

Experience of Self and the Negative Zone: Recognition and Freedom

Although the sexual revolution was supposed to be an expression of freedom, Lee's film appears to support an opposing view. The protagonists seem to be constricted by a climate of compulsive casualness. A conversation about the pornographic film *Deep Throat* (1972), for example, appears to be inflated, and the Halfords' key party is uncomfortable and embarrassing. Janey is the only one who represents a liberated woman, but she does not seem very happy either; she is too egocentric and therefore is in much the same condition as the other characters. Furthermore, it would appear that the protagonists are all condemned to return to a solitary position, where the other, necessary for the insurance of one's own freedom, is absent.[14]

Mutual recognition and sympathy, on both mental and physical levels, are the essential constituents of a love relationship, according to Hegelian-inspired theories of recognition. The recognition theory should therefore be juxtaposed with the dialogical concept of love. Love is a form or sphere of recognition. The subjects confirm their particular individuality in their sexuality, in the structure of their physical needs, and in institutionalized love relationships. Thus, the subjects experience a form of self-awareness, one that Hegel calls "knowing-oneself-in-the-other."[15] The love partners therefore help each other to attain a basic level of self-confidence.

Neither Janey and Jim nor Elena and Ben can lay claim to a physically, mentally, and emotionally shared, mutually insured "we" and the corresponding confirmation of their own individuality. Elena's lack of self-confidence is exemplary in this respect. For recognition theorists, mutual recognition in a love relationship is also a prerequisite for freedom. This means that part of the relationship is to guarantee the freedom of the other. Ideally, the partners support each other's ethical and moral development, help each other with existential decisions, confirm and help to formulate each other's personal identity, and satisfy each other's physical need for tenderness and sexuality. The partner in a love relationship is a source of self-discovery and an extension of the personality of the other.[16]

The protagonists in Lee's film are looking for all this in the wrong places: in an affair (Ben, Janey), in bicycle rides and lipstick theft (Elena), and in molecules (Mikey). However, Mikey seems to experience an extraordinarily happy and vibrant experience of the self shortly before, or perhaps during, the moment of his death: the tragic scene where he slides across the ice and hangs onto the railing, watching the dangling electricity cable, which will eventually kill him, dance in front of his awestruck eyes. The delicate sound of the ice represents the beauty of the moment; the subsequent silence is indicative of the molecular stagnation, which is the subject of so much fascination for Mikey. The dead body glides over the ice in almost total silence, in much the same way as it did when it was still full of life. However, Mikey now seems to be a thing, an object rather than a subject.

The next scene transports us back to the beginning of the film. Paul's train grinds to a halt before slowly resuming its journey. As a reminder, Paul's off-camera voice can be heard explaining that the family is the void you emerge from and the place you return to when you die.

This leads us to Sartre's negativistic interpretation and the further development of Hegel's theory of recognition. Of course, it is possible to use a more disillusioned approach to Lee's film than the one we have used thus far. In *Being and Nothingness,* Sartre associates intersubjectivity with negativity, recognition with the death of the original freedom of the subject; according to Sartre, the other's gaze[17] is associated with shame, objectification, and alienation. Although love is based on dialogical unity, it is doomed to fail. Love is a perpetual conflict because the lovers see or want to see the partners in a way they do not want to be seen. That is why love and seduction are associated with dislocation rather than with the mutual openness and corresponding freedom suggested above. Of course, this kind of reading can also be applied to Lee's film, when Paul talks about the negative zone of the Fantastic Four, for example:

> To find yourself in the negative zone, as The Fantastic Four often do, means that all everyday assumptions are inverted. Even the Invisible Girl herself becomes visible and so she loses the last semblance of her power. It seems to me that everyone exists partially on a negative zone level. Some people more than others. . . . But for some people there is something about the negative zone that tempts them. And then they're going in, going in all the way.

It could be argued that Mikey and Sandy are motivated by such a compulsion. Sandy destroys his toys by blowing them up with fireworks. Mikey is obsessed with molecular stagnation. He submits completely to the negative zone at the point of his death, assuming that death is the negation of life. However, Sartre's condition of recognition and love is also one in which the self experiences itself as self. The relationships described by the Carver and Hood families, however, are characterized by attitudes of indifference, ignorance, and (self-)deception.

Everything appears to change when Mikey dies, however. And so we come to the final section, in which I would like to explore the concept of sharing the experience of other people's suffering through empathy and sympathy.

The Reunion: Empathy and Sympathy

According to the phenomenologists Max Scheler and Edith Stein, the awareness of another subject is related to a process of empathy. This is a fundamental stage of interpersonal experiencing and understanding.[18] Empathy is not a fellow feeling, however, but—as a complex form of comprehension—a prerequisite for sympathy and compassion. Empathy and sympathy are to be distinguished from the aforementioned shared feeling. The complex structure can only be hinted at here. Nevertheless, I consider it important to use these phenomena in my philosophical examination of *The Ice Storm*. Interestingly, Scheler used the example of a father and mother, standing together beside the body of their dead child, for the explication of various forms of empathy and fellow feelings. The parents share the same feeling at this particular point. They experience emotional sharing, suffering the same pain at the same time. This phenomenon is different from the feeling a third party would have if he or she were to join the mourning parents. The third person sympathizes with the parents' suffering. He or she is not directly involved with mourning the loss of the child but is sad insofar as he feels compassion for the parents.

At this stage, there is an easy transition to *The Ice Storm*: Ben finds Mikey's dead body on the icy road on his way back from the Halfords' party. He brings the body to the Carvers' house, where Jim, the father, takes over. Jim buries his face in the dead body and weeps. It is interesting that this character, which had thitherto been confined to a secondary function, should suddenly play such a decisive role. His wife, Janey, is not there; she is lying in bed, where she can hear her husband's sobs and groans. No state of shared feeling has therefore been activated—at least not at that moment in time. Lee leaves the question open as to whether or not the event of the death of their son will reunify them. Jim is certainly alone in this situation. He even seems to be experiencing some kind of shame because, in his state of grief, he feels that he is at the mercy of the other person's gaze (which could be linked to Sartre once again). Ben, Elena, and Wendy stand there, expressing bewilderment and compassion; Wendy consoles Sandy by embracing him; Ben and Elena stand close together, even though they hardly look at each other. I believe Lee expresses something akin to optimism with the Hood family. The sun comes out and the icicles start to glitter when the Carvers leave. The Hoods go to meet their son, Paul, at the train station. The father becomes emotional and reveals his vulnerability by shedding tears in front of his family. Elena addresses her husband via his Christian name, Ben, and that is how the film ends.

I hope I have managed to illustrate how *The Ice Storm* raises ethical and existential questions. I have shown how the various philosophical approaches to love have been presented in the film, and I have declared my support for the dialogical model. Moreover, I have placed this model in relation to theories of recognition. In both respects, I have argued that the characters in the film represent the lack of dialogical love and mutual recognition necessary for the successful development of a reciprocal love relationship with a partner, a relationship of solidarity within the family, and a healthy relationship with oneself. Furthermore, I have also shown how empathy and sympathy can, in this instance, quite literally break the ice, creating opportunities for the rediscovery of recognition and love. In my opinion *The Ice Storm* is an impressing aesthetic–ethical paradigm for philosophical issues like these.

Notes

I would like to thank Philip Jacobs for the helpful support with the translation and Frank Hesse for his helpful comments.

1. Henry Sidgwick, *The Methods of Ethics* (Indianapolis, Ind.: Hackett, 1981), 244.

2. Robert Nozick, *The Examined Life: Philosophical Meditations* (New York: Simon & Schuster, 1989), 68–69.

3. David J. Velleman, "Love as a Moral Emotion," *Ethics* 109, no. 2 (1999): 362.

4. Iris Murdoch, *The Sovereignty of the Good* (New York: Routledge, 1970), 65.

5. Velleman, "Love as a Moral Emotion," 361.

6. Bennett Helm, "Love," in *Stanford Encyclopedia of Philosophy* (http://plato.stanford.edu); Angelika Krebs, "Dialogical Love, with a Response by Martha Nussbaum," in *The Philosophy of Martha Nussbaum,* ed. R. E. Auxier and Lewis E. Hahn (Chicago: Open Court, forthcoming).

7. See Helm, "Love."

8. Robert Solomon, *About Love: Reinventing Romance for Our Times* (Indianapolis, Ind.: Hackett, 2006), 36.

9. Ibid., 197; see also Nozick, *Examined Life,* 70.

10. Harry Frankfurt, *The Reasons of Love* (Princeton, N.J.: Princeton University Press, 2004), 61.

11. Roger Scruton, *Sexual Desire: A Philosophical Investigation* (London: Continuum Press, 2006).

12. Angelika Krebs, "The Phenomenology of Shared Feeling," *Appraisal* 8, no. 3 (2011): 35.

13. See Dan Zahavi, "Simulation, Projection, and Empathy," *Consciousness and Cognition* 17 (2008): 514–522.

14. See Axel Honneth, *The Struggle for Recognition: The Moral Grammar of Social Conflicts* (Cambridge, Mass.: MIT Press, 1995), and *Das Recht der Freiheit. Grundriß einer demokratischen Sittlichkeit* (Frankfurt am Main: Suhrkamp, 2011).

15. Honneth, *Struggle for Recognition*, 37.

16. Honneth, *Das Recht der Freiheit*, 270.

17. Jean-Paul Sartre, *L'être et le néant. Essai d'ontologie phénoménologique* (Paris: Gallimard, 1943), 310.

18. Max Scheler, *The Nature of Sympathy* (London: Routledge, 1954), 9.

IT'S EXISTENTIAL

Negative Space and Nothingness in *The Ice Storm*

David Koepsell

A Universe Devoid

Two of the most important philosophical movements of the nineteenth and twentieth centuries are also the least understood. Phenomenology and existentialism mark, in many ways, the cultural move from modernism to postmodernism and serve as the context for much of the twentieth century's significant and lasting contributions to our present world. Ang Lee's critically acclaimed film, *The Ice Storm* (1997), based on Rick Moody's 1994 novel of the same name, is an existential masterpiece, depicting the crossroads at which humanity stands through a story about a New England family in Nixon's America.

In light of the successes of science and technology, the emergence of the modern era is marked by a slow, though not always articulate, suspicion that we live in a universe devoid of theistic teleology and meaning. The feeling among some is that the universe does not care for us at all, and except for the meaning that we create through our myths and languages, there is no particular meaning or purpose to our existences, either individually or collectively.[1] Nevertheless, for French existential philosopher and playwright Jean-Paul Sartre (1905–1980), this is not cause for a terminal state of angst, but rather is the root of our freedom and humanity.

Existence Precedes Essence

Sartre's existentialism embraces the lack of inherent meaning or essence in existence, describes existence as preceding essence, and makes it thus the project of our life's work to create meaning. The meaninglessness and lack of essence to bare existence forces us into a state of freedom. We are so utterly free that we become nauseous when facing our bare, meaningless, existence: the "no-thing-ness" (of *Being and Nothingness*). We are thus much more responsible—in a broader political, moral, and aesthetic sense—for what comes of our lives than previous philosophies could accept. Sartre views many of us as living inauthentic existences, escaping the no-thing-ness we face by playing roles rather than being in the world and of it, facing existence with our freedom and making conscious authentic choices. He terms this condition bad faith. Living inauthentically, or in bad faith, is perhaps the worst sin for Sartre, and the existential project is, more than anything, to be authentic.[2]

Sartre's ontology makes the interaction of consciousness with existence the crux of the existential conundrum. But his project is a humanistic one, concerned not at all with describing the essences of the phenomenal world, but rather with the problem of how to live. While Sartre undermines traditional idealistic dualism in favor of a unity of being, being comes in several forms. Being in itself refers to being apart from consciousness, such as the being of a chair or any other nonconscious entity. The being of persons exists in a state of tension between being-for-itself (oneself) and being for others. Being in itself cannot be attained by persons, though we often fall into bad faith or inauthenticity in seeking it, which is essentially the same thing as seeking to be god. Being for itself is conscious being undirected toward any other. Only this type of being is capable of detachment from anything else, and thus of no-thing-ness. This is the consciousness of the cogito. Being for others causes us an eternal war of selves, as each self makes an object out of the other in order to recover its own being. The objectification of the other is necessary. The other objectifies us even as we objectify the other. The responsibility of freedom, given our no-thing-ness, is to avoid objectification of the other, to regard the other as a being for itself, to avoid alienation and inauthenticity. Our freedom is both limitless and a limit as we must acknowledge it, and respect it, and define from it our essence. Thus, essence follows existence, and we are free to create our essence.[3]

Sartre's philosophy is complex and evolves over the course of decades, but his role in defining modern existentialism is clear. Existentialism is a postmodern philosophy that extends humanity's godless, meaningless existence into an all-encompassing political, cultural, ontological, and personal way of living. Immersed as we are in existence, and faced with no-thing-ness, we have as our overriding challenge the responsibility to define our own essence and make meaning out of our lives. In Nixon's America, at the height of the Vietnam War and with the Watergate break-in as the context, *The Ice Storm* presents us with several personal and interpersonal examples of the existentialist dilemma of how to live. Let's explore some of these in context and see how the underlying philosophy of existentialism provides an answer rather than angst.

The Family and Negative Space

The use of fiction is common and particular to existentialist philosophy as a tool to investigate the human situation. Fiction allows us to examine humans (albeit fictional ones) existing. Rather than assuming an analytical posture, inquiring into language and its meanings, we are presented through fiction with human situations—characters and their inner lives—and allowed to experience vicariously the full range of human experience. In fleeting moments of good fiction, we transcend the dichotomy between us and the other, and we experience life as the other. *The Ice Storm* is an existential work, and arguably a masterpiece of existentialism, because it shows us a world of alienated others who manage, despite their hopeless context, to overcome their alienation, albeit through tragedy. It is also replete with existentialist themes and language.

In the opening few minutes of *The Ice Storm*, Paul Hood, commenting on Mister Fantastic of *The Fantastic Four*, reflects:

> And that's what it is to come from a family, if you analyze it closely. Each of them is negative matter for the other ones. And that's what dying is—dying is when your family, which is in fact your personal negative matter from which you emerge—it's when the family takes you back, thus hurling you back into negative space.

Negative space could well be the no-thing-ness of which Sartre writes when referring to the state of being itself. It is a place of existence without predication. Paul concludes: "So it's a paradox—the closer you're drawn back in, the further into the void you're thrown." And so we are thrust headlong into the central theme of Sartre's existentialism: the divide between being and no-thing-ness, and the paradoxical struggle to achieve disalienation or authenticity by directing our gaze upon others. From this moment, we are cast into the midst of a rather stereotypical New England family: WASPish, cold, and clearly all suffering from alienation under varying degrees of inauthenticity. Drugs, desire, and depression reign as each of the characters seeks desperately to surmount his or her despair. The backdrop is Nixon's America, in which the 1960s generation of peace, love, and harmony has been replaced with war, lies, and materialism. The "me" generation was gearing up to replace the freaks and hippies. Paul and his sister are perhaps the most authentic, but they are still distracted and alienated from their parents. Daydreaming in his English class, he listens to the object of his desire, a New York City upper-class nymph with some artistic and philosophical sensibilities, as she discusses Dostoyevsky: "What Dostoyevsky is saying here is that to be a Christian is to choose, because you have to choose of your own choice; but since you can't choose to be good because that would be too rational, you have to choose to be bad—it's existential."

This sets up the central moral theme. Between *The Fantastic Four* and Dostoyevsky, we have, within the very first few minutes of *The Ice Storm*, been presented with the existential conundrum facing the characters, their families, and their relations to each other: the question of negative space, the desire of the being for itself to become being for others and the tension between these two states of affairs. We see the Hood and Carver families as neighbors of a sort, in that they live in the same sparse, distant, rural suburb in New England. The Carver family reflects the alienation of the Hoods, with their own disaffected, distant children, cold marital climate, lies, and angst. From the safety of their material comfort, they engage over dinner in charming conversations about horrors, like the Vietnam War, gas lines from the energy crisis, and the infidelities of the local Unitarian minister. They do this bemusedly, judgmentally, and from their positions of privilege. Sartre could not be more sickened by their bourgeois patter, detached from responsibility as upper-middle-class patrons of the ruling class. This mastery, disdained by Sartre as the attempt to validate one's self as a being for itself (without regard for the other and anything but as an object), is all too apparent within their family. Wendy and Paul, the Hood kids, are liberals whose hatred of Nixon is hushed and countered by their father, Ben, while Elena—the stereotypical, June Cleaver–esque, ineffectual mother—remains quietly complicit.

The children are more or less left out of the parents' lives and conversations, except when there's a command or some requirement to be met. But they are affected by their parents' conversations, discussions of key parties, the movie *Deep Throat* (1972), and other subjects perhaps a bit too complicated for the Carver or Hood children. We then learn, as we follow the Hood family home, how alienated Elena and Ben are from one another. They don't share a bedroom, Ben refuses to seek counseling, and he has apparently not yet decided on whether to leave or stay. Seeking advice from his father—who remained married to his wife despite their hatred—is of no help. Ben's father blanches at being called "dad," and he advises Ben to leave his wife as he should have done, but Ben vacillates still, believing he maybe loves her. Meanwhile, Elena browses self-help books in a New England bookstore and gets hit on by the notorious Unitarian minister, who urges her over coffee to join his flock. At the same time, Wendy, who has been excoriating Nixon's lies and presumed thievery, is revealed to have a shoplifting problem. We also learn that Ben Hood and Janey Carver are having an affair. Alienation abounds.

The Carver kids have their own issues, as Mikey (the oldest) seems to have a penchant to daydream, or problems concentrating, or possibly a real affliction. He is good at geometry but little else. Sandy, the youngest, seems to be the only one with no real problems. Both kids barely notice their parents, who barely notice them. When the father, Jim, returns home from a business trip, Mikey asks, "You were gone?" Jim's return is treated with similar apathy by his own, cheating wife.

Elena's attempt to find some semblance of freedom by riding a bike she finds in her garage is stymied by a flat tire, leading to an awkward lift home provided by her husband's lover. It's clear Elena suspects, or even knows, but the pretense of civility is maintained, and then we learn that Elena too is a shoplifter. From there we return to Paul, who is on a train heading home for Thanksgiving, musing as he did at the beginning about the negative zone of *The Fantastic Four:* "To find yourself in the Negative Zone, as the Fantastic Four often do, means that all everyday assumptions are inverted—even the invisible girl herself becomes visible, and so she loses the last semblance of her power." It is commentary on this sordid family that he is returning to, and consequently on himself as a product of that family. The existential angst that pervades these characters is unresolved, and seemingly irresolvable. How can they possibly contact each other, connect across the void separating them each as being for themselves? How can they take responsibility for their freedom and act in the world as though the others exist?

Wendy, who has been meeting Mikey to make out, reveals herself to Mikey's prepubescent brother, Sandy, and they are both caught by Janey, who hypocritically and moralistically lectures them about the temple of their bodies. Mikey is betrayed and alone more than ever. Amid this sordid maelstrom, Paul returns home to nonsensical advice from his father that he listens to absently. Only marijuana can help Paul cope with his familial malaise. Ben retreats swiftly to his lover, Janey, who gets up and drives away abruptly after they have sex, leaving Ben to wander the (supposedly) empty house, only to find Mikey and Wendy making out in the basement. Now he, hypocritically and moralistically, lectures them both. Bringing her home in the rain and cold, he tells Elena what he found, forgetting that the "why" of the where he found her was his own dalliance. Finally totally aware of Ben's unfaithfulness, she confronts him as they prepare to attend a neighbor's party, having no real communication, no resolution, and no honesty at all. Paul leaves for New York City to pursue the rich girl, the object of his desire.

The Rain Continues, and It Grows Colder

Things come to a head at various parties. The Carvers and the Hoods both attend what is revealed to be a key party, where Elena and Ben finally have it out, resulting in an admission of sorts. Then Janey and Ben argue as well. Janey tells Ben she has become bored with him and she doesn't want to be used anymore. When she chooses the key of a young, attractive man, Ben launches into heavier drinking and passes out in a bathroom. Jim and Elena end up together, matched by the key in the bowl, and couple frantically in a car. Meanwhile Paul wades through a drug-addled daze at his party in the city, failing again to score with Libbets. Unsupervised, Wendy wanders through the icy rain to the Carvers', only to hear that Mikey has gone out in the growing ice storm. Wendy and the prepubescent Sandy end up drinking vodka and falling asleep naked in bed, while Mikey wanders the icy, abandoned suburban landscape, risking life and limb in the process. He totters on a slippery, iced-over springboard above an empty pool, somehow managing not to fall off it and kill himself. He then wanders the iced-over streets in genuine joy, reveling in the foreign landscape, sliding on the streets. Then the streetlights sputter and die. A power line has fallen. Sitting on a metal guardrail to take in the wondrously beautiful world covered in ice, he doesn't notice the snaking electrical cable that meets the guardrail, electrocuting him as he quietly says, "Oh shit." His lifeless body falls, then slides unceremoniously down the iced-over street.

Elena leaves Ben at the party, and Ben, walking home in the dawn, discovers Mikey's body.

The ice storm has passed and left behind some hope, amid the horror.

The ice storm is pure, mindless, meaningless being-in-itself, pure existence without consciousness. Nature cares not for us, nor is there a god to watch over us. But in the ice storm, and through Mikey's death, two important existentialist moments are shown. The first is that Mikey revels in the storm: he exists. He takes experience as it is directly given to him. His abstract mind is caught up in concrete existence. It is wonderful, joyous, and he is, briefly, free. In those fleeting instants, we see what existence is about—or at least Mikey has made meaning out of this natural wonder and found in it both delight and play. More than any other character at any other time in the movie, Mikey overcomes angst, rejoices in his existence, and transcends his ego. His is a solution to the existentialist problem, but it proves fatal for him. Like so many tragic, existential heroes (including the lead character in Sartre's *Nausea* [1938]), he is overwhelmed by existence. Unlike Antoine Roquentin, Mikey dies without having had an opportunity to come to grips with the responsibilities of freedom.

The second important moment for the hope of overcoming the existentialist angst into which the other characters have fallen comes in the resolution of the movie. While Paul waits in a train, stranded by the power outage, he reads his *Fantastic Four:* "DON'T YOU SEE, SUE? HE WAS TOO POWERFUL . . . IF HIS ENERGY HAD CONTINUED TO BUILD, HE WOULD HAVE DESTROYED THE WORLD!" Existence is overwhelming: like electricity, it is too powerful to touch. In a rare, human moment, Mikey's father wails in loss, though he is alone. But Wendy, seeing Sandy, breaks through his momentary rage and hugs Sandy, defusing the moment. Human contact—not words, reason, or logic—has disalienated the two briefly. As the Hoods pick up Paul at the train station, Ben finally acts like a father: he is finally present, in that moment, being both for himself and for others, and begins to cry as he presumably starts to inform Paul of the night's tragic events.

Negative Space and No-thing-ness

Sartre's philosophy is sometimes wrongly criticized for being negative. Some believe he is fatalistically hopeless or despairing. But no-thing-ness is not hopelessness. We, as beings in ourselves, recognize that we are not things, not objects, not like the world of being in itself. But we are rather utterly, perfectly free to recast ourselves. We are not essences; we play roles, but we are not those roles. Death, for Sartre, turns us into being in itself, and we thus become like the rest of the nonconscious world. We can never truly know existence as being in itself, for to do so is to die, as Mikey has done. But we can become present as beings for ourselves and for others. To do so, we must cease to objectify the other. We cannot use the other simply as a means to have power over ourselves, to verify ourselves in the absence of some universal power.

We are consciousness. The cogito is true. But we are not consciousness apart from the world. We exist in the world, and the world is full of existence. Learning how to reconcile the seemingly irreconcilable divergence between being in itself and being for itself, and closing the chasm among beings for themselves, is the great responsibility of our freedom. Sartre has no particular answer for this moral quandary. Perhaps we find this answer in fleeting moments, as the characters in *The Ice Storm* do, when existence intrudes upon our alienation and breaks it briefly. Perhaps in a momentary embrace at a moment of loss, or enraptured in joyous wonder at nature's beauty, we find a way to deal with existence. Sartre did not believe in the separate existence of universals, and so no all-encompassing theory will do to explain the solution to the problem. But in his fiction and philosophical works, we can see clearly what we are not to do. The Hoods exhibit this clearly too, and they promise at the end of *The Ice Storm* to remake themselves, as they are free to do, in a way that can cope with existence more authentically. It is something the rest of us can hope for, and maybe even attain, if we understand the failures we are shown in existentialist masterpieces like *The Ice Storm*.

Notes

1. For more on this worldview and explanations concerning existentialism, see Jean-Paul Sartre, *Being and Nothingness: A Phenomenological Essay on Ontology,* trans. Hazel Barnes (New York: Washington Square Press, 1992); *The Transcendence of the Ego: An Existentialist Theory of Consciousness,* trans. Forrest Williams and Robert Kirkpatrick (New York: Hill and Wang, 1960); and *Existentialism Is a Humanism,* trans. Carol Macomber (New Haven, Conn.: Yale University Press, 2007); Jack Reynolds, *Understanding Existentialism* (London: Acumen, 2006); Thomas Flynn, *Existentialism: A Very Short Introduction* (Oxford: Oxford University Press, 2006); Julian Baggini, *Atheism: A Very Short Introduction* (Oxford: Oxford University Press, 2003).

2. Thomas Flynn, "Jean-Paul Sartre," and Steven Crowell, "Existentialism," both in *Stanford Encyclopedia of Philosophy* (http://plato.stanford.edu).

3. See Joseph S. Catalano, *A Commentary on Jean-Paul Sartre's* Being and Nothingness (Chicago: University of Chicago Press, 1985), 10–11.

THE ICE STORM

What Is Impending?

George T. Hole

Opening Scene: Prophecy

The Ice Storm (1997) opens, we feel we are moving, but the scene is dark and unidentifiable. Credits appear; some letters are out of focus, and then slowly become clear. The moving image becomes distinct. We have been following railroad tracks, and we see icicles hanging underneath a train car. We next view a page of a comic book, then the young boy reading it in a commuter train. The car's overhead lights flicker. We are outside the train, slowly beginning to move with grinding sounds. Above the train, sparks fly in the night sky. Back inside, a conductor calls out "good morning" and announces the next station. (A single flute is playing wistful notes.) A voice, presumably the young boy's, tells us that the father of *The Fantastic Four* comic has used an antimatter weapon on his own son, turning him into a human atom bomb. He explains that the Fantastic Four are like a family. The more power they have, the more harm they do to each other. A family is like your own anti-matter: "It is the void from which you emerge and where you return when you die. And that is the paradox: The more you're drawn in, the deeper into the void you go." The scene shifts to two adults and a young girl, presumably together, waiting at the commuter station, looking solemn. The boy emerges from the train and smiles. The final credits appear, against a dark, blank background, and again they gain clarity after being out of focus. Four minutes have elapsed. Now the film truly begins.

When the film ends, it will be evident that this opening was prophetic, foretelling the harm the family does to each other and the void in which they live and into which each will return. An exploration of this impending uncertainty and loss is the theme of this chapter, which draws from existentialism, Zen Buddhism, and Daoism to argue that significance is obtained only by viewing one's existence as a life film, a work of art that culminates in one's demise.

Plot: A Question

The film closely follows the 1994 novel *The Ice Storm,* by Rick Moody, who presents a scathing portrait of decadent suburban culture circa 1970. He lays bare the lifestyle of two families during the Thanksgiving holiday, as if they were under a magnifying glass in sunlight, burning. The film's action involves the intersecting plots of the four members of the Hood family: the adulterous father, Ben (Kevin Kline); his quietly suffering wife, Elena (Joan Allen); Paul (Tobey Maguire), about to turn sixteen years old, whom we met on the commuter train reading a comic book; and his younger sister, Wendy (Christina Ricci), fourteen years old. She is the one who points out hypocrisies. For grace at Thanksgiving dinner, she gives thanks for "all the material possessions we enjoy" and then lists national disgraces: "Letting us white people kill all the Indians and steal their tribal lands and stuff ourselves like pigs while children in Africa and Asia are napalmed." The other family is the Carvers: the father is Jim (Jamey Sheridan), mostly absent; the wife is Jane (Sigourney Weaver), who is having an affair with Ben Hood, and their two sons, Mikey (Elijah Wood) and Sandy (Adam Hann-Byrd), the same ages as Paul and Wendy, both of whom have significant interactions with Wendy.

In current moralistic–sociological language, both families, upper-middle-class affluent, would be diagnosed as dysfunctional. Each family member is searching for a way out of everyday malaise. Ben and Janey seek solace in an affair, and the four Hood and Weaver adults participate in a swinger's party, a version of hooking up, where women fish car keys out of a bowl and leave with the keys' male owners for sex. Elena shoplifts. The kids experiment with sex too, and do drugs. Wendy propositions Sandy: "I'll show mine if you show me yours." Paul takes the tranquilizer Seconal from Libbets's parents' medicine cabinet to sedate his roommate, Francis, whom he considers a rival for her affections. Sandy likes to blow up his military toys. Along with adultery, there are the usual deceptions of the adulterer to his spouse and himself. To keep life calm, there is heavy alcohol use. There is boredom: lying in bed after having sex, Ben complains to Janey about his golf game, comparing it to a rival's at work. She responds almost without feeling, "You are boring me. I already have a husband. I don't particularly have the need for another." Ben tries awkwardly to give advice about masturbation to his embarrassed son, Paul: "Don't do it in the shower; it wastes water and electricity." Without such doses of comic relief, the characters would be stick figures, instructive as psychological case studies.

Just as the family is troubled, so is the nation. Through the television, we are given access to the unsettling political world of the Nixon Watergate scandal and the Vietnam War. Television also gives us weather updates, news of the world of nature. Film director Ang Lee masterfully interweaves the worlds of the families, the nation, nature, and comic book fantasy. It is spooky, for example, to see Wendy, wearing a Nixon mask, being dry-humped by Mikey.

Actions occurring at the same time are juxtaposed as the drama slowly moves toward anticipated sexual fulfillment for the couples, Ben and Janey, for the key couples, for Paul and Libbets, and for Wendy and Sandy, not her boyfriend, Mikey. The weather reports increase in frequency and seriousness. Ice is forming on everything outside, beautifully and dangerously. Sandy's toy soldier will not stop warning, "Mayday. Mayday." No one heeds these ominous warnings. Sexual expectations culminate in disappointment and humiliation. Janey does not pick Ben's key, so he ends up drunk and nauseated and in the bathroom. Elena picks Jim's (Janey's husband) key, and has awkward, quick sex with him in the front seat of his car. So that he can have sex with Libbets, Paul drugs his roommate, who is unexpectedly present with Libbets at her parents' apartment. But Libbets inadvertently takes the drug too. Ironically, when she passes out, her head falls onto Paul's groin. Wendy and naive Sandy drink vodka, take off their clothes in bed, and fall asleep.

While others are suffering sexual disappointment, Mikey has been having fun alone, outside in the ice storm. Sliding on the ice-covered road, he sees the downed wire, alive, dancing dangerously close. Feeling safe, he sits on the guardrail, unaware that the wire is touching it. He is, seemingly by chance, electrocuted. His death will radically change the Hood and Carver families. Turning away from the movie toward ourselves, how does the ending affect us, the audience? The ending is sad, perhaps tragic. Does the film challenge us in any way? What, if anything, does it warn us about? We are back to our hunt for what is impending.

When we think of examples of what is impending, we could put them into two evaluative containers: those that we look forward to, like graduation, a great job, and an even greater love life. In the other container we put exams, paying off debts, and healing a broken heart. These examples of what is impending point to what might be realized in the future. The impending we are tracking is, curiously, in the present. First, consider the way in which the past is impending.

Suffering: A Zen Buddhist Story

The Hood and Carver families are suffering. According to the Four Noble Truths of Buddhism, suffering has a cause, involving desires, and a cure. But is it possible to end all desires? Even to attempt this feat would arise from a desire, so the project is self-defeating. In addition to the reality of suffering, classical Buddhism asks us to understand impermanence and the nature of what we think our self is. In regard to suffering there is a more sophisticated understanding of desire, according to which our attachment to our desires is the cause of suffering. Attachment is exemplified in the following Zen Buddhist[1] story:

> Two monks on a religious pilgrimage have taken a vow of strict celibacy, not to touch a woman in any way. They come upon a swollen river and meet a beautiful woman who is unable to cross it. One monk picks her up and carries her to the other side. When they arrived at their night lodging one monk says to the other, "Why did you touch that woman? It is contrary to our vows." The other monk replies, "I left her at the river. Why are you still carrying her?"

The monk carried his judgments against the other monk for breaking his vow. At what cost? As he replayed judgments about the monk's vow breaking, he was not present to experience much of his journey because he was preoccupied with his ruminations. He missed, for example, experience of the scenery. He was also replaying his judgments from a point of view of himself as pure and righteous.

Our minds, like the monk's, can become cluttered with all kinds of judgments and mental activity tied to the past like regret, guilt, fear, and even memories of happy times, all interfering with our experience of our present reality. In a sense, these mental activities impend from our history into our present. A source of clutter, indistinct, dark, and out of focus like the film opening, is our attachment to images of our selves, shaped in complex and inscrutable ways by our previous experiences and hopes for our future. In effect, we often act and live in hypothetical dramas in mental space, dramas featuring our self-image. A danger with attachment to our self-image is that we hold on to multiple, inflexible images, and what does not fit with them causes conflict. So to maintain the image, discrepancies must be ignored, rejected, or annihilated. This is a truth gleaned from Paul's comic book: the father in the story, aptly named Annihilus, saw his son as a rival threatening his image of himself; therefore, he had to be annihilated. The adults in *The Ice Storm* struggle with their images of themselves and have stereotypical images of what their children are supposed to be. At the same time, their children are struggling to break free of parental images and find an acceptable image for themselves.

As we see, our past is impending in our lives. We carry, like the monk, all kinds of burdens and ruminate about them in many dramatic ways. As a consequence, we block and distort experience of our present. Adults in the film are attached to desires and to their concerns about them to the point their actions seem like malaise-infected rituals. Their kids might say that their parents do not have a clue what is going on in their lives. In the world of the comic book, they all sense a void in their worlds. Others in their family do not fill the void. They are attached to each other in typical family roles and are devoid of affection for each other. So the family members are in a force field of rejection. Like the Fantastic Four family, they exert a repulsive force against each other and seek outside attachments, to free themselves from the repulsive force. They are attached to a desire for something else, indefinite, a desire arising in a deep dissatisfaction, a desire to fill some void in their lives. Fortunately there is humor and irony in their repulsive force field and voidness. It is both humorous and sad when Jim Carver comes home from a business trip and greets his two sons: "Hey guys, I'm back." Both look at him, confused, and Mikey answers quizzically, "You were gone?" Without comic relief, the characters would be repulsive, not only to each other, but also to the audience.

Change and Synchronicity

What is impending points us obviously to the future. Not surprisingly, we would like to know our future—if good, to wish it would come quickly, like our birthday and gifts; if bad, to wish to avoid it. Consider an ancient way to tell the future, the Chinese classic *I Ching* (Book of Changes). It presents a template for relationships between the individual and larger macrocosm. By contrast, in Western culture, we place almost exclusive emphasis on the individual, independent of larger dimensions of life. The book describes how to use a hexagram composed of six straight lines, unbroken or broken, stable or moving. Originally a soothsayer would cast sticks to generate one of the sixty-four hexagrams, in order to predict a person's future. A modern use is to guide a person in making a decision by bringing into alignment the outer/ objective and inner/subjective worlds. While hexagrams do not appear in *The Ice Storm*, the underlying concept of synchronicity does.

We are accustomed to view the relation of events in terms of causality in the natural world and in terms of choice, or chance or coincidence in the human world. Carl Jung, in his preface to the *I Ching*, offers a third option: synchronicity:

> Synchronicity takes the coincidence of events in space and time as meaning something more than mere chance, namely, a peculiar interdependence of objective events among themselves as well as with the subjective (psychic) states of the observer or observers.[2]

Another related Chinese philosophical concept, from Daoism, is embedded in the *I Ching*. The *dào* is the mysterious flow of the natural world.[3] Water in a stream is an apt metaphor for it: we can flow with the current or fight it. To know the difference requires sensitivity, like a continuous appreciation of what is present, so that one can harmonize the flow inside oneself with the flow outside. In sports terminology, flow is being in the zone, where effort feels effortless. (The Daoist name for this experience is *wú-wéi,* doing without doing.) Flow often happens in our activities when we are not standing as if on the outside of our experience, trying to make something happen positively for ego gain, and distrustful how it might happen negatively for ego deflation. In *The Karate Kid* (1984), Mister Miyagi teaches karate indirectly to the impatient kid, Daniel, by having him do mundane tasks like waxing his car so he will learn how to pay attention to flow, which is vitally important to karate as a martial art and an art of living. Synchronicity and flow are close to the Buddhist concept of dependent origination, according to which all phenomena arise together in a mutually interdependent web of cause and effect. In other words, everything is interconnected; hence everything affects everything else. We are in a flow with everything else. But we focus on what is particular for us, our individuality, which we hope will emerge into clear focus for others and ourselves, like the credits at the film's opening.

The phenomenon of an ice storm, an important metaphor for what is impending, involves a synchronicity of rain, temperature, and elevations. For an ice storm to occur, conditions must be just right. When frozen precipitation from an upper layer in the sky meets a warm layer and melts, then falls through another cold layer, the melted precipitation refreezes. If the precipitation is only partially melted, it becomes sleet, snow, or rain. If the melted rain droplets fall through a bottom layer with a temperature below freezing, in this rare condition, they pass into what is called a supercooled state. They do not freeze while falling, but when they strike the warmer ground, they form a film of ice. This is an apt metaphor for the repulsive force in the two families. The adults have layers of cold. When affection passes through one cold layer, meets a warm layer, melts, and then passes through another supercooling layer, affection lands in a film of ice over themselves and their world. They live in a synchronistic system, each person mutually affecting and being affected by others' repulsive forces and their own. "Repulsive force" is Paul's term from *The Fantastic Four* for the power family members have to harm each other; they flow against each other, out of harmony, even with themselves.

How might synchronicity apply not just in the physical world, but also in the human world where we have the power to make choices? It seems that Mikey's electrocution was a fluke, a matter of chance. The immediate physical cause was sitting on the guardrail, made of conductive metal, that touched the downed wire. From the perspective of moral responsibility, were any of the characters a cause of his death through their actions or inactions? The parents may not have been good parents because they were so wrapped up in their own lives. Nonetheless, are they responsible because they should have heeded the storm warning and stayed home? Mikey phones Wendy to invite her to go out into the storm with him. Instead, she has a rendezvous with Sandy. Is she in some way responsible? Is Sandy responsible, because he could have gone with his brother Mikey or convinced him to say home? Is Mikey responsible because he made the choice to go into the storm? These questions can be answered, if at all, by philosophically examining complex issues about the nature and meaning of responsibility and knowing all the facts of the situations. Philosophy aside, if Mikey were a member of one's own family, it would be difficult to accept and understand that the cause of his death was simply a downed wire touching a guardrail that he happened to touch. We would plead for an answer to "why?" In hindsight, there seems to be a synchronicity in which all the characters are involved in the death of Mikey. Like the formation of the ice storm, the conditions were ripe for this unforeseen event.

Mikey's death touches on an existential theme: contingency, or the sense that life has a deeply disconcerting randomness. We have a strong demand for order, and violations of it are difficult to understand and accept. For example, when a person laments, "Why did my loved one die?" there is a plea that life should have an intelligible order, and better yet, an order obedient to our profound wishes. All the characters were aware of the impending ice storm—at least aware of the announcement of it. They neglected what was impending. How we neglect what is impending brings us to Heidegger, and one of the most anxiety-producing existential themes.

Anxiety: Existentialism

Existentialists focus on basic aspects of human existence as it is lived.[4] They reject traditional philosophy that is overly rational and obsessed with the pursuit of abstract truths that are out of touch with the disturbing realities of human experience. They insist on living authentically and expose the ways in which inauthenticity comes at a great cost in our lives. Choice is one existential reality. We like to have choices. Many choices feel easy and enhancing, like buying new clothes. Some are distressingly difficult, like choosing a college or career path. We face them with an unsettling air of anxiety about making "the right choice."[5]

Choice (and its evasion) is a central theme that characterizes the malaise of the film's characters. Elena is the adult most visibly constricted by her life role, made painful by her suspicion that her husband is having an affair. She faces a significant decision about her marriage and, most decisively, who she will become by her choice. Any choice, even to stay in her marriage and suffer in silence with angry outbursts, poses huge risks. She takes an unexpected risk by shoplifting cosmetics in the drugstore and gets caught. Her impulsive choice to shoplift may be a substitute for her choice about her marriage. Getting caught may actually give her relief, and she might conclude that impulsive choices turn out badly, so she should stay in the marriage. If so, she feels responsible for this critical choice. Later at the key party, she deliberately chooses to pick a set of keys, thereby consenting to have sex with their owner. It might appear that her choice is one for which she takes full responsibility. But she might think that she was coerced by her husband's eagerness to have his keys chosen by Janey, thus denying her full responsibility for her choice. Furthermore, she might have an unacknowledged desire to punish him. She can justify to herself that he is guilty of betrayal and fate punishes him as he lies drunk and sexually disappointed in the bathroom. Thus, by some maneuver out of conscious focus, she can wiggle free of responsibility for her choice. If true, Sartre would conclude she is acting in bad faith, his name for self-deception.

Kierkegaard exposes a different self-deception in regard to religious faith. Faith in God implies a degree of uncertainty and hence anxiety. For a believer, uncertainty creates an anxiety that can be dissolved by reshaping faith into comfortable knowledge—the believer knows that God exists. Kierkegaard states that belief in a Christian God, who became incarnate in the world as a human, died, and becomes God again, is absurd. Realizing the absurdity and yet believing it is a leap of faith—a leap into the irrational. To be authentically faithful, according to Kierkegaard, one must hold onto the absurdity of Christianity and yet believe in it with fear and trembling. Anxiety for an existentialist is like suffering for a Buddhist; it condenses in a single word a profound character of human existence. Anxiety and suffering are strong motivators for seeking comfort by locking the door and jumping in bed under the covers.[6]

We want to be happy. Nietzsche tells us how: "The secret of the greatest joy in existence is to live dangerously."[7] At first glance, this seems dangerous, even immoral. We want to be individuals. Nietzsche dares us to "become who [we] are."[8] Likely we have heard another quote from Nietzsche, easier to say than live: "What does not destroy me, makes me stronger."[9] He offers an explanation of how we act as a group, as a moral herd. We resent individuals who live outside the herd, who act from a "will to power."[10] The will to power refers to the power to be true to oneself, not a power over others. Nietzsche alleges that we create rules to suppress others—and ourselves—who dare to create a flourishing life. In their different ways, existentialists hold a mirror up to the way we live and ask us to look and answer whether we are living authentically.

Existential themes appear in Paul's *Fantastic Four* paradox. His view of the void, where we come from and into which we go, being sucked further into it by family, is like the existentialist view that we are thrown into existence. We did not choose to be here. We are like aliens arriving in a strange world, aware that we live among others and yet separate from them, aware of being influenced by their demands on us, and yet free to make our own life-defining choices. Moreover, knowing we will eventually leave this world behind makes us aliens of a different sort. The void has no characteristics, so it might not seem threatening. Insofar as it suggests the void of death, it can appear even more menacing and give our lives an uncanny sense of being alien.

What Is Uniquely Impending Right Now?

Heidegger gives us the answer to what is impending in our present: our death. Understandably, thinking about our own death can generate anxiety. On the positive side, Heidegger explores the authenticity we gain if we do think it through, in a special way, not go around or over it. There are two radically different kinds of death: that of others, and that of our own. Our death does not occur, for us, in the world. We experience the death of others; we cannot experience our own death, even though we might imagine it for maudlin purposes. Death, our own, is the one event that is uniquely impending for each of us. But it does not impend like the ice storm. Our death, we might mistakenly believe, is impending only in a vague sense, as sometime in the future; consequently, it can be ignored now. Death, as Heidegger defines it, is the possibility of one's absolute impossibility.[11] Our death will completely sever us from all relations to our world. We cannot experience it. Our death is the end of our experience. The thought of this inescapable, inevitable end generates anxiety. We project our lives' possibilities, projects and hopes, into the future, so ironically, we live with our future death in the midst of our life. In the future, they are our not-yets. Our death, as Heidegger argues, is uniquely impending, our final not-yet. We have ways to tranquilize anxiety about our own death. Death, when it occurs, is always someone else's death. Death is not a threat when it belongs to no one in particular arriving from somewhere, not yet present for oneself. Everyone—the "they," as Heidegger refers to us collectively—gives a public interpretation of death, and we talk about it with varying degrees of concern for the one who has died. This public expropriation of death resembles a conspiratorial synchronicity. Socially, we are in harmony about how we should conceal death, especially its significance for ourselves. So unless we are persistent in our philosophical inquiry into what is impending, we might chant, "We're not scared." Our death is really impending now. It is as if we have locked the door on this possibility and we hide under the covers.

Why think about our death? In what way is it impending in the present and not impending in the future, as we mistakenly assume? Heidegger's argument depends on three unique characteristics of our death. Death cannot be outstripped; it cannot be outrun or avoided. It is nonrelational in that no one can be a substitute for our own death, and our death undoes all relations with the world. Succinctly, our death is our "ownmost," wholly unique in our lives. We might say "so what," except for the stunning connection with our death and our being. The core of our lives, our being, has the same three characteristics as our death. Our being, our authentic being, cannot be outstripped, in spite of the ways we compromise it to fit in with others and, as a consequence, we become lost to ourselves. Our being is nonrelation in that it is the source and task of our lives, and no one else's. And our being is not a summation of other's ideas and our relations to them—our being is, finally, our ownmost being. Thus emerges Heidegger's provocative insight. Because our being and our death share the same three characteristics, ownmost, not to be outstripped, nonrelational, when we flee from and alienate our ownmost death, we flee from and alienate our ownmost being. Our death is impending in the same way our potential for being is impending—not later, but now. Both are in the present, and how we choose to actualize them, these two sides of the same coin, makes all the difference.

The death of Mikey brings the Hoods and Weavers painfully close to death, but not their own. As long as they believe their own death is not impending, their potential for being is not impending either. It seems odd to confess thinking about one's own death. But facing the reality of one's death is sobering and a great motivation to live closer to the heart of one's being. As much as the Hoods and Carvers experiment to find happy lives, they are caught in the currents of other's expectations and cowardice by avoiding their ownmost being. Because others are avoiding their ownmost being also, there exists a collective synchronicity of individuals in denial of their ownmost death and their ownmost being.

Not-Yet: Just a Film?

We can debate the meaning of the movie in many ways, from aesthetic to moral. How artistic was Ang Lee in his adaptation of the novel? Is it tragic that Mikey dies from a random event? Such questions avoid Heidegger's question about our distinctly impending death and what it means for how we live our lives. In effect, Heidegger asks us to look at our lives as a film, including its ultimate end when the main character, our self, is as dead as Mikey. Is this my own life film? Or am I in the trance of watching a film about my life, while dreaming of a better, more authentic way to live? Heidegger is correct about our death being distinctively impending. He is insightful to link our ownmost death with our ownmost life. However, our ownmost life can in fact be outstripped, unlike our death. We can suddenly die still waiting for the right conditions—rarer conditions than for an ice storm—to start living our ownmost life. We may be like the monk who is still carrying the woman. In this case, we are carrying the dream of our ownmost life while complaining about or envying others' lives. It as if we have made a vow not to participate fully in our lives, until, when conditions are just right, our ownmost true self will simply emerge. Watching a film can be one of many ways to tranquilize ourselves, avoiding the anxiety of choosing to live our lives with full responsibility. We can say, "Death is not-yet," and live in a daze, ignoring storm warnings and maydays. Thus we ignore our ownmost life, ignore taking responsibility for choosing our lives.

In films, we are able to empathetically project into others' lives and briefly live another life. Eastern philosophy and existentialism remind us to live our lives empathetically before our life film ends. It will end. Our life film is not just a film. Nevertheless, we can meet our impending death and discover its relation to our ownmost living. At this point, we are on our own, within the drama of our own lives, facing a choice about how authentically we choose to live. There is no conclusion, only a choice.

Not-Yet: Getting Personal

A close encounter with one's own death can lead to dramatic life revisions. People who recover from heart attacks or face terminal cancer often purge their lives of what now seems unimportant, and they become passionate about what counts the most. For example, a survivor of the plane that landed in the Hudson River tells how, feeling the plane lose power and falling toward his death by crash, he vowed to change his life if he survived.[12] He survived, and true to the promise to himself, he gave up negativity and devoted himself to being the best parent possible. Heidegger is right: when some people face their ownmost death, they do make a life-altering choice to live in their ownmost way. They free themselves from attachments to what others think and free themselves from an immortal image of themselves to live more passionately. But not all passengers on that flight made significant life changes.

Of course, not flying anymore is a way of avoiding one's death by airplane crash. Getting personal, I might consider whether there is strong evidence for Heidegger's view of the intimate connection of one's death and one's life. From an existential perspective, evidence does not matter. Waiting for sufficient evidence about such a critical life matter becomes, in effect, a death-and-life delay. So I must ask, what is my view of my ownmost death and life?

I believe Heidegger is right. To live as if I am not going to die dilutes how I act and what I value. If I had a brush with death like the crash survivor, perhaps I would take my life more seriously. Yet I believe I do live seriously. Nonetheless, I feel compelled to ask whether I am living seriously the fullness of my ownmost being. In the last five years I have had two serious surgeries. Still, I live on in my usual way, though with troublesome side effects from the surgeries. Recently, I had a sudden and frightening weakness on the right side of my body, indicating a stroke. Fortunately, I did not have a full-blown stoke. But I had and still have a blood clot totally blocking a major artery in my brain. If it moves, it might kill me. Even if it did not kill me, it would kill so many brain cells that I would have major losses in functioning—a grotesque possibility. Nothing medically can be done about the clot. In spite of these physical warnings, I have not made significant life changes. I am not bored and disillusioned like the Hood and Weaver adults. It is easy to be like the righteous monk, to become attached to being philosophical about how others live. Heidegger would be right to point out that examining others' lives involves making comparisons, when I should be looking at my death and life nonrelationally. I can delay, even aware, given my age, that my death could be immanently impending. It certainly will not be outstripped. While I agree with the Socratic ideal of "the examined life" as the one worth living, I have discovered that my ownmost life is beyond the grasp of my reason. To create my ownmost life, I definitely sense what Nietzsche means by living dangerously and what Kierkegaard means by a leap into something seemingly absurd.

Notes

1. See Allen Watts, *The Way of Zen* (New York: Vintage Books, 1957).

2. *I Ching,* trans. Richard Wilhelm (Princeton, N.J.: Princeton University Press, 1950), xxiv.

3. For a detailed exposition of the key tenets of Daoism, including *dào* and *wú-wéi,* see James McRae, Chapter 1, this volume.

4. For more information on the philosophy of existentialism, see Chapters 10 and 14 in this volume. See Diane Raymond, *Existentialism and the Philosophical Tradition* (Upper Saddle River, N.J.: Prentice-Hall, 1991).

5. Jean-Paul Sartre, "Existentialism is a Humanism," in *Existentialism from Dostoevsky to Sartre,* ed. and trans. Walter Kaufman (New York: Penguin, 1956), 351.

6. See Søren Kierkegaard, *Fear and Trembling (with Repetition),* trans. and ed. Howard V. Hong and Edna H. Hong (Princeton, N.J.: Princeton University Press, 1983).

7. Friedrich Nietzsche, *The Portable Nietzsche,* trans. and ed. Walter Kaufmann (New York: Penguin, 1976), 97.

8. Ibid., 657–660.

9. Ibid., 467.

10. Ibid., 44, 170, 446.

11. See sections 50–52 in Martin Heidegger, *Being and Time,* trans. John Macquarrie and Edward Robinson (New York: Harper & Row, 1962).

12. See Ric Elias, "3 Things I Learned While My Plane Crashed" (Ted.com).

All's Fair in Love and War?

Machiavelli and Ang Lee's *Ride with the Devil*

James Edwin Mahon

Ang Lee's *Ride with the Devil* (1999) is a film about war and love. It is a common belief, captured in the proverb "All's fair in love and war,"[1] that when it comes to war and love, there are no rules.[2] The ends—winning the war, and winning the heart of one's beloved—are supposed to justify any means whatsoever. In particular, they are supposed to justify deception.[3] In this chapter I will address the question of whether *Ride with the Devil* endorses the view that when it comes to war and love, deception is justified.

In *Ride with the Devil,* the war in question is the U.S. Civil War—in particular, the border war between the antislavery Kansas jayhawkers and proslavery Missouri bushwhackers. The love in question is that between a young widow and an immigrant German boy fighting for the Southern bushwhackers. I shall first provide some historical context to this war, explain why this war interests Lee, and why he is sympathetic to the Southerners. I shall then argue that his true sympathy is for the outsiders on the Southern side and show that it is these individuals who form the moral core of the film. Because these same people engage in deception, I shall consider what the film has to say about deception. I shall argue that unlike the great Chinese military strategist Sunzi, the film does not endorse the view that all deception is justified in war and love. Instead, it can be shown to agree with Machiavelli that even in war, there are limits on when deception can be practiced. It can also be shown to suggest that in love, it is honesty that is ultimately required. According to Ang Lee's *Ride with the Devil,* all is not fair in love and war.

General Lee, or Yanqui Go Home

The War between the States, otherwise known as the Civil War,[4] is thought of as a war fought in the South and the East of the United States. However, the prospect of the creation of new slave states in the Midwest contributed to the outbreak of the Civil War, and the war was also fought in the Midwest. Before the war, a dispute over whether Kansas should be a slave state or a free state led to a series of violent clashes between Southern (largely Missourian) pro-slavery Border Ruffians, and Northern antislavery Free Soilers or Free Staters settlers, in what is referred to as Bleeding Kansas, Bloody Kansas, or the Border War. Although the violence had abated by 1859 and Kansas entered the Union as a free state in January 1861, with the commencement of the Civil War in 1861, the border war erupted again. Missouri did not secede from the Union, but the governor refused Lincoln's call to send volunteers to invade the South. The governor and the state legislature were deposed, and they fled in order to avoid arrest. The Missouri state guard actually fought against the federalized militia. As another commentator has said, "Only a massive build-up of Union troops and a lack of support from the Confederate government in Richmond kept Missouri in the Union. In an effort to preserve their lives, property, and sacred honor, many rural Missourians either joined the Confederate army or fought their own guerilla war against the invading forces."[5] Those who fought their own guerilla war against the invading forces of pro-Union irregular jayhawkers, as well as the Union federals, were known as the bushwhackers.[6]

Ang Lee's film about this border war between the jayhawkers and the bushwhackers came about by chance. In 1987, a woman named Amy Carey read Daniel Woodrell's *Woe to Live On* (1987),[7] a novel about three people—an immigrant, a former slave, and a young widow—caught up in the cross-border fighting.[8] Years later, Carey was working for a production company associated with Lee and gave him the novel. Lee read it "in 1994 while attending a screening in Deauvile, France, of his recently completed *Eat Drink Man Woman* [1994]."[9] According to James Schamus, Lee's longtime collaborator and the author of the screenplay, "he got so engrossed in it that it interrupted his reading of the script for *Sense and Sensibility* [1994]. He knew right away that he had to make this movie."[10] As Woodrell himself tells the story, Lee wanted to get out of making domestic dramas: "He said he'd like to make a film that wasn't all domestic drama, she gave him the book, he read it in one night and they bought it."[11] Another author has even said that Lee "wanted to make a macho film."[12] Lee confirmed that he had wanted to do a movie that had action in it, but he said that the adaptation gave him the chance to combine action with domestic drama: "At first I wanted to get away from a family drama and do something with more action and scope, but it turns out [*Woe to Live On*] does both. Family values and the social system are tested by war. It's a family drama, but one where the characters represent a larger kind of 'family'—the warring factions of the Civil War and the divisions in the national character."[13, 14]

The focus of the film is on the bushwhackers. They were fighting in what James Schamus has called an American Vietnam:

> Once the war got underway, Missouri ended up as something of an American Vietnam, occupied by Union forces and under martial law during most of the conflict, with local populations giving support and cover to loosely organized gangs of Southern "Bushwhackers." These guerillas terrorized Union sympathizers and preyed on Northern patrols and supply lines.[15]

As he points out, these bushwhackers "became increasingly desperate and bloodthirsty, devolving eventually into criminal gangs that had little interest in or regard for the politics of the conflict that spawned them."[16] From the bushwhackers came some of the most notorious criminals of the West, including the Younger Brothers and the James gang.

It should be noted, however, that the jayhawkers they fought against were not principally, or even particularly, interested in abolishing slavery. As the novel puts it, from the mouth of the protagonist, Jake Roedel, "Jayhawkers said they raided to free slaves, but mostly they freed horseflesh from riders, furniture from houses, cattle from pastures, precious jewelry from family troves and wives from husbands. Sometimes they had so much plunder niggers were needed to haul it, so they took a few along. This, they said, made them abolitionists."[17] It can be agreed by all that in his adaptation of Woodrell's novel, "Lee's sympathies are clearly with the bushwhackers."[18] *Ride with the Devil* is a movie that, as one author has put it (presumably with no play on words intended), "adopts the unusual position of focusing on the losers of the American Civil War."[19] Why would Lee make such a movie? One possible reason is that Lee himself was a loser in another civil war.

Lee's family members were wealthy landlords in Kiangsi province in mainland China. At the end of the Chinese civil war in 1949, however, the Communist Party of China defeated the governing Chinese Nationalist Party and divided China into the People's Republic of China (mainland China) and the Republic of China (Taiwan, which had been under the control of Japan until the end of World War II in 1945). The entire family of Sheng

Lee, Ang Lee's father, was executed. Sheng Lee, himself a district commissioner, managed to escape the communist forces who were after him, and he fled to Taiwan. There he married another orphaned survivor from mainland China, Su-Tsang Yang. Together they started a family, the eldest child of which is Ang Lee.

Ang Lee has often said that he does not consider himself to be a native son of anywhere. He is not a native son of Taiwan, where his parents fled after the communist revolution; he is not a native son of communist China, where his parents would have been killed had they stayed; and he is not a native son of the United States, his adopted home: "To me I'm a mixture of many things and a confusion of many things. I'm not native Taiwanese, so we're alien in a way in Taiwan today, with the native Taiwanese pushing for independence. But when we go back to China, we're Taiwanese. Then, I live in the States; I'm a sort of foreigner everywhere. It's hard to find a real identity."[20]

As another author has pointed out, "Lee's outsider status is something he jealously guards, although in the past it was a great burden. He assiduously maintains his Chinese roots, never having applied for American citizenship."[21] With his dispossessed family background in Taiwan and his immigrant status in the United States, Lee's choice to direct a movie about dispossessed Southerners looks less surprising. Indeed, Lee has said that he identifies with the Southerners against the Yankee invasion:

I grew up in Taiwan, where older people always complained that kids are becoming Americanized—they don't follow tradition and so we are losing our culture. As I got the chance to go around a big part of the world with my films, I heard the same complaints. It seems so much of the world is becoming Americanized. And when I read the book *Woe to Live On*, on which we based our movie, I realized the American Civil War was, in a way, where it all started. It was where the Yankees won not only territory but, in a sense, a victory for a whole way of life and of thinking. The Yankee invasion has not only a surface meaning—Yankees continue to win militarily and economically—but also an internal meaning. It changes you, in a kind of unstoppable way. Everyone is equal, everyone has the right to fulfill themselves—this is the Yankee principle. . . . This is what the Civil War meant to me—and I think it meant this as well to the boys in the movie, who are also non-Yankees. So the Civil War is not only on the surface, of blood and guts, it is also a personal war that leads to the new world in which we are living today—the world of democracy and capitalism.[22]

There is a scene in *Ride with the Devil* that would appear to capture Lee's sentiment about the Yankee invasion. Mr. Evans, the father-in-law of Sue Lee Shelley, is a loyal Southerner (he has already lost his son in the war) who agrees to let the bushwhackers wait out the bitter winter on his land. He invites them to his house for supper one night. There he tells them an anecdote about the Yankification of the entire country:

> Have you ever been to Lawrence, Kansas, young man? . . . Before this war began my business took me there often. And as I saw those Northerners build that town, I witnessed the seeds of our destruction being sown. . . . It was the schoolhouse. Before they built a church even, they built that schoolhouse, and lettered every tailor's son and farmer's daughter in that country. . . . My point is merely—that they rounded every pup up into that schoolhouse, because they fancied that everyone should think and talk the same freethinking way that they do, with no regard for station, custom, or propriety. And that is why they will win—because they believe that everyone should live and think just like them. And we shall lose because we don't care one way or the other about how they live or think, we just worry about ourselves.[23]

Lee's displacement from his native China and his critical attitude toward America has the result that *Ride with the Devil* "presents the southern side of the war with greater sympathy and comprehension than has been attempted in the past."[24] The audience "is asked to side with the losers who are, to our current way of thinking, in the wrong. These Southerners genuinely feel they were losing their freedom to prejudiced, corrupt, racist and psychotic Yankees."[25]

Band of Outsiders

Although Lee does sympathize with the Southerners, he is most sympathetic to the misfits among them—those Southerners who are not fully accepted by the other Southerners. All of the main characters of the film are, in some way, outsiders.

Jakob "Jake" Roedel, the sixteen-year-old protagonist of the film, is called "Dutchy" by the other bushwhackers. His nickname is a corruption of "Deutsche" because his father, Otto Roedel, is a German immigrant who settled in Missouri. Otto works at the mill owned by the Chiles family, and he remains loyal to the Union.[26] Jake refuses to go to St. Louis with a friend of his father for safety, telling him, "I told you, I'm not goin' to huddle with all the other Lincoln-loving Germans in St. Louis" because "these are my people." His father insists, "You will always be a Deutschman, a German, to them, no matter with who you are friends." [27] Although he was born in Germany, Jake grew up in Missouri, and he considers himself a Southerner, like the other natives.

After Asa Chiles, the father of Jack Bull Chiles, is killed by jayhawkers and Jack joins the bushwhackers, Jake turns his back on his father and joins the bushwhackers too, fighting the jayhawkers and the Union troops.[28] His estranged father, Otto, is later killed by a Union soldier (released as a result of Jake's intervention) because, as Jake is later told, "he was mainly known as your father, Dutchy. You got a reputation now."[29] Despite his fighting for the bushwhackers and the loss of his father to a Union soldier, the other bushwhackers continue to call him Dutchy, and some continue to question his allegiance to their cause.

Daniel Holt, a character who gradually becomes Jake's close friend, is a former slave who rides with his former master, George Clyde, whose life he has saved in the past. Despite the fact that Holt is a free man and is clearly loyal to his former master, Holt is not trusted.[30] He is still considered "Clyde's pet nigger, but don't call him that in front of George. No, George don't like that." He is not allowed to carry a gun unless Clyde gives him one: "He's a damn fine scout, and spy—and, when George tosses him a gun, a good Yankee-killer, too." He is even mistrusted, originally, by Jake himself, who says that "a nigger with guns—it still is a nervous thing to me."[31]

Both Jake and Holt, then, are outsiders: "Roedel is a German immigrant seeking to gain acceptance into the world of southern civility, and Daniel Holt is a free Southern slave who travels with his former owner."[32] Among the bushwhackers, their outsider status is clear: "They soon realize that they are outsiders, both in this war and in the South. They both entered the war out of a misguided sense of loyalty to a side that despised them."[33] The outsider status of both Jake and Holt is confirmed in a gruesome game of poker played by the other bushwhackers. When they run out of money, they continue to play using the captured scalps of blacks and immigrants: "That's two nigger scalps—I'll see you with one Dutch scalp."[34]

Finally, Sue Lee Shelley is a young, native, white Southerner—but she is also a widow, her husband killed in the Civil War after being married to her for only three weeks. She is also an unmarried single mother, with a baby girl out of wedlock by Jack Bull Chiles (who himself is killed before his daughter is born). Although the Brown family takes her in, they will not stand for her to remain unmarried. As Orton Brown says, "I can't have it in my house the way it is."[35] She must be married.

The three main characters, then, make up an outgroup of misfits. Indeed, Lee himself has characterized the main characters of the film as outsiders: "The story starts with the Southern boys' point of view; the perspective of those who will lose to the Yankees. But then it gradually changes to focus on the points of view of the two outsiders the German immigrant and the black slave—as well as that of the young woman. Through them we come to experience the changes that freedom will bring. It is their emancipation that the film becomes about, their coming of age. So, as a Taiwanese, I can identify with the Southerners as the Yankees change their way of life forever, but I also identify more strongly with these outsiders, who grasp at freedom, and fight for it."[36]

The story of the film is the development of the relationship between the three people, who, if not literally orphans, do not have a home and come to rely on each other: "Issues dividing the North and the South are not what primarily motivate these three; it is their loyalty to one another and their fight to stay alive in a world gone mad."[37] Jake and Holt become good friends, and they become more disaffected with the bushwhackers, who eventually try to kill Jake. After their friends are killed in the fighting and they themselves get injured, they join Sue Lee and the Browns to recuperate. Eventually, they decide not to rejoin the bushwhackers. Jake marries Sue Lee and becomes a stepfather to Chiles's daughter. They head off to California to start a new life. Holt joins them for part of the way, then leaves for Texas to find and free his slave mother.

There is a stark generation gap between these three people and the parental figures that surround them. In consequence, they become a family themselves: "Although on one level *Ride with the Devil* operates as a butch, manly film with shoot-outs and big battle scenes, it is still basically an intimate family drama. The 'family' are not related by blood but are brought together by their emotional journey."[38] This new family—the immigrant, the young widowed mother, and the former slave—appears to be a metaphor for the new America. As Lee says, "So our story is about the very heart of America, even as this heart was—and still so often is—torn apart by racial and other conflicts."[39]

In the end, *Ride with the Devil* is about the creation of a new American identity, free of the past and old family ties: "Over and over again Lee shows us how cultural, national, family and individual identities contradict each other. This sensibility creates the underlying focus of Lee's work—that of identity."[40] In that sense, *Ride with the Devil* is like other classic westerns, such as *How the West Was Won* (John Ford, Henry Hathaway, and George Marshall, 1962). As Schamus says, it is "a kind of un-Western, a rereading of the myth of the West in light of the violent racial and regional and sexual politics that informed it."[41]

Sympathy for the Devil

Jack Bull Chiles and George Clyde, both Southern gentry, become bushwhackers because their families are killed by jayhawkers. Jake and Holt join the Southern bushwhackers out of loyalty to these friends. However, their friendships with Chiles and Clyde respectively become strained because the bushwhackers are not welcoming to outsiders: "In their small-town environments they could be friends, but once they leave their home environment it becomes all too clear that a 'dutchy' and a 'nigger' are not Southerners. There is a strong level of discrimination against foreigners."[42]

There is also an important difference in moral outlook between Jake and the other bushwhackers. A number of incidents reveal this. Early on in the film, the bushwhackers trick a group of Union soldiers at a store into thinking that they are Union soldiers, then shoot them. They also shoot the storekeeper for "doin' business with the Yankee invaders." Although they refuse to shoot the storekeeper's wife, they—in particular, Pitt Mackeson—decide to burn the store down. They are deaf to Jake's pleading on her behalf: "We took her man. Leave her the store."[43]

Later in the film, at a bushwhacker encampment, Jake sees that a former neighbor from his hometown, Alf Bowden, is now a Union soldier and is being held prisoner. The leader of Jake's group of bushwhackers, Black John, wants to secure the release of two bushwhackers who are being held by the Union forces. Jake persuades Black John to send a prisoner to the Union forces with the offer of an exchange of prisoners. He releases Bowden and gives him the message to give to the Union soldiers, telling him, "You are spared, Alf."[44] (Seeing what has happened, Mackeson says, "I am on to you, Roedel."[45])

What these two incidents reveal is that Jake is merciful and will try to help those he can. Jake is also the only bushwhacker who knows how to read and write. When a sack of Union mail is found, he refuses to read the letters aloud to the others, on the grounds that "it's someone else's letter."[46] Threatened by Mackeson, and encouraged by others who say that there may be military secrets in the letters, Jake does read one letter aloud, from a Northern mother to her Unionist son. The effect of reading aloud the letter is to convince listeners that, as one young bushwhacker says, "She sounds about like my mother,"[47] and that the true differences between the young men fighting on opposite sides are negligible. Importantly, Jake's initial refusal to read other people's private mail indicates his greater respect for the rights of others than the rest of the bushwhackers.

The incident that most reveals his difference in moral outlook from the other bushwhackers, however, is the raid on Lawrence, Kansas. This occurs in the summer, after Chiles has died from a gunshot wound. William Clarke Quantrill, the leader of all of the "sons of Missouri,"[48] and, at least according to some, the devil of the title,[49] gives a rousing speech to the bushwhackers. Responding to the news that a number of women who were sisters or cousins of the bushwhackers were killed or injured when the jail in which they were being held collapsed[50] (the bushwhackers themselves do not keep women prisoners and have a "code of honor where women will not be harmed"[51]), he says to them: "Men of the South! Our enemies are sleeping. Just as our sisters slept in that Kansas City jail until the walls fell down and crushed the breath right out of them. Good women whose lives were cut short by Yankee treachery. But now our Southern sisters' souls fly forth to transmogrify into the fire and steel that will destroy our enemies! Yes, my boys, the abolitionists of Lawrence sleep under the heavy blanket of guilt that covers their shame."[52] He convinces them to follow him in a dawn raid on the Union town of Lawrence, Kansas, fifty miles away, in what seems like a suicide mission. However, when the 440-odd bushwhackers arrive, they completely surprise the town and are met with little or no armed force.[53] They proceed to kill at least 184 men and boys (whoever was judged old enough to carry a rifle), to loot the town, to rob the bank, and to burn down most of the town's buildings. In the midst of this carnage and slaughter, Jake, accompanied by Holt, decides to get breakfast. One of the raiders, drunk, tries to knock Holt down. Only Jake's cry—"It's George Clyde's nigger, you fool"—stops him.[54] While having breakfast in a boarding house, a group of bushwhackers, led by Mackeson, bursts into the boarding house and tries to bring an old man and a young boy out into the street to be executed. Jake pulls a gun on Mackeson and tells him to leave them alone. Mackeson backs down and leaves the boarding house with the others. Riding back to Missouri, however, Black John tells Jake, "I told you not to spare."[55] George Clyde promises to do what he can for Jake, but in the ensuing fight with the pursuing Union cavalry, Clyde is killed. Mackeson also deliberately shoots at Jake.

Jake and Holt, both injured, manage to escape and make it to the farm where Sue Lee now lives with the Brown family. After they have recovered from their injuries, they decide not to rejoin the bushwhackers. Jake says to Holt, "You know, I probably got only one more fight in me—I'm gonna kill Pitt Mackeson, either when he comes here or when I can get up to find him out," but when asked by Holt about joining the fight again, he says, "Fight for the cause? What about you?"[56]

The raid on Lawrence is the turning point for Jake. He no longer has any sympathy for the bushwhackers and their cause. For Holt, the turning point comes immediately after the raid, with the death of his former master, Clyde. As he says, "I don't right understand it, but it come to the day George Clyde took that Yankee bullet, *that* was when it made me feel the somethin' new. . . . What I felt was diff'rent. What I felt was now—now I was gonna be free. Oh that George Clyde—I loved him sure. But his friend was no diff'rent from being his nigger—and Roedel—I never, never again gonna be nobody's nigger."[57] Holt finally asserts his freedom. He decides that he is going to go his own way, for once in his life. He will not return to the bushwhackers. That was his former master's cause, not his. He is "going to find [his] mama. I believe she was sold to Texas, so that is where I will begin. If she was sold there, I will go there and pay for her freedom."[58]

Jake's moral development in the film, and his development from boy to man, dictates that he take two further steps. First, he marries Sue Lee. He becomes a husband and a stepfather, and he accepts responsibility for a family. Second, although he is eventually provided with a chance to kill Mackeson, the man who tried to kill him, he decides to spare him. As he says to Holt, "It ain't right and it ain't wrong. It just is."[59] By now, Jake has cut off his hair, one of the marks of being a bushwhacker, as he said he would do: "I said I'd never cut my hair 'til I was finished with the war."[60] His transformation is complete. As another author has said: "Over the course of the film,

Jake Roedel is transformed very realistically from naive boy to emotionally mature man. In addition, both Roedel and Holt exhibit traits of mercy, gratitude and civility which make them stand apart from the other characters . . . the two stand out from the crowd as the true vestige of decency and integrity in a world turned upside down by war and conflicting loyalties."[61]

The Blue and the Gray

James Schamus has said of *Ride with the Devil*, "The movie doesn't present the usual image of the Civil War, of easily identifiable hordes of gray- and blue-clad soldiers clashing on the field of honor in the fight either for or against slavery,"[62] and another commentator has written, "Ang Lee avoids the clichés of a typical gunpowder-and-uniform Civil War movie."[63] There is a great irony in the claim that the film does not depict Civil War battles between one side wearing blue uniforms and another side wearing gray uniforms. The irony is that the main tactic used by the bushwhackers is to wear the blue uniforms of the Union army, and to hide their long hair under their blue army hats.

The first sentence of *Woe to Live On* is, "We rode across the hillocks and vales of Missouri, hiding in the uniforms of Yankee blue."[64] By wearing the blue uniforms, the bushwhackers can move across the state without getting fired on. In the opening chapter, they encounter an immigrant family while wearing the blue uniforms. Jake relates, "Our uniforms were a relief to them, for they did not look too closely at our mismatched trousers and our hats that had rebel locks trailing below them. This was a common mistake and we took pleasure in prompting it."[65] They interrogate the father, a barrel maker, as to whether he is a "Southern man" who supports seceding from the Union. He tells them, in his German accent, that no, he is "Union man."[66] When they are about to hang him, he speaks in German to Jake, and Jake relates to Black John, "He says he is not a Union man," and "He was codded by our costumes." Black John replies, without a hint of irony, "Well, he should've hung by his convictions rather than live by the lie."[67] The man is hanged, and his young son is also killed—a boy who had been "beginning to study our uniforms."[68]

Wearing the blue uniform of the Union soldiers also allows the bushwhackers to ambush smaller numbers of enemy soldiers. In *Ride with the Devil*, the bushwhackers trick a group of Union soldiers at a general store into thinking that they are fellow Union soldiers, and then, having surprised them, shoot them. Afterward, in writing a letter to Mrs. Chiles, Jake reveals that these men were the men who killed Asa Chiles—her husband and Jack Bull Chiles's father. As it is narrated: "Often we don the Union blue to lull the federals into a false serenity, and the Yanks pay dearly for their belief in appearances. Under the disguise we wear our Bushwhacker vestments close to our hearts. They may not be regular army uniforms as there is no army out here for us to join, but where we find true Missouri men we make our own army." This narrated letter, which is not in the film's screenplay, and the scene of the bushwhackers tricking the Union soldiers that precedes it are inspired by passages from the novel such as the following:

> For a while we went back to wearing Yankee blue uniforms. They were so easy to come by. The trick of it was so simple, but it worked peachy. Twenty or thirty of us would ride up to a scout of Federals and George Clyde would say, "How is rebel hunting today, lieuten-ant?" and before an answer could be uttered or suspicions raised on closer inspection, we would cut open on them point-blank and pass them through to the next world. The treachery of it was not too noble, but it was a rare day when it failed.[69]

It is important to note that Jake characterizes their wearing the enemy uni-forms as treachery, which is not noble. He recognizes the deception that they are practicing. As he says early on in the novel, "In the morning we shed our blue sheep's clothing. Our border shirts came out of satchels and onto out backs. We preferred this means of dress, for it was more flat-out and honest."[70]

When the 440-strong force of bushwhackers rides to Lawrence, they do so wearing the blue uniforms of Union soldiers. Concerning the raid on Lawrence, it has been said by one writer: "Any true Southerner should thrill at the beautifully filmed scenes of Quantrill's men, dressed in navy blue jackets for disguise, riding into Kansas, assembling on Mt. Oread above the town, shedding their jackets, forming into battle lines, and then swooping down with rebel yells on the radical Republican stronghold."[71] What is curious about this description of a scene that should thrill any true Southerner is that it is a scene depicting Southerners wearing the uni-form of the North. It is a scene depicting Southerners wearing a disguise, concealing their Southern identity. It is a scene depicting the Southerners engaged in deception.

Machiavelli on Perfidy and Ruses of War

In *The Art of Warfare*, Sunzi (Sun-tzu) says, "Warfare is the art of deceit. Therefore, when able, seem to be unable; when ready, seem unready; when nearby, seem far away; and when far away, seem near. If the enemy seeks some advantage, entice him with it. If he is in disorder, attack him and take him. If he is formidable, prepare against him. If he is strong, evade him. If he is humble, encourage his arrogance. If he is rested, wear him down. If he is internally harmonious, sow divisiveness in his ranks. Attack where he is not prepared; go by way of places where it would never occur to him you would go."[72] Sunzi seems to equate waging war with (certain forms of) deception. He does not draw a line between different kinds of deception in war.[73] Not all authors, however, refuse to discriminate between different kinds of deception in war.

In the *Discourses on Livy*, Machiavelli says, "Although deceit is detestable in other things, yet in the conduct of war it is laudable and honorable."[74] Although this may seem like a blanket approval of all deception practiced in war, Machiavelli distinguishes between deception in general and the special case of perfidy: "I do not confound such deceit with perfidy, which breaks pledged faith treaties; for although states and kingdoms may at times be won by perfidy, yet will it ever bring dishonor with it."[75] Perfidy, on Machiavelli's account, means explicitly pledging, as a combatant, to act in some way with the intention of breaking that pledge in order to kill, injure, or capture the adversary. Acts of perfidy would include raising a white flag of surrender and then shooting at the opposing forces as soon as they emerge from their hiding place, or making a treaty with the enemy and then attacking. Perfidy in war is dishonorable.

The kind of honorable deception in war that Machiavelli is talking about is "those feints and stratagems which you employ against an enemy that distrusts you, and in the employment of which properly consists the art of war."[76] He provides, as an example, Hannibal's deception: "Such was that practiced by Hannibal when he feigned flight on the lake of Perugia (Thrasimene), for the purpose of hemming in the Consul and the Roman army."[77] Machiavelli considers such deceptions to be a normal part of war, as he reveals in his *The Art of War*:

> To avoid being drawn into an ambuscade by the enemy, you must
> be very cautious of trusting to flattering appearance: for instance, if

the enemy should leave considerable booty in your way, you should suspect there is a hook in the bait; or if a strong party of the enemy should fly before a few of your men, or a few of his men should attack a strong party of your army; or if the enemy suddenly runs away, without any apparent cause, it is reasonable to imagine there is some artifice in it and that he knows very well what he is doing; so, the weaker and more remiss he seems to be, the more it behooves you to be upon your guard, if you would avoid falling into his snares.[78]

The act of feigning a retreat or flight, in order to lure an enemy into an ambush, is an example of an act of deception that is called a ruse of war (*une ruse de guerre*). Ruses of war include disguising weapons, supplies, or men (when not fighting), creating dummy targets, sending troops or supplies in the wrong direction, pretending to communicate with nonexistent troops or reinforcements, and simulating inactivity. These ruses of war make use of indices—that is, signs whose meanings are established by experience. They do not involve the use of symbols, or signs whose meanings are established by human convention.[79] A beard, for example, is an index of being male and adult; the disguise of a false beard may be used to deceive people into thinking that you are a man. To make the assertion, "I am a grown man," when one is female or a child, with the intention that another believe it to be true, would be to attempt to deceive using symbols (language). Withdrawing troops from a battlefield in order to lure an enemy into an ambush involves making use of an index of retreat (a natural sign of retreat) rather than a symbol of retreat (such as a declaration to the enemy that one is retreating).

Not all ruses of war are limited to the use of indices or natural signs, however. Transmitting falsehoods over the radio or telephone, moving signs to indicate incorrect locations, planting false battle plans, and using spies and agents—all are ruses of war that involve the use of symbols or linguistic signs.

In the *Discourses,* Machiavelli provides another example of an honorable deception in war:

Such also was the stratagem of Pontius, general of the Samnites, to draw the Romans into the defiles of the Caudine Forks. Having concealed his army behind a mountain, he sent a number of his soldiers disguised as herdsmen with droves of cattle into the plains. These, on being captured and interrogated by the Romans as to the whereabouts of the Samnite army, answered, according to the instructions of Pontius, that it was engaged in the siege of the town of Nocera. The Consuls, believing it, entered the defiles of Caudium, where they were promptly hemmed in by the Samnites.[80]

Here the Samnite soldiers wear the disguise of herdsmen, allow themselves to be captured, and then lie to the Roman army in order to trap the Roman army in the Caudine Forks. Machiavelli does not consider the soldiers' disguising themselves as noncombatant civilians or the soldiers' lying to the Roman army to be examples of perfidy. What he does not comment on is whether wearing the disguise of the enemy's clothing or armor—that is, wearing its uniform—is an example of perfidy.

According to the Hague Convention of 1907, under "abuse of flag and uniform," it is forbidden "to make improper use of a flag of truce, of the national flag or of the military insignia and uniform of the enemy, as well as the distinctive badges of the Geneva Convention." This is to be distinguished from "ruses of war and the employment of measures necessary for obtaining information about the enemy and the country," which are permissible.[81] Although the language of "improper use" might suggest that "the article does not definitely prohibit" the use of "the enemy's uniform to deceive him, so long as the disguise is abandoned before actual contact and fighting with the enemies begins,"[82] it has been argued conclusively that the convention does prohibit the wearing of the uniform of the enemy as a means of deceiving the enemy at any time, and not only in open combat.[83]

The 1977 protocol, which was added to the Geneva Conventions of 1949, states, in "Prohibition of Perfidy," that "it is prohibited to kill, injure or capture an adversary by resort to perfidy." It further states, "Ruses of war are not prohibited" and gives as examples of ruses of war "the use of camouflage, decoys, mock operations and misinformation."[84] As examples of perfidy, it includes "the feigning of civilian, non-combatant status" as well as "the feigning of protected status by the use of signs, emblems or uniforms of the United Nations or of neutral or other States not Parties to the conflict."[85] Under "Emblems of Nationality," it says, "It is prohibited to make use in an armed conflict of the flags or military emblems, insignia or uniforms of neutral or other States not Parties to the conflict," then goes on to say, "It is prohibited to make use of the flags or military emblems, insignia or uniforms of adverse Parties while engaging in attacks or in order to shield, favor, protect or impede military operations."[86] It does add, "Nothing . . . shall affect the existing generally recognized rules of international law applicable to espionage or to the use of flags in the conduct of armed conflict at sea."[87]

By the Hague and Geneva conventions, therefore, feigning civilian, non-combatant status and wearing the uniform of the enemy "while engaging in attacks or in order to shield, favor, protect or impede military operations" are acts of (illegal) perfidy, and not (legally permitted) ruses of war. Because Machiavelli does not consider the feigning of civilian, noncombatant status to be perfidy, he can be said to reject this first portion of both conventions. Although his position on the wearing of the uniforms of the enemy is not certain, it can at least be argued that he would not consider the wearing of the uniform of the enemy to be perfidy either. That is, were the Samnites to trick the Romans by wearing Roman armor, he would, it seems, count that as honorable deception, not perfidy. If this is correct, then Machiavelli would defend the bushwhackers' deceptive wearing of enemy uniforms in fighting jayhawkers and Union forces.

This does not mean that there is not a distinction to be drawn between perfidy, or impermissible deception in war, and ruses of war, or permissible deception in war, by Machiavelli and the bushwhackers. At one point in *Ride with the Devil,* the bushwhackers are eating in the house of Mrs. Clark and her twelve-year-old daughter. After eating, Jake sits on the porch alone to rest. There are two horses tied up in front of the house. Two Union soldiers creep up on him and draw their guns. One of them asks, "Where's the other one, you devil?" Jake responds by lying, "I am alone. That's my daddy's horse—he was shot off it three days back."[88] Such a lie, it seems, would count as permissible deception by Machiavelli.

The soldiers believe Jake is lying to them, but just as they are about to shoot him, the other bushwhackers shoot them from inside the house. The house is now surrounded by Union soldiers. Jake tries to get the horses, but the horses are shot dead, and as he runs into the house, his pinkie finger is also shot off. Inside, he joins the other bushwhackers in shooting at the Union soldiers. From inside, Black John calls a cease-fire and shouts, "Do you kill women? There's women in here!" The response from the Union soldiers is, "You know we don't kill women! Send them out now and they'll be safe-passaged!" The Union soldiers cease firing. One of the bushwhackers says to Mrs. Clark, "Please, ma'am, you and your daughter got to go."[89] She walks with her daughter to the door, gingerly opens the door, and then walks briskly with her daughter away from the house. Once they are far enough away, the soldiers resume shooting.

What the bushwhackers do not contemplate doing is using this opportunity to ambush the Union soldiers. If, instead of sending out the mother and the daughter, the bushwhackers had burst out of the door shooting at the Union soldiers, then it seems fair to say that all involved would count this as an act of (impermissible) perfidy, and not a (permissible) ruse of war, and likewise if the Union soldiers had started shooting as the mother and daughter opened the door. It seems that Machiavelli would agree, too. The film does not, then, endorse all deception in war.

Of Human Bondage and Shotgun Weddings

Ride with the Devil is bookended by weddings. It opens with the wedding of Jack Bull Chiles's sister, Sally Chiles, to Horton Lee Jr. It closes (or nearly closes) with the wedding of Jake to Sue Lee. Nevertheless, what the male protagonists say about weddings (or really, marriage), and especially what Jake says about it, is extremely negative.

During his sister's wedding at the beginning of the film, Jack Bull refers to "my sister's funeral—I mean wedding," jokingly characterizing his sister's wedding as her death.[90] Afterward, Jake says that a wedding is a "peculiar thing." Jack Bull says that it is "no more peculiar, Jake, than slavery." To this Jake replies, "That is certain. And that is why I have often wondered for what cause those Northerners are so anxious to change our Southern institutions. For in both North and South men are every day enslaved at the altar, regardless of their state and color." Jack Bull responds, "It is a type of subjugation. We shall avoid it, Jake," to which Jake responds in turn, "Happily, my poverty ensures my freedom from such a fate."[91]

Jake considers marriage to be a form of bondage. Toward the end of the film, Jake goes to Orton Brown's house to recover from his wounds. He is now living under the same roof as Sue Lee, a single mother with a daughter, Grace, by Jack Bull. He is told to marry Sue Lee by Cave Wyatt, another bushwhacker and the nephew of the Browns: "Ort tells me that when you brung that girl here she was already pregnant. You better marry her, boy. It ain't right not to." To this Jake replies, "Me? No, not me. I don't got to marry nobody."[92]

Cave believes that Jake is the father of Sue Lee's baby and that Jake should do the honorable thing and marry her. However, Holt, who knows that Jake is not the father, also believes that Jake should marry Sue Lee. In a scene from the original screenplay that is not included in the film, Holt tells Jake,

"Could be you ought to . . . I've thunk about it from several sides, and could be she'd make you a fine wife."[93] Jake's response is to say, "Even if I *did* want to marry her," nevertheless "there is one lil' thing we ain't mentioning here. It might just be she don't *want* to marry me."[94]

At this same time, Sue Lee confronts Jake and asks him, "Jake, what's this trash I hear about you being my fiancé?" Jake tells her that Cave and the Browns believe that he is the father of her baby. Sue Lee then asks him, "Do you figure I ought to be married?" Jake says, "Yes, if you want to keep fingers from waggin' in your face," and also, "They got a name for kids without daddies, you know. It's not a good one."[95] Sue Lee, however, is not concerned about her own disgrace, although she does care about her daughter being called a bastard. Her next question is more intimate. "So, do you want to marry me?" she asks Jake, in the closest she has ever come to proposing to him.[96]

It is clear from everything that Sue Lee says, and does not say, that she wants to marry Jake. She is also too proud to tell him this. It is clear from everything that Jake says that he does not know that she wants to marry him. He is also extremely deferential and shy around women (he is a virgin). His ignorance as to her intentions, coupled with his shyness, leads him to say in response to her quasi-proposal, "Naw. Not too bad." His response produces a classic example of "the lady doth protest too much, methinks" from Sue Lee, who, after a pause, snaps, "Good. That's good news. 'Cause I wouldn't marry you for a wagonload of gold. . . . I wouldn't marry you even if you weren't a runty Dutchman with a nubbin for a finger."[97] To this Jake himself snaps back, "Fine! That's damned fine. I wouldn't want a wife who didn't keep her place. Anyhow, it is a proven thing that being your man is just plain bad luck, and I don't need to marry any of that."[98]

If the matter were left up to them, then perhaps Jake and Sue Lee would never get married. Later, when Jake tells Sue Lee, "You know, that girl needs her a daddy," Sue Lee (still angry with him, it seems) snaps back, "She had a daddy, Jake, and you ain't it."[99] However, Orton and Wilma Brown do not leave the matter up to the young couple. Orton leaves on horseback for Hartwell. He tells Jake to stay behind and doesn't tell him where he is going. When Jake asks Wilma why she is preparing a chicken for dinner, she tells him, "Why, nothing. I just know Orton will be mighty tired tonight when he gets back from his ride. I intend to feed him well."[100] The conspiracy of the Browns allows them to spring a wedding on Jake. Orton returns with the Reverend Horace Wright, and, while still holding his shotgun, tells Jake,

"You're getting' married today, Dutchy. You're getting' married or you're get-ting' out." In a last attempt to free himself from the bondage of marriage, Jake shouts out to Holt to saddle his horse. Holt replies, "Oh, no. You should do right, Jake."[101] While not in on the deception, Holt concurs with it.

It is at this point that Sue Lee, who was not in on the deception either, but who does want to marry Jake, brings him around to the side of the house and asks him, "Are you going to or not?" They have the following exchange:

JAKE: I thought you said you wouldn't marry me for a wagonload
      of gold 'cause I'm a nubbin'-fingered runt of a Dutchman. I
      remember you saying that.
SUE LEE: Well, I guess I lied.
JAKE: Are you lying again now?
SUE LEE: No. I wouldn't lie to you, Jake.
JAKE: You just told me you lied to me before.
SUE LEE: That was different. That was romance.
JAKE: And now is what?
SUE LEE: Now is the truth. This here now is the truth.[102]

Having established that she does indeed want to marry him, Jake marries Sue Lee.[103]

Sue Lee makes a distinction between lying in romance, where it is per-mitted, perhaps even expected, and lying at the moment of truth in a rela-tionship, where honesty about one's feelings is demanded. Jake is unpracticed in the ways of romance and does not understand the use of deception by lovers. What he demands of her, in the end, is honesty about her feelings for him. Only if she drops her pretense will he agree to marry her.

Insofar as the film appears to endorse the deception of Jake by the Browns—and even, it seems, appears to side with Sue Lee in judging Jake to be naive about romance—it can be said to endorse a certain amount of deception for the sake of love. However, insofar as the film seems to endorse Jake's request for honesty from Sue Lee, it can be said to reject the view that all deception in romance is justified. Honesty, in the end, is required.

In this chapter, I argued that Lee's sympathy in *Ride with the Devil* is for the outsiders caught up in the Civil War. They form the conscience of the film. Because they engage in deception in their fighting and in their romance, it raises the question of whether all deception in war and love is justified. I argue that the film rejects this view. Instead, it can be said to agree with Machiavelli that even in war, there are limits on when deception can be practiced. It can also be said to suggest that in love, honesty is finally required. Despite what people may think, all is not fair in love and war.

Notes

Research for this chapter was conducted at Princeton University in the summer of 2011 and at Yale University in the fall of 2011. I would especially like to thank the staffs at the Sterling Memorial Library, the Bass Library, and the Film Study Center at Yale University for their assistance. Many years ago I was encouraged to take Machiavelli more seriously as a thinker by Hein Goemans. I would like to take this opportunity to thank Hein for his good advice.

1. Several sources are possible for this proverb, including "Anye impietie may lawfully be committed in love, which is lawlesse" (from *Euphues,* 1578, by John Lyly) and "Love and warre are all one. . . . It is lawful to use sleights and stratagems to . . . attaine the wished end" (from *Don Quixote,* rev. ed., trans. Thomas Shelton, 1620). *Wordsworth Dictionary of Proverbs,* ed. G. L. Apperson, Stephen J. Curtis, and Martin H. Manser (Hertfordshire: Wordsworth Editions, 1993), 355.

2. In *Butch Cassidy and the Sundance Kid* (George Roy Hill, 1969), Harvey Logan challenges Butch to a knife fight for the leadership of the Wild Bunch gang. Butch is handed a knife, but he waves it away, saying, "Not 'til me and Harvey get the rules straightened out." Harvey drops his guard and says, "Rules? In a knife fight? No rules!" Butch then kicks Harvey as hard as he can in the balls, and Harvey doubles up in pain. Then Butch knocks him out.

3. Note that the claim is that deception in war and love is justified, and not merely that it is excused. For more on the distinction between justifying deception and excusing deception, see my "To Catch a Thief: The Ethics of Deceiving Bad People," in *The Girl with the Dragon Tattoo and Philosophy,* ed. Eric Bronson (Hoboken, N.J.: Wiley-Blackwell, 2011), 198–210.

4. It was referred to as the War of the Rebellion by the Northern Unionists and the War for Southern Independence by the Southern Confederates. Other names include the War for the Union and the War of Southern Aggression (on the Northern side), and the War of Secession and the War of Northern Aggression (on the Southern side).

5. Mark Winchell, *God, Man, and Hollywood: Politically Incorrect Cinema from The Birth of a Nation to The Passion of the Christ* (New York: Intercollegiate Press, 2008), 182–183.

6. The terms *bushwhacker* and *jayhawk* predate the Civil War. The origin of *bushwhacker* remains obscure, although it implied "woodsmen who knew how to fend for themselves in rugged terrain." "Jayhawkers and Bushwhackers," in *Encyclopedia of Arkan-*

sas History and Culture (http://encyclopediaofarkansas.net). According to John C. Tibbetts, "Historian Stephen Starr (1973) has said that the term *jayhawk* was first applied to Kansas raiders 'whose sudden and unexpected incursions into Missouri were like the swoop of a hawk pouncing on an unsuspecting and less capably larcenous bluejay.'" Jayhawkers were also referred to as "red legs" because they wore red leggings. Tibbetts, "'Plains' Speaking: Sound, Sense, and Sensibility in Ang Lee's *Ride with the Devil*," in *The Literature/Film Reader: Issues of Adaptation* (Lanham, Md.: Scarecrow, 2007), 319n3. The citations are from Stephen Z. Starr, *Jennison's Jayhawkers: A Civil War Cavalry Regiment and Its Commander* (Baton Rouge: Louisiana State University Press, 1973). More generally, *jayhawking* came to mean theft.

7. Daniel Woodrell, *Woe to Live On* (New York: Holt, 1987). Woodrell's novel was originally a short story that appeared in the *Missouri Review* in 1983. It was divided into three sections, "Coleman Younger, The Last Is Gone—1916," "I Have Been Found in History Books," and "Only for Them." According to Tibbetts, "The narrator is Jakob Roedel, a second-generation German American who lives with his son, Jefferson, and grandson, Karl, in Saint Bruno, Missouri. Jake has just learned that his old friend and comrade in arms, Coleman Younger, has passed away. Younger's demise triggers Jake's memories of those bloody days of the early 1860s when conflicts between Missouri pro-Southern bushwhackers and Kansas Free-State Jayhawkers resulted in the slaughter of thousands of citizens and soldiers and divided the loyalties of many families. The subsequent novelization appeared in 1987. It expanded the central section of the story and confined the action to the years 1861–1863." Tibbetts, "'Plains' Speaking," 321n11. The novel's title was bought, along with the rights to adapt it, but as a studio president at Universal Pictures is supposed to have said, "I'm not spending millions of dollars on a movie with the word *Woe* in the title." James Schamus, "Fragments towards an Introduction," *Ride with the Devil* (New York: Faber and Faber, 1999), xii.

8. The opening crawl of the film reads, "Allegiance to either side was dangerous, but it was more dangerous still to find oneself caught in the middle." The implication here, of course, is that even those characters in the film who join the bushwhackers are caught in the middle of the two sides.

9. Tibbetts, "'Plains' Speaking," 312.

10. Ibid., from Tibbetts's interview with James Schamus, March 14, 1988, Kansas City, Missouri.

11. Liz Rowlinson, "A Quick Chat with Daniel Woodrell," *Richmond Review*, 1999, quoted in Whitney Crothers Dilley, *The Cinema of Ang Lee: The Other Side of the Screen* (New York: Wallflower Press, 2007), 115.

12. Ellen Cheshire, *The Pocket Essential Ang Lee* (Harpenden, U.K.: Pocket Essentials, 2001), 65.

13. Tibbetts, "'Plains' Speaking," 312, from Tibbetts's interview with Ang Lee, March 24, 1988, Kansas City, Missouri.

14. Even though the film had a veritable Brat Pack of a cast, including Tobey Magu-

ire, Jeffrey Wright, Skeet Ulrich, Jonathan Rhys-Meyers, and James Caviezel, as well as singer-songwriter Jewel (Kilcher), Tom Wilkinson, and Mark Ruffalo in minor roles, and even though the film cost $35 million to make, its main release was canceled after being shown in only sixty theaters. Universal Pictures sent it to video in January 2000. The explanation given by Lee was that the movie had poor test screenings. (Lee no longer allows his films to be test screened as a result.) Lee himself could not do any publicity for the film because he was doing preproduction for *Crouching Tiger, Hidden Dragon* (2000). Indeed, Lee was dissatisfied with a number of the decisions made by Universal Pictures, the company who cut the film for distribution. It did not help matters that *Ride with the Devil* was a slow-paced, difficult-to-follow three-hour period movie, with imitation nineteenth-century speech and few battle scenes about a relatively obscure part of the Civil War. Quite apart from finding it overlong and hard to follow, some U.S. critics considered it to be reactionary because it was sympathetic to the plight of the Southerners. The film received better notices in Britain. Perhaps because of its lack of narrative structure, its length, and its dialogue, or perhaps because of its incorrect politics, or perhaps for all of these reasons, this film is considered to be one of Lee's misfires, and it has suffered somewhat from popular and scholarly neglect, although it has become a cult favorite among certain (Southern) audiences.

15. Schamus, "Fragments," xvi.
16. Ibid.
17. Woodrell, *Woe to Live On*, 49–50.
18. Winchell, *God, Man, and Hollywood*, 183.
19. Cheshire, *Pocket Essential Ang Lee*, 63.
20. Ibid., 15 (from *Cinemaya*, no. 21, 1993).
21. Emilie Yueh-yu Yeh and Darrell W. Davis, *Taiwan Film Directors: A Treasure Island* (New York: Columbia University Press, 2005), quoted in Dilley, *Cinema of Ang Lee*, 28.
22. Ang Lee, foreword to James Schamus, *Ride with the Devil* (New York: Faber and Faber, 1999), ix.
23. Schamus, "Fragments," 53–54.
24. Dilley, *Cinema of Ang Lee*, 125.
25. Cheshire, *Pocket Essential Ang Lee*, 63.
26. As Schamus says about such German settlers, most of them "were radical '48-ers'—men and women who had fled Germany after the failed 1848 revolution," and they "were violently opposed to slavery. These Germans . . . were crucial Northern allies in Missouri, and were especially loathed by pro-Confederate Missourians." Schamus, "Fragments," xv–xvi.
27. Ibid., 8.
28. As Woodrell says, "There are things about the Border Wars that might surprise some people. For many of those involved, on both sides of the state line, it was more a question of family . . . than ideology. Even a famous bushwhacker family, like the Youngers, who had started out pro-Union, turned against Free-Staters when they were

roughed up by Union militia. We forget that most of these guys were teenagers. They were coming of age at the wrong time. For another, German immigrants who came to America, like Jake's family, were 90 percent pro-Union, and they were not liked by the Southern side. Therefore, Jake's decision to ride with the bushwhackers is almost as strange, seemingly, as Holt's. Both Jake and Holt were outsiders in the cause, but they both acted on personal loyalties to their mutual friend, George Clyde. My research has revealed that, historically, there were really such characters." Woodrell, quoted in Tibbetts, "'Plains' Speaking," 314.

29. Ibid., 43.

30. There were free as well as slave African Americans who fought on the side of the Confederates during the war, although their reasons for fighting differed. As Schamus says, "Some wanted to prove to white Southerners that blacks could be as loyal and trustworthy as whites, in the hope that after the war, if the South won, the treatment of blacks would improve. Some were fiercely loyal to white friends or masters, whom they often served as manservants. Others saw service in the war as welcome relief from the drudgery of plantation life. And probably for the vast majority, being near the front lines meant being that much nearer the North—and when they got the chance, they crossed the lines and joined forces with the Union army. Some of them performed in active combat duty, though this was rare. But there are numerous accounts of armed blacks fighting for the South, although, politically, Southern leaders were loath to admit their presence in the ranks, no matter how small. Most often, though, blacks served as laborers, valets or teamsters. Many in the South were afraid to arm large numbers of blacks, though by the end of the war, even the President of the Confederacy was admitting that arming blacks was the only way the South had a chance to win. It's often been said that if the South had armed its blacks earlier, it might indeed have won. Ironically, it was wealthy Southern slave-owners who were the most vociferous in their arguments against blacks being mustered into active duty—they were worried about their valuable property bring killed in action" (xviii). The character of Daniel Holt is an amalgam of actual historical characters, including John Nolan, who served as a spy and scout for the bushwhacker William Quantrill, who led the raid on Lawrence. As Woodrell himself says about the original source materials he found during his research at the Kansas University Spencer Research Library and the Lawrence Historical Society and Museum, "All the time I had been thinking and reading about the Border Wars, I realized I had a lot of feelings about it and wanted to write about it. The letters, diaries, and other first-person accounts I found at KU were particularly amazing. For instance, there was a hand-written letter from a black man who had ridden with the bushwhackers against Lawrence. That was off, I thought at first—a black man riding with pro-slavery guerilas. But I can understand that. He wasn't thinking about the big political issues, he was thinking about his friends." Tibbetts, "'Plains' Speaking," 315–316. Tibbetts adds, "Historian Edward E. Leslie (1996) mentions at least three African Americans who rode with Quantrill: John Lobb, Henry Wilson, and John Noland ('Noland was especially well liked by his white

fellow veterans and was described by them as a "man among men'")." Tibbetts, "'Plains' Speaking," 321–322. The citation is from Edward E. Leslie, *The Devil Knows How to Ride* (New York: Random House, 1996), 86. For more on African Americans fighting for the Confederacy, see Ervin L. Jordan's *Black Confederates and the Afro-Yankees in Civil War Virginia* (Charlottesville: University of Virginia Press, 1995).

31. Schamus, *Ride*, 16.

32. Dilley, *Cinema of Ang Lee*, 116–117.

33. Cheshire, *Pocket Essential Ang Lee*, 68.

34. Schamus, *Ride*, 87.

35. Ibid., 130.

36. Lee, foreword to Schamus, *Ride*, ix.

37. Tibbetts, "'Plains' Speaking," 313.

38. Ibid., 66.

39. Lee, foreword to Schamus, *Ride*, x.

40. Cheshire, *Pocket Essential Ang Lee*, 13.

41. Schamus, "Fragments," xiii.

42. Cheshire, *Pocket Essential Ang Lee*, 67–68.

43. Schamus, *Ride*, 13.

44. Ibid., 35.

45. Ibid., 35.

46. Ibid., 39.

47. Ibid., 39.

48. Quantrill was born in Ohio, although he lied about his birthplace. He may or may not have been a deserter from the Missouri state guard.

49. There is some ambiguity here. According to Winchell, "Quantrill has been so demonized in historical writing and popular culture (including at least ten previous films dating back to 1914) that he is clearly the evil referred to in the film's title." Winchell, *God, Man, and Hollywood*, 185. There is also a biography of Quantrill entitled *The Devil Knows How to Ride*, by Edward E. Leslie (New York: Random House, 1996). However, in the 1940 movie *Dark Command*, Quantrill is accused by his mother of "fighting for the hosts of Darkness [with] the Devil riding beside you" (Tibbetts, "'Plains' Speaking," 309). That would mean that Quantrill rode with the devil, not that he was the devil.

50. As Tibbetts says, "On 14 August [1863] several women were killed and many others were badly injured during the collapse of a Kansas City jail. Three of them were sisters of [William T.] 'Bloody Bill' Anderson and another was a cousin of Cole Younger." Tibbetts, "'Plains' Speaking," 321n14.

51. Cheshire, *Pocket Essential Ang Lee*, 67.

52. Schamus, *Ride*, 88.

53. The actual raid took place on August 21, 1863.

54. Schamus, *Ride*, 102.

55. Ibid., 109.

56. Ibid., 125.

57. Ibid.

58. Ibid., 137.

59. Ibid., 142.

60. Ibid., 138.

61. Dilley, *Cinema of Ang Lee,* 117. It should be noted that the character of Jake in the film is more merciful than the character of Jake in the novel. In the novel, Jake kills a fourteen-year-old boy, the son of a German immigrant barrel maker, in front of his mother and sister, to prove that he is on the side of the Southerners. He tells the other bushwhackers, who are somewhat shocked, "Pups make hounds." Woodrell, *Woe to Live On,* 8.

62. Schamus, "Fragments," xv.

63. Dilley, *Cinema of Ang Lee,* 116.

64. Woodrell, *Woe to Live On,* 3.

65. Ibid., 4.

66. Ibid., 5.

67. Ibid., 7.

68. In the novel, it is Jake who kills the young boy.

69. Woodrell, *Woe to Live On,* 155.

70. Ibid., 19.

71. H. Archer Scott Trask, "A Southern Braveheart," *Chronicles: A Magazine of American Culture,* October 2000, 51, quoted in Winchell, *God, Man, and Hollywood,* 185.

72. Sun-tzu, *The Art of Warfare,* trans. and ed. Roger T. Ames (New York: Ballantine Books), 95–96.

73. To be fair, all of Sunzi's examples of deception could be understood as examples of (mere) ruses of war. Hence, he has no need to discriminate between them. The distinction between such ruses, as well as perfidy, may be implicit.

74. Niccolò Machiavelli, *Discourses on the First Ten Books of Titus Livius,* trans. Christian E. Detmold, ed. Max Lerner (New York: Modern Library, 1950), 526.

75. Ibid.

76. Ibid.

77. Ibid.

78. Niccolò Machiavelli, *The Art of War,* trans. Ellis Farnworth, ed. Neal Wood (Indianapolis, Ind.: Bobbs-Merrill, 1965), 143.

79. Icons are signs whose meanings are established by resemblance. For the distinction between index, icon, and symbol, see Charles S. Peirce, "Logic as Semiotic: The Theory of Signs," in *Philosophical Writings of Peirce,* ed. Justus Buchler (New York: Dover, 1955), 98–119. For more on the relevance of the distinction to lies and deception, see my entry, "The Definition of Lying and Deception," in *Stanford Encyclopedia of Philosophy* (http://plato.stanford.edu).

80. Machiavelli, *Art of War,* 526–527.

81. "Convention (IV) Respecting the Laws and Customs of War on Land" (http://www.au.af.mil).

82. Valentine Jobst III, "Is the Wearing of the Enemy's Uniform a Violation of the Laws of War?" *American Journal of International Law* 35 (1941): 437.

83. Ibid., 435–442.

84. "Protocol Additional to the Geneva Conventions of 12 August 1949, and relating to the Protection of Victims of International Armed Conflicts (Protocol I), 8 June 1977" (http://www.icrc.org).

85. Ibid.

86. Ibid.

87. Ibid.

88. Schamus, *Ride,* 22.

89. Ibid., 23.

90. Ibid., 4.

91. Ibid., 6.

92. Ibid., 117.

93. Ibid., 117–118.

94. Ibid., 118.

95. Ibid., 119.

96. In the original screenplay, the "you" is italicized, and her question is: "So, do *you* want to marry me?" (ibid., 119). However, in the film, the question is asked softly, without any emphasis on "you." The result is that it sounds as though Sue Lee is proposing to Jake.

97. Ibid., 119.

98. Ibid.

99. Ibid., 128.

100. Ibid., 129.

101. Ibid., 129–130.

102. Ibid., 131.

103. In the original screenplay, Jake says, "Jack Bull would have wanted that girl to have a daddy. He was like a brother. I guess I'll do it" (ibid.). The implication of what he says is that he is doing the right thing out of loyalty to his friend. However, in the film, there is no reference to Jack Bull. Jake is supposed to be marrying Sue Lee out of love.

ACKNOWLEDGMENTS

Robert Arp: Thanks to Adam and Jim for their work on this book; Mark Conard, editor of the Philosophy of Popular Culture series at the University Press of Kentucky (UPK); and Anne Dean Watkins, acquisitions editor at UPK.

Adam Barkman: Thanks to my coeditors, Rob and Jim, for their generous and cooperative spirit on this project; Redeemer University College, for a Grant in Aid of Publication to assist in indexing this book; and our indexers, Kyle Alkema and my wife, Ashley.

James McRae: I would like to humbly thank my research assistants, Geneva Steck, Graeme Cave, and Andrew Robertson, for their tireless work on this project; Brett Houska, for his helpful comments on my *Crouching Tiger, Hidden Dragon* chapter; J. Baird Callicott, for his support and friendship as I worked to finish two books simultaneously; and finally, Robert Arp and Adam Barkman, for inviting me to work with them on this project. *Mahalo nui loa.*

GLOSSARY OF CHINESE TERMS

Term	Chinese	English Translation
Cáng Lóng Wò Hǔ	藏龍臥虎	*Crouching Tiger, Hidden Dragon* (film title; literally, "Hidden Dragon, Crouching Tiger")
chéng	成	Completion; actualization
dào	道	Road; path; way of nature (the Dao)
dé	德	Excellence; virtue; function
è	惡	Evil; wicked
Giang Hu (Jiānghú)	江湖	Warrior underworld
Jiāo Lóng	嬌龍	"Delicate dragon" (Jen's full name)
jūnzǐ	君子	Exemplary person (Confucianism)
lǐ	禮	Ritual; customs; rites; etiquette
qì	氣	Psycho-physical energy
rén	仁	Benevolence; humanity; authoritative conduct
róu	柔	Suppleness; yielding strength
Sè, Jiè	色，戒	*Lust, Caution* (film title)
shèngrén	聖人	Sage (Confucianism)
shì	士	Scholar-apprentice
tàijítú	太極圖	Diagram of ultimate power (Daoism)
tiān	天	Heaven; inherent order of the natural world
tiānmìng	天命	Propensity of circumstances; natural tendencies
Tuī Shǒu	推手	*Pushing Hands* (film title)
wú-wéi	無為	Non-interference; non-assertive action

wǔxiá	武俠	Chinese literary tradition
xìao	孝	Filial piety
Xiǎo Hǔ	小虎	"Little tiger" (Lo/Dark Cloud's full name)
xiǎorén	小人	Petty people
xīn	心	Heart; mind
xìn	信	Truthfulness; sincerity; integrity
xìng	性	Nature
xìngshàn	性善	Natural goodness (Mencius)
Xǐyàn	喜宴	*The Wedding Banquet* (film title)
yáng	陽	Positive; bright; dominant; creative; opposite of *yīn*
yì	義	Appropriateness
yīn	陰	Negative; dark; recessive; destructive; opposite of *yáng*
Yǐn Shí Nán Nǔ	飲食男女	*Eat Drink Man Woman* (film title)
zhèngmíng	正名	Rectification of names
zhēnrén	真人	Sage; genuine person (Daoism)
zhī	知	Realization
zhìchéng	至誠	Creativity; utmost sincerity
zìrán	自然	Natural; nature

CONTRIBUTORS

Robert Arp, Ph.D. (http://robertarp.webs.com/), is a philosopher and ontologist with interests in philosophy of biology, ontology in the information science sense, and philosophy and popular culture. He has authored and edited numerous books and articles.

Adam Barkman, Ph.D., is associate professor of philosophy at Redeemer University College. He is the author of *C. S. Lewis and Philosophy as a Way of Life* (2009) and *Through Common Things*, and is coeditor of *Manga and Philosophy* (2010).

Patricia Brace, Ph.D., is professor of art at Southwest Minnesota State University. She has a strong interest in the aesthetic analysis of popular culture. She contributed chapters to Dexter *and Philosophy* and *The Philosophy of Joss Whedon,* among several others.

Jeff Bush is a Ph.D. candidate in philosophy at the University of Liverpool, where he was the John Lennon Memorial Scholar in 2007 and 2008. His research interests are interdisciplinary, and he is specifically interested in the areas where phenomenology, psychoanalysis, and linguistics meet.

Timothy M. Dale, Ph.D., is assistant professor of political science at the University of Wisconsin, La Crosse. His primary research interest is democratic theory, and he has written on the subjects of inclusion and democracy, civil society, and political messaging in popular culture. He is coeditor of *Homer Simpson Marches on Washington: Dissent in American Popular Culture* (2010) with Joseph Foy, and coauthor of *Political Thinking, Political Theory, and Civil Society* (2009).

Carl J. Dull, Ph.D., is a philosopher who specializes in classical Chinese philosophy with interests in South Asian philosophy and comparative philosophy. His current work involves adapting classical Chinese models of emotional well-being for contemporary discussions of moral psychology.

Joseph J. Foy, Ph.D., is associate professor in the department of political science at the University of Wisconsin, Waukesha. He is the editor of *Homer Simpson Goes to Washington: American Politics through Popular Culture* (2009) and *SpongeBob SquarePants and Philosophy: Soaking Up Secrets under the Sea* (2011), and coeditor of *Homer Simpson Marches on Washington: Dissent through American Popular Culture* (2010) with Timothy Dale.

George T. Hole, Ph.D., is distinguished teaching professor of philosophy through State University of New York with interests in existentialism, Zen Buddhism, philosophical counseling, and poetry.

Misty Jameson, Ph.D., is assistant professor of English and film studies at Lander University in Greenwood, South Carolina. She has previously published articles on works by Vladimir Nabokov and William Gaddis.

Nancy Kang, Ph.D., is an assistant professor of English at the University of Baltimore. A former postdoctoral fellow in the interdisciplinary humanities and Asian American studies at Syracuse University, Kang teaches and publishes in ethnic American literatures and cultures.

David Koepsell, J.D., Ph.D., teaches ethics at the Delft University of Technology, faculty of values and technology, in the Netherlands. He has published and edited numerous articles and books on ethics, religion, legal philosophy, technology, and culture, including *Who Owns You? The Corporate Gold Rush to Patent your Genes* (2009) and *Innovation and Nanotechnology* (2011).

Renée Köhler-Ryan, Ph.D., is senior lecturer in philosophy at the Sydney campus of the University of Notre Dame, Australia. Her areas of interest, teaching, and publications include philosophy of culture, ethics, philosophical theology, and metaphysics. Her publications focus on how questions about transcendence are expressed both culturally and ethically.

Basileios Kroustallis, Ph.D., is a philosopher and teaching fellow at Hellenic Open University, Greece. He has published research articles in philosophy of mind, British empiricism, and philosophy of film.

James Edwin Mahon, Ph.D., is associate professor of philosophy at Washington and Lee University. His primary research interests are in moral philosophy and early modern philosophy.

James McRae, Ph.D., is associate professor of Asian philosophy and religion and the coordinator for Asian studies at Westminster College in Fulton, Missouri. He is a coeditor of *Environmental Philosophy in the Asian Traditions of Thought* (forthcoming) with J. Baird Callicott, and his work is included in anthologies such as *Value and Values* (forthcoming, edited by Roger T. Ames and Peter Hershock), *Rethinking the Nonhuman* (forthcoming, edited by Neil Dalal and Chloe Taylor), and *Introducing Philosophy through Pop Culture* (edited by William Irwin and David Kyle Johnson, 2010).

Sydney Palmer, Ph.D., is a theologian who focuses on theological exegesis but whose interests also include literature, literary criticism, film criticism, and art.

Ronda Lee Roberts, M.A., is an independent scholar and editorial consultant. She contributed a chapter to Avatar *and Philosophy* using Levinas's discussion of the face of the other. She specializes in social and political philosophy, and her current focus involves looking at collective responsibility and the interactions between states and their citizens.

Susanne Schmetkamp, D.Phil., is senior teaching and research associate at the department of Philosophy at the University of Basel, Switzerland. Her areas of research and interest include film philosophy; the relation between aesthetics, emotions, and ethics; and contemporary moral and political philosophy.

Michael Thompson, Ph.D., is lecturer at the University of North Texas. His primary interests are Kant, the imagination, consciousness, and architecture of the mind.

David Zietsma, Ph.D., is assistant professor of history at Redeemer University College. His interests include representations of American national identity in film, the role of religion in U.S. foreign relations, and the function of violence in personal and collective identity.

INDEX

and, 81; cultural identity in, 8; and
globalization/modernity, 5, 147–48;
and individualism, 256; patriarchy
in, 6; sexuality in, 89–90; value
system of, 7, 11, 86–87, 143
wǒ, 25
World War II, 151, 195, 267
Wudang, 181, 182
wú-wéi, 7–8, 32, 256
wǔxiá, 9, 33–34, 46

xìao, 7, 26, 44, 142–43
xīn (heart and mind), 82, 92, 133
xìn (integrity), 26, 34
Xunzi, 66–69, 74, 122, 130, 132–35,
139.

yáng, 7, 25, 28, 95–96, 109–10, 116–17,
159
yì, 6, 25–26, 31, 33, 74, 76n12, 83–84,
87, 142–43, 149
yīn, 7, 28, 95–96, 109–10, 116–17, 159

Zhànguó Shídài. *See* Warring States
period
zhēnrén, 29–30
zhī, 24, 27, 83–84, 90, 92
Zhou dynasty, 6, 20
Zhuangzi, 28–30
Žižek, Slavoj, 192–93, 207

The Philosophy of Popular Culture

The books published in the Philosophy of Popular Culture series will illuminate and explore philosophical themes and ideas that occur in popular culture. The goal of this series is to demonstrate how philosophical inquiry has been reinvigorated by increased scholarly interest in the intersection of popular culture and philosophy, as well as to explore through philosophical analysis beloved modes of entertainment, such as movies, TV shows, and music. Philosophical concepts will be made accessible to the general reader through examples in popular culture. This series seeks to publish both established and emerging scholars who will engage a major area of popular culture for philosophical interpretation and examine the philosophical underpinnings of its themes. Eschewing ephemeral trends of philosophical and cultural theory, authors will establish and elaborate on connections between traditional philosophical ideas from important thinkers and the ever-expanding world of popular culture.

SERIES EDITOR

Mark T. Conard, Marymount Manhattan College, NY

BOOKS IN THE SERIES

The Philosophy of Stanley Kubrick, edited by Jerold J. Abrams
The Philosophy of Ang Lee, edited by Robert Arp, Adam Barkman, and
　　James McRae
Football and Philosophy, edited by Michael W. Austin
Tennis and Philosophy, edited by David Baggett
The Philosophy of Film Noir, edited by Mark T. Conard
The Philosophy of Martin Scorsese, edited by Mark T. Conard
The Philosophy of Neo-Noir, edited by Mark T. Conard
The Philosophy of Spike Lee, edited by Mark T. Conard
The Philosophy of the Coen Brothers, edited by Mark T. Conard
The Philosophy of David Lynch, edited by William J. Devlin and Shai
　　Biderman

The Philosophy of the Beats, edited by Sharin N. Elkholy
The Philosophy of Horror, edited by Thomas Fahy
The Philosophy of The X-Files, edited by Dean A. Kowalski
Steven Spielberg and Philosophy, edited by Dean A. Kowalski
The Philosophy of Joss Whedon, edited by Dean A. Kowalski and S. Evan
    Kreider
The Philosophy of Charlie Kaufman, edited by David LaRocca
The Philosophy of the Western, edited by Jennifer L. McMahon and
    B. Steve Csaki
The Philosophy of Steven Soderbergh, edited by R. Barton Palmer and
    Steven M. Sanders
The Olympics and Philosophy, edited by Heather L. Reid and Michael
    W. Austin
The Philosophy of David Cronenberg, edited by Simon Riches
The Philosophy of Science Fiction Film, edited by Steven M. Sanders
The Philosophy of TV Noir, edited by Steven M. Sanders and Aeon
    J. Skoble
The Philosophy of Sherlock Holmes, edited by Philip Tallon and David
    Baggett
Basketball and Philosophy, edited by Jerry L. Walls and Gregory Bassham
Golf and Philosophy, edited by Andy Wible

CPSIA information can be obtained at www.ICGtesting.com
Printed in the USA
BVOW042057010413

317011BV00002B/2/P

9 780813 141664